Simon Mohler Landis

An Entirely New Feature of a Thrilling Novel!

Entitled, The Social War of the Year 1900

Simon Mohler Landis

An Entirely New Feature of a Thrilling Novel!
Entitled, The Social War of the Year 1900

ISBN/EAN: 9783337009441

Printed in Europe, USA, Canada, Australia, Japan

Cover: Foto ©ninafisch / pixelio.de

More available books at **www.hansebooks.com**

AN ENTIRELY NEW FEATURE

OF

A THRILLING NOVEL!

ENTITLED,

THE SOCIAL WAR

OF THE YEAR

1900;

OR,

THE CONSPIRATORS AND LOVERS!

BY

S. M. LANDIS, M.D., D.D.,

AUTHOR OF "SECRETS OF GENERATION," "SENSE AND NONSENSE,"
"MESMER, THE TERROR OF THE RICH," "COURTSHIP AND
MARRIAGE," "KEY TO LOVE," "KEY TO HEAVEN," ETC.

A LESSON FOR SAINTS AND SINNERS!

PUBLISHED BY "LANDIS PUBLISHING SOCIETY,"
No. 13 NORTH ELEVENTH STREET,
PHILADELPHIA, PA.
1872.

Entered according to Act of Congress, in the year 1872, by
SIMON M. LANDIS, M.D., D.D.,
In the Office of the Librarian of Congress, at Washington, D. C.

PREFACE.

OF late years my enemies have driven me to conclude that fixed truths are stumbling blocks to the consummation of established usages and modernized human life. Whenever I have advertised a lecture, sermon, book or apparatus of a useful, scientific character, I have had only a few patrons; but, when I made an impression, by my advertisements, that I was going into the *veriest* mysteries of human nature, was going to teach the public how to enjoy the feeling propensities without danger of exposition, was going to shake the devil by his horns and knock *particular* thunder out of ordinary things, I have always had an abundance of customers!

Therefore I have drawn a heavy picture in the novel before us; and, whilst all phases of humanity are portrayed, I think I have not overstepped the modesty of nature, nor left any thing undone to satiate all classes of people; whilst sensation, history, comedy and tragedy loom up truthfully, and I hope to the satisfaction of all who admire either devil, or nature and nature's God!

To furnish the reader with a diet that is palatable to his omnivorous taste, and yet to smother the most unpalatable though healthful dishes by his favorite hash, is the aim of this novel. By so doing, I am persuaded that the reader may learn, sooner or later, that the viand which was most distasteful was after all the most needful and desirable, and then he will distinguish truth from error, or a natural from an unnatural life. This done, and the masses will return to truth, nature, sound sense and solid logic. I have also dramatized this novel, and I hope and pray that my labors have not been in vain, but I trust that millions may be saved from all sorts of misery through this feeble effort to entertain and instruct the people.

THE AUTHOR.

CONTENTS.

CHAPTER	PAGE
PREFACE........	3
I.—THE HERO RESCUES THE HEROINE......	11
II.—THE SOLEMN OATH OF THE CONSPIRATORS.........	15
III.—DEACON STEW RAVES AT LUCINDA'S LOVE FOR VICTOR.........	20
IV.—PAT O'CONNER BLARNEYS THE DEACON............	24
V.—THE BLOODY CONSPIRATORS POISON VICTOR JUNO	28
VI.—THE SERPENT AT LUCINDA'S BEDSIDE.............	31
VII.—NANCY CLOVER, FAILING TO CAPTIVATE GENERAL ARMINGTON, BECOMES REVENGEFUL.........	36
VIII.—LUCINDA IN DISGUISE SAVES VICTOR'S LIFE.......	39
IX.—VICTOR AND LUCINDA BETROTHED	43
X.—FOUL CONNIVING OF THE BLOODY CONSPIRATORS.	47
XI.—SHREWD EXPOSE OF COSMOPOLITAN RASCALITY...	51
XII.—VICTOR JUNO'S SCATHING SERMON IN THE THEATRE........	53
XIII.—LUCINDA ABDUCTED AND IMPRISONED...............	57
XIV.—VICTOR ABDUCTED AND IMPRISONED..........	61
XV.—REPORTED ELOPEMENT AND SEDUCTION OF LUCINDA BY VICTOR........	66

CONTENTS.

CHAPTER		PAGE
XVI.	Lucinda's Thrilling Prayer and Lamentation in Prison	70
XVII.	General Armington searching for his Seduced Daughter in Europe	75
XVIII.	Jemmy discovers Victor and Lucinda	79
XIX.	Deacon Stew threatens to shoot Jemmy	83
XX.	Lucinda nearly murders the Deacon in her Cell	87
XXI.	Victor's Vision, in a Dream, in his Dungeon	89
XXII.	Victor's Terrific Struggle with the Night-Watchman	95
XXIII.	Thrilling Prison Scene between Lucinda and Deacon Stew	100
XXIV.	Dr. Victor Juno's Escape from his Dungeon	105
XXV.	Dr. Juno locked out of Concert Hall, which caused a Riot	109
XXVI.	Most Thrilling and Demoniacal Plotting of the Conspirators	113
XXVII.	General Armington turns Insane	117
XXVIII.	Dr. Juno arrested in his Pulpit for selling "Obscene" Books	121
XXIX.	The Insane General Armington nearly murders the Physician-in-Chief	124
XXX.	Harry Gossimer condemned to Death	129
XXXI.	Harry Gossimer's Heroic and Thrilling Speech before they drown him	133
XXXII.	Dr. Juno convicted, imprisoned, and Attempts made to poison him	137
XXXIII.	Dr. Juno's first Sharp shooting Sermon on Ministers and Doctors	141

CHAPTER	PAGE
XXXIV.—Pat O'Conner saves Harry Gossimer from drowning but are both arrested	146
XXXV.—Dr. Juno's Second Startling Sermon on Doctors and Ministers	150
XXXVI.—The Bloody Conspirators in Fear, and fight amongst Themselves	156
XXXVII.—Dr. Juno again in the Insane Asylum	161
XXXVIII.—Deacon Stew frantic with Delirium	164
XXXIX.—Nancy Clover makes a Master Speech to the Conspirators	167
XL.—Dr. Juno, Pat O'Conner, and Judy M'Crea in Private Council	171
XLI.—Dr. Juno's Stunning Sermon on the Improvement of Church and State	175
XLII.—Dr. Juno's Scathing Sermon continued	179
XLIII.—The Bloody Conspirators mobbed	183
XLIV.—Dr. Juno informed where Lucinda is imprisoned	187
XLV.—Dr. Juno organizes the "Secret Order of Naturalists"	191
XLVI.—Lucinda shoots Deacon Stew in her Cell and escapes	195
XLVII.—Lucinda is re-arrested before she escapes	199
XLVIII.—The Bloody Conspirators in Terrible Fear of Dr. Juno	203
XLIX.—Lucinda doffs the Deacon's Clothes and threatens to shoot the Conspirators	207
L.—The Leading Bloody Conspirators at Loggerheads	211

CHAPTER	PAGE
LI.—Nancy Clover lecturing Deacon Stew	214
LII.—Lucinda bites Deacon Stew's Ear nearly off	218
LIII.—Dr. Juno's Stirring Speech to the "Secret Order of Naturalists."	222
LIV.—Dr. Juno mobs the Insane Asylum and frees Lucinda	226
LV.—Meeting of Victor and Lucinda in her Cell	229
LVI.—Dr. Juno offers Amnesty to the Conspirators	233
LVII.—Lucinda Free and at her own Home again	236
LVIII.—Pathetic Interview between Lucinda and Victor	240
LIX.—Dr. Juno performs a Serious Operation on Deacon Stew	243
LX.—The Bloody Conspirators bothered and arrested	247
LXI.—Love Scene between Victor and Lucinda	251
LXII.—The Fight between the Naturalists and Conspirators	255
LXIII.—Dr. Juno's Conciliatory and Black Flag Speech to the Conspirators	259
LXIV.—Conference between Dr. Juno and Conspirators	263
LXV.—A Pleasing Interview between Victor and Lucinda	267
LXVI.—Victor and Lucinda visit and restore Gen. Armington	270
LXVII.—Dr. Juno's Plans laid before the "Secret Order of Naturalists."	274

CONTENTS.

CHAPTER		PAGE
LXVIII.	Efforts to arrest Dr. Juno for Riot and Murder	277
LXIX.	Desperate Efforts of Deacon Stew and Nancy Clover	281
LXX.	What the Newspapers said of the Riot.	284
LXXI.	The Editors of the Conspirators' Newspapers receive Documents asking them to leave the Country.	290
LXXII.	Futile Efforts to arrest Dr. Juno—his Wedding instead	292
LXXIII.	Night of the Wedding—Dr. Juno shot..	295
LXXIV.	All the Guests examined, and the Assassin detected	298
LXXV.	The Attempted Assassination of Dr. Juno by Nancy Clover caused a Terrible Public Wrath	302
LXXVI.	Dr. Juno and Lucinda Armington making Love	305
LXXVII.	Congress mobbed for recognizing God in the Constitution	309
LXXVIII.	Dr. Juno's First Great War Proclamation	312
LXXIX.	Dr. Juno's Terrible Army Orders	315
LXXX.	Retaliatory Means of the Conspirators' Army	319
LXXXI.	Captured Conspirators shot dead.	322
LXXXII.	The Religious Conspirators dumbfounded	325
LXXXIII.	Dr. Juno writes to his Lucinda.	329
LXXXIV.	The Fear and Distress of the Conspirators	332

CONTENTS.

CHAPTER	PAGE
LXXXV.—Terrible Battle fought—Dr. Juno shot and lost	335
LXXXVI.—Miss Armington takes the Field when she finds that Dr. Juno is gone	338
LXXXVII.—The Trial by Court Martial of Dr. Juno	342
LXXXVIII.—The Court Martial tries Juno	346
LXXXIX.—Hon. Bluster Gibbons' Speech before the Court Martial	352
XC.—Dr. Juno's Great Defiant Defence	356
XCI.—The Verdict and its Effect	360
XCII.—The Shooting of Dr. Juno and the Last Battle	365
XCIII.—Pathetic Meeting of Victor and Lucinda after the Battle	369
XCIV.—Dr. Juno's astounding Peace Proclamation	372
XCV.—Dr. Juno, with his Picked Soldiers, brands the Pharisees	376
XCVI.—Disposal of Nancy Clover and Company, and Preparation for the Marriage of Victor and Lucinda	380
XCVII.—The Wedding	385
XCVIII.—Famine and Pestilence come to the Aid of the Naturalists	389
XCIX.—The New Constitution	394
C.—Dawn of the Millennium	397
Moral	400
Dr. Landis' Reformatory Enterprises	403

THE SOCIAL WAR

OF THE YEAR

1900;

OR,

THE CONSPIRATORS AND LOVERS!

CHAPTER I.

THE HERO RESCUES THE HEROINE.

IN one of the oldest settlements of Pennsylvania, where nature has developed many curious phenomena, and where beautiful mountains, hills, groves and valleys abound, was born, in an humble Christian family, a son whose goodness, greatness and peculiar power amongst men were herculean. This humble but heroic son of toil was an out-growth, as will be seen from the indomitable passions, love and barbarous cruelty which he possessed.

His parents were uneducated, though sincerely pious, orthodox, religious people, who did not believe in education; therefore, opposed schooling, deeming hard physical labor and devotion to gaining an honest living the extent of their zeal and ambition; however, the hero of our plot could not and would not see things in this light; but, he saw a mirror in nature which overshadowed the valley of life and death, and he concluded to go through life in a natural manner, enjoying all the God-ordained manifestations and blessings, or fight like an indomitable fiend to win the victory, or die the death of a martyr!

VICTOR JUNO was a God-loving youth, an admirer of the beautiful, the natural; a lover of the fair sex, an admirer of pristine loveliness, and an adorer of handsome babies! He beheld in his mind's eye, whilst quite a youth, what very few people ever see during a lifetime, namely: That all the world is a stage, and all the men, women and children simply actors, who play a Farce, Tragedy, or Cupid's Melo-Drama!

He was the worshipper of the latter; because, he looked upon a normal or godly human life as being a boon that should vouchsafe unto man one continual round of pleasures, joys and delights, hooped together by a living love for the immutable Creator and his creatures, Adams and Eves in Eden gladness, surrounded by angels and baptized with talismanic darts of celestial love!

To him such a world, and such a life, was worth living and dying for; and he despised the rational creature who could not aid in the advancement of this soul-enchanting and body-beautifying cause.

In his childhood he sought, by day and by night, the means whereby the hallowed ends, which he beheld in the mirror of nature, could be attained. Bred and reared amongst the illiterate and uncouth, with no opportunity to obtain a necessarily liberal book education, he strove to obtain from nature what others sought in collegiate tuition; and whilst he meditated almost continually over the wonderful works of the Creator, he became the more enamored with the bountiful goodness of the beneficent Most High, and beheld in the normal Elysium of Nature the mirror which radiantly illumined the soul with effulgent joy and delight.

To the high blue firmament he vowed to live a pure and healthy life, eschewing all useless and injurious habits, and as long as God gave him breath, he should not cease to promulgate and agitate the fundamental principles upon which humanity must depend for succor and salvation.

Moved by intuition, instead of man's tuition, he grew up to manhood, and whilst having been thrown among his fellows, who did not comprehend nor esteem his Cupid God, he saw that his Elysium of Nature was beneath par, and that his life most surely should not be the one which he saw unfolded to his senses in early childhood, as the design of the unchangeable Creator was being marred, and all living human creatures were acting a farce or tragedy, whereby they laid traps to catch each other, fearing that by being too natural and generous they might become too happy, and thereby lose the boon of salvation.

One day, as our hero was seated by the road-side of the celebrated Wissahickon, suddenly a two-horse equipage was driven along, when the horses took fright, ran up an embankment and upset the magnificent coach. Quick as lightning Victor Juno appeared upon the spot, when he found one horse lying flat on his side and kicking with fury, while the other beast stood trembling with fright, the coachman was lying about six feet aside of the coach, and all that he saw was an old gray-bearded sire's face, who was entangled somehow under the upturned equipage; the moment he saw Victor he cried vehemently:

"Young man, for God's sake, save my daughter!"

Victor Juno being very courageous, at once began cutting the harness away from the horses, but how to undo the traces of the kicking horse, without help from any one, was more than mortal strength and ingenuity of one man could accomplish; however, he soon contrived to so entangle the kicking horse in the lines, that one foot was fastened, when he vigorously grasped the other foot in his herculean hand, and held it whilst he leaned over and cut the traces; but, just as he did so, the horse sprang to his feet, and throwing the hero about twenty feet vigorously against a fence, fractured his arm and scarified his handsome face severely. The horses ran furiously away; Victor sprang back to the coach, and with the strength of a giant rolled the equipage aside, which relieved the sire; but, Oh! horror, there was the most gloriously beautiful daughter, for whom the sire prayed for a safe deliverance, dead to all appearances; quickly Victor Juno raised her to his arms, and being a physician, took a small vial from his pocket, and placed to her lips a few drops of unfermented vegetable liquid, which immediately caused slight signs of life!

"Sire," cried Victor Juno, "shall I take the liberty to do my utmost—I am a physician—to restore your daughter?"

"Ten thousand dollars and an everlasting indebtedness to you, sir, for her restoration," responded the old gentleman.

"I'll save her without dollars or indebtedness, or I am not a normal Naturalist," ejaculated Victor Juno.

The hero now speedily removes the jewels, satins and silks from her swan-like neck and Venus chest, and applies his powerfully magnetic hand upon the nape of the neck, and centring his giant will into his fingers, sends messengers of grace to the nervous centre of the prostrate form of the loveliest of her kind, and in a moment Miss Lucinda Armington opened her eyes, and gave a benignant look into the fiery and heaven-inspired eyes of our hero; and thus the life of the one became the joy and resurrection of the other.

Victor Juno was, however, considerably embarrassed, when he found the long sought idol of his great soul lying in his arms, with her beautiful curly dishevelled hair hanging over her bare shoulders, and he apologized in the most affable manner possible for the position and inopportune condition in which he found her.

She said: "Where am I?"

"Here, sound and safe, in the hands of a most skilful physician, my darling!" cried the father.

Victor Juno bowed his head gracefully in acknowledgment of this compliment, and said:
"It is a joy to serve my fellows, and more particularly when danger threatens the pure and innocent angels of our souls. With your permission, fair lady, I will now leave you for a few minutes, and go to my home and send my coach to convey you to comfortable quarters."

CHAPTER II.

THE SOLEMN OATH OF THE CONSPIRATORS.

N the year 18— there arose in the city of Philadelphia a monstrous agitation and strife among the Religious Classes, in which war, to the hilt, was carried on for ten or twelve months; but, finally the money-power conquered, the orthodox classes having possession of the filthy lucre. In sooth, the same selfish and bigoted spirit that makes people orthodox, makes them also penurious; because, there is neither progression nor generosity in orthodoxy, therefore these kind of people believe in hoarding up and retaining their hoardings, whether in stereotyped religious rites or lucre; whilst, on the other hand, the progressive and generous thinkers do not place so much value in religious ordinances nor in lucre, hence, become poorer in purse and selfishness, but richer in mind and spirit.

The leaders of a similar bloody conspiracy, that is now breeding, consist of three persons : Rob Stew, Joe Pier and Nancy Clover.

ROB STEW is a man of robust build, with a smooth tongue, whose eye can sparkle like an angel's when endeavoring to dupe any one, but flash fire and fury when cornered or disappointed. He is what the New Testament would call a Judas Iscariot, a viper, scribe, hypocrite and pharisee. A man who can dissemble and adapt himself to any kind of villany, who goes about praying and exhorting, claiming to be a chosen vessel of the Lord! A domineering and self-righteous saint, whose exterior humility deceives thousands, and when one listens to his public prayers and exhortations, he feels as though brother Stew really was a holy saint without blemish.

It is probably this power to dissemble, that deceives almost every one who comes within reach of his influence, that gives him an immense sovereignty over the people. Nearly every one who knows him, or knows of him, believes Deacon Stew to be a perfect saint, who could not be guilty of any evil act; but, as we pass on, it will be shown that he has two sides, one of which is well hid under a smooth exterior.

JOE PIER is a very finely organized man, of medium size, who is the beloved of the fair sex, a minister of the gospel, who presides over the former—Deacon Stew—but who is nevertheless the submissive tool of Rob Stew.

Rev. Joe Pier has many refined, tender and noble feelings, but, being one of those milk-and-water creatures who has no mind of his own, nor enough talent to succeed in life without some one to keep him stiff in the back bone, he is just the miserable, though useful, instrument in the hands of a Judas—like Deacon Rob Stew—to aid in proselyting millions to the faith of blue-stocking orthodoxy.

NANCY CLOVER is a finely formed female, of profound talent and wheedling capacity. She has the faculty of LOVE OF POWER immensely developed, in addition to a mountain of Self-conceit, which makes her bold and dauntless. Moreover, she possesses almost a talismanic power to make every one fall in love with her, whether man or woman, and she always plays upon the lute-strings of affection of those whom she wishes to control, before she attempts to use her LOVE OF POWER over them. Rev. Joe Pier deems her to be a goddess, and even old Deacon Stew is under her gigantic influence; still, the latter often combats vehemently with sister Clover, and whilst the charming sister permits the saintly Judas to frequently digress from the even path of orthodox piety, she nevertheless frequently, in secret, admonishes him until he feels ashamed of himself, and sister Clover well knows that this is the only way to hold the old deacon in her power; for it must be evident to any one, if you would be made respect a person, you must look UP to such a one; and Nancy Clover fully understands human nature, and also knows how to torture and hold in subjection every one she takes a mind to wheedle.

The leading conspirators, in company with a few of the faithful, are now in private conclave, plotting the destruction of Victor Juno's influence with General Washington Armington, the millionaire and father of Miss Lucinda Armington, or, if it be necessary, to murder him privately; at any rate he MUST cease the agitation of his Melo-dramatic reform, or the orthodox doctrines will lose prestige with the people.

They met in Tabernacle Hall on a rainy night, Rev. Joe Pier in the chair. After the meeting was called to order, Deacon Rob Stew said:

"Mr. President, I have a very important matter to lay before you this evening, which requires immediate action without fear or favor, and I hope that the brotherhood is ready to use any means to accomplish what I shall have to propose. Should there be any chicken-hearted brothers or sisters present, I move that they be expelled, or swear renewed allegiance to the form of our beloved cause"—

Here he was interrupted by a surly fellow, who disputed the deacon's right to be so rigorous and mighty as to demand the expulsion of any member of our cause for the purpose of consummating any of his cherished secret plots, which evidently had a close connection with the love-scrape he had with Miss Armington—

"Stop, Mr. Grumbler," ejaculated Deacon Stew, "you are a suspicious and faithless fool, who is not to be trusted with any important work of our cause. I move, Mr. President—I say, EMPHATICALLY, Mr. President—that brother Grumbler shall at once leave the room, or, if he go not voluntarily, then he shall be expelled by force."

"I will leave this matter to the majority of the friends," said the President.

Nancy Clover rose to the floor and said: "Brothers, I am grieved at your silly conduct; are we not a unit, does not a house divided against itself fall, and shall we quarrel amongst ourselves whilst a dangerous enemy is entering into our family, who, if his course is not summarily checked, will destroy our influence and beloved cause entirely? I repeat, brothers, as you love one another and our common and holy cause, cease these worthless bickerings and remain a unit, remembering that he who holds out to the end shall be saved."

This lofty speech of so good, pure and faithful a disciple as the beautiful sister, had a tranquillising effect, and the whole membership became a unit.

"As each member is ready to act his part in the contemplated plot of our worthy deacon, I now call for the question and plans of Deacon Stew," said the President.

The deacon arose and spoke as follows:

"Beloved saints, our cause is just and holy; moreover, as we are the elect and chosen vessels of the Creator, it behooves us to use any means to keep innovators and reprobates away from our path. *First*, we shall use moderate, but effectual means; if, however, they fail, or *if we even entertain a doubt of failure*, we shall, *secondly*, drive the bullet or dagger to the inner recesses of the heart of the defiler of the brotherhood.

"There is a man in our midst who has always held sentiments antagonistic to, and dangerously at variance with, our common and holy cause, who has gained great influence in the family of our most heroic and wealthy co-laborer—I mean the family of General Armington.

"This innovator, by some act of his, has obtained access to the heart and home of the general, and aims to obtain the hand of Miss Lucinda Armington, which, should he be successful, would ruin our peace, comfort and safety in all time to come. I am informed that this vile innovator is a very magnificent looking young man, who can proclaim with a Demosthenic tongue, and charm even the most devoted disciple of our faith; in sooth, he has already turned the heads of our staunch Armington family, therefore we are compelled to work very cunningly and deeply, keeping our noble and heroic general in the dark until we contrive some mighty plan for the certain ruination of this Victor Juno—a romantic (?) name for the intended husband of Miss Armington.

"By the heaven above me—and I invoke the powers that be to aid me—I'll trap him, and make him rue the hour that sent him to set his foot in my path! Brothers and sisters, do you comprehend our condition, and do you swear renewed allegiance to our cause and the work I propose? If so, say, each one of you, I will, and raise your left hand toward heaven, whilst you place your right hand upon your beating heart, and pronounce the following solemn words after me; repeating each his or her own name:

"I, Rob Stew, solemnly swear to keep perfectly secret all the plans, acts and operations of the cause of our sainthood, and should I divulge anything or neglect to do the portion of work assigned me, I agree to have my upraised (left) hand burned into cinders; my right hand, which now clasps my beating heart, cut into fragments, and my heart torn out by its roots; moreover, should I fail to do as before stated, I hope to have my soul cast into outer darkness, where there shall be weeping, wailing and gnashing of teeth forever, and where the devil and his boon associates shall hiss at me, and pour pestiferous reptiles, with envenomed darts, upon my sensibilities, lashing and torturing me beyond the expression of language! This do I *voluntarily* swear, and hope for no other destiny should I fail in the fulfilment of each part of our sacred covenant. So help me God!

"Brethren and sisters of the sacred tie, you have renewed your vows, and I can now confide my bloody plans to your heads and hands; therefore, we shall at once dispatch this sacrilegious innovator, whose very name curdles my blood, and fits me to do such bitter business as would cause the devil to quake!"

CHAPTER III.

DEACON STEW RAVES AT LUCINDA'S LOVE FOR VICTOR.

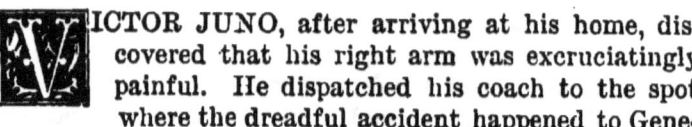ICTOR JUNO, after arriving at his home, discovered that his right arm was excruciatingly painful. He dispatched his coach to the spot where the dreadful accident happened to General Washington Armington and his lovely daughter, Lucinda, requesting his coachman to serve them to their liking, and telling the latter to make an apology to them for not accompanying the coach, as unavoidable circumstances prevented his attendance at that moment.

He sent for a brother physician, who discovered a neglected compound fracture of Victor's arm, which was already swollen to alarming dimensions, and lest he instantly retired to bed, mortification might end his days suddenly; notwithstanding this most painful condition, which was brought about through the humanitarian act of saving, and restoring to life, the angelic form of a creature whose very existence was a gigantic balm of Gilead to the lacerated body of our hero, and, in a half delirious state of mind, he felt like leaping mountains to raise prostrate female forms, and to become blessed with hymeneal joys of the most glorious character; but, his imagination soon forsook him, and a raging fever, accompanied by the most violent deadly delirium, ensued, which lasted a fortnight.

It may be interesting to learn, that Victor Juno was a

perfectly sound man of magnificently formed dimensions, erect in stature, six feet in his stockings, and, in fact, he was almost god-like in every feature.

His face was of the Roman cast, with a most happy and indomitably energetic and affectionate disposition. He possessed a full, round and well proportioned forehead, with eyes black and like sparkling diamonds; nose, mouth, chin, cheeks and complexion in the image of God, or after the acme of perfection, the whole central globe of the soul surrounded with hyperion curls, which hung gracefully over the superbly shaped head, and his trunk and extremities harmonized with these features.

Victor Juno had many warm friends, although there were few who dared, *in such perilous sectarian times*, stand by him openly, which he regretted very much; but yet he was most hopeful of living down all opposition, and conquering every element of strife. However kind, loving and generous he was toward friend and foe, he possessed the faculty of hardening his manly heart toward everybody, if such was necessary to gain a natural end.

He reasoned *thus:*—"What would it profit a man if he gained the whole world and lost his own soul; his own manhood and self-respect; and why should not we be willing to sacrifice the few, and the good of the few, for the many, and for the improvement of the race of mankind; for the perpetual good of a god-like and fixed law-abiding race?" Our hero was truly a man, and we fear we shall *not* look upon his like again; he loved the sinner, but despised his erroneous ways; he would not prosecute any one for money and worldly glory, but would slay millions for justice and principle, and he taught as one having authority, and not as the scribes, hypocrites, or pharisees.

The weakest point of his character, to live amongst haughty sinners, was his wonderful benevolence, which caused him to confide too much in what people said,—he believed everybody was honest, like himself, until he had gone through the fiery ordeal of martyrdom, when he turned his heart into adamant, and treated everybody as a viper and hypocrite. But, notwithstanding all his doubts and suspicions of adults, he had a never-failing faith in nature and nature's God, and looked always lovingly and confidingly to little children ; for, said he often, of such is the kingdom of heaven.

This latter quality still proved that the man was a genuine naturalist, who lost nothing by the storms through which he had passed ; but yet he lost faith in adults, whilst he continued to cherish the pure and innocent of God's heritage.

The family physician of Victor Juno had his doubts about the recovery of our hero, until the second week, when his symptoms seemed to become more favorable ; at this time General Armington had learned for the first time that the saviour of his daughter's life was lying in a dangerous condition, which was caused by the herculean and humanitarian efforts the noble Victor made in behalf of the family of the general ; when the latter instantly repaired to the home of the delirious man, and asking it as a particular favor to see the hero, was, by special favor, admitted to his bedside, when, in apparent agony, he was compelled to listen to the recital of the love he bore, and pain he underwent, for the daughter of General Armington on the occasion of the accident.

The general at once desired to render any assistance in his power to alleviate the precarious and painful state of Victor Juno.

The nurse thanked the general, but said that his physician did all for him that was possible, and he thought that a change for the better was apparent, at least so said the skilful doctor a few hours previous.

The general returned to his home to his daughter, who was also lying on a bed, suffering of severe nervous prostration, and who should be sitting by Miss Lucinda Armington's bedside but Deacon Rob Stew, who did his utmost to exhort and encourage the fair damsel, who was the apple of his evil eye.

General Armington related all he had seen at Victor Juno's bedside in the hearing of his daughter and Deacon Stew. The latter sat with eyes and mouth wide open, however, with a distressed look on his face, and upon close inspection by an expert, it would have shown that a fiendish expression passed spasmodically over his harrowed phiz, whilst he observed with what great interest, grief and sincere sorrow Miss Armington listened to the story that her father was relating.

The deacon saw that betimes Miss Armington was enchanted, especially when the father related what Victor Juno said of his daughter's rescue; whilst, on the other hand, she looked downcast when her father spoke of Victor's dangerous condition. The deacon—Judas-like—hid his feelings thoroughly from the gaze of either the general or his daughter; the latter, however, always felt uncomfortable in the presence of Deacon Stew; in fact, she despised the man, but after all respected him on account of his high position in their church, as also for his religious graces.

After carefully listening to the general's recital of what occurred, as well as to the praises which General Armington gave in behalf of the noble Victor Juno, the deacon said in the most solemn manner:

"General, I am deeply grieved at the sad story of this young physician, as well as being sorrowful to find your noble daughter sick after such a providential escape; it is my heartfelt prayer that all may come right very speedily, and I hope it will"—

"Thank you," interrupted Miss Armington. "I am *sure* the excellent young gentleman who has been so brave and unselfish will soon be restored to health, for God would not permit such a noble benefactor to pass away so early, whilst he is capacitated to do mountains of generous acts toward his fellows."

"Daughter, I am delighted to hear you express yourself so gratefully and kindly toward this heroic gentleman, for you seldom have anything favorable to say of the male gender," responded General Armington.

To these sentiments the deacon *ironically* replied: "Certainly Miss Armington could not well feel otherwise toward a man who saved her life, for he must be a brave and worthy (?) creature."

"Thanks, Deacon Stew," she said. "I am not ungrateful; moreover, dear father, I feel that we should employ the best medical talent to save Mr. Juno from a tedious and protracted illness."

"You are very thoughtful, my darling," responded the parent. "I think the deacon is about the best judge who is skilful in the medical profession; moreover, brother Stew, you would be the ablest man to select a good, *pious* doctor, as I believe greatly in the virtue of grace, which you know must be attended with heavenly results."

"General, your wisdom, and Christian worth and valor charm me, and whilst you were speaking, my mind was directed to a plan, or rather to a very eminent Christian physician, who never fails in the fulfilment of anything he undertakes; that is, if it is in the power of sinful mortal to perform," responded the jealous and hypocritical deacon.

CHAPTER IV.

PAT O'CONNER BLARNEYS THE DEACON.

WHILST Deacon Rob Stew was conjuring up a lot of shrewd deviltry, and preparing himself to win to his heart the fine Lady Armington, another scene was being enacted in the house of General Washington Armington.

Pat O'Conner, a peculiar disciple of the Roman Catholic Faith, was conspiring with Judy McCrea, both servants to General Armington, who hated Deacon Rob Stew with a bitter hatred; and their cunning plots to oust his deaconship were novel, and proved equally effectual when the time arrived for the fulfilment of their conniving.

As Deacon Stew was preparing to leave the bedside of Miss Lucinda Armington, Judy McCrea was relating to Pat O'Conner what a fancy the deacon had taken to her young lady, stating that Miss Lucinda despised the old hypocrite, when the following dialogue was held between the twain:

"Och! Judy, darlin', an' ye mane that dirty ould blackgard is in luv wid the purty Miss Armington?" said Pat O'Conner.

"An' shure I do," responded Judy McCrea.

"Be me sowl, I'll trap 'im, the squally old hypocret," said Pat.

"What will ye do to him, darlin' Pat? Be kereful of yerself, for the masther belaves him to be a parfect saint," replied Judy.

"Och, and ye nivir mind, but sind the ould curmudgon through the side doore, whin I'll plaster his nist for him. Mark, you kape dark on the matter," said Pat..

"I'll do it," responded Judy, and passed toward the bedchamber of Miss Armington; and who should she meet but the general and the deacon, on their way to the library.

They conversed for a moment, when Judy McCrea repaired to the library door and knocked, and, upon being asked in, she said, that Miss Lucinda desired her father to go to her as soon as possible, when the deacon was shown out by Judy through the side door, where another hypocrite—the faithful coachman, Pat O'Conner—was busily at work, who placed himself in such a position as to accidentally run against the deacon whilst the latter turned the corner of the house. Pat knocked the pious deacon under his chin, with the top of his head, sending the lover of Miss Armington reeling like a lightning-struck bull; and no sooner had the deacon recovered his balance than Pat humbly apologized:

"Och, murdher, yer honor, and I didn't mane to do it; will ye plaze to pardon an awkward Irishman? I whas a pullen up a big shtone out of the ground, whin I slipt, and fallen, struck yer honor," said Pat.

"I will pardon you for what you could not help doing," replied the deacon.

"Tanks, meny tanks; but, yer honor, how have ye found Miss Armington?" said Pat.

"Very much better, Pat," responded the deacon.

"Yer honor, plaze, if ye should not consider me impertinent, I could tell ye somethin' ye ought fur to know," said Pat.

"Certainly, I would not consider it impertinent for you to tell me what I ought to know; but, I would be very grateful to you for telling me, and if it is of any value to me, I would cheerfully compensate you for it," replied the deacon.

"Yer honor, plaze do not mention compensation, fur I would sarve ye charefully, if I tought ye would kape it a sacret," said Pat, humiliatingly.

"Most certáinly I shall keep anything secret that you propose to tell me as confidential; but what is it you have to tell me, I am anxious to know it?" ejaculated the deacon.

"I will tell yer honor, if ye tink it not too bould an' foolish; and if yer honor do hould it as silly, what I shall tell ye, an' ye will still kape it sacret—will ye?" said Pat, looking sheepish.

The deacon responded impatiently: "Pat, I have told you before, that I would not divulge your secret, so speak it out like a good man, without hesitation."

"We-ll, yer honor, I have larned lately that the Miss Lucinda Armington bees desparately in luv wid ye, an' she bees; yer honor will kape me sacret, will ye?" stammered Pat.

"Yes, yes, most profoundly secret; go on, and finish what you have to say," almost furiously ejaculated Deacon Stew.

"On me sowl, ye will kape yer own counsel on this matter?" mumbled Pat.

"Patrick, you insult me by your prevarication; speak straight out, and don't be silly," said the deacon.

"I will, yer honor; an' do ye tink it, Miss Armington bees in great dishtress becase ye do not axe her to marry ye?" said Pat.

"I am confounded with delight," meditated the deacon, and continued aloud:

"Pat, how do you know all this? Who told you?"

"Och, an' don't me darlin, Judy McCrea, tell me awl aboot it; yis, an' what's more, the ould gintleman wants his daughter to set her cap fur that Mr. Juno chap, what has saved me young lady whin me horses runned away wid me, an' almost killed us all. Now, yer honor, that young man bees a grate man in the eyes of the gineral," said Pat.

"Curse that Juno," meditated the deacon, and mildly asked Pat:

"Do you think Miss Armington loves Mr. Juno?"

"Well, yer honor, ye must know that she luv yer honor; but then she be a fathful daughter; an' should the gineral persist in the incouragment of Mr. Juno, she might turn her affectins from ye to him," said Pat.

The deacon was almost frantic with delight about Miss Armington loving him at last; but, again, he was in agony about the general being favorable to this infernal Victor Juno. In sooth, the Irishman's conjuring proved effectual, in creating in the deacon renewed ambition to gain the hand of Miss Armington, whilst his determination to destroy Victor Juno was becoming more desperate.

CHAPTER V.

THE BLOODY CONSPIRATORS POISON VICTOR JUNO.

E shall now be necessitated to go back to Tabernacle Hall, on the rainy night, where the bloody conspirators were laying their first plans to destroy Victor Juno's influence with General Washington Armington and family.

It will be remembered that Deacon Rob Stew, Rev. Joe Pier and Nancy Clover were the leaders of the sectarian ring, who had sufficient influence, cunning and craft to wield whatever power they saw fit to exercise over the orthodox religious classes of all denominations; for it must be again remembered, that although sectarian denominations seem to hate each other, nevertheless, when any innovator attacks *one* sect, or part of a sect or its tenets, they are *all* a unit to subdue and quiet the aggressor.

Deacon Stew—whose blood had curdled in his veins, on account of Victor Juno having gained access, and a most dangerous hold upon the affections of General Armington, who already had urged his daughter to receive the attentions of this rude innovator, and as the deacon was himself convinced from what he saw with his own eyes at the bedside of Miss Lucinda Armington, when her father related what he had seen at Mr. Juno's house, called for vigorous action, therefore—proposed that one of the most trustworthy physicians belonging to the cause be apprised of the necessity to attend instantly at Tabernacle Hall, to receive instructions to attend this Mr. Juno in consultation with the family physician of Mr. Juno, at the request of General Washington Armington and his amiable daughter Lucinda.

The president, Rev. Joe Pier, said: "Beloved saints, we certainly have arduous duties to perform, and they are of such a character as to cause me to tremble in my boots, unless the most zealous followers of the craft are selected to enact the work now in contemplation; I should be happy to hear the plan of operation laid before this meeting by Deacon Stew, whilst Mr. Grumbler will be dispatched to summon either Dr. Toy Pancy or Dr. Lewis Williams to come with him instantly to this hall."

Deacon Stew took the floor, and said: "It gives me much joy to be able to propose an effectual plan for the speedy and safe removal of that enemy to God's elect. I have been chosen by General Armington to select a physician for this man, Juno, and if we can induce, with perfect safety, either of the physicians, whom our worthy president just sent for, to slyly administer some fatal drug to this great admirer of heathendom, I am convinced that our task will be easy, sure and sound.

"Whilst the brother physicist is in consultation with Mr. Juno's family doctor, he must evince a monstrous anxiety to restore the sick man speedily; and propose, that if his prayers and attentions will do anything toward saving him, nothing shall lack on his part to accomplish the work of convalescence. Moreover, the entire religious brotherhood, sisters included, should be exhorted to pray for the restoration of the worthy hero who saved the lives of General Armington and daughter; and the members shall be solicited to call upon Mr. Juno continually, and be thankful to God that this noble youth had the courage to save the beloved brother Armington and daughter, whilst, of course, they will lament this sickness, that was caused by this generous act of Victor Juno.

"Beloved saints, it is always wise and better to pray much, long and often in public, as it shuts up the eyes completely of many worldlings, and, in fact, makes some or most of our own members, and other Christians, more respectful to, and confiding in us."

Sister Nancy Clover rose and spoke as follows: "The noble and indomitable brother Rob Stew has given us all that could be desired, even from an angel; therefore, I rise to say amen to it all, and may the power that always shields the elect stand by and see this holy work speedily executed "—

A knock at the door interrupted the sister, and, upon opening it, Mr. Grumbler and Dr. Toy Pancy stood ready to walk in and take seats.

The president said: "Brother Pancy, we are delighted to see you with us upon such short notice."

"At your service, brethren," responded the doctor. "What is your pleasure?"

"Dear doctor, we have a *most* important little job for you, which requires perfect secresy and great shrewdness. Our worthy president has selected you as the most trustworthy and able physician of the brotherhood to do what has been planned by us," said Deacon Stew.

"Brethren, I am highly complimented, and I assure our most excellent president that I appreciate his confidence, which he has so liberally placed in the skill and trustworthiness of my humble self, and I assure him that, if it is in my power, I shall perform whatever task is assigned me. So help me God!" responded Dr. T. Pancy.

"May the blessing of heaven continually abide with so faithful a disciple," said the president, and continued: "Deacon Stew will give you your instructions privately, and should you refuse to comply, after listening to the requirements demanded of you, I shall be happy to learn your objections, and whether you accept it or not, you are sworn to secresy until death."

"Certainly, your reverence," said the doctor.

"Deacon Stew will now conduct the doctor into the ante-room, and explain his work," commanded the pious Reverend and President Joe Pier.

The deacon related to Dr. Pancy what the reader already knows, only he exaggerated everything, and got the doctor to swear particular allegiance to *him* in this work of deviltry; fearing that he probably might need him to dose

Miss Lucinda Armington for the purpose of bringing her to terms of connubial submission, should any part of his programme fail.

The doctor seemed to be highly pleased with all that the deacon proposed, and showed himself as one of the most ambitious disciples of the elect to purge the brotherhood of all innovators; because, allopathic physicians are hand in glove with orthodox saints.

The doctor was conducted by the deacon to General Armington's house, but was told that the latter must be in total ignorance of the plans in consideration; the general received him kindly, and at once offered to conduct him to Victor Juno's residence and bedside, whilst Deacon Rob Stew was to summon Victor's family doctor to meet him forthwith.

A consultation was soon held, when Dr. Toy Pancy solicited to be ordered by the family physician to remain that night with the sick man, as the latter must be worn out; for this great kindness the family doctor was truly grateful; however, he deemed his patient much better, now, being conscious of all that transpired, yet Victor was very feeble and dangerously ill.

Dr. Toy Pancy returned to his own office, and prepared a slow poison, which he took with him in the evening for the purpose of administering portions of it to Victor Juno during the night.

CHAPTER VI.

THE SERPENT AT LUCINDA'S BEDSIDE.

MISS LUCINDA ARMINGTON was a beautiful young lady, of medium size; she had heavenly blue eyes, a brow like an angel; and altogether the face of a seraph.

Her form was slender, but magnificently cut; a bust of wonderful symmetry, and beautiful arms and hands. Her hair chestnut brown, and beautifully curly; whilst her disposition was of that benevolent and frank character which would curl or entwine itself around every one, of either sex, who came in contact with the fair damsel. She loved the beautiful in nature, and adored gentlemen who were governed by principle, instead of policy.

In other words, she was the *fac simile* of Victor Juno in sentiment and spirit.

After she had learned of the deep interest that Victor Juno took in her; his unselfish acts in rescuing her and her father; and when she knew that he suffered so excruciatingly on her account, she seemed to get well almost at once.

She said to her father, a few days after his recital of the condition in which he found the young hero:

"Father, why should not I be equally brave and determined to save Victor Juno's life as he was to save mine?"

"My darling, I should be pleased to see you use every effort to do so," responded the father.

The day that General Armington accompanied Dr. Toy Pancy to Victor Juno's house, Deacon Rob Stew, after sending his servant for Victor's family doctor, went to visit Miss Lucinda Armington, and said:

"Miss Lucinda, I hope you are pleased with my selection of a physician for your courageous (?) young saviour—I mean Mr. Juno." Almost sneeringly and savagely he uttered these words, which caused Miss Armington to start and ejaculate:

"Deacon, I am very much indebted to you for going to so much trouble; had I known that it would have inconvenienced you so much, I should not have spoken of a physician in your presence, as I did, then father would not have thought of burdening you to select an eminent doctor."

"My dear Miss Lucinda, you do not understand me; I have not said, nor felt, it was the least trouble to serve you, or this young gentleman; but, when I spoke, an idea, not pleasing, concerning another matter entirely, flashed through my mind, which caused me to express myself a little emphatic, which I humbly pray you to pardon, for you must be aware that we are all sinners; but, thank God that his grace is abundant toward his elect," humbly responded Deacon Rob Stew.

"Your apology is accepted, and I am glad that I have not asked too much of you; but, when I come to think, it was not my intention to have you select a physician, but it was father's doings, who has such unfeigned confidence in your worth and goodness," said Miss Armington.

"I appreciate this compliment, and shall endeavor to merit it, if God is willing," replied the deacon.

After exchanging many words with Miss Lucinda, the over-rated deacon departed, but accidentally met Pat O'Conner again, just as he was leaving the piazza, when the deacon said:

"Pat, how do you find things to-day; have you heard anything lately of this Mr. Juno?"

"Shurely yer honor must know more than I doos of what am goin' on in this house, or at Mr. Juno's plaze. Ye are a cunnin' gintleman; be jabers, ye make hay, I belave, while the sun shines. Will yer honor have the graceousness to kape my secret away from Miss Armington?" said Pat.

"Pat, never fear me; but, to convince you of my trustworthiness, I will tell *you* a great secret, if you promise to hold it sacred and will serve me," replied the deacon.

"Och, murdher, yer honor, don't be a placin' me on aquality wid your holy self, I am only a poor workin' Irishman; howsomever, I kin kape sacrets, I warrant ye, an' if I kin sarve ye, will do it widout tanks," said Pat.

"I believe you, Pat, and as you confided in me without solicitation on my part, I will now return the compliment, and tell you that I hate that Victor Juno. He is a heathen, a heretic and an impudent innovator; and although, good Pat, you and I do not agree in religion exactly, yet we are Christians, whom this Mr. Juno tries to undermine and ruin by his worldly notions; therefore, Pat, will you help us to put him where he belongs?" questioned Deacon Rob Stew.

"We-ll, yer honor, I bees at yer sarvice to do anyting that bees not too indacant, an' I am atinkin' where this Juno chap belongs. Will yer honor plaze tell me?" said Pat.

"Why, sir, he belongs to the ground from whence he came, and I have a plan at work that will place him forever beyond stepping into my, or your, path," ejaculated the deacon, in reckless anger.

"Och, howly Moses!" meditated Pat, "I shmell a mighty big rat, or I'm no man," and said: "Yer honor knows what's best, an' I will be sacret and sarve ye in any manner; but here comes Judy McCrea, so good day to yer honor."

"Judy, darlin', an' I have a sacret to confide to yer bossom, could I but fale sartin that me darlin' could kape a dredful sacret," said Pat.

"Why, Pat, ye spakes like a crazy man; do ye tink I've become a tratress and vaggabone, and have ye lost fath in yer Judy?" angrily said Judy.

"No, me darlin', be me sowl ye air accusin' of me wrongly; howsomever, I hav a monstrous sacret to tell ye, an' if ye promise to kape it good, I will give it ye, an' I want ye to hilp me to worry the matter out," said Pat.

"An' shure, I'll do it all as ye plaze, dear Pat," responded Judy.

"Open yer eyes, then, Judy, darlin', an' listen; do ye know that ould hypocret, Dacon Stew, bees manin' harm to the brave young lord, Victor Juno?" said Pat.

"Ye do not mane that?" replied Judy.

"Mane it, begorra I knows it; but I'll fix the dirty ould blackgard, or I'm no man; Judy, darlin', will ye hilp me to watch the squally curmudgon?" said Pat.

"Cartainly I will," responded Judy.

"A blazin idee strikes me mind; and that bees, we must tell Miss Armington of the attampt this dacon bees makin' to murdher Victor Juno," said Pat.

"Murdher Juno!" ejaculated Judy.

"Yis, bluddy murdher, jist now abreedin'. Ye git Miss Armington to consult wid ye an' me, and do it quick," said Pat, as though new danger fired up his soul.

Judy McCrea was a faithful nurse, who would have willingly lost her own life for her mistress, and she was already aware that Miss Lucinda Armington loved Victor Juno; therefore she hurried to find her ladyship, to bring her to Pat O'Conner, for the purpose of giving her the news.

Miss Armington said: "Judy, what does Pat want with me?"

"Och, my swate lady, an' he has a parcil to tell ye what will make yer blood fraze," nervously replied Judy.

"Tell me, what does he mean?" said Miss Armington.

"Indade, an' I couldn't tell ye, becase I do not know much aboot it," responded Judy.

"Well, Judy, I'll go with you in a moment to hear what Pat has to say," said Miss Armington.

They passed out together to consult Pat, who bowed profoundly to Miss Armington, and said:

"Do the lady desire to larn of the diviltry that am a hatchin'?"

"Yes, Pat, I am curious to know the news," replied Miss Armington.

"Yer ladyship," said Pat, after suspiciously looking all around, "I could not tell ye here, but let us go to some sacret plaze, whin I'll tache ye a wonder."

"Come, then, let us go into the library," responded Miss Armington.

CHAPTER VII.

NANCY CLOVER, FAILING TO CAPTIVATE GENERAL ARMINGTON, BECOMES REVENGEFUL.

SISTER NANCY CLOVER is a deep maiden lady, who speaks seldom, unless she sees a sure chance to make an impression in her own behalf. General Washington Armington is the idol of her soul, and although the general is not a marrying man, being a widower of nearly fifty summers, she has had a hope of capturing him without much trouble.

The general has always treated her with more than ordinary respect, probably on account of her zeal in the work of Christianity; because he was himself no hypocrite, but a sincere believer in, and follower of, orthodox religious creeds.

General Armington was a liberal orthodox saint, who looked upon every religious sect with charity, love and respect; in fact, it made little or no difference to him whether a man was a Presbyterian, Methodist, or Catholic; so long as he had faith in Jesus Christ, and led a good moral life, he esteemed such a one as his brother.

Nancy Clover understood the views of the general thoroughly, and as she was very conceited, and delighted in controlling every one, thought that it would be an easy task to bring him to terms after a seasonable time had passed after the death of his wife; but Nancy found that she was shamefully mistaken; therefore her *love of power* was aroused to its highest bend, and she determined to conquer or die.

She meditated as follows:—" I have done everything in my power for the last two years to get General Armington to propose to me; I have courted the society of his hateful daughter Lucinda; I have endeavored to make him jealous of others, after he paid me more than ordinary attentions, but all failed to cause the least impression on his mind. Now, I see but one effectual way of bringing him to my feet. I must cause the ruination of his daughter's reputation, and whilst I will link her fall with this innovator, Victor Juno, I will kill two birds with one stone, by causing a wide-spread prejudice amongst the saints of all denominations against both of them, and at the same time I will prove the most sympathetic bosom friend of both the general and his despicable daughter.

"This may seem to be serving God and Satan, but, as long as the elect cannot sin, and as long as I can wheedle the entire brotherhood, I am safe. Truly, my unsuspicious and innocent general, I'll turn your head around this way; and you shall see the hypocrisy of others, whilst you will be hated and suspected by many saints, who, however, for your money and position's sake, will do you homage; yet I will prove to be your *only* reliable friend, and when your family troubles bow your head, and those in whom you most trusted have proved false to your knowledge, I *still* will show my fidelity to yourself and daughter; but beware when the tigress once has the opportunity to close her teeth upon her prey, how she will make the huntsman, who fails to respect her life, howl!"

At this moment some one gently knocked at the door, and, on opening it, one of the servants announced that Rev. Joe Pier was in the parlor, desiring to see her.

"What does he want?" asked Nancy.

"I cannot say, my lady," responded the servant.

"Tell him I'll be there in a few moments," said Nancy, and murmured to herself: "That stupid mush-head is continually boring me; I wish Satan had him, the poor love-sick fool. If ever anything can disgust one, it is to have a sap-head like Joe Pier trotting after one, for whom one has neither love, fear nor respect; well, well, he may be of some valuable service to me, and I shall take advantage of this visit and use him to accomplish my purposes, if it kills him! The silly dunce seems to be happy when I give him one kind look; but, after all, I pity him, because he loves me as I have loved General Washington Armington; but, do to him what I would, he could never have enough wit, courage and spirit to revenge himself on me. Thus we are alike in loving what we cannot get, but unlike in revenging our wrongs.

"I will conquer or revenge myself, whilst poor Joe will fail to conquer me, and, instead of revenging himself on me, undoubtedly will conclude, parson and hypocrite-like, that it was the will of the Lord. After all, I despise these mush and milk saints, who possess neither manliness nor valor. But I must go to cozy and smile around my dupe, he may become tired waiting."

Sister Nancy Clover now entered her parlor, where the Rev. Joe Pier meditated over the future, when he should possess this richly adorned establishment, with the jewel of a woman as its presiding genius.

"Good morning, brother Pier, you are an early disciple of the Lord; I hope I have not kept you waiting; I was just completing my devotions and heavenly meditations, when the servant informed me of your presence," said Nancy Clover.

"My dear sister, you have always been a pattern of saint-hood, and I often think what a glorious world this would be if we had more sisters like your noble self," responded the Rev. Joe Pier.

"Thanks, brother Pier, for the compliment; but I *assure* you that I always seek to do my duty as an humble follower of the lowly Redeemer," ejaculated the influential and revengeful Nancy Clover.

"By the way of changing our conversation, may I ask, what is your opinion of General Washington Armington, as regards the fancy he has taken to Victor Juno? Do you not fear that the general will be carried away from the faithful if that innovator is allowed to get well, and continue to hold converse with the generous and unsuspecting general?" said Joe Pier.

"Indeed, brother Pier, my peace of mind has been much exercised about this matter, and I fear and tremble when I think of the abyss over which our beloved and truly pious general is inclining. We must exhort all the religious denominations to unite in carrying out some of my plans, which I shall ask *you* to weave into your sermons, as well as go amongst the members personally and exhort them of the danger that is brooding," said Nancy Clover, with a double meaning.

"Oh, angel sister! you do me so much good by your deep and holy thoughts. Will you please give me your plans of operation?" responded Joe Pier.

"Certainly, with pleasure, dear brother; but listen, some one is ringing the bell," said Nancy Clover, when a messenger arrived from General Armington.

CHAPTER VIII.

LUCINDA, IN DISGUISE, SAVES VICTOR'S LIFE.

IN the library of General Washington Armington, Pat O'Conner was relating to Miss Lucinda Armington, in the presence of Judy McCrea, what he had learned from Deacon Rob Stew about putting Victor Juno "where he belongs," namely, "to the ground." Pat continued to relate what the reader already knows, and added his own conclusions and plans. Said he:

"Miss Armington, after havin' yer promise to kape this intire matter sacret, and also yer promise to relate to Mr. Juno the danger what treatens him, wid *his* promise to kape it sacret, I'll jist unhitch me sowl of the burden of me hart," said Pat O'Conner.

"Well, go on, Pat, and let me hear it," responded Miss Armington.

"Me lady, ye know ye and yer father axed Dacon Stew

to git a doctor for to trate Mr. Juno; an' I had me idees rubbed up that this Dacon Stew, what luvs yer lady, an' hates Mr. Juno, becase ye luv, or raspect, Mr. Juno more than he like to sea; I mane, that Dacon Stew has played ye an' yer father false, by gittin' a tricky doctor what will pison Mr. Juno!" said Pat, with great agitation.

"Oh, Pat, you surely cannot think that of Deacon Rob Stew! He is a *good* Christian, and would not do such a foul act as to employ a murdering physician," ejaculated Miss Armington, with an internal shudder.

"Be me sowl, Miss Armington, may I stop to belave me own senses, ef it aint the trooth," said Pat, earnestly.

"But, Pat, how do you suspect or know all these things?" responded Miss Armington.

"Good lady, only kape sacret, an' I'll tell ye. That day whin Dacon Rob Stew was at yer bedside, whin ye axed yer father to imploy a doctor for Mr. Juno, I tould Judy McCrea, who tould me somethin' aboot him what strengthened me suspicions, that I wanted her to sind Dacon Rob Stew out by the side doore, whin I runned accidentallee against his honor, which made him spake to me; I humbly apologist, an' axed him aboot Victor Juno in a mannor what made him belave I hated Mr. Juno, whin the ould curmudg—beg yer pardon for forgittin' meself"—stammered Pat, when Miss Armington interruptingly said: "Go on."

"Well, yer ladyship, I was agoin' to say, Dacon Stew spake confidenge to me, an' said: 'Pat, if I could trust ye, I have a job that would make ye rich.' I suspected his diviltry, whin I blarneyed him, an' what ye tink, he unbossomed the dirtiest plans of his hypocretcal hart to meself, and I tought, be jabers, Pat, here bees a way to larn sacrets that will be of sarvice to me luvly mishtress, whin I swore, wid one eye shut an' a mental resarves, to lade him into the faild of battle.

"He tould me anough to conclude that he meant to pison Mr. Juno; an' me plans air, that ye sacretly go to

Mr. Juno's house, an' kape an eye on that doctor chap," said Pat.

"Oh, Pat, how can I believe or do all this?" gloomily responded Miss Armington.

"Be me sowl, I have tould ye only what am good trooth; ye can axe Judy McCrea, here, what kin tell ye I am spakin' only the trooth," ejaculated Pat.

"Fath, me swate lady, Pat O'Conner spake the holy trooth, so far as I knows," responded Judy.

Miss Armington was in great distress, and soliloquized as follows, after she excused herself and was left alone for prayerful meditation:

"O Lord, what *shall* I do? I cannot let father know of this conspiracy to murder Victor Juno; nor can I allow them to poison him, since I can save him. How shall I manage this matter, O, how must I act? Great powers above, guide my distressed soul aright.

"I have it; I have it. I will go in disguise to the house of Victor Juno, and request to see him as an old aunt of his; I understand he has an only relative, and that is an elderly aunt. I'll personate her to the people in his home, and when I once reach his bedside, I'll manage to make him understand me. This will be his salvation, although it may prove my ruination."

Miss Lucinda Armington waited until about seven o'clock in the evening, when she dressed herself in some of her mother's old clothes, which she had preserved from her death, and quietly left by the side door, thinking that she would not be seen so readily by leaving the house by that direction (it must be remembered that this was the door through which Deacon Rob Stew mostly visited the house of General Armington); she made her way to Victor Juno's residence, and as she rang the door bell, Dr. Toy Pancy drove up, and also stepped upon the step, waiting for the door to open; presently a very polite male servant received them, the doctor passing to the patient's room direct, whilst Miss Armington, in her disguise, was politely invited into the handsome parlor, which embarrassed her very much, causing a singular shudder to come over her system; the waiter noticed that the lady was somewhat nervous, hence he did not speak for a moment, when Miss Lucinda Armington said:

"Mr. Victor Juno lives here, does he not?"

"Yes, ma'am, at your service," responded the servant.

"Will you have the kindness to inform him that his aunt desires to see him?" said Miss Armington.

"Yes, ma'am, but he is very ill; however, he may desire to see his aunt; I'll go to him," responded the servant.

Miss Armington now had a flash of horror fly across her mind, thinking: "Oh, gracious heaven! should I be detected; monstrous, should this servant know the *real* aunt, and go to Victor Juno or Dr. Toy Pancy, and announce the fact that a lady is in the parlor who says she is Victor Juno's aunt, but that she is not the aunt that he knows, when Victor probably might be strong enough to state that he has only one aunt, or something to that effect. My, my, O, my head! I think I had better leave at once; because, should Dr. Toy Pancy find out who I was, or even suspicion of a mysterious person being in the parlor, he would be on the alert, and hence my mission be a failure, and most likely father, Deacon Stew and all the rest would discover that something was not right. Never was I in such misery; never was I so undecided what I had better do; and should any one come to me now, my face would be a mirror, wherein guilt and confusion could be plainly seen. I must compose myself; hark, I hear a step."

The door opened, and the same polite servant returned saying that Mr. Juno would see her in a few moments; moreover, that the housekeeper would come to the parlor in a few minutes.

She begged of the servant not to send any one to her, as she would patiently wait until Victor was ready to have him (this servant) conduct her to his side.

When Victor Juno heard the announcement that his

aunt was in the parlor, his countenance brightened up, and he solicited the doctor to permit his aunt to sit by him this night, and hinted he had better leave; which he did, although reluctantly.

The servant then conducted Miss Lucinda Armington, the bogus aunt, to Victor Juno's bedside.

CHAPTER IX.

VICTOR AND LUCINDA BETROTHED.

HEN Miss Lucinda Armington presented herself at the bedside of Victor Juno, he seemed to have known what was coming, he therefore spoke first, and said:

"I feel as though an angel from on high, in disguise, was before me," and took both her hands into his transparent ones, when she replied:

"Mr. Juno, I hope you will pardon me for appearing before you in this peculiar manner?"

"Certainly, my brave young lady, I feel from my inmost soul that you are here on a mission of mercy. And, if it were possible, I would relate to you what I saw in a dream last night," said Victor Juno, with a deep and exhausted sigh.

"Mr. Juno, please do not exhaust yourself; but, if you are not too weak, I will relate to you why I came here, and in this disguise," responded Miss Armington.

"Speak, O speak, sweet lady; your presence electrifies and strengthens me, and I am quite well enough to listen to anything that your charming voice may relate," quite vigorously said Victor Juno.

"Friend Juno, beg your pardon, *Mr.* Juno," stammered Miss Armington.

"Dear angel, use the former, and believe me that my very soul is yours, and I feel assured, by your presence at this hour, and in this disguise, that your heart beats in unison with mine, or you would not be thus," most affectionately spoke Victor Juno, looking worlds of love into her soul-enchanting eyes.

"May you never doubt my sincerity and motives, but still I am almost a perfect stranger to you," ejaculated Lucinda; but Victor interrupted her, and said solemnly:

"My beloved lady, why should you feel in the least embarrassed or backward in the presence of a man who would lose his life ten thousand times to give you one meagre joy?"

"Speak no more, dear friend, you have indeed saved my miserable life, at triple the danger of losing your own, therefore I would *indeed* be an ingrate to withhold anything from you," modestly responded Lucinda.

"Thanks, *many* thanks, for this delicious candor, and will you now be kind enough to relate what you spoke of, and, after so doing, I will tell you my dream," said Victor.

"Oh! I have some horrible things to tell you, which may not be any benefit to your shattered nerves; but, there is a greater danger overhanging you than my story can produce, should you be kept in ignorance of what I know. You will, therefore, find that my presence at this hour, and in this awkward disguise, may save your precious life, which, if such will be the case, will at least repay you for the great services you have done me and my father," said Lucinda.

"Beloved angel of my soul, why do you mention what *I* did? You certainly cannot deem me so selfish as to hope I labored for compensation," sadly responded Victor.

"Oh, no! certainly not, I did not mean that, but"— hesitatingly she continued—"I sup-pose it was"—

"Love," ejaculated Victor, "that prompted the wholesome act; say so, sweetest lady, and I'll believe you!"

"Yes, sir, indeed it was," she said, softly but earnestly.

"My soul is rejoiced that my never-ceasing affection for you is reciprocated, if I may be so bold as to esteem myself so blessed," responded Victor.

Lucinda modestly bowed her head and said: "This, truly, is the happiest moment of my life."

Instantly Victor drew her toward him and kissed her affectionately, after which he said:

"My darling, I should be pleased now to listen to 'the horrible things' of which you spoke."

"I will tell you, but hope you will see the necessity of keeping the whole matter a sacred secret, otherwise ruination might befall us both," said she.

"No, darling, have more faith in my Cupid God; but let me not interrupt you any more," responded Victor.

"Well, my noble friend, you will see the good of being cautious about making known my visit, disguise and story," said Lucinda.

"Of course, sweet love, I shall be perfectly silent, especially as you desire it, even if I saw it was better to make it public," ejaculated Victor.

"Thanks, blessed Victor. But to the point; I have a faithful servant at home, who has overheard a secret plot to murder you, and that by people whom you have never injured, and of whom you would not think that they could be guilty of such dark deeds," said Lucinda.

Victor interrupted her, and said: "My darling, allow me to ask who these parties are, and whether your servant really is reliable?"

"Yes, good Victor, my servant *is* reliable; moreover, there are a train of circumstances, of which I know, that convince me of the existence of such a plot; and, further, when I tell you all, you may be able to conjure up some matters that happened in this chamber, by which you also will know the truth of what I shall relate.

"My father is a good, honest man, and a great admirer of yourself; I make this remark because, when I tell you my story, you might conceive the matter in such a manner as to cause an impression on your mind that dear father had something to do with this vile work; because, you certainly must know that Dr. Toy Pancy was employed by father and myself," said Lucinda.

"What say you, Dr. Toy Pancy?" ejaculated Victor.

"Yes, Dr. Toy Pancy is a villain, who has evidently been trying to poison you whilst he was sitting up with you at night, without your own family doctor knowing anything about it," said Lucinda.

"Indeed," muttered Victor, and meditated a moment, then said—"I can now know why he was so uneasy and anxious to be alone with me; surely, my dream was not all a dream; but, then, I have again interrupted you before you have finished your story, please go on and tell me all."

"I will, dear Victor, but you may not clearly understand why myself and father would send you such a villain of a physician, unless I explain to you how he happened to be selected. I myself first proposed to furnish you with additional medical aid, and my father and Deacon Rob Stew sat by my bedside when I asked father to employ a doctor for you; at once father said to the deacon that he, the latter, was best acquainted with physicians, and would ask it as a *special* favor if Deacon Stew would select a physician; the deacon did so, and this is the manner in which Dr. Toy Pancy came to your bedside," said Lucinda.

"But, my beloved angel, how could such a course cause Dr. Toy Pancy to have designs upon my life?" exclaimed Victor.

"You may deem me immodest, but, nevertheless, as we have become so well acquainted and love each other, I may tell you that Deacon Rob Stew has been suing for my hand the last year; but, I hate his advances, and have always rejected him, yet have never been rude to him, because I always esteemed him a good Christian, until I learned that he connived with Pat O'Connor, our coachman, to murder you. Pat, irish-like, suspicioned this wolf in sheep's clothing, when he dissembled and acted as though he also hated you, knowing that the deacon detested you, because you are his successful rival," said Lucinda.

"Is it possible that Dr. Toy Pancy and Deacon Rob Stew attempted to take my life? Surely, I well remember that I had grown weaker the few days that Dr. Pancy was by my side, and my family doctor remarked several times, in the presence of Dr. Toy Pancy, that he could not clearly comprehend why I should not get stronger instead of weaker. My arm is nearly well, and I seem to see it all now; and it is *you*, my most precious darling, who saved my life; but, now I'll have an eye on these vile conspirators, and I see the necessity of secrecy, as you asked it," responded Victor.

"Dear Victor, I am exceedingly happy to see you so much better, and able to protect yourself against the danger which threatened your precious life; but, please tell me your dream, when I must go home," said Lucinda.

"Well, I dreamt three or four times last night you were by my bedside, as you are, and that we had pledged our mutual vows of love; but, every time that we wanted to consummate our nuptial ties, some obstacles were thrown into our path by deep designing enemies. This was all I remember of it, but, O, the horror and despair that I felt was almost unendurable," exclaimed Victor.

"It was, of course, only a dream, yet a very peculiar one, to say the least, and I shall be in continual dread of these men, who certainly have commenced in earnest"—said Lucinda, when a knock at the door interrupted their conversation; and when Miss Armington opened the door, the servant stood trembling and stammering: "O, good lady, the house is surrounded by an army of men."

CHAPTER X.

FOUL CONNIVING OF THE BLOODY CONSPIRATORS.

THE bloody conspirators have met again at Tabernacle Hall, Rev. Joe Pier in the chair.

Nancy Clover took the floor and said:

"Brothers, as no one but the faithful and *élite* are present, and as it will benefit you all to know my '*plans*,' which, when you are acquainted with them, may open the door to some new operations "—

The president ejaculated: "Dear sister, I have been almost dying to learn your 'plans and operations,' as you proposed them the last time we met, when General Washington Armington's messenger interrupted us."

"Mr. President, I have a word to say which will aid a speedy conclusion of plans," exclaimed Deacon Rob Stew.

"Brother Stew, our noble sister Nancy Clover has the right to the floor," interrupted the president and Rev. Joe Pier.

"Pardon me, dear sister, I did not intend to be rude, but thought if I could hint it to you, ere you speak, that I discovered Miss Lucinda Armington leave the general's— her father's—house, in disguise, last night, to go to Victor Juno's residence, you would be better prepared to draw your plans up in speedy order," said Deacon Rob Stew.

"Thanks, valiant brother Stew, you verily have done me a service, and as I am now prepared to give you my *plans and operations* for consummating this holy work of purging our cause of all unfaithful members, apostates and innovators, you will remember, that we have one common interest, and if we cannot gain our *individual* points, we nevertheless are a perfect unit in obtaining our combined ends.

"I find that several of those whom we love and respect are being led astray, who would rather play falsely toward us than adhere to the principles we espouse.

"*Firstly*, then, General Washington Armington is in dangerous hands, whilst surrounded by this Mr. Juno; therefore we must devote time, money, muscle and brains to break the link that binds the general and this Juno together. The best plan is to cause a sanctimonious anxiety for the general amongst all religious people; that done, then our united attention must be earnestly exercised to ruin the reputation, in the general's mind, of Victor Juno, who has escaped us, and is now beyond reach of the plan that was laid for his death through the faithful brother, Dr. Toy Pancy.

"*Secondly*, we must generate a hue and cry that Miss Lucinda Armington has compromised her reputation by injudicious familiarities, having, in disguise and at an improper hour, visited Mr. Juno's residence.

"*Thirdly*, that, having failed in our first attempt to forever quiet Victor Juno, we must now work more amongst the masses of saints of all colors, than aim directly at the life of this vile innovator; and by setting up a howl amongst the brethren, setting forth the great danger to our cause, provided this man Juno is not quieted or degraded. This is our next best step—what thinks brother Stew?" said Nancy Clover, whose words sank deep into the hearts of all present.

Deacon Rob Stew now arose and spoke as follows:

"Beloved saints, I have listened with great interest to our valued sister's glorious plans of operations, and have come to the conclusion, what she does *not* know is not *worth* knowing.

"Let us, therefore, act upon her plans, and to do so effectually, each one must be assigned his or her portion of the work, otherwise we might cause the chains to clank to our disadvantage, by drawing attention to matters with the same persons, and thereby cause suspicions. I mean, that each one shall know in what field he is to operate; because we shall have to influence the Standard Medical Fraternity; the Editorial Fraternity; the Municipal Ring; the moral, literary, charitable and religious organizations, such as the Young Men's Christian Associations, Sabbath schools, Bible societies, tract and the numerous charitable societies. And I propose the following order of work for our members:

"Rev. Joe Pier, among the Editorial and Municipal Rings.

"Dr. Toy Pancy, among the Standard Medical Fraternity and Druggists.

"Sister Nancy Clover, among the charitable and literary associations; and I will take to the tract, Bible, Sabbath schools and Young Men's Christian Associations.

"I would also here relate what I did last night, after I learned that Miss Lucinda Armington repaired in disguise to Victor Juno's residence. I called twenty of the faithful to disguise themselves, and join me to surround the house of Victor Juno; and getting Dr. Toy Pancy to arrive also at such a moment as to force his way accidentally into Mr. Juno's house, and go directly to his bedroom for the purpose of detecting whether this reputed aunt who visited her nephew—Mr. Juno—last night, was not the veritable disguised Lucinda Armington.

"I concluded, should we find her there, we would abduct her, and take good care that the wretched apostate would never more come between us and our enemy; but, from some cause or other, we missed our prey."

"You were not very sharp," said Nancy Clover.

"Well, as bad luck would have it, they were apprised by Mr. Juno's servant that we were surrounding the house, before Dr. Toy Pancy could enter the house, which evidently caused Miss Armington to escape; but, how she got through our lines, as we besieged the house, is miraculous," responded Deacon Stew.

"How do you know that she escaped; why may she not have been hid away, somewhere about the immense mansion of Mr. Juno; did you search the house?" said the president, Rev. Joe Pier.

"No sir, we did not search the house at all; but, when I found that Dr. Toy Pancy failed to find her, or the bogus aunt, I drew my comrades aside, and directed them to scatter a little, until I would go to visit General Washington Armington's residence, and announce to the general and daughter the precarious condition in which Mr. Victor Juno was found when Dr. Toy Pancy returned to his bedside; and behold her ladyship—Miss Lucinda Armington—was aroused from her own bed, as though nothing had happened; this caused us to disband for the present," exclaimed Deacon Stew.

The reader will remember that Miss Lucinda Armington was by Victor's bedside the moment Dr. Toy Pancy entered the front door, but she at once ran down stairs and out at the back door before the disguised conspirators dreamt that their presence was detected, and before they had taken their proper stations, as besiegers, she had fled.

Victor Juno, although not a dissembler, for the lady's sake, at once feigned to be awfully ill, and called for Dr. Toy Pancy and his family physician. Dr. Toy Pancy was told by Victor Juno's civil servant that something very horrible was breeding around this neighborhood.

CHAPTER XI.

SHREWD EXPOSE OF COSMOPOLITAN RASCALITY.

THE work of sanctimonious deviltry, as well as the melo-dramatic acting, was now about being commenced on both sides; and as Victor Juno was about restored to comparative good health, sent his agents to lease the Philadelphia Walnut Street Theatre for Sunday evening preaching, which aroused the *bloody conspirators* to renewed efforts to conquer him, by either disgracing or killing him.

Victor Juno advertised in all the daily, weekly and Sunday newspapers that he should preach next Sunday evening in the Walnut Street Theatre, on the "*Rock upon which* '*The Church*' *Split*," in which he should advocate the running of the street cars in Philadelphia on Sunday. This announcement was hailed by the great majority of "the people" with delight; which was proved by the immense crowd of the *élite* and humble that filled the theatre from "pit to dome," whilst from five to ten thousand ladies and gentlemen could not gain admission.

This popularity was excruciatingly nauseating to the *bloody conspirators*, as well as distasteful to the more generous and sincere religionists; however, the latter would not have thought of interfering or menacing Victor Juno, although violently opposed to having the street cars running on their holy Sabbath, had not the *bloody conspirators* thrown firebrands amongst the denominational cliques; who were thereby persuaded, almost to a man, that there was violent danger in the atmosphere, or the good Rev. Joe Pier, Deacon Rob Stew, Nancy Clover and company should not have warned the believers.

There were now various elements at work: The sincere, but misled followers of the flock were in wonderful earnestness; the medical clique also were so bitter that their sincerity to destroy the influence of, or Mr. Juno himself, could not be doubted; the editorial staff laid back until they could *learn* who would win, for they cared not a whit for either party, on account of principle, or love for their "hobbies," as they styled their causes, but they were after the *filthy lucre* and high positions amongst men, whilst the worldlings rather relished the battle that was breeding in the air.

The latter are *always* in the majority, and they are also ever ready to investigate anything that is not too indecent or inconsistent; still, they are not a class, under existing morbid civilized life, to be relied upon for succor; because, having been misled and humbugged from infancy to old age, by the professed saints, medical lights, political honorables and *lucre* grubbing editorial cliques, as a natural consequence, are equally suspicious of innovators.

Moreover, "the people," not being educated in sound human science, do very little or no thinking, from duty, upon the fixed laws of nature and nature's God; hence are naturally suspicious, irreverent and recklessly impious; therefore reformers always labor under very unfavorable circumstances, which is the reason that all *genuine* reformers are only appreciated many years after they have gone beyond this shoal of tears.

The staunch and sincere followers of the sectarian churches are afraid of reformers; the standard medical profession is too dignified and learned (?) in potions and fine classic terms to be annoyed by rude naturalists, or less scientific charlatans; the *bloody conspirators*, claiming to possess ownership, by might if not by right, of everything, entwine themselves around the hearts of the unsuspecting and innocent, whilst they swear allegiance to orthodoxy in medicine and religion, and bitterly detest innovators; the newspaper fraternity and municipal rings neither fear nor hate orthodoxy or liberalists, provided the pile of stamps is balanced; but, when the precious jingling stuff inclines one way, then they behold more respectability, decency and godliness on that side of the house.

With the foregoing illustration of the position of Victor Juno, the reader may be able to realize the unenviable state of a heroic reformer; but, the power of the *bona fide* natural Christian, or normal man, is *immense* over the weak minds of a sickly nation, as will be seen by the way Victor Juno holds the entire community uneasy, causing thousands to quake in their boots.

He takes his enemies by storm and rends asunder the sophistries of century-born customs, which shakes the foundations of falsely erected houses, until amazement stultifies the human mind.

CHAPTER XII.

VICTOR JUNO'S SCATHING SERMON IN THE THEATRE.

(NOTE. *The reader must peruse each of Victor Juno's Discourses or he cannot understand the plot.*)

BELOVED FRIENDS—I will speak to you this evening on "*The Rock upon which 'The Church' Split.*" I have nothing new to offer, but as Shakespeare says: "Old things wax new when lovers grow cold," and I argue that the love for a natural

Creator, who has made everything for our pleasure, joy and perpetual bliss, has grown *very* cold. In sooth, God and nature are esteemed vulgar monitors, if we accept the actions of the professed saints as criterions to go by.

The Old and New Testaments teach sound logic, when we have the key to unlock the meaning of the mandates of this Bible. It is very much a book like the arithmetic, and as long as it is read by everybody, without anybody having the key by which alone a natural or scientific religion can be discovered, "*The Church*" of God (which is composed of all the wonderful works and fixed laws of God) will be continually split into new isms and schisms, and

> "Each stupid sect, in error bound,
> Think they the only road have found
> To paradise complete."

There exists only *one* church, namely, the Holy Catholic, or Universal, or Natural Church of God, and Jesus Christ was the Naturalist who established it.

There are no such things in God's, or Christ's, or nature's vocabulary as "churches." Moreover, a "church" is not a house made of bricks, mortar, wood and cushioned seats, with gilded candlesticks and gaudy or plain fixtures, blasphemously *dedicated to Almighty God* (as commonly called) by the pharisees and blind leaders of the blind; but, a "church," or "THE CHURCH," is composed of law, order, principle, heavens, earth, air and all the multitudinous little injunctions of the Creator, with Jesus Christ's simple, pure and resolute mind at the head, representing himself as the *chief corner stone;* whilst the Holy Spirit is the motive power that incites the mind to a full understanding and *bona fide* appreciation of the Creator's fixed laws; hence, the Father, Son and Holy Spirit are in one work—or are actually one—and yet three distinct heads, or principles.

Therefore, "The Church" cannot be dedicated by man who is born and bred in false relations to life—it is the height of presumption to talk such stuff; but man can dedicate, or consecrate, or devote himself *to* "The Church," if he chooses to repent of his bad habits, and is willing to seek and find wisdom inside of God's fixed laws of life and health both of body and soul.

Knowing, therefore, what "The Church of God" is, we can soon behold what split this hallowed natural institution, namely:

"Reading the Bible, without first understanding the science of human life, or laws of nature, hence not being able to cypher out the meaning of God and nature."

One must understand the multiplication table before he can use the arithmetic to advantage; so also one must comprehend a *true* anatomy and physiology before he can understand that the Bible and fixed laws of nature and nature's God agree.

Beloved friends, having given you the key to the Bible, namely, a knowledge of the *science of life;* and having shown that God's kingdom suffers violence through ignorance of his fixed laws of life; therefore this ignorance is the "Rock upon which 'The Church' Split."

Let me reiterate, that the bigoted sectarian and partisan spirit is given pre-eminence over God and nature. God makes the beautiful natural country, but sinful man makes the city; the latter is composed of the abuse of the Creator's goodness, is a heap of brick-and-mortar, like the sectarian brick-and-mortar churches, but has no keen conception of Christ-like sympathy for the poor, the fallen and the leprous. No, those who should be cared for, who should be raised, healed and saved, are made the tools and serfs of the *lucre kings*, who, pharisee-like, can ride to their gilded brick-and-mortar churches, or anywhere else, in handsome coaches on Sunday; but the poor laborer, who is the bone and sinew of the city, is not allowed to have *his* carriage run through the streets of this immense city on the only day of rest; I say the street cars *shall* be made to run on Sunday in this great heap of brick-and-mortar.

Friends of free, noble America, are you going to allow the meanest monarchy on earth to rob you of your inalienable rights,—I mean the sectarian money-monarchy,—are you going to stand by, rubbing your bloodshot eyes, and blaming God for the miseries and serfdom you suffer, whilst cunning, craft, hypocrisy and the most cruel deceptions are continually practiced upon you by these false interpreters of the Bible, who would have you dance to their fiddle or see you suffer the veriest slavery; but, withal, howl of freedom and American liberty?

Why, my dear friends, there are leaders at the head of these misled enthusiasts who would enter into any foul conspiracies for the purpose of gaining their pharisaical ends. The bloodiest conspirators of all ages are at the helm of this sanctimonious work of deviltry. They crucify Christ anew, and connive to slay the faithful follower of truth, because they, claiming to be the chosen people of the Lord, think they own heaven, earth, man and his liberty to serve God.

Was not Jesus Christ arrested on the Sabbath day for doing good, the same as these modern vipers arrest all men who desire to think and act as they deem it right? Did Jesus ever use trickery like this to subjugate sinners? Did he delight in domineering, lucre-grubbing and sanctimony? Nay, nay; but he pronounced the following terrible woes upon such scoundrels:

"Wo unto you scribes and pharisees, hypocrites, for ye devour widows' houses, and for a pretence make long prayer; therefore ye shall receive the greater damnation. Ye fools and blind guides, who strain at a gnat and swallow a camel.

"Ye serpents, ye generation of vipers, how can ye escape the damnation of hell."

With Jesus Christ, God and nature, I cry aloud and spare not him who sets himself against the fixed laws of an unchangeable Creator, and I exhort and *pray you*, instead of God, to rise up as one man and slay the hydra-headed monster that would stay the stream of a God-ordained piety.

I ask you to lead natural physiological lives, returning to nature, truth and sound sense, and unless you fight for principle and justice, you cannot expect salvation.

> "I live to hail that season,
> By gifted men foretold,
> When men shall live by reason,
> And not alone by gold!
> When man to man united,
> And every wrong thing righted;
> The whole world shall be lighted,
> As Eden was of old!"

At this moment the meeting was interrupted by dirk knives being thrown from the galleries at Victor Juno, when a terrible riot arose.

CHAPTER XIII.

LUCINDA ABDUCTED AND IMPRISONED.

THE house of General Washington Armington was besieged by visitors from the sainthood; and although the faithful Pat O'Conner and Judy McCrea were not suspected of either knowing anything of the troubles that were breeding, or of being participants in the diabolical work of overthrowing the sacred temple of the elect; yet, truly, they were in secret conclave with Miss Lucinda Armington, doing bold acts, whilst the sincere and bloody conspirators were trying to inveigle the general into a plot to discard Victor Juno.

Deacon Rob Stew said: "General, are you not afraid that your beautiful daughter will get a bad name by associating with Victor Juno, because, my dear brother, you must know that an immense odium is attached to that man?"

"I cannot see what he has ever done to cause such gossip about the brave young hero; I certainly admire him *very* much, and shall stand by him until I learn of acts by him that are unmanly," exclaimed the general.

Pat O'Conner has such long ears that he was overhearing this little conversation, and he at once said:

"Me lady, that divil of a dacon is a puttin' mischafe unto yer father's head; but I'll shtop him strate, if ye want me to do it."

"I do, Pat, if you can do so in a judicious and effectual manner," ejaculated Miss Armington.

"Bedad, lave that to me, an' I'll rattle his mutton fur the ould hypocret," said Pat.

Pat now hurried to the library, where the general and deacon were secretly conversing, and impatiently knocked at the door, whilst he almost simultaneously cried with a loud voice:

"Me honored good mashter, I was tould by a gintleman on the sthreet that ye were violantly callin' an' sarchin' fur me; here I bees, at yer sarvice."

General Armington told him to *come in*, when Pat rattled off a lot of Irish that might have done homage to a king, whilst he bowed profoundly to Deacon Rob Stew and said:

"May it plaze yer honor, if I say to ye, that the worthless paople are assaultin' the howly saints; I mane yer frinds, way down by Jabob's plantation, an' the Riverend Joe Pier and Miss Nancy Clover tould me to ax ye, should I see ye, to come home quickly, fur they belave a riot am abrakin' out."

"I'll hasten, general, if you'll excuse me," exclaimed the deacon, frightened lest Victor Juno was arousing the people to do great violence to the believers.

"Good mashter, I have somethin' to tell ye, if I tought ye would not tink me too bould," said Pat.

"Not at all, Pat, go on and tell me," replied the general, recklessly, with however more than ordinary anxiety.

"We-ll, ye may not belave me, but shure as life be in me, the dacon, what jist lift, is no frind of me Mishtress Lucinda; becase, I heerd him spake to a stranger the other evenin' what was not true, nor kind to spake of a nice lady like Mishtress Lucinda," said Pat.

"What was it, Pat?" demanded General Armington.

"An' shure, good mashter, he said tow the stranger: 'Well, brother, I have discivered that Miss Lucinda Armington is a fast young lady, becase she has visited Victor Juno in they dark night,'" exclaimed Pat, angrily.

"How does it come, Pat, that he would make such a remark in your hearing; he knows that you live with us, and would not utter such words in your presence, fearing you might tell us? Where was this?" indignantly ejaculated General Armington, who thought, "Pat, you are either lying, or the deacon is a hypocrite."

"Good mashter, belave me, an' he said that very ting; but it was one dark night, whin I heerd many noises along the rood as I was acomin' home from Judy's father's," said Pat, without hesitation.

"Surely, Pat, I cannot understand this; but I will see by and by what it means," responded General Armington.

Pat now sought his Judy and Miss Armington, to tell them how he worked the deacon's mutton. He said: "Och, be me howly Moses, but I worked the dacon's mutton; I jist made him belave that there was a fight down by Jabob's plantation, atween his howly saints an' the worthless paople, an' mind ye, he belaved every word uv it, an' clared right strate away from yer noble father; whin I tould yer good father, what will cause him to look to the ould curmudg—excuse me, I mane hypocret," jocularly said Pat.

"We must be very cautious not to expose our secret workings, or our plans will prove futile, and dear father then might be turned against Victor Juno," sadly responded Miss Armington.

"But, have ye herd of the riot last Sunday evenin' at

the Walnut Street Theatre ? The dirty ould dacon, I'se sartin, were at it every bit," said Pat.

"O, yes, I have learned from a friend who was there, that these blood thirsty conspirators had sent some detectives in citizens' clothes, as well as had sprinkled throughout the theatre some of their own disciples, for the *especial* purpose of breaking the peace, so that the mayor could find a legal cause to arrest Mr. Juno. But they were unable to cause the audience to be clamorous, hence, toward the close of his discourse, threw several dirks from the galleries toward Mr. Juno, which missed him, thank God, but sank deep into the boards of the floor all around him; and as soon as the *people* saw this outrage, they made for the scoundrels who were seen throwing the knives.

"The enemies to Mr. Juno were too few to stand a battle, therefore the apparent riot was soon calmed; but the mayor and bloody conspirators were afraid of the *people*, who were well pleased with Mr. Juno's sermon, otherwise he would have been arrested," said Miss Armington.

It was now getting late in the evening, and the general having retired to bed, Miss Lucinda Armington, Pat O'Conner and Judy McCrea were still talking over these exciting times; because Miss Armington had now no trustworthy friends, amongst all her many *élite* acquaintances, in whom she dared to trust; only her faithful servants were left her.

These humble, but cunning, Irish lovers grew in Miss Armington's esteem to a wonderful degree of respectability and moral worth, when she compared them to all her pious (?) friends, who were now determined to have her desert Mr. Juno, or they should desert her. However, death would be preferable to unfaithfulness to her betrothed husband.

At last the servants also retired to rest, but Miss Lucinda remained in the dining room alone, meditating over what she should or could do to be of service to her beloved Victor.

After sitting for an hour in a meditative mood, she thoughtlessly opened a door that led to the fine garden, and whilst thinking only of Victor, she found herself walking under the magnificent trees, which were interwoven with shrubbery, and, O, horror! suddenly she felt something thrown over her head, which was the last she remembered that night.

CHAPTER XIV.

VICTOR ABDUCTED AND IMPRISONED.

THE *bloody conspirators* worked hard and faithfully to influence their people, besides throwing baits and firebrands amongst those who were in less reputable pursuits, such as rum, tobacco, perfumery dealers and patent medicine venders; showing plainly, that if Victor Juno's teachings were accepted by *the people*, there would be an end to orthodox creeds; and medical doctors, medicines, rum, tobacco, toilet articles and the thousand-and-one fashionable make-ups and unnecessary artificial paraphernalia would be useless, and the manufacture and sale of these articles would totally cease; therefore the thousands of people who make a good livelihood at these trades would lose the means of making a living through such doctrines as Victor Juno advocated.

This kind of logic was convincing to those who cannot see God in natural things; but, who are born, bred and educated under artificial logic, artificial habits, and as Victor Juno says: "They live by art, doctor by art, and expect to fly to glory on golden wings."

The *bloody conspirators* are not idiots nor simpletons, but deep, cunning villains, who understand all about the power of God's holy laws; and whilst they are not able to teach sound doctrines, they can nevertheless comprehend what such doctrines imply when presented to their senses by the true naturalist. Therefore they are envious and jealous beyond endurance of the man who dare present sounder and holier teachings than have been advocated and followed by themselves.

Here, then, is a bugbear that must be removed at all hazards, and as the followers of the sectarian creeds are not so wide-awake and apt to comprehend good and evil as the *bloody conspirators*, the latter find it no trouble at all to control and wheedle these sincere and innocent followers of the believers; hence, in one short week, these four *bloody conspirators*—Rev. Joe Pier, Deacon Rob Stew, Sister Nancy Clover and Dr. Toy Pancy—have the whole religious community in a blaze of earnest zeal for the rescue of sinners from the infidel and heretical teachings of this vile innovator, who thinks nothing of preaching his profligate doctrines in a play-house on the holy Sabbath day, there to urge on the masses of worldlings to violate the holy Lord's day by running the street cars on the Sabbath.

The following Sunday the great majority of ministers preached special sermons on this man Juno, denouncing him in the most severe terms that it was possible for them to utter and seem saintly. They urged their people to use every means to destroy the influence of this sacrilegious innovator; and also requested their Sabbath school teachers to command and exhort their pupils not to go where Victor Juno was, nor to dare to read or touch any of his books or advertisements.

Any reasonable free thinker, who does his own thinking, may at a glance behold the power that these *bloody conspirators* were wielding; but this was only a drop in Victor Juno's cup, and truly thus, " Bad begins, but worse remains behind."

Deacon Rob Stew, failing to impress General Washington Armington favorably, when he had a secret interview, in the general's library, with him; and having it from the general's own lips, that he should stand by Mr. Juno until he saw improper acts on the part of Victor Juno, caused the *bloody conspirators* to abduct both him and Miss Armington, and announce to the general that Victor Juno had eloped with his faithful daughter Lucinda.

They telegraphed to Pittsburg, and later to Chicago, to their sectarian equals, to send telegrams back, stating that a Mr. Juno and the handsome daughter of General Washington Armington were seen in those places; thus having *bona fide* proofs to present to the general's own eyes, that his daughter was seduced and carried away by this ruthless person.

When the general received this sad news, he was almost paralyzed with amazement; but Pat O'Conner and Judy McCrea, who had been faithful servants for long years, whispered earnest comfort into the general's ears, and even exposed some tangible deviltry of some of the pious clique; however, Pat was too wise and cunning to open his secrets too far to any one; because he had unbounded confidence in Victor Juno, Miss Lucinda Armington and a just God; therefore felt certain that everything would turn out right in the end.

The general was between two fires, as he was inclined to believe the *bloody conspirators;* in fact, they gave him convincing proof; but, on the other hand, he had too much faith in his beautiful and affectionate daughter to believe she would play so wickedly; and he also believed what Pat O'Conner and Judy McCrea whispered to him. At any rate, he was persuading himself that his fair daughter was not the girl that the saints made her appear; and he made up his mind to remain unprejudiced, but wait and watch.

He set himself to work to learn when Victor Juno left his own house; and by applying to Mr. Juno's civil male servant, the latter told him that his master was last seen going down Chestnut street, about eleven o'clock in the evening of last Thursday.

On that very Thursday night Miss Armington also disappeared; so, according to this statement, they left, or were disposed of, at the same time.

Victor Juno was not a suspicious man, but rather believed that people were more honest than their actions proved; and, on account of his immense benevolence, he very readily trusted those whom he should have shunned, and by so doing he was very easily led into a perfect trap. As he turned the corner of Fourth and Chestnut streets, he spied a gentlemanly looking man coming straight toward him, who bowed profoundly and said:

"You are Dr. Victor Juno, are you not?"

"Yes, sir, that is my name," responded Dr. Juno.

(Hereafter we shall preface Victor Juno's name with Doctor.)

"Mr. Wm. T. Josephs, of Kingsessing, sent me in great haste to bring you to his residence, his daughter is very ill, and he desires your services," exclaimed the stranger.

"I should be happy to go, but how shall we go; at present my carriage is not home?" said Dr. Juno.

"Mr. Josephs' close carriage is waiting at a friend's in Walnut street. I am to bring a male servant with me also, and whilst he was packing up his duds, I proposed to go direct to your office, and ask you to get ready to go, and I thought by the time the driver got around to your office, you might be ready to jump in, and thus we should not lose any time," interposed the stranger.

"Certainly," said Dr. Juno.

"But, doctor, as I have found you here, if you have the kindness, you would better accompany me down to Walnut street, where we can get into the carriage, and stop at your office on our way out there, if you choose to stop there," interposed the stranger.

"I will do so; nor is it necessary for me to stop at my

office, but we had better hurry to Mr. Josephs', if his daughter is so sick," said Dr. Juno.

"Thank you, sir; here comes the carriage already," responded the stranger.

The gentlemanly man, whose face was somewhat familiar to Dr. Juno, motioned to the driver to drive to the curb, which was in a rather illy lit part of the street; the driver jumped from his box, opened the carriage door, when the male servant stepped out, and Dr. Juno was politely invited to step in, the stranger and pretended servant following, the driver closed the door, and off rolled the vehicle.

All were silent; but in a few moments Dr. Juno felt some strange sensations, and looking around the carriage saw what seemed to be a bundle of clothes, which he thought was the servant's wardrobe, when suddenly, as they turned a dark corner, he was vigorously grasped and gagged, and bound hand and foot, so that he was entirely powerless.

The carriage was rattled along speedily, turning an innumerable quantity of corners, until, after driving for what seemed an age to Dr. Juno, it ceased to rattle, having struck a country road, and after continuing straight ahead for what seemed a long time, a few turns were made, when the team was stopped, and in great darkness he was roughly seized by four men and carried into a damp apartment, and dumped on a hard cemented floor, when a voice said:

"Have you got him safe and sound?"

"All right," responded another brutal voice; then they all departed, and the last that Dr. Juno heard of them that night was the rattling of several immense keys as they locked the doors.

CHAPTER XV.

REPORTED ELOPEMENT AND SEDUCTION OF LUCINDA BY VICTOR.

SISTER NANCY CLOVER had been spreading secretly amongst her circle of saints the delightful gossiping news that Miss Lucinda Armington was not what she ought to be, having been too intimate with this *roué*, Victor Juno, and, of course, since both Dr. Victor Juno and Miss Lucinda Armington disappeared at the same time, the entire community believed that an elopement was certain.

A great deal of sympathy was felt and expressed for General Washington Armington, and whilst many saints innately rejoiced at the calamity that had befallen the general, they nevertheless were free with their expressions of pity for the poor misled daughter, whilst they denounced to General Armington's face this profligate son of toil, whose "out-growth" was plainly to be seen in this ungrateful act to his benefactor and intended father-in-law.

The general would not allow any one to say anything cruel of his daughter or Dr. Juno; because he believed them innocent of crime. He soliloquized thus: "Why should my faithful and loving daughter elope with Victor Juno, or why should *he* desire to do so, as long as I encouraged their union?"

Whilst the general was thus in deep meditation, Deacon Rob Stew was ushered into the library of the former, where the general sat with downcast countenance.

"Good morning," cheerfully said Deacon Stew.

"Good morning," coldly replied the general.

"My dear brother, do not take this elopement so seriously to heart, for I have rather good news for you"—

"What is it?" interposed the general, impatiently.

"Why, sir, I have just received a letter from New York, from a faithful brother, who says that he saw a lady and gentleman answering to the description of Miss Lucinda and Dr. Juno, take passage on a vessel for Liverpool last week," responded Deacon Rob Stew.

"Indeed, sir; but I don't believe it," said the unsuspicious general.

"Don't believe it; what reason have you to doubt it? surely they have eloped "—

"Silence, Deacon Stew," furiously and frantically ejaculated the general, and continued, "I believe that there is some foul plot at work to remove these innocent young people from my presence; they were not opposed by me in their desire to become man and wife; then why should they elope, I want to know?"

"General, you confound my ideas; but if you had not lost patience with me, I think I could set your mind at ease on this subject," said Deacon Stew, tremblingly and much frightened.

"Well, sir, I am all patience, speak," replied the general.

"Pardon me when I say that I am confident that Miss Armington was pure; but Dr. Juno did not desire marriage with your daughter, he had other designs upon the lovely and unsuspecting daughter of your house; and this is the reason that he eloped with her, very likely promising marriage," said the deacon.

"Oh, horrible! horrible!!" exclaimed the general.

"Dear brother, please be consoled, and trust in the Lord," solemnly said the bloody deacon.

"Oh, deacon! I have never dreamt of what you just insinuated; but I now feel that my poor child has fallen into the hands of a monster!" exclaimed the general, with great tears in his eyes.

"If you desire it, dear brother, I will do my utmost to arrest this demon; or, probably, it would be as well for us to telegraph to Liverpool, and request the authorities there to arrest him, when he arrives," said the deacon.

"No, good brother; I think I had better at once get ready and follow these truant children. I will take two good male servants with me, and start for Liverpool tomorrow, for I have no heart to live here whilst disgrace and ruination—yes, and probably desertion—may befall my dear child.

"Oh, daughter! daughter! what have you done? I have centred my whole life, soul and spirit on you, and for you to be thus snatched from me is more than an old man can endure. God, O God! aid and comfort my bleeding heart!" exclaimed the heart-broken general.

The deacon was internally spoiling with delight to think that his plans had worked so very excellently, and thought he:

"When Sister Nancy Clover learns the real state of things she will fairly glut over the success of our plot, and be doubly delighted at the distress of the general, and discomfiture of his hateful daughter.

"She will seek the general, and offer her saintliest sympathy and most energetic assistance; but when the general is gone to Europe, we shall have a clear track before us; truly, wont I go to the proud, stuck-up and apostate Miss Lucinda Armington's prison, and dictate my own terms of peace. Ha! ha! my caged bird, I'll save you the trouble of disguising yourself again, for the purpose of acting the aunt, to spoil our holy plans; and as for the heroic and celebrated Dr. (?) Juno, he shall feed on slim victuals, whilst a lingering death shall be his *most certain* portion this time; yea, verily, and I shall let him know that it was I,—Deacon Rob Stew,—of the Orthodox Faith, who instigated and managed his ruin for molesting the elect in their God-ordained work of Christianity."

The deacon now repaired to headquarters of the bloody conspirators, to inform them of the state of General Armington's mind; whilst the general was at work making preparations to leave for Liverpool. He called Pat O'Connor and Judy McCrea to his side, and told them that he was going to Europe to seek his daughter, and as they had always been faithful servants, he should give everything into their charge, and he hoped and felt confident that they would prove faithful to him in his hour of sore distress. Here Pat could not hold his peace any longer, and, interrupting the general, said :

"Fath, me good mashter, an' may me sowl rot ef I don't be tru to ye ; an' whats morer, I'll sake fur Mishtress Lucinda meself, an' fur good young Mishter Juno."

"Pat, never mention the name of that villain, Juno, again, if you do not want to insult me," in great agitation responded the general.

"Howly Sant Patrick, but me mashter is desaved by that ould divil, Dacon Stew," meditated Pat, and said aloud, "Och, good mashter, yer ould servant meant no harm whin I spok ov Mishter J——, pardon me, I didn't mane to spake that name agin ; but I'll do as ye plaze, an' Judy will hilp me, wont ye, Judy ?" said Pat.

"An' shure I will, wid all me hart," responded Judy.

Pat and Judy now saw that the deepest kind of villany was at work, and he said to Judy:

"Judy, darlin', I sees, be me sowl, that these dirty vaggabones have hided away Miss Armington an' Dr. Juno, an' may I sace to be an Irishman ef I don't blarney them till I diskiver all their diviltry an' find me swate mishtress."

"Och, Pat, an' I pray Sant Patrick that ye may not fale tow do it, an' I'll hilp ye do it, ef I die," earnestly said Judy McCrea.

The general left the next day amid the sympathies of the many who bade him adieu and God-speed. But he did not seem to care or notice anything, except his anxiety to get off as speedily as possible.

No sooner had he departed until Deacon Rob Stew went to General Armington's residence, to pump Pat O'Conner and Judy McCrea, for the purpose of ascertaining if they knew or even suspected anything of the abduction of these young lovers. He said to Pat :

"Good Pat, your master has now gone to Europe on a great mission of mercy to his poor child, and he told me to look after things whilst he is away; of course, you are to have charge of everything"—

"So I tought," interposed Pat, a little surly.

"But you must know that the general was in such a distressed state of mind that he did not realize the responsibility you had resting on your shoulders in his and his daughter's absence," gently and sympathetically responded the deacon.

"Shure, yer honor, ye are right, an' I'd be a miserable divil to not belave ye had the good ov us at hart," humbly said Pat.

"Where is Judy, and what does she think of this elopement?" exclaimed the deacon.

"What should she tink ov it, yer honor, but that Mishter Juno bees a dirty blackgard," impatiently and indignantly said Pat; but, thought he, "If only Judy will not cum here now, becase this ould curmudgon mite smuggle some wrong idees out ov her innocence."

At that moment Judy McCrea was heard in another part of the house, screaming *murder* at the top of her voice!

CHAPTER XVI.

LUCINDA'S THRILLING PRAYER AND LAMENTATIONS IN PRISON.

ON the night that Miss Lucinda Armington was abducted from the lawn of her father, there were great preparations being made at a celebrated insane asylum near West Philadelphia, for the reception of two dangerous and incurable lunatics.

For one of these insane persons an underground dungeon was being rapidly finished; because the physician-in-chief at the asylum was informed that this patient could not bear the light of the sun and constellations without disturbing the peace of his own and other people's minds. Darkness, total darkness, and perfect solitude were the only panaceas to quiet his nerves and cause a serene state of human conscience.

Moreover, the sound of human voice proved an injury to this most peculiarly affected lunatic; therefore an immensely thick wall, and correspondingly heavy laded doors were constructed for such patients, which was a necessity only of very recent occurrence.

In another portion of this same pious and generous orthodox insane asylum, on the third floor, was prepared an extra private, strong, but comfortable cell for a patient who could not endure human sounds, but was benefited by light and comfort.

This cell was not accessible by any one except the highest officials and Deacon Rob Stew; the latter was the most powerful man in the entire community of the elect saints.

The physician-in-chief of this humanitarian asylum was a faithful brother of the faith, who fully confided in the little secret prayers and holy plans of the *bloody conspirators:* and all his assistants and servants, excepting one Irishman, were equally faithful; for convenience' sake, we will call this unfaithful to the faithful, Jemmy, who was a man of strong sympathies for the fallen, depraved and miserable, and whose honesty had no flaw in its composition. Jemmy was the most trustworthy servant in the asylum, and the physician-in-chief invariably commanded Jemmy to watch the other keepers and the help; making him a kind of superintendent or overseer amongst the many employés, and therefore the latter dreaded Jemmy, because whatever report of delinquency and disobedience he would make to the head of the place would be accepted as truth, from which no appeal would benefit aught.

We might here state that Jemmy was a bosom friend of Pat O'Conner, and a distant relative of Judy McCrea, who frequently visited Pat and Judy at General Washington

Armington's residence; therefore he had often seen Miss Lucinda Armington, and Pat on several occasions pointed out Dr. Victor Juno to Jemmy as being the accepted lover of Miss Lucinda Armington.

Jemmy believed that their asylum was a model humanitarian institution, whose physician-in-chief, and the managers thereof, were the best men living; and, although he was a Roman Catholic, he believed that his employers were as near saints as Protestants could be.

On numerous occasions he told Pat O'Conner that these gentlemen were very pious, being also continually devoted to acts of charity, and besides prayed and worshipped God zealously, which he (Jemmy) esteemed the highest attributes of Christianity, even if they were not Catholics.

Pat, however, had less faith in such men, after he became acquainted with Deacon Rob Stew, who was the president of the insane asylum.

Nearly all the leading orthodox religionists, except the Roman Catholics, had. an interest in this philanthropic asylum for the insane, and no doubt nearly all of them esteemed it a most Christian and exemplary institution. They had formed themselves into a guardianship; hence, were privileged members of the asylum to visit every portion of it, except those few departments where incurable lunatics were confined, whose idiosyncrasies were of that peculiar character that human voices, etc., could not be endured by them; to these departments no one had access except the physician-in-chief, a few of the *bloody conspirators*, and the servants.

Few of the latter were even permitted to enter upon these sacred parts of the asylum. The cells of these departments were seldom cleaned by any one except the prisoners themselves; who, by a confidential announcement, we may say, were never too crazy or ill, from the onset of their incarceration, to do their own work. And these lunatics were fed through a peculiarly contrived apparatus, which prevented the waiter or keeper from seeing the patient.

The basement cells were complete dungeons, where total darkness prevailed; but the third-story cells of these departments were supplied with a good degree of light; however, shutters were so constructed to the windows that total darkness could be produced in a moment, which seemed often necessary when peculiar examinations of patients were required.

Many of the patients who were confined in these sacredly secret cells were females, who would not submit to certain tutorage on open *terra firma*, and who could be more thoroughly managed, subdued and cured by total darkness, shielding the disciplinarian from unpleasant recognition, than by permitting the light of heaven to co-operate in the consummating of the holy work.

It was seldom necessary to introduce instruments of torment into this department of the asylum; but, solemnized religious worship,—prayer, exhortation, and singing by the saints,—was frequently introduced with signal success.

It is almost beyond the conception of mortals how peculiarly zealous some of these *bloody conspirators* were in the work of subjugating those whom they loved with a wicked hatred.

The female cells also had several secret doors to them, which were an auxiliary to the work of restoring sanity to the heads and hearts of the fair sex, who were victims to these sacred apartments of the elect.

Miss Lucinda Armington first opened her eyes to consciousness, after appearing in her father's lawn on the night of her abduction, in one of these female cells, on the third floor of this insane asylum. She could not imagine where she was, and for what purpose she would be in this unpleasant place. She rose from her neat little couch, and surveyed the tidy little apartment, which was neatly and very comfortably furnished, but withal there was an air of horror connected with the appearance of things.

She examined the door, which she found was locked; next, she examined the floor and walls, but found them solid and sound; and as to the window, she could not examine it, because it was a skylight, situated directly overhead, and although there was a table, chair and bed in the room, she piled them upon each other, and managed to climb on top of them; but she was then a few feet too short to reach to the skylight. She replaced her furniture, and began to pound on the floor, door and walls, but all sounded dead and dull, without the least response from any one. Next, she screamed at the top of her voice, but to no effect; when she thought:

"Oh, great heaven! why am I thus confined in this living tomb? Can this be a prison? But why should I be confined in it? Where was I to my last recollection? Let me think; O, yes, I remember; Pat O'Conner, Judy McCrea and myself sat in our dining-room, conversing over the outrage that had happened to dear Victor at the theatre; and I now remember of having gone out into the lawn, when suddenly something nasty was thrown over my head, whilst at the same moment some strong hands grasped my body, and I knew nothing more.

"Surely, I was then carried to this prison. Oh, horror! horror! What may, what *will* become of me? Great powers of glory protect me, and deliver me from my bondage! Who could have been so cruel as to abduct and incarcerate me thus? Great Lord! an idea flashes through my half frenzied brain! It was the same *bloody conspirators*, who tried to poison my beloved Victor, that have sent me to this place; but, what will they do with me? This is horrible, most horrible! Because, any one who is bad enough to have me thus abducted and imprisoned, is also vile enough to abuse and murder me, if that suits his pleasure and plans best.

"What, really, have I done to merit such foul treatment? Let me think; I have always been kind to every one; have no enemies that I know of; but, now it flashes upon my distressed soul, I have stood by the side of dear Victor, I have conspired with Pat and Judy to save my beloved. Oh, darling Victor! save, save me now from the impending danger that awaits your unprotected Lucinda! My persecutors are monsters, or they could not tear me away from my dear old father, and from my dearly beloved Victor. God, if thou ever hearest the prayers of mortals, hear mine:

"Infinite and all-powerful Creator, I invoke Thee, and all Thy vitalizing influences, to stultify and deaden the head and hand that has brought me to this cruel place. I pray Thee, heavenly Father, to shield the just and faithful, whilst Thou wilt confound the wicked conspirators who have sought to ruin and destroy me and mine; and, O God, look with compassion on Thy distressed servant, who would freely offer up her life, in purity and innocence, for the good of heaven's righteous cause!

"Moreover, I humbly pray Thee, O Lord of Hosts, send Thy messengers of grace to guard and protect my beloved and heroic Victor, whose strifes and struggles, on behalf of his race, are herculean! God, grant me this humble supplication, and Thy name shall have all the glory for ever and ever. Amen!"

A terrible noise, as it were rattling of chains, unbolting of gigantic doors, and groans of the most horrible character, now disturbed the suppliant; and suddenly the door, entering her cell, flew open, when she beheld a man in disguise, standing before her; she swooned away.

CHAPTER XVII.

GENERAL ARMINGTON SEARCHING FOR HIS SEDUCED DAUGHTER IN EUROPE.

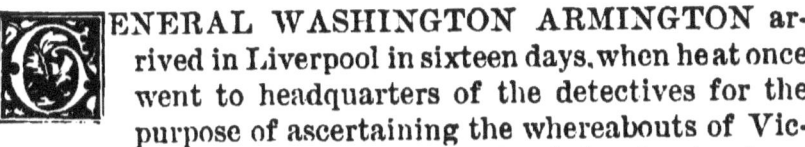ENERAL WASHINGTON ARMINGTON arrived in Liverpool in sixteen days, when he at once went to headquarters of the detectives for the purpose of ascertaining the whereabouts of Victor Juno and his amiable daughter, Lucinda; having been

informed, before he left New York, that his truant child and her paramour were seen on consecutive days to reside at the Hotel De La Breau, on Grange street, Liverpool; but on inquiry for such persons, a negative answer was given; because, there were no persons, nor had been, stopping there that would answer the description in any way.

This was a terrible disappointment to the general, and what to do was beyond his capacity to contrive; however, upon consultation with the chief of police, he was encouraged by the advice the chief gave him. Said he to the general:

"You had better consult with Louis Kingdom, one of our foremost detectives, and although his price is extortionate, but, if your people can be found, he can do it, provided they are on this continent."

"I am fully persuaded that they sailed several weeks ago from New York to Liverpool, in the Scotia, and I was told that they had been repeatedly seen at the Hotel De La Breau; but, upon examination, I failed to ascertain of their whereabouts; however, as the man is a cunning rogue, I fear that he has bribed the proprietors of the hotel not to divulge anything concerning their appearance," said General Armington.

The general engaged Louis Kingdom, the detective, to search for the elopists, and find his daughter, if it cost ten thousand dollars. The detective said:

"If they are on this globe, I will find them, and shortly."

This assurance from so great an expert gave the general full satisfaction, so far as the securing of his daughter was concerned; but yet the general's mind was in one continually agitated and disturbed state.

He endeavored to console himself by renewed devotion to the church, but whenever he approached the orthodox religionists, something seemed to warn him, and almost tell him, that this class of persons were the ones who caused all his trouble.

Nevertheless, he continued to go amongst them, making

many acquaintances, and very soon he received a long letter from Rev. Joe Pier, which consoled him amazingly, whilst at the same time a very pious deacon of his own faith called upon the general and told him that he was well acquainted with Deacon Rob Stew, of America, who had very often mentioned the general's name to him when he was sojourning in America.

The general took a wonderful pleasure in this English deacon's acquaintance, whilst the wily deacon was simply the co-conspirator of Deacon Rob Stew and the *bloody conspirators*.

We will now call attention to the operations of the *bloody conspirators*, who had been holding several special meetings recently at Tabernacle Hall, for the purpose of keeping the general in Europe until Dr. Victor Juno was in his grave, or at the bottom of the ocean, where worms or sharks will devour his mouldering clay, as he endeavored to devour the doctrines of the elect saints.

As for Miss Lucinda Armington, no one but Deacon Rob Stew seemed to care what became of her, whether she lived or died; neither did they care a straw about the general, so long as they were safe from molestation by this Victor Juno. The deacon said:

"Holy saints, I will promise you to take good care of Miss Lucinda Armington, so she shall be no trouble to the cause, nor to you personally. I have always loved the dear, innocent (?) child, and take my holy word, I'll fix her to the advantage of all parties, and to her own satisfaction."

"Surely, our beloved and faithful deacon understands the charitable and nurturing business thoroughly, hence, I assure you, he will do what pleases the Lord," said Nancy Clover.

"But, brethren, we must contrive some plan by which we can banish all suspicion of the abduction business, should some one get wind of it, or the thing in any way prove a failure; you are all aware that I fear and tremble, when I think of the bold work which we have taken into our hands; and although the elect cannot sin, still, they are not infallible, else Victor Juno would have died at the hands of our faithful brother and doctor, Toy Pancy," exclaimed Rev. Joe Pier in an agitated state of mind.

"Truly, good brother Pier, your remarks are wise and spoken at an opportune hour," said Dr. Toy Pancy, "for you must know that there are many infidels and atheists in this world, who would delight in acting as spies for the purpose of betraying us to '*the people*,' and I am sure one ounce of prevention is worth a pound of cure; moreover, if all things turn out right, there cannot arise any injury from the exercise of extreme precautionary measures.

"Supposing this vile agitator and coarse innovator should escape us"—

"Nonsense!" interposed Deacon Rob Stew, in an indignant and boisterous manner.

"Patience, brother Stew, I have the floor; please, therefore, let me finish what I proposed to say," said Dr. Toy Pancy.

"Go on," exclaimed the Rev. Joe Pier.

"Well, I was going to say, supposing Mr. or Dr. Juno should escape us, he would undoubtedly be bold and daring enough to at once mount the rostrum again, and expose our conduct toward him, when '*the people*' would very likely join him and mob us," said Dr. Toy Pancy.

"Nonsense! you are a poor chicken-hearted dunce to reason thus. Have you no faith in God and in his elect? And do you suppose I have been idle all these days, and have done nothing to guard against such contingencies? You must take me to be a faithless fool. I have it in my power to ruin this Juno; yes, a simple stroke from my pen will disgrace and quiet this innovator any time; but, it must not be known publicly that I would stoop to undermine republican liberties; because I am an advocate of republicanism, and as you all know that the republican party believes me to be a perfect saint, hence I hold them

THE CONSPIRATORS AND LOVERS. 79

in the hollow of my hand so long as I can keep my secret acts away from them. We are told by Christ to pray and act in secret; hence, I never throw such holy things before dogs, nor cast pearls before swine," exclaimed the holy deacon.

A knock at the outer door caused all to remain quiet for a moment, until the sentinel should see who sought admission, when the physician-in-chief of the insane asylum rushed into the hall in an awfully excited state of mind, and said: " Victor Juno has escaped!"

CHAPTER XVIII.

JEMMY DISCOVERS VICTOR AND LUCINDA.

IT may be remembered that Pat O'Conner's wits were heavily exercised about this reported elopement affair. He could not see any philosophy in such an act on the part of either Dr. Juno or Miss Armington; therefore he did not believe that they eloped, but he feared some foul play; and who but Deacon Rob Stew was guilty, hence Pat endeavored to blarney the deacon, so that he could get deeper into the latter's confidence.

In fact, the deacon never suspicioned Pat of infidelity to him, but thought Pat O'Conner was his tried, true friend. Pat knew this, and therefore he said:

"Dacon, yer honor, I have heerd sich talk aboot this Mishter Juno chap what maks me blood run coold; but, yer honor will not spake agen ov this mattar, will ye?"

"Certainly not, Pat; but will you tell me what it is?" asked the deacon.

"Och, be Sant Patrick, I belave that son of they wicked paople stharted a talk that ye were the cause of Miss Lucinda, me mishtress, aloped wid them Juno chap; becase ye would not axe her to marry ye," said Pat.

"Is that what you have heard?" interposed the deacon.

"Yis, yer honor, that's it," said Pat.

"Sure, Pat, you have heard nothing more; and you do not believe that, do you?" responded the deacon.

"Howly Moses, yer honor, I do belave that Miss Armington was mad wid ye, becase ye would not axe her fur to marry ye; an' fur to shpite ye, she runned away wid this Mishter Juno; do ye mind that?" said Pat.

"No, my faithful Pat; but as you are a true friend of mine, in whom I feel *sure* I could entrust my life, I will give you a little insight into this matter. But, Pat, you must be secretive, and not mention it to a living soul," responded the deacon.

"Howly Sant Patrick, I would not spake ov it to any parson, an' ef it would smash me life into smithereens; belave me, yer honor," said Pat.

"O, I do, good fellow. Well, Pat, Miss Lucinda Armington and Victor Juno did not elope; but they were abducted by some of the medical opponents of Victor Juno," ejaculated the deacon.

"Abdoocted, yer honor; bedad, an' ye are shure on that, are ye?" said Pat.

"Yes, Pat, I *am* sure of it," responded the deacon.

"Howly saints, an' ye know that me mishtress be murdhered, an' ye would not tell me mashter, but let him go to Europe fur to hunt his murdhered child; O, ye bloody curmudgon, what do ye expect will becom ov ye?" furiously ejaculated Pat, who was now ready for a fight with the deacon.

"Pat, Pat, you do not understand me," replied the deacon.

"Begorrah! an' I do undershtand ye; abdoocted, ye murdherin' hypocret, an' may the divil swallow me whoul body an' sowl ef I don't tell on ye, an' that this very hour, ye squally murdherer, for ahelpin' to abdooct me swate mishtress! An' will ye tell me where ye have buried her?" exclaimed Pat.

THE CONSPIRATORS AND LOVERS. 81

"Pat, you are crazy; listen to me, she is not dead," replied the deacon, half scared to death, lest Pat might expose the whole matter in his excitable state of mind, for he saw Pat was ready for a fight.

"Not dead!" exclaimed Pat, looking amazed, and continued, "how could she be abdoocted, an' be not dead?"

"Now, Pat, calm yourself, and I will explain to you all about it; she is living, healthy and will evidently be happy when I shall see her and offer myself in marriage to her," said the deacon.

"Yer honor am not hoaxin', am ye?" exclaimed Pat, his countenance lighting up with delight.

"Certainly not, good Pat, you evidently do not understand the meaning of abduction. Abduction means, carefully taken away from danger," said the deacon.

"Do it, yer honor? an' I am plazed it manes that; but, be jabers, I tought it mant murdher," responded Pat.

"Well, Pat, you are now satisfied, are you not? And you will keep the secret, for I promise you, all will be for the best," said Deacon Rob Stew.

"Yis, sur, I am yer fathful sarvant, as ye plaze to have me," ejaculated Pat, good humoredly and apparently satisfied.

Pat returned to Judy McCrea, and cautiously told her that he suspected Deacon Rob Stew to be a dirty villain, when they agreed to watch the deacon's movements. On Saturday afternoon, Jemmy, the overseer of the insane asylum, generally visited Pat and Judy.

The three were sitting in the dining room of General Washington Armington's residence, discussing the question of the day. Pat said:

"Jemmy, ye have a fine plaze fur the poor lunatick, an' whin ye showed meself an' Judy darlin' the inner ov the asylum, why did ye not take us tow them other parts?"

"Shure, I'd like tow see all ov thim," said Judy.

"Pat, it is not allowed to take strangers into the private departments," replied Jemmy.

"Privat divils; I belave that ye kape thim places fur to smuggle dacent paople away," ejaculated Pat.

"Pat, now do ye think we are cut-throats in our asylum?" angrily responded Jemmy.

"Jemmy, dear," said Judy, "excuse Pat, fur ye knows he bees much worred aboot the good darlin' Mishtress Lucinda, who he belaves is smuggled up in that plaze."

"Yis, Jemmy, will ye do me one kind favor?" asked Pat.

"Certainly, dear Pat, I will," responded Jemmy.

"Thin, kape an eye on thim privat plazes, an' ye may sea me mishtress in thare," said Pat.

"Pat, in faith, ye are mistaken; but I'll do it, an' tell ye of it, if I see anything," replied Jemmy.

These three parted good friends, and although Jemmy could not harbor a thought in his mind that would reflect upon the virtuous conduct of the managers of the asylum, but, thought he, "it cannot do any harm for me to peep around and satisfy my mind, and should I find anything wrong, I might help to right it, and should I find all straight, no harm is done."

The following Sunday Jemmy was ordered by the physician-in-chief to oversee the private departments, as the latter should be compelled to leave the asylum that day. This pleased Jemmy, and he took the first opportunity afforded him to see who occupied the cell on the third floor, where Deacon Rob Stew recently visited so often; for sure, if Miss Lucinda Armington should be in the asylum, that is the place where she would be confined. With little trouble he unbolted the outside doors, which gave him an opportunity to peep quietly into her cell, and, to his amazement, there he beheld, reclining on the neat little cot, Miss Armington, sleeping sweetly.

This almost stunned Jemmy's sensibilities, and he was now ready to believe anything and everything that might be said either of the asylum or of its managers. He quietly retired from the spot, and at once made his way to the basement dungeons, where, however, he could not peep, because there was no light in those cells; but he went to the door of the dungeon and tried to unbolt it, when he heard a peculiar noise in a distant part of the corridor, which scared him away from his intended design for the present.

He went up stairs and found that they had brought a very crazy patient into the asylum, and, after he was stored safely away, he got another lot of keys and returned to the dungeon, and succeeded in opening the outside door, which gave him access to call the prisoner. He said:

"Victor Juno! Victor Juno!" then listened, when he heard a low, stifled voice reply:

"Who calls me? I am Victor Juno."

CHAPTER XIX.

DEACON STEW THREATENS TO SHOOT JEMMY.

IT will be remembered that on a preceding occasion, when Pat O'Conner and Deacon Rob Stew were in conversation at General Armington's house, Judy McCrea suddenly screamed murder in another part of the mansion, which disturbed the two connivers in carrying out their deviltry. Pat O'Conner, who was blarneying Deacon Rob Stew, was delighted that something happened to distract the attention of the deacon's mind from the subject that was then under discussion, and it may have been a God-send that Judy McCrea was caused to scream murder at the top of her voice.

Pat and the deacon at once repaired to the spot, where Judy was imagining that she was being in a terrible conflict with bloody murderers; but they discovered nothing, except that Judy said she had been tired, and whilst reclining on a lounge fell asleep, and had a horrible dream.

No one inquired about the dream, and even Judy herself seemed then not to care or think it of any moment; however, a few weeks later, Judy's mind one day was bewildered, and when Pat asked her what was the matter, she said, that the dream she had a few weeks ago impressed her mind so strangely that she could not rest, but she could not tell exactly what the dream was like. Pat said:

"Me darlin', ken ye not tell yer Pat what ye seed in yer dream?"

"Yis, dear Pat, the ting jist now com to me mind; I tought I was atalkin' wid me luvly mishtress, whin a dirty, ruf man com along, an' trowin' a murderin' cap over her head, what choked me darlin' mishtress, whin she could not spake, an' I tried to hilp her, but me body was werry stiff, an' I could not do nothin' fur her, whin they tooked her off on a waggon," said Judy McCrea.

"Darlin' Judy, why did ye not spake of it bafore now?" exclaimed Pat.

"I have not tought ov it, an' I am sartin that me lady bees in that plaze where Jemmy bees, ovur yander in West Philadelphy, fur I mind now that I seed her taked in the waggon tow that plaze, an' carried up tree shtares, an' put in a small room what luks as a prison morer than an asylum," said Judy.

"Och, Judy, ye bees adreamin' jist now," laughingly replied Pat.

"No, Pat, ef ye luv me, belave me, fur I sees me swate lady jist now settin' all alone by herself aweepin' as a child," said Judy, with tears in her eyes, and sniffling as though she really was in sympathy with the poor young lady.

It may seem curious, but it was nevertheless true, that the spirit of Judy was hovering around Miss Lucinda Armington in a clairvoyant state, and whilst Judy and Pat were talking over these matters, Jemmy, the overseer, knocked at the door, and being asked into the room, at once said:

"My good friends, I have news to tell ye. I have watched my chance at the asylum, and when I was authorized to superintend the secret departments, I looked into one of the third story cells, where, to my sorrow and surprise, I seen yer luvly Mistress Armington."

"Och, murdher, Pat, an' have I not tould ye so, but ye would not belave," ejaculated Judy.

"Jemmy, bedad, ye confound me wid sich news; howsomever, I tought that yer squally dacon was up to any diviltry, an' shure, sartin he was the chafe apostle in this work ov Satin; an' shure, it am quare that me darlin' Judy should be dramcing all aboot it," responded Pat.

"Dear Jemmy, did ye spake to me lady?" asked Judy.

"No, Judy dear, I only was wantin' to know if she were there. She were asleep when I peeped through the door hole," responded Jemmy.

"Well, Jemmy, an' do ye now belave me, whin I sed them chaps were hypocrets?" said Pat.

"Yis, dear Pat, I belave anything, after having seen Miss Lucinda Armington lying on a cot, tight asleep in that cozy cell. I would tell ye that I have also diskivered that Mr. Victor Juno be in the new dungeon, in the basement," replied Jemmy.

"Bloody murdher! be me sowl, ye knock me branes strait out by tellin' me all sich talk! Do ye mane to say that Dr. Victor Juno am caged up widin that cellar dungon?" said Pat, half crazed and furiously indignant.

"Yis, Pat, he is there, but he wont be long coming out of it, if I knows it," exclaimed Jemmy.

Jemmy, being a good, honest Christian, would not cooperate with any one, or work for any one, whom he found to be dishonest and criminal; therefore he made up his mind to set Victor Juno and Miss Lucinda Armington at liberty, after which he would leave the asylum. But how to go about this without being exposed, and without danger to the prisoners' lives and future prosperity, was a puzzling question.

He planned in various ways to cause the escape of Victor Juno, but always failed to see his way clear; however, he might furnish the half starved man with better and more food, until he regained his strength, when a cold chisel and heavy hammer might answer his purpose; besides, he might leave the bolts in Victor Juno's dungeon doors slipped, a few days previous to his attempt to escape, when he would not be working in that department on the time Victor should make his escape; this would remove suspicion from Jemmy.

Moreover, he might furnish Victor Juno with a rope, which undoubtedly should be of great service to him. All this Jemmy did, and he informed Victor which way to leave the asylum, on what day and in the middle of the night as near as he could do so.

Jemmy did not worry so much about Miss Lucinda Armington as he did over Victor Juno, because she had comfortable quarters, besides, her father was in Europe; but Victor was in a dark, damp, sickly cell, where death surely would end his miseries in a short time, unless he was set at liberty; moreover, his business was suffering by this most foul incarceration.

When Jemmy had given Victor Juno all the trappings and information, he made an excuse to visit some of his relatives in the country, who were sick, and the physician-in-chief, being willing to grant any favor to his most faithful overseer, permitted Jemmy a week's leave of absence.

As Jemmy was about quitting the asylum for the purpose of making his visit, Deacon Rob Stew entered the institution, and at once confronted Jemmy, and said:

"Come with me, instantly, and hesitate not, or I'll blow your Irish brains out with this pistol, you vile conspirator!"

CHAPTER XX.

LUCINDA NEARLY MURDERS THE DEACON IN HER CELL.

N the cell where Miss Lucinda Armington was confined there was but one window, a skylight, which had shutters that could be closed in a moment by the keepers and managers; and when the man in disguise appeared before Miss Armington, and he saw that she swooned away, he suddenly darkened the cell by closing said shutters, thinking that she would be more readily restored and conquered in darkness than in light; moreover, she might detect the disguised person if too much light shone upon him.

He laid her on the cot, and when she came to, he said:

"I have come to offer you freedom and my heart and hand in marriage, and I hope you will not refuse me this request," said the disguised monster.

"Sir, who are you, that dares to insult me thus, and why have you darkened this prison cell? Are your intentions so dark and foul that you cannot present them in the light of day?" exclaimed Miss Armington.

"I am a man of tender affections toward you, but as I have lately noticed you to conspire with a vile atheist, I felt it my duty to separate you from him until you have time to repent"—

"Fiend, that you are, do you suppose for one moment that a woman could or would yield to a man's wishes, who can be guilty of so foul a deed?" interposed Miss Armington; and continued, "Further, I would like to know by whose authority, and by what august power you have taken this outrageous task upon yourself to abduct, and cast me into this prison?"

"Dear lady, you are haughty; I really admire your high toned spirit; but, your desire to be stubborn or sarcastic will not profit you aught; neither will you receive your liberty until you yield to my desires!" said the disguised man.

"Monster, have you lost your manhood, and how could you expect a woman to accept the proposals of a man or beast, which uses such criminal measures to gain the hand of woman?" responded Miss Armington.

"Go on, with your sophistries, but methinks you will be very glad to accept my offer; now come let us understand each other; I am handsome, rich, influential, religious and only fifteen or twenty years your senior," said the monster, quite coolly.

"You are handsome, rich, influential, religious and only fifteen or twenty years my senior; why is it then that you cause total darkness in this cell, and disguise yourself? You should show your beauty, and give the woman of your philanthropic choice an opportunity to behold that handsome person, whose wealth, influence and religion are so prominent! Indeed, your acts exhibit very holy (?) attributes of piety; but as to wealth and riches, I have not the least doubt, that by your demoniacal deeds you are capacitated to wring money from the thousands, and with its corrupting power, influence whole communities of your equals in crime!" sharply exclaimed Miss Armington, without fear or falter.

"Heigh-ho! but you are a philosopher, as well as a charming damsel; by my soul, I am taking renewed fancies for the jewel which I have found," ejaculated the disguised man.

"Do you think, sir, that you can conquer me? Do you dare to beard the tigress in her den? You have brought me here, from some motive best known to yourself, and whilst you have not the manly courage to show me your features in the light, you may think that you have me in your power, and can badger and insult me as you choose; but, I now *warn* you to beware how you provoke me, lest by some miraculous power I strike you to my feet, and bruise your venomous head!" furiously ejaculated Miss Armington.

"Sweet Lady, you would not do all that, at one time, would you, darling of my heart?" responded the intruder sarcastically, whilst he took hold of her arm. This latter act so enraged the helpless lady, that she sprang to her feet, and quick as lightning made for the monster's head and face, tearing his mask and disguise from him with herculean strength, whilst she dealt him blow after blow upon his mouth and nose, until the hot blood flew in every direction.

He was not prepared for such summary chastisement, hence, before he knew what he was about, he was apparently helpless; when he humbly begged her pardon! But, she said, furiously:

"Go, leave me, or I'll murder you, before you will be able to gain help!"

He humbly responded: "I'll go, give me a moment to collect my senses."

"Go," she ejaculated in a voice that meant a second beating. He instantly disappeared through a secret door, and as he was closing it exclaimed:

"I'll be a match for you when I call again!"

She ran to the secret door, but found it closed and bolted, seeming like a wall of adamant.

CHAPTER XXI.

VICTOR'S VISION, IN A DREAM, IN HIS DUNGEON.

DOCTOR VICTOR JUNO, was left all night lying on the hard, damp, cemented floor of the dungeon, without removing even as much as the gag; but, about eight o'clock in the morning, several rough men came to his presence, when they removed the shackles, and left him without saying a word. He asked them what was the object of this malicious conduct, but not a syllable was answered, and the men left him to surmise what was in store for him.

He now got upon his feet; however, it was as much as he could do to stand erect without tumbling to the ground, and managed to stagger to the place where the men seemed to come in and go out; but, upon closely examining it, he found nothing but a small offset, and a rough iron door without a single aperture in its construction.

He next followed the wall around, examining every inch from the ground floor to as high as he could reach; but, alas, nothing was detected except a roughly plastered wall; and after a long search for a spot from which air or light might be received, he found himself back again to the doorway.

Now he laid down on the floor, stretching his hands and feet in every direction, trying to measure his prison-house, and also for the purpose of ascertaining if any furniture or opening could be discovered; but, O, horror! horror! nothing but one blank, dark dungeon was surrounding this son of toil.

He sat himself as comfortably as possible on the floor, inclining his back against the wall, and listened for what seemed to him nearly an hour, but all was as silent as the tomb. He was getting thirsty and hungry, and he wondered if this was a plan to starve him to death, or what can be the object of this foul conspiracy to incarcerate him in this horrible dungeon; presently he fell into a sleep, when he dreamed that he was travelling over the continent of Europe, where he met General Washington Armington, who was in terrible distress about the loss of his daughter Lucinda, and when he and the general met face to face, the latter at once accused him (Dr. Juno) of being the seducer of his lovely daughter, and said to him:

"Dr. Juno, prepare yourself to meet your God, for I am going to shoot you forthwith."

"My dear general, you greatly wrong me, I have always treated your daughter with profound respect; moreover, you forget that I have jeopardized my miserable life to save hers, and I would do so a thousand times over for the fair virtuous damsel; why, then, do you accuse me of ruining your child, have you no more confidence in me than that?" spoke Victor Juno to the general; to which the latter seemed to smile and walked away. Suddenly there appeared an angel before Dr. Juno, who had several beautiful emblems in his right hand, and the angel held up one of them and said:

"This represents a youth whose wisdom excels his vanity, and who, if he prove true to his intuitive gifts, will be compelled to go through a fiery furnace for a brief season; but, if he continues to trust in an over-ruling, just and infinite God, will have this crown set upon his head;" and now the angel presented another emblem, which appeared to look like a rainbow, inside of which hosts of cherubims were embracing each other, until the entire brotherhood of mankind seemed to be enchanted with the power and hallowed blessedness of the beneficent Creator of all things.

In the left hand the angel held a dark ring, which had unsightly, leprous spots upon it, and which poured forth fiery vipers. The angel said:

"If you prove faithless and fearful, you will inherit this crown, which is prepared for all who flag and faint in the hour of persecution."

The angel disappeared, and the prisoner woke up, amazed to find himself thus.

He continued a long time in the same position, on the damp cemented floor, and meditated as follows:

"I have had a peculiar dream, a beautiful dream; but what is there in dreams? Great God, since I am deserted by man, I thank Thee for having permitted an angel from yonder realms of the blessed to come unto me, and direct me what course I shall pursue to accomplish my work. I shall heed the admonition, and bear patiently all that my persecutors can heap upon me; knowing that I am in the right, I must also be convinced that God will not permit me to die for naught; and what can it matter to the naturalist whether he is sacrificed in one way or another, only so that his beloved cause may prosper."

The man philosophized in this manner for hours, forgetting thereby that he was in a dungeon and powerless; but he imagined that he was growing stronger and of more moment hourly, until finally he changed his bodily position, when hunger and thirst seemed to overpower him; but presently he heard a noise, his prison gates were moving, and a keeper brought him a loaf of bread and a mug of water. O, how grateful to God and his persecutors was he for this little kindness, for, thought he, "They don't mean to starve me, and I hope for a safe deliverance from this dungeon; and should I escape and see my beloved Lucinda again, I would be too happy; yes, and I should preach to the people once more my beloved sentiments, and also inform them of my sufferings on their behalf.

"Truly, had I done as my persecutors desire all men to do, I would now be the successful pastor of some wealthy congregation, with plenty of wealth and more glory of men than any of the rest: because, with my knowledge of human nature, I could be the greatest hypocrite and saintliest pharisee; but my zeal runs in an opposite direction, and I shall hold out faithfully to the end, and though my wounded soul bleeds to exhaustion.

"I have already suffered much for my audacity, in presenting a purer and more Christ-like piety than the fashionable sectarian world upholds, but yet I have not endured what Jesus and his apostles had to undergo. This is a consolation, that there is a hereafter, where we shall be rewarded according to the deeds, not the blind faith, done in the body."

It must not be forgotten that Dr. Juno had comparatively few friends who cared enough for him and his doctrines to put themselves out of the way for him, except Miss Lucinda Armington, who, however, was as firmly locked up in the asylum as he was himself.

Probably because they were so near to each other, yet

unaware of the fact, caused them to be more buoyant than they would have been had they been far apart.

Both of them felt certain that the other was being persecuted at the selfsame hour; because the *bloody conspirators* knew all about their love for each other, hence this persecution.

Victor Juno loved her dearly, in fact, he worshipped the ground she walked on; but, notwithstanding all this, he was more deeply concerned about his cause of reform. He considered the improvement of the human race as preeminently of more moment than the happiness of the few; and as his religion convinced his mind that God was just, if man was unjust, he deemed it of little importance whether he suffered martyrdom or not.

He was receiving no attention in his dungeon beside a loaf of bread and a mug of water daily, which was no deprivation to a vegetarian, like himself, although the *bloody conspirators* thought that he would soon sink and starve to death on such a regimen; but, instead of that, he gained solid flesh, and when Jemmy had learned that he was a prisoner there, he increased the quantity and improved the quality of his food.

Although Dr. Juno gained in flesh, he became more tender, and often felt prostrated, probably more on account of the vitiated atmosphere which he was bound to inhale than from anything else.

One day, after he had been feeling particularly prostrated, Jemmy made this discovery, that Dr. Juno was a prisoner within that most terrible dungeon; and whilst Jemmy was cogitating what he had better do to save the benefactor, he overheard two jealous servants of the asylum say to one another, that they suspected Jemmy of being engaged in a plot to ruin their reputation with the managers, and that they would set a trap for him, and turn the tables on him, if they could.

They watched their opportunity to get a chance to speak to Deacon Rob Stew, who was their particular friend, as he was instrumental in getting them into the institution, because they were Protestant saints; and when they saw the deacon, one of them said to him:

"Brother Stew, George and myself have discovered a deep plot, which is now being worked up, by several of the Catholic help, which will greatly injure the Asylum, if it succeeds!"

"What is it, William?" asked the deacon.

"You will not expose us, if we tell you; for the Irish Catholics are wicked enough to murder us, should they find out that we told on them," said George.

"Never fear your deacon," responded the viper, feeling terribly nervous, because the guilty conscience needs no accuser.

"Well, it is this: Jemmy, the Irish overseer, is trying to have all Protestant help removed from the various wards of the Asylum, and have Catholics installed in our stead! He thinks that there are now some secret matters going on in this institution, that could not occur were they to occupy the entire control of the prisoners," said William.

"Great God," meditated the deacon, "can Jemmy know that Victor Juno and Miss Lucinda Armington are confined within these walls! I must contrive a plan to have him forthwith arrested and removed from the Asylum, and also deprive him of his liberty, or I am ruined; in fact, the whole brotherhood would be disgraced!

"Never mind Jemmy, what cannot I do, to prevent my plans from failing, and your arrest and speedy conviction is a fixed fact."

It will be remembered that Jemmy was arrested by the deacon himself, as he was leaving the Asylum to visit his country friends; but, as the inauspicious moment would have it, Pat O'Conner and Judy McCrea, excited and awfully indignant, met the deacon and Jemmy just as the latter twain were in angry consultation, when Pat blustered forth:

"Dacon, yer honor, by gorrah! I'll have satesfaction, or I'll expose the whole ting."

CHAPTER XXII.

VICTOR'S TERRIFIC STRUGGLE WITH THE NIGHT WATCHMAN.

ALTHOUGH Jemmy aroused the suspicion of the Managers of the Insane Asylum concerning Victor Juno and Miss Lucinda Armington's incarceration, they nevertheless did not for one moment suspicion that he had done anything to aid the escape of Dr. Juno.

The only thing then that was to be done, was to silence Jemmy from spreading the news; neither were they certain that Jemmy knew of the imprisonment of these reported elopists.

The physician-in-chief did not believe, would not believe, that Jemmy could be unfaithful to him or to the welfare of the Asylum; moreover, he had no access to any of the secret cells to ascertain who was therein confined; how then could he know anything about it?

Deacon Rob Stew said he arrested Jemmy, because George and William told him of a plot which would greatly injure the Asylum, and he came to the conclusion that it was nothing long or short of an *exposé* of the incarceration of Dr. Juno and Miss Armington; and what confirmed his suspicions, was that Jemmy, Pat O'Conner and Judy McCrea were very intimate friends; moreover, when Pat and Judy came to the Asylum in a rage, threatening to "expose the whole ting," what other opinion could a guilty man arrive at, except that there was a knowledge afloat of the inner workings of this holy (?) institution!

The physician-in-chief requested that an investigation should be made forthwith; in fact, Jemmy should receive a secret trial by the brotherhood, and if found guilty should speedily be convicted in the court of sessions before a certain pious (?) judge, who belongs to the bloody clique, and who would rule out any evidence that would be favorable to Jemmy, misconstrue the law, and sentence him for life to the penitentiary.

Whilst the secret trial of Jemmy took place, the time arrived for Dr. Victor Juno to make his escape. Precisely at midnight Dr. Juno tied the rope around his stalwart form, and taking his cold-chisel in one hand and the hammer in the other, he quietly opened the unbolted doors of his cell, and in a moment stood in the corridor without a thought of being unsuccessful in making good his escape; but, he had to do some dreadful work before he was on free soil.

He walked up a short flight of winding stairs, but his progress was impeded by a huge iron door. What to do was a puzzle, because it was so dark that he could not see anything, nor could he detect any bolt, lock or hinges to this door, and it was utterly impossible to hew down the same; he however tried to find a place by which his cold-chisel might be used to pry it open; still all attempts proved a failure.

Now, what should he do? He placed his ear to the keyhole, which was the only aperture he could find, and listened, but all was quiet. He then soliloquized thus: "I have gained a great point in getting out of my dungeon, but how to make my way out of this corridor is more than I know, which is in itself a perfect prison. I shall not be expected here, much less does any one but Jemmy dream that I have these implements of destruction in my possession. Truly, I might wait here until morning, and when the keeper comes, could easily dispatch him, but I do not desire to become a murderer; but, wait, I have it—I'll prepare this rope, by cutting it into pieces with this chisel, and as soon as the keeper opens the door I'll grab and bind him; but, if he attempts to create a noise, I'll be compelled to dispatch him like a bullock; but I shall tell him first to be silent, when I wont harm a hair on his head. But, should there be two or three of them together, what then will best be done? I have it—surely; I will knock them all dumb with this flat cold-chisel, and before they will be able to come to, I will have them bound hand and foot, and if I can, shall lock them in this corridor; still I have nothing wherewith to gag them, and they might scream loud enough to attract others to aid them. Ha! I have got it—I'll drag them into my dungeon and bolt the door on them; that is, if I can find the key to it; I'll go and see if there is any key in either door, or if there are any means of fastening the same without a key. Here it is, an outside bolt!

"I will now return and wait behind the stair door until morning; but why could I not create some noise to arouse the night-watchman? He might not be far away, and without hesitation unbolt the door to see what was wrong.

"I'll try a deep, distant moan by ventriloquism, as if some dungeon prisoners were very ill, and if this fail, I'll increase the sounds until I shall bring some one or more."

He now groaned in a deep voice through the key-hole, and in a moment he heard some one approach the door, who seemed to listen for a few minutes, when he repeated his moan, throwing it into his cell; this caused the night-watchman to unbolt the huge iron door, when he went directly toward Juno's dungeon, and opening the feed-slide, placed his ear evidently to it to listen to the groans. Now was Dr. Juno's time to quiet his keeper; but, he first quietly took the key which the latter let remain in the outside of the stair door, and placed it inside of the lock, closed the door, bolted it, and pocketed the key; then he quietly went in the direction of his dungeon, and before he knew what he was about he struck his head against the keeper's, and quick as lightning they grappled, but being somewhat feeble, found that he had a pretty good match in the diminutive keeper.

They scuffled about the place in a most terrible manner, one moment one being on the top and the next minute the other, until Victor Juno got his hand into the long hair

7

of his antagonist, when the keeper asked for mercy. Victor Juno could not continue to punish his victim uselessly, and as he felt nearly done-over himself, said:

"If I let you loose, will you promise me to be docile and perfectly quiet—I mean, make no noise?"

"Certainly I will," responded the keeper.

But he was no sooner loose, than he made for the stair door, thinking:

"I shall lock you devil or lunatic up, until you can be secured."

But, O horror! the lunatic had locked the door of exit, and what could he do but face the demon or scream for help? Victor Juno heard him scramble for the door, when he said, in a low tone:

"Sir, you are not as good as your word, therefore I shall be under the disagreeable necessity of *compelling* you to be silent."

The poor trembling keeper interposed: "What do you want me to do?"

"Sir, I want your promise to keep silent, and come over here and sit quietly down on the floor until daylight," said Victor Juno in a commanding and stern voice, which thrilled the scared victim, and although he had no weapon of defence with him, he nevertheless ejaculated:

"If you come near me again, I will shoot or stab you; I have both a revolver and a dirk ready for action."

"Indeed, sir, then I shall be compelled to beat your brains out with the huge hammer which I hold in my hand; so you see that two can play at this little game," exclaimed Victor Juno.

"Tell me, who are you, and what do you want? You seem to be sane," said the keeper.

"Yes, sir, I fear that I am too sane and powerful for you; but, who and what I am, or want here, can be no affair of yours this night, so you better obey my orders, when not a hair on your head shall be harmed," kindly responded Victor Juno.

THE CONSPIRATORS AND LOVERS.

"Great God, he is mad!" thought the poor victim, and said aloud: "Did you bolt this door?"

"Yes, sir, I did, and have the key of it in my possession," replied Victor Juno, and continued earnestly: "I say, will you obey me; speak and act, or I'll send you swift as lightning into the next world?"

This caused the half frightened keeper to scream murder, when Victor made one leap in the direction of the voice, and struck him on the temple with his fist, which caused him to reel and spin like a top. Thus Victor Juno sent his victim away into the dark corridor beyond his reach; therefore he began to fish and reach for the sickened and scared watchman cautiously, dreading the pistol or dirk of which he spoke.

After searching for several minutes, Victor listened with ears and mouth wide open, when he heard the keeper breathe; cautiously he neared the breathing apparatus, and when he was sure that he was within the distance of arm's length, he reached for his throat, whilst he managed to grab him simultaneously by the shoulder, and reeled him around, and with lightning velocity grasped his arms by the elbows and forced them together, when he took a piece of rope and bound them securely, and said:

"Now, sir, I think your pistol and dirk won't avail you much, and I implore you give them to me, or I'll handle you very roughly," furiously exclaimed Victor Juno.

"I have neither pistol nor dirk," stammered the victim.

"Then, I'll send you to my cell," and no sooner said than he moved him along the corridor to where Victor's cell door was, and, opening it, ushered him uncouthly forth into the cell, and closed and bolted the same.

CHAPTER XXIII.

THRILLING PRISON SCENE BETWEEN LUCINDA AND DEACON STEW.

ISS LUCINDA ARMINGTON was not visited or molested by any one for several days after the disguised and whipped monster suddenly disappeared from her presence, through a secret door; therefore she had time for reflection. She thought almost continually about her beloved Victor. What was he doing, or where might he be, at that moment! O, if she could only meet him once more, only for a short hour, how happy she would be!

Her appetite failed her, and she could not sleep without continually dreaming the most horrible things, and her dear Victor would always appear in her dreams, who was surrounded by reptiles and vermin of the nastiest character, which did their best to bite and sting him to the heart, when he would weep and wail for assistance; and although she saw it all, and he begged her to assist him, she was entirely powerless and could not as much as say a kind word to him, or keep these venomous pests away from him.

After waking from these awful dreams, she always felt that her betrothed and dearly beloved Victor was surrounded by fiends, or was even then undergoing severe punishment for serving God and man. She endeavored to console herself by Scriptural passages, but she had not the nerve and faith that were necessary to face such martyrdom. Although, she was not thinking of her own sufferings, but of the dangers and tortures that threatened dear Victor.

Whilst in the midst of these meditations, early in the morning, a private door opened, and Deacon Rob Stew stood before her; at first she felt like flying to him and embracing him, because he was the old friend of the family and good deacon. The deacon saw that she looked kindly upon him, which made him bold, when he advanced toward her and said:

"My dear Lucinda, I am delighted to see you, although very sorry to find you in this place."

Like lightning the thought flashed through her brain: "You scoundrel, can dissemble beautifully"—and her countenance changed to a frown, and hatred looked out of her determined eyes, when the pious deacon asked:

"What is the matter with my sweet child? Do not look so distressed, I have come to offer you freedom and my heart and hand in marriage."

"Avaunt! you fiend! I know you now, and you need not dissemble and act the hypocrite any longer! I say you had better be gone, or I'll give you another beating that will leave worse marks than the one you now carry on your nose! Do you hear me? Be gone!" furiously ejaculated Miss Armington, who was fully convinced that the disguised man whom she had pummelled a few days before in this cell, and that in the dark, was this saintly deacon.

He now flew into a passion, and said:

"Miss Armington, how dare you insult me in this way, when I came to you in the kindest manner, and with the holiest intentions? You are an ingrate, who deserves no better treatment than you are receiving in this cell, and I shall leave you in a moment, as you request it; but, before I go, let me say, that I am Deacon Rob Stew, and I would have you know that my power and influence is greater than any monarch in Europe, therefore, beware how you insult and cast me off."

"You are Deacon Rob Stew, the powerful and influential saint; yes, and you were 'handsome' before I destroyed your beautiful nose the other day, when I beat you like a howling cur"—

"You beat me like a howling cur," interposed the deacon. "When, and how was that?"

"If you don't leave me, I will show you how," exclaimed Miss Armington, her eyes flashing fire and fury.

The deacon rather winced, and feared that she might make another onslaught on his saintly carcass, when he changed the conversation and said, very sanctimoniously:

"My dear young sister, now come, let us be serious, and talk like Christians, not like sinners; for you must know that I love you, have always hoped you would become my wife. And had it not been for that profligate innovator, Victor Juno, I undoubtedly would have remained foremost in your affections"—

"May the curse of an avenging God fall upon your leprous tongue, and the spirit of unrest never cease to molest and torture your wicked soul, until you retract every word that you have ever spoken against that honorable gentleman! Yes, may God sow thorns and thistles in your path, that your body may be pricked and torn to pieces by them, as you have endeavored to lacerate mine and the noble Victor's hearts by your bloody conspiracies against us both! You are a detestable villain, and I wonder that you are not afraid that God will strike you dead forthwith, and send your loathsome soul into the regions of everlasting torment! Do you hear that?

"Now, you have my sentiments, therefore leave me instantly!" interposed Miss Armington, in a manner that meant mischief.

"I pray you, listen for a moment to me, and then, if you are not satisfied, I will quit you forever," down-heartedly said the deacon.

"Well, say on then; but no more insults, remember that," responded Miss Armington.

"You blame me for things of which I am entirely innocent. I have never conspired against you, but I cannot say that much for Victor Juno"—

"Accursed falsifier that you are; would you damn your own hypocritical soul over and over by adding insult to injury?" interrupted she.

"Hear me through," said he, "before you become so severe; I do not wish to shield myself from any crime or sin that I may have committed on your behalf"—

"What do you mean," interrupted Miss Armington, "by saying that you have committed crime or sin in my behalf?"

"My dear Lucinda, I *love* you, and love is blind to everything. It was this extreme affection for you, sweet lady, that drove me to commit acts that nothing else in the world could have driven me to do," sorrowfully said the deacon.

"I have never done anything to encourage you in that direction; and if what you say is true, of which I have my doubts, I pity you; but that is *all* the consolation you can ever expect from me. Even had I possessed any regard for you, the acts which you have committed against him whose very footprints I love more than the entire existence of thousands like yourself, would have caused me to spurn you," indignantly ejaculated Miss Armington.

"Is there, then, no hope for me? I was told by Pat O'Conner that you only took to Victor Juno because I did not propose marriage to you," said he.

"And you were fool enough to believe what my servant told you!" she exclaimed.

"Why should I not have believed it? Did you not always treat me kindly, and appeared glad to see me at your house, until that innovator made his appearance?" said Deacon Stew.

"Sir, if you desire my audience even in this prison cell, cease to call my beloved Victor names, or I'll refuse to listen to you," proudly exclaimed Miss Armington, looking at him as if she really detested him.

"Well, proud lady," said he, "I then shall be compelled to remove this 'beloved Victor' from your reach; and, unless you promise to lend me your ear and give me some hope, I shall cause his death!"

"What! Would you become a murderer? Would you

add this foul crime to your already blackened deeds done in the body? Avaunt! I say; or I'll tear you limb from limb, you miserable fiend, and save you the trouble or pleasure of injuring my beloved Victor," most furiously exclaimed Miss Armington, who was now almost insane with fear and horror, lest her faithful betrothed should be made to suffer tortures on her account. She thought:

"For aught I know, he is now enduring the pangs of a lingering death; because I am sure this vile deacon would be guilty of anything to gain his selfish and brutal ends. Oh, Victor! Victor! may the Infinite hand of Jehovah protect and guard you against the wiles, plots and conspiracies of these bloody people. What have you ever done to injure them? What have you ever done to injure any one? You are so noble, so benevolent, so very generous and so zealous to improve your race, that I cannot see what benefit it is to a man to do good in this world."

After looking upon her for a few minutes with dumbfounded amazement, the deacon said:

"What are you thinking about, Miss Armington? Do you not feel well? If I have caused you pain, I humbly ask your pardon, and if my presence distresses you, I will leave you; but, can I not hope for a little encouragement?"

"No, you cannot; but, you can drive me mad, and then you may be able to justify yourself before your brethren, and the world, for placing me in this cell! This may be the object of your visits here, so now then, please leave me," when she fainted dead away.

CHAPTER XXIV.

DR. VICTOR JUNO'S ESCAPE FROM HIS DUNGEON.

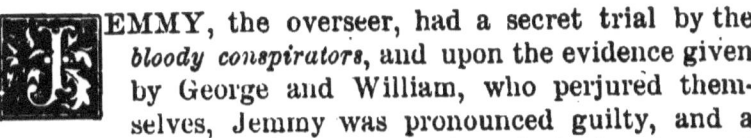EMMY, the overseer, had a secret trial by the *bloody conspirators*, and upon the evidence given by George and William, who perjured themselves, Jemmy was pronounced guilty, and a true bill of indictment was found against him the next day, when he was tried in the court of sessions, before a judge and prosecuting attorney, who belonged to the bloody clique.

However, it must be remembered, that Victor Juno escaped before Jemmy's public trial took place, which confirmed Deacon Rob Stew's former suspicion of the guilt of Jemmy, and therefore additional witnesses were placed upon the stand. The night-watchman, whom Dr. Juno locked up in his cell the night of the tussle, was a first-class witness for the conspirators, and of course, Jemmy was found guilty of felony, and sentenced forthwith, for life to solitary confinement in the eastern penitentiary.

This gave a quietus to the only man who really knew anything positive of the workings of the asylum, except Pat O'Conner and Judy McCrea, and when they learned how summarily Jemmy was dispatched, they very likely would be silent, lest they might be served in the same way.

Deacon Rob Stew sought an interview with Pat O'Conner as soon as he had an opportunity, after he met him and Judy McCrea at the asylum when he had arrested Jemmy, and said :

"Pat, I want to know what you meant by coming into my presence in the asylum, and ejaculating so furiously that you would '*expose the whole thing,*' the day that I arrested Jemmy, the conspirator? Was it you who was in conspiracy with Jemmy "—

"Och! be Sant Patrick, yer honor should know me better than that," said Pat.

"What did you mean, when you said you would '*expose the whole thing*'?" responded the deacon.

"Expose the whole ting," ejaculated Pat, and stammering, "we-ll I was tould by that Mishter Juno's sarvant that ye had murhdered me Mistress Armington, an' that Mishter Juno camed home from visitin' a sick person along ways away; this is what was the hole ting what I was sayin' I'd expose."

"Pat, are you telling the truth?" asked the deacon.

"An' may me sowl sace to liv ef it aint," solemnly said Pat, who however had other ideas, but he considered an ounce of policy might be worth ten thousand pounds of truth, just now. And he knew well enough, if the deacon had the least suspicion of him being informed of Miss Lucinda Armington and Dr. Victor Juno being, or having been in their philanthropic insane asylum, he would cause his and Judy McCrea's arrest, conviction and imprisonment; and, although as Dr. Juno is at liberty, he had better not be seen in Juno's company, else mischief might befall him and his Judy.

Pat was no fool in reasoning thus; and especially as the deacon looked determined and spoke very theateningly, Pat considered discretion the better part of valor.

The *bloody conspirators*, at this stage of proceedings, had to make powerful efforts to stigmatize Dr. Juno as a wicked monster and awful liar, for they felt certain that he would at once pounce upon the rostrum and expose all he knew; but the influence of all the religious denominations, who believe every thing the *bloody conspirators* say, was immense; and by the hue and cry against Dr. Juno as the seducer, eloper and deserter of Miss Lucinda Armington, he could be held up to such scorn and contempt, that his practice as a physician would be utterly ruined, and few, if any, would dare to go near him.

There was only one thing to be dreaded, his tongue in the rostrum; for the wicked and curious "people" *will* go to hear him, and he has a way of addressing them that convinces thousands that he is in the right. Now, something must be done to stop him from preaching in large halls, or theatres, or they (the conspirators) would as sure be ruined as water runs down hill.

They could easily prevent their followers, and even the great majority of the worldlings, from believing anything that Dr. Juno might say, so far as his incarceration was concerned; but, when he gets a chance to preach, or write for a paper, he argues in such a manner as to positively show his auditors and readers that his doctrines are sound, and prove to every one that all the religionists' views and teachings are anti-Christ and anti-Natural! Although the very hearers or readers who are convinced that his logic is correct, nevertheless may not believe him to be an honest or truthful man; hence, it is no trouble for the elect to say that he has been away with Miss Armington, if he should say that the saints abducted him or Miss Armington and imprisoned them in the insane asylum.

Pat O'Conner and Judy McCrea made up their minds that they would remain quietly at home and attend to their business, and would positively not have any intercourse with Dr. Juno; but, if the general would return, they would confide the matter to him.

The general was still in Liverpool at this time; and as soon as Victor Juno had escaped, the bloody conspirators managed to write to him at once, and gave him the sore information that Dr. Juno had returned home, evidently having deserted his daughter, Miss Lucinda Armington.

That unless they gave the general the first information of it, and some one else would do so, he might suspicion his faithful (?) brethren, and lose faith in their integrity.

They told the general, in their letter, that they learned that Miss Lucinda was then in London, the mother of a little son, and that he had better direct his steps there, for she was evidently in poverty and great distress.

The poor general went almost mad when he received this news, and concluded that he would go to London, and diligently search for his misled child; and if he failed to find her in a certain period, he would sail for his home in America; for he felt as though his beloved daughter was near his own home; at any rate, he was nearly insane, and he would return to revenge himself on Victor Juno; and he would seek him, and with a loaded revolver pointed at Dr. Juno's breast, he would make him confess or shoot him dead.

Whenever General Washington Armington made up his mind to do anything, he would never cease thinking of it until he had fulfilled his mental promises. He therefore went to London in company with his expert detective; but, after a fortnight's diligent search, they gave it up as a failure. The detective told the general that he felt certain that neither his daughter nor Dr. Juno had been in Europe, as reported; but that he believed, and he claimed his judgment to be good, that his daughter was hid away not far from the general's own home; this coincided exactly with the general's own views. The latter, therefore, started for America, and arrived at his residence in a very brief season, where the faithful servants were found when he arrived.

Pat O'Conner intended to confide what he knew at once to his master; but the general was in such an agitated state of mind that he would not give Pat an opportunity to say anything to him. The only thing he asked Pat was:

"Is Victor Juno at his home?"

"Yis," said Pat.

"My God!" retorted the general, and asked Pat to leave him.

He now prepared a six-shooter, and at once sat out to seek Dr. Victor Juno; he found the doctor in his medical office, when he accosted him thus:

"Now, you infernal rascal, where is my daughter?"

"That is just what I want to know," said Dr. Juno, anxiously, but coolly. This so enraged the general, that he presented his revolver to Dr. Juno's breast, and fired.

CHAPTER XXV.

DR. JUNO LOCKED OUT OF CONCERT HALL, WHICH CAUSED A RIOT.

DOCTOR VICTOR JUNO, after running the night watchman into his cell and bolting the door, had very little trouble in making his way out of the asylum. He unbolted the iron stair door, and after he passed through it, locked it again and pocketed the key, thinking that he might need it elsewhere.

Since he now had the keeper or watchman stored away where he could not be heard should he scream with all his might, he felt almost certain that no one else was in that part of the institution ; but, for fear there might be, he was cautious in his advancement, and although he put the keeper's hat on, he was too large to look like him.

As he arrived on the first floor, where lights shone dimly, he beheld a man in a distant part of that corridor, who called to Dr. Juno :

"Jeremiah, will you take charge of this ward for the balance of the night?"

When Dr. Juno replied, "Certainly I will."

The man instantly passed through a door, and disappeared. He evidently mistook Dr. Juno for the legitimate watchman. The Doctor now followed the advice which Jemmy gave him, and with a slight effort pried the only door open that was locked, until he reached the open yard of the asylum; and with his rope, chisel and hammer, he readily scaled the wall, and in an hour he was in his office.

Having been away for several weeks, he must at once begin his lectures again ; and when he retired to his bed, could not sleep for thinking what he had better do. He soliloquized as follows:

"When I last preached in the Walnut Street Theatre, the pharisees colluded together to create a riot, and failing in that, they influenced the mayor to solicit the proprietor of the theatre to not let me have it again, as a monstrous breach of the peace was threatened ; then, when I returned to my own small hall in the northern part of the city, and had immense crowds of people follow me who could not gain admission on account of my room being too small, the pharisees were displeased with even that success, when they literally bought off all the daily newspaper proprietors—requesting them to cease taking a single advertisement from me, and even refuse to insert my name for love or money into their columns.

"They thought, of course, that, if I was deprived of the use of the theatres, large public halls, and the newspaper advertising columns, I would be compelled to starve or leave the city, and now as I have been abducted and confined in that hell-hole of an insane asylum, these *bloody conspirators* will make a handle of it, or at least in some way construe my absence into something that will speak against me!

"I have my own newspaper, '*The Sharp-Shooter, and Anti-Fogy,*' which they dread awfully, and I have my own hall, that will seat three hundred people ; but, my hall is not large nor fashionable enough for the *elite* to enter it ; at any rate, a small audience cannot be fired up and made enthusiastic like a large one ; hence, I will hunt around to-morrow and see if I cannot find some large public hall or theatre that has not been bought off by the pharisees.

"I shall go to see my darling Lucinda the first thing in the morning ; she will be delighted to see me! The poor girl, I wonder if she dreams of the persecution that I have suffered ? I'll ask the general to advise and aid me to get a large hall to preach in next Sunday evening !"

In the morning Dr. Juno's servant told him what the report was about him whilst he was gone ; that most of the people, who had been his former friends, really believed that he had eloped with Miss Lucinda Armington.

"What?" ejaculated the astonished doctor, "eloped

with Miss Lucinda Armington ? Great Heavens! Has she been also away in my absence ?"

"Certainly, she disappeared the same night that you did, and has not been heard of since," said his servant.

"This is monstrous! O God! this is *truly* unendurable! Jack, leave me to meditate over this outrage," exclaimed Dr. Juno in agony.

"I am confounded, and scarcely know what course to pursue; but I cannot lose much time in thinking. I'll go and see the general, and tell him all about my incarceration; but these confounded conspirators assuredly have turned him against me. Truly, I see it all. They have abducted dear Lucinda the very night that I was kidnapped, and very likely she is confined in the same lunatic asylum from which I escaped.

"What can I do to find her? I dare not be rash or imprudent in the matter, because these bloody monsters have everything their own way just now; therefore, I must work cautiously, but energetically."

Dr. Juno looked around for a large centrally located public hall to preach in. He first went to Concert Hall, which was the largest and most fashionable place in the city, knowing that a new proprietor had it for rent, and verily, he agreed to lease it to Dr. Juno for a year to preach in on Sunday evenings; therefore, he at once had his posters and circulars printed and distributed, and also sent his advertisement to the only independent newspapers, (the Sunday papers), to which he always had access in common with the community at large.

The moment it was noticed by the religious bigots that Dr. Juno was advertising to speak in Concert Hall on the following Sunday, they went to the new and inexperienced proprietor of the hall, and told him to prevent Victor Juno from preaching in his hall, or they would withdraw their patronage and operate against him, which would have literally ruined the proprietor. The latter, therefore, went to the mayor, and said to him:

"Your honor, I have leased Concert Hall to Dr. Juno, for the purpose of preaching by himself, and the Young Men's Association, opposite, say that if I let him speak only one night in the place, that they will throw up their engagements for the winter and do all against me that is in their power, and this would surely ruin me, for the influence of the religious community is *the* power of our city. Now, sir, I have come to ask you what I had better do to-morrow?"

"Do? Close the doors against him of course; but you have time to inform him to-day that he cannot have it," said his honor, the pious, or make believe saint, Mayor M——l.

"My dear sir, I have already informed Dr. Juno that he cannot have it, but he insists on having it, as he has paid for it, and has also freely advertised the same, which undoubtedly will bring a crowd to-morrow, Sunday evening," exclaimed the proprietor of the hall.

"Ah! Indeed, he defies you, does he? Very well, we will see. You bolt the doors as strongly as you can, and I will have a *posse* of police there to guard and protect you thoroughly," responded the excellent mayor.

"Many thanks, noble sir; I shall follow your advice strictly," said the proprietor.

When Sunday evening arrived it rained heavily, being a settled rain, but notwithstanding this rain, and then no street cars running on the "Sabbath-Day," there was an immense crowd of people congregated in front of the hall; but the doors were closed, and a large force of policemen lining the entrance to the same.

The people wanted to know what this all meant, the answer came from the police officers, that Juno was prohibited from preaching therein on this occasion; and as soon as this got noised throughout the four to five thousand people that were patiently waiting to see the doors open, they became impatient and rebellious, and cried aloud:

"Dr. Juno! Dr. Juno!"

He got on a step and said in a loud voice:

"The pharisees are determined that you shall not be allowed to hear me preach to you; I have paid for the hall in advance, and you see the rest yourselves."

Then an immense uproar burst upon the air:

"Mob the police! mob the police!" And a most terrible riot ensued.

CHAPTER XXVI.

MOST THRILLING AND DEMONIACAL PLOTTING OF THE CONSPIRATORS.

THE bloody conspirators had now increased their number of members largely, and a special meeting had been called for Wednesday evening, sharp, at eight o'clock, in Tabernacle Hall. Rev. Joe Pier, the President, in the chair, who called the members to order, when the doors were securely locked, and business was commenced.

Deacon Rob Stew was the first man who took the floor, and spoke as follows:

"Beloved saints, I have a great deal to say to you this evening that is to be kept sacredly secret; and I therefore again assert, that if there is any chicken-hearted brother or sister present, whoever it is, he or she may at once be removed. Will the President challenge the new members, who are not so fully indoctrinated into our plans and mottos as is necessary?"

"Certainly, dear Brother Stew; I will do as you say, for you all know that I tremble when I think of the arduous work that it is our holy mission to fulfil; therefore, I order all the members to rise to their feet, and repeat our pledge after me," responded Rev. Joe Pier.

After the terrible oath was repeated by each new member separately (the reader knows what that oath is; has read it in the second chapter), Deacon Stew continued:

"Feeling again safe in confiding my bloody plans to your hearts and hands, I shall briefly state what I have secretly learned, and what I propose *shall* be done; I say *shall*, because I am ordained by the Church to see to financial and secular matters as well as to assist in conducting religious worship. Dr. Juno has again escaped us, which is the most unfortunate thing that could have befallen the saints; and he has already advertised to speak in Concert Hall, next Sabbath evening; but I have fixed matters for him already, so that he will be locked out of the hall when his hour for discourse appears. I have managed this through the Young Men's Association, who have great influence with the proprietor of Concert Hall. But, whilst this will deprive him from speaking on that occasion, it will not stop him from trying it elsewhere; moreover, he has a small hall of his own, where he holds his physiological lectures to the sexes; but, I am sure I have a plan in view which will entrap him, if it is rigidly carried out by our religious people, and by the secret conclave. It is this: We must have the cry vigorously circulated, far and near, that Victor Juno is an awful *roué*, who is proved such already in public esteem, by the reputation we gave him—by the seduction of, and elopement with, Miss Lucinda Armington. Therefore, we shall hire a few fascinating single ladies, who must go to his medical office for professional advice, and endeavor to get him to make improper advances toward them; and if they cannot succeed, will, nevertheless, be willing to swear before a public tribunal that he insulted them."

"I do not think that such a plan will work successfully; but, why not concoct some method by which we can either imprison or hang him?" said Dr. Toy Pancy.

"No, sir; your plan would be dangerous at present, for we dare not make too many bold attempts at his life so closely together; because, you must all know that *the people* are looking sharply on, and when they should find out that this man was being too roughly handled, they might arouse the hue and cry: 'Persecution and Republicanism subjugated,' which might cause mob law and rebellion, a thing we shall avoid by quietly, but cunningly, working in the way I have proposed. However, I have not given you my whole plans as yet. Dr. Juno is not a suspicious man, but a fearless dog; hence, several married ladies should be hired to visit his medical office also, and seek domestic advice; and if they cannot induce him to make improper overtures to them, they must, nevertheless, go home to their husbands (and for this purpose we must select handsome women, whose husbands are already jealous of their wives, and who are not afraid to shoot him), and tell their jealous better-halves that Dr. Juno grossly insulted them, and if they had not accidentally escaped him, they would have been ruined," said Deacon Stew.

"I have still a better plan," responded Dr. Toy Pancy; "that is, a plan that is more likely to succeed, and will be far more plausible. It must be very certain that Dr. Juno needs money, for we have already impoverished him by our past course, and he is heavily in debt, which he dreads awfully; therefore, we should send some unprincipled females to him, with five hundred or a thousand dollars a piece, to offer him for producing abortion on them, which, very likely, he would do. He is skilful in surgery, and should, undoubtedly, conclude that this would be an easy way of making large sums of money"—

"This is the best plan," interrupted Sister Nancy Clover; "and afterwards arrest him and have him sent to the penitentiary for twenty or thirty years, which would ruin him thoroughly and forever, even though he should be pardoned by some weak-minded Governor."

"Oh! Holy Sister Nancy Clover, you are such a deep saint that my soul swells when I hear you sanction such safe and cautious plans," said Rev. Joe Pier, solemnly.

"I have still another plan should he again attempt to speak in a large public hall, where we should fail to control the proprietor thereof; and you will all agree with me that it will succeed in convicting him for a misdemeanor that gives him one year in the county prison, and five hundred dollars fine.

"Dr. Juno publishes and sells several medical books; one of them is on the '*Physiology of Marriage*,' and we can readily cry it down as an 'Obscene' publication, and all we have to do is to apply to our good natured and sincerely pious mayor, who will arrest him just before he steps on the rostrum to preach, and convey him to the Central Station, where, in some rude cell, he will stay until the following Monday morning; because there will be no officer there on Sabbath evening to give him a hearing or take bail.

"By the morning following, all the newspapers will delight in filling their columns with the arrest of Dr. Juno for selling 'Obscene' books and giving indecent sermons," said Deacon Rob Stew.

"Excellent! excellent! most excellent!!" exclaimed Sister Nancy Clover, and added, "and I am *sure*, if we can once get him before a grand jury, he will be indicted forthwith; and our exemplary District Attorney, Charlson, who is a member of several leagues of pious and republican orders, will work for his conviction with all his pious shrewdness, and we can easily manage to get Judge Sanctiblower on the bench, who will conspire with the District Attorney, Charlson, and rule out all of Dr. Juno's testimony, misconstrue the law to the jury, and sentence him to the full extent of the law, and deem it a religious duty becoming the elect."

"Mr. President, and brothers and sisters, I am a tyro in this work of deviltry, which you are conspiring to carry out under the cloak of holy religion; now, whilst I shall not violate my oath, which I have been compelled to take this evening, I nevertheless am not willing to co-operate with you in the fulfilment of this nefarious work," said Harry Gossimer, earnestly and with a derisive countenance.

"Great Mars! may I never live to see to-morrow if this

wretched apostate shall leave this hall to-night until we settle his benignant conscience!" furiously exclaimed Deacon Rob Stew. "Such miserable devils as Brother Harry Gossimer should learn to understand upon what ground they stand, when they enter our secret order!"

"Sir, Mr. Rob Stew need not fear that I shall betray the holy saint, whom I now behold in his true colors "—

"Cease your sarcasm," furiously exclaimed Deacon Stew, interrupting the speaker, whilst he continued, "Mr. President, I order this vile apostate to be at once arrested, tried, convicted and sentenced by this court of secrecy, according to our oath. What say the brothers and sisters?"

"Arrest him! Arrest him!" was the unanimous cry; when he was pounced upon by the entire brotherhood, who knocked him senseless to the floor, and cast him into their dungeon.

CHAPTER XXVII.

GENERAL ARMINGTON TURNS INSANE.

JUST as General Washington Armington fired, Dr. Victor Juno knocked the pistol aside, when the bullet barely grazed his skin; but the general, not satisfied, immediately attempted to shoot again, when Dr. Juno wrung the pistol from his hand, and said:

"Now sir, general, if I were the man you would believe me to be, I might, and most likely would shoot *you;* but you cruelly wrong me, as well as your own faithful daughter! Great heaven! could I only find out where she is!" exclaimed Dr. Juno, with great tears in his eyes, which fairly changed the general's ideas, when he asked:

"Tell me, then, where have you been all the time, that no one knew of your whereabouts?"

"I was kidnapped one Thursday evening, as I was walking down Chestnut street, and carried to the insane asylum in West Philadelphia, and cast into a most dreadful dungeon, and only made my escape by a miracle—through a faithful servant, whose name I vowed not to mention. I believe that your daughter is confined in the same asylum," said Dr. Juno.

"O God! you have opened my senses to an awful suspicion"—

"Yes, sir, and the very deacon who stands so high in the church, and who is also president of this asylum, is in love with your child; and very likely he is torturing her inside of those walls; but this is only a suspicion; I know nothing about it, and am sorry I have no chance to find out whether she is there or not; but it is only a matter of time!" responded Dr. Juno, sympathetically.

"Oh! my dear son, this will set me crazy; for I now believe that I have wronged you altogether—I am *sure* of it, and feel convinced that we have all been wronged by the very people in whom I had the utmost confidence; but, let me invoke you, young man, to remain steadfast in principle and honor, come what may; for the day of reckoning will come, and God is just and immutably impartial—remember that!" sadly replied the general.

"Yes, sir, you are right, and I prefer death to dishonor; moreover, principle with me is everything"—

"I know it, I know it; but, I have greatly wronged you, for which I ask ten thousand pardons," said the general, interrupting Dr. Juno, who continued:

"Nay, do not ask pardon of me, because you have only done what any good father would do; and had you done less, I could not respect and love you, as I now do."

"Young man, you break my poor, distressed heart! I have suffered a million of deaths since last we have seen each other happy together—I mean, my beloved daughter and myself! Lord! O Lord! comfort an old bereft, desolate man's soul, in this bitter hour of sorrow! But, where, O where is my daughter, my daughter?" which were the last sane words that General Washington Arnington spoke.

Dr. Juno called his servant, and requested him to join him in conducting the old man to his home, as he esteemed him in such a febrile state of mind, as to be unsafe to let him go unattended. When they arrived at the general's residence, Pat O'Conner and Judy McCrea were thunderstruck to see their master in such a distressed state of mind; but they feared danger very much to have Dr. Juno found at their home; therefore, Pat proposed to send for sister Nancy Clover, who was the general's best friend, and in whom the general always had wonderful confidence. Dr. Juno said nothing, but did not wish to meet Nancy Clover, for his heart throbbed when he heard her name mentioned. The doctor therefore left the house, saying to Judy McCrea, if his services were wanted, to send for him; she responded:

"Yis, sir."

The moment sister Nancy Clover arrived, she said:

"The general is insane, and he must at once be taken to the West Philadelphia Insane Asylum."

"Och! murhder," almost audibly mumbled Pat O'Conner, and said aloud, "Yer lady would not tak me good mashter away from home, would ye?"

"Why not?" indignantly responded Nancy Clover, "he is insane, and our asylum for such invalids is the proper place."

Pat and Judy withdrew from the presence of the pious sister, when Pat said:

"Judy darlin, what ye tink ov this doins? Be Sant Patrick, I be dumb sthruck wid this work."

"Och! Pat, an' I be sick ov this asylum; jis tink, Pat darlin, what these peoples may do to me mashter an' mishtress, whin they hav them in that divilish place!" said Judy.

These faithful servants were in great distress to find their master insane, who should share the fate of his poor daughter; and what would become of the general's property, was a puzzle to them; but, very likely, the bloody clique would become the guardians of the estate, and use his money under the pretence that they support him in their asylum ; thus they will become owners of the bodies, souls and property of the Armington family ; but, thought Pat O'Conner :

"I'll expose the whole ting, at the rite plaze, an' I be awachin' me chance to do it."

It may be necessary to say here, that the riot which took place on the Sunday evening, when Dr. Juno was locked out of Concert Hall, was instigated by the interfering of these *bloody conspirators;* it having been the work of Deacon Rob Stew ; and the police who were injured could blame no one but these vipers and their co-conspirators, the mayor and Young Men's Association. They never tried to arrest, or even accuse, Dr. Juno for causing this riot ; because they knew too well where their bread was buttered.

Had Dr. Juno been arrested for causing a breach of the peace, which a former mayor tried his best to bring about on several occasions, when Dr. Juno preached in the theatre, it would have turned in favor of the latter, as there were too many fearless witnesses ready to expose the dastardly outrage that was practised by those who claim to be the city fathers and guardians of the inalienable liberties of men.

There are times in the affairs of human events when even the religious bigots, however mighty they are, cannot master everything, and we prophesy that before half a century is gone by, these *bloody conspirators* and false interpreters of the Bible, and misrepresentatives of Jesus Christ, God and Nature, will be looked upon as the offscouring of the earth, and greatest blasphemers of all the heathen ages.

CHAPTER XXVIII.

DOCTOR JUNO ARRESTED IN HIS PULPIT FOR SELLING "OBSCENE" BOOKS.

DOCTOR JUNO was too wide awake to take to the baits which the *bloody conspirators* cast before him. He was not a law-breaker, but rather a law-maker, and he practised what he preached, which proved a perfect safeguard against such traps as were set for him; and, therefore, the only possible way to imprison or kill him was to use foul means.

Several novel, but unsuccessful, plans were instituted against him. The conspirators connived with several policemen to shoot him some night, as it were, by accident. The following was the designed manner of making all things safe and sound:

Two policemen were to keep an eye on him, and when he would be called out some dark night, they should be pretending to be tracking a thief, and just as he leaves his door, they should fire at him with perfect aim, and shoot him dead in a mistake for a burglar, which would remove Dr. Juno, and acquit the policemen, who would be lauded for their vigilance, whilst very few persons would regret the accidental death of Juno.

The foregoing was the plot established and actually carried out by Deacon Rob Stew and two policemen. These public guardians of private citizens shot—as stated—five bullets, well aimed, one night at Dr. Juno, as he was called to see a patient. As soon as he left his door-step, these policemen fired, and continued firing at him, whilst he took to running in the direction of his patient, until five shots exhausted their ammunition; but they failed to touch him.

The neighborhood was aroused, and when the report spread, at two o'clock in the night, that a policeman had shot five well aimed bullets at Dr. Juno, mistaking him for a thief, but utterly failing to hit the doctor, all sorts of sentiments were then and there expressed. His friends denounced these policemen, whilst his enemies abused them for being such poor shots.

One officer did all the shooting, and he told Dr. Juno himself, afterwards, that he took special aim three times, and whilst he could nine times out of ten hit a ten-cent piece at thirty paces, he had been within ten paces of Dr. Juno when he stopped to aim. This was a miraculous escape. The officer said:

"Doctor, should I have killed you, I would have had no trouble to be acquitted, because I was *sure* you were a thief who came out of your house."

Again Dr. Juno escaped miraculously, and the conspirators became superstitious, because nothing can kill this innovator. He was repeatedly annoyed by those who proffered their advice; but nothing insulted him more than to have any one suggest how he should act or what he had better do. Inducements were next presented to him to leave the city; even several thousand dollars were offered him if he would leave the place for a year, but all such movements were treated with disdain, and the propounder felt cheaper than ever in his life. Because Dr. Juno would reply to all such propositions:

"No, sir, the pharisees of Philadelphia require to have one fearless and competent man over them, who can expose their heinousness."

It may be seen from the foregoing history of the antagonistic parties, that neither of them were idle, nor did grass grow under any of their feet. Each was determined to conquer or die; which was a noble determination for the side which had right to back it.

The religionists had the *lucre*, position and seven-eighths majority, which gave them immense power and influence; whilst the single-handed reformer—Dr. Juno—stood comparatively alone, and his only power rested in his oratorical capacity, and tact in explaining fixed laws; therefore the public rostrum was his proper sphere to cause a successful battle with his opponents; he consequently searched for another large public hall, of central location, to preach in; and, as luck would have it, an old German theatre had burned down some months prior, which was rebuilt by a Jew, and at this time this new establishment was just being then inaugurated, and Dr. Juno succeeded in leasing it for Sunday evening preaching. As soon as the *bloody conspirators* found out that Dr. Juno had rented the magnificent new Theatrical Hall, in Callowhill near Fifth street, they sent a committee of three retired gentlemen to the proprietor of this hall to buy him off.

They addressed him as follows:

"Mr. S———r, we have learned that Dr. Juno has leased your magnificent new establishment for Sabbath evening preaching?"

"Yes, sir, he has," said the proprietor.

"Do you not suppose that if you permit him to preach in it, that it will ruin the reputation of your place?"

"No, sir, I do not," sharply replied the proprietor.

"Well, my dear friend," said the chairman of the committee, "may be you do not know the odium that is attached to this man."

"No, sir, I do not, and I don't care as long as he has paid me my price; and so long as he continues to do so, I care nothing further what attaches to him, or to you. Who are you, any way?" indignantly exclaimed the proprietor.

"We are a committee of Christians, sent by the Young Men's Association, to consult you on this matter," said the chairman.

"Sir, I am a Jew, not a Christian, hence I spurn your proposals! Good day," ejaculated the proprietor, and walked away. This ended the interference in that quarter.

Deacon Rob Stew's course was now resorted to; so this committee of *retired gentlemen* saints called upon the pious and obliging mayor, and told his honor that Dr. Juno had engaged the magnificent new hall in Callowhill street, and had advertised to preach there the following Sabbath evening; that they had been to see the proprietor to persuade him not to permit Juno to speak therein, but before they could finish their proposal, he told them sharply that he was a Jew, and that Dr. Juno could have it as long as he paid his price for it; that they were just going to offer to pay the said price, if he would not let Juno have it, when he said: "Good day," and walked away.

That the only thing now left for them to do was for the mayor to send forthwith one of his detectives to Dr. Juno's office, to buy from him a copy of each of his publications, as he published and sold an "Obscene book," and if the mayor would have a warrant issued, after having said books, and direct his officers to retain that warrant until Sabbath evening, just before Dr. Juno would commence to preach, they should arrest him and lock him up all night in a cell in the Central Station, giving the particulars to the newspapers, which would cause a tumultuous hue and cry the following morning, which would turn the entire community against the prisoner.

The holy mayor coincided with this plan, and, true as preaching, he had it carried out to the letter, and Dr. Juno was cast into a cold, close cell, with a horse thief.

CHAPTER XXIX.

THE INSANE GENERAL ARMINGTON NEARLY MURDERS THE PHYSICIAN-IN-CHIEF.

IT will be remembered that when Deacon Rob Stew last visited Miss Lucinda Armington in her prison-house, he tormented her until she fainted dead away, when he was frightened, for he really thought he had killed her, and, although if she were dead, he would not need to fear anything except Jemmy, who might be brought some day from his cell to testify in a court of justice ; because politics change men, and, in sooth, men themselves are changeable ; therefore, he shuddered at the idea of having caused Miss Lucinda Armington's death! The deacon at once went to the physician-in-chief of the asylum, and told him that he had just visited Miss Armington, and he believed that she was dead!

Although the physician-in-chief was in rapport with the *bloody conspirators*, and was in fact a member of the bloody clique, he did not know that the pious deacon had ever loved the girl, that he had been jilted by her, or that he tortured the poor creature, whilst he made his frequent visits to her cell. The physician-in-chief rather thought that the generous deacon was kindly inclined toward Miss Armington ; hence, he did not dream of anything occurring through his (deacon's) visits that was disagreeable to the young lady, whom the physician-in-chief was inclined to love, respect, and treat with more than ordinary kindness ; because she was the daughter of his old friend and schoolmate, General Washington Armington, who was now really insane on account of this very daughter of his.

The physician-in-chief instantly went to her cell, asking the deacon to accompany him, but he excused himself, fearing she might not be dead, and might cause an unpleasant onslaught on his deaconship ; and when the doctor entered her cell she was seated on her chair, looking somewhat stupefied, but seeming rational and talkative.

Miss Armington at once asked him :

"Doctor, why am I confined in this place, and why do you permit Deacon Rob Stew to enter my prison-house to insult and torture me ? "

"My dear Miss Armington, I hope the deacon does not treat you rudely. Is it not your imagination only, that he treats you badly ? " said the physician-in-chief.

"No, sir ; I imagine nothing ; but know of what I speak.

He has insulted me awfully, and one time he came to me in disguise, and after making this cell dark, offered the grossest indignities, until he so enraged me, that I beat him furiously, which may have seemed insane in me; but being in an insane asylum, it must be excusable; because I might as well have the game as the name. This place is enough to make one crazy; but will you please inform me why I am incarcerated here?" exclaimed Miss Armington.

"My poor girl, your father ordered you to be placed here for your own good, fearing you would be led astray by that Dr. Victor Juno, who really is out of his natural senses, or he would not set himself against all the usages of society. He pitches into everything and everybody, and that shows that he is a lunatic, who ought to be confined in prison or an insane institution like this. He will sooner or later come to grief, because you cannot find anybody who approves of his course of action," said the doctor.

"Sir, you wrong him; he is a scientific man and sincere Christian, with a most benevolent heart; and you said that no one approves of his course of action; let me disabuse your mind on that question—I heartily approve of all he does, and, if some of the bigots, who claim more nicety than they possess wisdom, would attend to their own business, and let him alone, he would make many sound bodies and expansive minds, who would become members of the Christian church.

"Yes, sir; he is in the right, and his persecutors know it, and *the people*, whom the pharisees dread, also know it. The latter would gladly receive the natural teachings of Dr. Juno, but there are so many ignorant, bigoted and self-righteous sinners in this world, who are envious, selfish and jealous of a man who is so far their superior, that they would murder him for being what he cannot help to be, namely, a genuine benefactor and natural Christian," responded Miss Armington, greatly relieved.

"You are quite a trumpeter for this Dr. Juno," rather sarcastically said the doctor.

"I only speak the holy truth, which some of you cannot appreciate, nor dare you maintain it like my noble Victor," haughtily she exclaimed.

"Indeed! I think your actions prove you to be as insane as he, and your own father evidently saw that, hence, placed you in this asylum," said he.

"Monster! do you say that my father had anything to do with this foul act? Never, never; but I fear that my poor old father, and probably my dear Victor, are even now both incarcerated not far from here. You start! You know it, then, to be a fact! O, fiend! you also belong to those *bloody conspirators!*" she said, in agony.

"Miss Armington, you insult me, and I now see why the deacon has been pronounced cruel and insulting by you. You first insulted him as you do me," responded the doctor.

"Am I not your prisoner; your slave? Let me have my freedom, and you may offer me any insult you choose, and I will not retaliate; but to be thus innocently confined in a mad-house, whose inner walls are polluted by men of seared minds and blackened hearts, is more than mortal can bear without expressing the scorn and loathing that prompts the tongue of its victim to speed," ejaculated Miss Armington.

"You, then, are of the opinion that we try to abuse and insult you, which certainly is not the case. As for Deacon Rob Stew, I cannot speak; but I assure you, that, with my consent, neither he nor any one else shall abuse or insult you, and I would like you to feel more pleasantly toward me than you have expressed in your remarks," said the doctor.

"I will think over the matter," she said, in a mood that was indicative of deep thought.

The physician-in-chief bade her good-day, and left the unhappy prisoner, thinking about Deacon Rob Stew:

"What could he mean by abusing the dear, beautiful girl? Why should he visit her in disguise, and darken the cell? I am suspicious, and shall keep my eye on his saint-ship. After all, these pious deacons have their failings and passions like other men; but he shall not insult her any more. She is beautiful, and if I were not a married man, I should be tempted myself to make love to her, and undoubtedly this is what the deacon did, when she refused his overtures and spoke lovingly of Dr. Juno. Confound it, I love the darling. little minx myself, married or not, and it is a great temptation to have her thus in one's power; at any rate, I shall not allow the old deacon to insult her any more. I shall visit her soon again."

The physician-in-chief called on General Washington Armington, to ascertain if he was comfortable in his apartment, and learn, also, if he had any symptoms of sanity. He found the general perfectly crazy, talking continually about his abducted daughter, and fairly raved over the outrage of slandering Victor Juno. He said:

"Yes, these devils wear the livery of heaven to serve the devil; they have abducted Victor Juno and my beloved daughter, and now they ravish them both in their dungeons. Heaven above me, protect them! save them! Away, you murdering hypocrites! You shut up the kingdom of heaven against men, for you neither go in, nor permit others to enter therein! I see the beginning of your heinous end, and won't I laugh at your calamity when the tables have turned! Ha! ha!! ha!!!"

Just then the crazy general took notice for the first time that some one was with him, when he cried out:

"Ha-a-a! you are one of them," and sprang upon the doctor like an infuriated fiend.

CHAPTER XXX.

HARRY GOSSIMER CONDEMNED TO DEATH.

THE bloody conspirators found Brother Harry Gossimer guilty of internal rebellion, perjury and threatened exposure; they therefore sentenced him to death. Whilst the prisoner was confined in the dungeon, unlike open courts, they convened a court martial, and in his absence tried him without any defence, because he as good as pleaded guilty to all the charges, by his bold words to the brotherhood; and the principal speech that was made Deacon Rob Stew delivered. He said:

"Brothers and sisters of the sacredly secret conclave, I am grieved at heart, as you may well know, that I am compelled to call upon you to pronounce a unanimous verdict upon our apostate brother, Harry Gossimer, who had the reckless audacity to defy us, and threatened to leave the brotherhood, after he voluntarily took our solemn oath; and I consider it a most dangerous thing to permit any member to faint and flag after he or she has remained at our special meetings, and has listened to all our holy work. I therefore propose to act quickly, and, without prevarication, convict, sentence and execute the sentence forthwith, of Harry Gossimer, for the wavering disposition he has exhibited a few minutes since before us all. If we do not act summarily in such cases, we shall ere long find the rope around our own necks!"—

"I do not fancy that," interrupted Rev. Joe Pier, "and therefore I hope to see this case instantly and permanently disposed of; because, I shake in my boots when I think of the responsible work of piety we are compelled to perform."

"I say," continued the deacon, "that our only salvation, individually and collectively, mark you, lies in visiting the penalty of death upon each and every one who falters in the performance of duty. Instead of Brother Gossimer standing up in our sacred hall, and saying: 'I am not willing to co-operate with you in the fulfilment of this nefarious work,' he ought to have encouraged the brotherhood to go on, and if he did not wish to act in his capacity of an active member, should not have joined us.

"He is a chicken-hearted scoundrel, or a faithless and unprincipled dog, who shall not be allowed to bark and bite us, if I know what I am about. Brethren, our holy cause demands, especially at this auspicious moment, most vigorous unanimous action; because we have our hands full. Look, for instance, there is Dr. Juno preaching publicly and privately in his own hall, and he shortly hopes to address immense crowds again down in the centre of the city; again, there is Miss Armington, who is as rebellious as the devil could make her, and although she is incarcerated where she cannot harm us now, yet I fear, unless vigorous action is had in her case, she may do a deal of injury sooner or later to our sainthood; moreover, all the pious denominations and wordlings must be watched and kept blindfolded, which, when we cast only a cursory glance at the immense work before us, we may see the necessity of being a unit inside of our secret conclave. Brothers, are you therefore ready to cast a unanimous vote in favor of despatching Harry Gossimer this very night before we adjourn?"

"I rise to ask our loyal and energetic deacon a question, if he will permit me to do so?" said Dr. Toy Pancy.

"Certainly, Brother Pancy, go on," responded the deacon.

"Do you think, dear brother, that it would be wise to execute Brother Gossimer, who evidently thought that as long as we are all sworn to perfect secresy, he could speak out his heartfelt sentiments? I know the brother thoroughly; he is an exemplary man; noble, liberal and energetic. I wish to ask the brotherhood, with the permission of our worthy deacon, whether it would not be better to be lenient, and permit Brother Gossimer to make a defence; at least, let him make a speech before this court martial?"

"I object to it," interrupted Deacon Rob Stew, "for if we are to be as lenient and slow to act as Brother Toy Pancy proposes, we might as well already consider our saintly work stopped, and run the risk of being mobbed by the advocates and followers of Dr. Juno. I say, brothers and sisters, we cannot entertain such propositions, and I now call for the unanimous vote of the conclave to a verdict of death in the case of the defendant," said the deacon, terribly agitated and ready for a fight to the hilt with any one who would dissent from his views.

The physician-in-chief of the insane asylum now rose to the floor, and asked permission to say a few words. He said:

"Mr. President and holy saints, I claim to be a faithful laborer in the common cause which we espouse; but, as a Christian, I cannot join in a work that sends a man, who may differ from me, so summarily into the presence of his Maker. Brother Stew is an enthusiast, and although a noble and zealous worker, who has more influence than any dozen of our best men combined, we should remember that he can err as well as other men, and therefore he should take the counsel of some who are as old and faithful to our cause as he"—

"Silence!" ejaculated the deacon. "You are an old drone; you are not now dealing with a lot of lunatics, who are compelled to obey your mandates, or even regard your charitable (?) advice. If our lenient doctor-in-chief will point out one act of mine that was uncharitable toward any one of our cause, or that what I did proved an injury to any good member of the faith, whether in active service in the secret conclave or not, I will yield to him"—

"I'll take you at your word," exclaimed the physician-in-chief. "Have you not acted in an 'uncharitable' manner toward our misled, but faithful sister, Lucinda Armington, not a year since, in our asylum; moreover, a word to the wise will suffice?"

"Curse your trifling, and may the marrow in your stereotyped bones rot, for intruding into the private workings of this conclave! What under the sun has the business of the insane asylum to do with this apostate? Mr. President! I emphatically say (in a mood that means work or death)—Mr. President! I command you to order all dissenting harangues as being irrelevant to the subject in consideration! I demand this under the penalty of our solemn oath; and I add, 'if *your* beating heart' is not to be torn out by its roots forthwith, you will heed my admonition and act determinedly! I say, speak!"

"Ye-s, I—I—I agree with Brother Stew, an—and rule that all that has been said, by those who differ with our worthy deacon, is irrelevant to the subject under consideration, and this I order under the penalty of having the *beating heart* of each disputant torn out by its roots! So help us God!" stammeringly responded Rev. Joe Pier.

Nancy Clover now jumped to the floor, as if she meant mischief, and said:

"Brothers, I have listened patiently, and I see that unless you have a determined principle to be governed by, you won't agree to advantage. Now, I am not a woman of words, nor do I stand with folded hands to see those who ought to have one object in view, namely, the subjugation of innovators and advancement of the cause of the elect, quarrel, bicker and bite each other, without trying to stop them in their mad career. Is not our cause just? Is its prosperity not a mutual benefit? Why, then, fight over trifles, like schoolboys?

"I say, do as Brother Rob Stew says, even if it goes against your beautiful, tender feelings, else you may be compelled to take what will be ten thousand times worse! Do you understand me? Act in unison, and dispatch this apostate, who undoubtedly would betray us, especially since you have beaten and thrown him into our nasty dungeon."

Sister Clover's neat little speech made the members a unit, and immediately Harry Gossimer was condemned to die.

CHAPTER XXXI.

HARRY GOSSIMER'S HEROIC AND THRILLING SPEECH BEFORE THEY DROWN HIM.

HE President, Rev. Joe. Pier, ordered the sentinel to bring the prisoner—Harry Gossimer—before him, that he may receive his sentence, which was death; however, with his choice of hanging or drowning.

The president then addressed him as follows:

"Harry Gossimer, the brothers and sisters have convened themselves into a court martial, and have found you guilty of violating the solemn oath of our secret conclave, and you must know that the penalty is death; but the court unanimously agreed that you should not be treated to the full punishment as avowed in our solemn oath, but that you may choose between hanging and drowning. This favor was granted you because you have not done any mischief as yet, otherwise, you would have had your '*left hand burned into cinders; your right hand cut into fragments*, and *your beating heart torn out by its roots.*'

"I am sorrowful and heavily grieved at this terrible state of affairs, but there is no appeal from this tribunal; therefore, if you have anything to say, now is your time."

The distressed and horror-stricken Harry Gossimer rose to his feet and said, in a tremulous voice:

"I suppose I have deserved some punishment, but this I did not expect, nor do I merit it; still, as there can be no appeal from this august and holy tribunal, I hope God will pardon you for this dastardly crime! I hope I am not intruding nor violating any more sacred pledges, so that your noble deacon might have this humane sentence revoked, and re-commit me for trial, and then give me the full blast of the terrible and accursed oath that I was compelled to take,"—

"Go on, noble apostate," interrupted the deacon, "we care little what you say to us, so long as you die before you can divulge any of our secret plans."

"May I then say what I choose, without having my verdict changed?" asked the convict.

"Yes, sir," responded the Rev. Joe Pier.

"Hear me, then," said the prisoner. "I have always despised hypocrites and pharisees, and believed that they were the most blasphemous wretches living,—thus agreeing with Jesus Christ,—but I did not think that such a bloody, villanous, accursed set of vipers could breathe the breath of life who were one tithe as wicked as the elated Deacon Rob Stew, Sister Nancy Clover and the dastardly Rev. Joe Pier; a trinity that outvies the blackest imps of the infernal regions!

"When such perfidious monsters can rule a nation, then is doomsday near at hand; and I can die happy when I reflect upon the heinous crime I have committed when I became a member of this sacredly secret conclave! So sacred (?) as to prefer to murder an innocent person in cold blood, than that a noble hero, like Dr. Victor Juno, should be permitted to succeed in the amelioration and elevation of the human race, which could not harm any one except those who are a scab upon society, and a pestiferous stench in the presence of God and man.

"If you, or your likes, go to heaven, I want to go to hell; because, the very sight of such loathsome vermin would destroy my happiness, and turn the realms of the blessed into regions of despair! You all have my keenest contempt, and I am now ready to be sentenced to be drowned at once, or later, if it suits your despicable natures better! Farewell, until we meet again, for we shall at a future hour see the glory of God by observing retribution visiting your worthless souls!"

Preparations were now being made to drown the apostate in the depth of the sea. He was gagged securely, and tightly bound by cords, so that it was utterly impossible to be relieved; then he was put into a large salt sack, in the bottom of which iron weights were placed; and this done, he was nailed up in a dry-goods box and instantly carried to the Delaware river in Deacon Rob Stew's charity wagon, which everybody almost knew, and when the same reached the wharf, the box was at once placed upon a speedy little schooner and carried to the ocean, where the box was quickly opened, and the salt sack with its iron and human weight dropped quietly overboard, which sank like lead!

Thus was the sentence executed, and the sharks or worms of the briny deep would feast their carnivorous natures upon the carcass of Harry Gossimer, the apostate!

The schooner immediately set sail for its own harbor, and the faithful sentinel rejoiced with six brethren and one sister of the sacredly secret conclave; but they did not dream that a wakeful Irishman was watching the proceedings regularly at Tabernacle Hall, and when the deacon's charity wagon was being rapidly driven toward the wharf, Pat O'Conner smelled a mouse; he therefore ran in the rear of the wagon, and when he saw them remove the box to the schooner, he at once went to a friend who lived in a shanty about ten squares down the Delaware wharf, who made his living by boating, and, as good luck would have it, the boatman was just about anchoring his fastest row boat. Pat O'Conner said to him:

"Patrick, kin I git ye to hire me yer best and fastest row boat, what one man kin row?"

"Yis, sir; why, Pat O'Conner, is that you?" responded the boatman.

"An' to-be-shure it be meself awantin' to do a leetle night work fur meself," said Pat.

He forthwith jumped into the row boat, and, sure as fate, there, just a little ahead of him, sailed the well known pious vessel, making good speed toward the sea.

"We-ll," mumbled Pat O'Conner to himself, as he pulled his oars with ease, "I'll be atter ye blooddee curmudgon, an' see what ye air adoin' on the river this time o'night."

Pat O'Conner had no trouble to row as fast as the schooner sailed, and as the night was rather dark, there was no danger of him being seen after they had gone beyond the reach of the city lights; he therefore crept near to the schooner, watching it closely, for fear it might stop suddenly, when he might be detected. The ocean was tame, and therefore all things favored Pat. When the schooner had passed about a quarter of a mile from the mouth of the river, it stopped, so did Pat O'Conner's boat; and after turning something overboard, the schooner sailed off, and, making a circle, steered homeward; but Pat did not sail off, nor steer homeward just then; but he went as near to the spot as he could where the salt sack, filled with iron and flesh, was thrown into the ocean; and, as fate would have it, Harry Gossimer got one of his hands at liberty before they reached the wharf, and he managed with it to get his knife out of his pocket; however, he was so tightly packed into the box that he could not open the blade until he was removed from the same; when thus liberated, he instantly opened the knife with his teeth of the lower jaw, and by the time he sank a few feet, he had his rope and salt sack cut to pieces, which gave him the use of his two hands, whilst his feet were bound until Pat O'Conner reached forth and drew him into his row boat.

CHAPTER XXXII.

DR. JUNO CONVICTED, IMPRISONED AND ATTEMPTS MADE TO POISON HIM.

OCTOR VICTOR JUNO was compelled to spend that Sunday night in the filthy, cold cell, with the horse thief, where he took an awful cold; but at nine o'clock Monday morning he was brought before the presiding magistrate, although he waived a hearing and entered bail in two thousand dollars to appear at the Court of Sessions. In six days he was arraigned and tried before the pious Judge Sanctiblower, who conspired with the sanctimonious District Attorney Charlson, to rule out all the evidence that Dr. Juno might produce.

The district attorney argued that all the evidence that could be relevant was for the Commonwealth to prove that this book on the "Physiology of Marriage" had been bought from Dr. Juno, and the book itself was to be given to the jury—which was composed of picked ringleaders from the saintly crowd—and the jurymen alone, unaided by experts, or law, or anything else, should decide if it were an *obscene book* or not.

Dr. Juno had twenty experts in court; eight of these twenty eminent physicians were professors of medical colleges; he also had over two hundred additional witnesses in court. By the former he wished to prove the scientific correctness of the book, and show by the latter that the book had benefited them in various ways; but the district attorney objected to hearing any of Dr. Juno's witnesses except for purity of character, which was proved beyond a doubt, and the august Judge Sanctiblower ruled to suit the district attorney.

The counsel for the defence produced the following law points, but his honor dodged them all, and gave instead his own opinion, viz:

"If the jury believe the defendant have in view the benefit of society—however wrong the ideas or objectionable the language—there is no malice, and he should be acquitted."

Again, "If the design of the book was to benefit society, it does not show malice to take measures to extend its circulation."

Again, "If the production was honestly meant to inform the public mind, and warn them against supposed dangers in society—though the subject may have been treated erroneously—then, however the judgment of the jury may incline them to think individually, they should acquit the defendant. If the jury doubt of the criminal intention, then, also, the law pronounces that he should be acquitted."

The few witnesses who were permitted to testify to the excellent character of Dr. Juno, shrewdly worked in that the book in question had benefited them *very* much; and when such evidence slipped in before it could be stopped by the district attorney, the old pious Judge Sanctiblower would yell out:

"That is purely a question for the jury to decide."

The counsel for Dr. Juno then quoted the following law points:

"In a criminal prosecution for a libel, the defendant may repel the charge by proving that the publication was for a justifiable purpose, and not malicious, nor with the intention to defame any man. And there may be many cases where the defendant, having proved the purpose justifiable, may give in evidence the truth of the words, when such evidence will tend to negative the malice and intent to defame."—*Commonwealth vs. Clapp*, 4 *Mass.* 163.

Again, the Supreme Court of the United States decided that: "Whenever the author or publisher of the alleged slander acted in the *bona fide* discharge of a public or private duty, legal or moral, such communication is privileged."—*White and Nicholls*, 3 *Howard*, 267.

Again, "As the offence of publishing a libel consists in the malicious publication of it, which, as already stated, is in general inferred from the words of the alleged libel itself, it is competent to the defendant, *in all cases*, to show the absence of malice on his part."—*Roscoe's Criminal Evidence*, 528.

To all this, and much more equally strong law points, Judge Sanctiblower paid no attention at all; because he told the Young Men's Association previously to bring Dr. Juno into the Court of Sessions and he would "fix him?"

The jury obeyed the judge and district attorney, and of course convicted Dr. Juno, in spite of law, evidence and their oaths to decide according to law and evidence. The judge then sentenced him to the full extent of the law for publishing an "obscene libel," which was one year in the County Prison and five hundred dollars fine.

He was at once closely confined in a felon's cell, but the Governor of the Commonwealth was a man of honor, and when a friend of Dr. Juno called upon his excellency with a copy of the book on the "Physiology of Marriage," and also a copy of the fully printed trial, the Governor at once pardoned and even exonerated Dr. Juno, which set him free after having served four months of his time.

Whilst Dr. Juno was incarcerated, the newspaper oracle of the *bloody conspirators* libeled him awfully; also the minor daily newspapers howled dreadfully, seeing a chance now to gain some note at the expense of Dr. Juno. They called him everything but decent names. Had he been a sot, *roué*, brawler, glutton, miser, gambler, liar, politician, hypocrite, pharisee, viper or cut-throat, he would have been a decent man compared with the character the *public press* of Philadelphia gave this martyred man.

And when Governor Golden pardoned him, the holy saints and newspaper scribes were over-awed, horrified and amazed, for they believed that there was no power on earth that could induce the Governor to pardon him.

The bloody clique went repeatedly to the Executive and

requested him not to pardon Dr. Juno for the life of him. He himself told the person to whom he gave said pardon, that the prejudice against Dr. Juno was immense, which he could not understand, and the Governor said:

"If there was not so much prejudice against the man, I would not pardon him, for prejudice is the child of envy, and not of crime."

Dr. Juno was not in prison a week until the bloody clique sent their friends, who belong to the prison society, to visit him in his cell, and they appeared very kind, giving him apples, figs, cakes, etc.; the doctor did not trust these nice people, he therefore placed these articles aside for inspection, and, upon examination, he discovered arsenic piled snugly inside of a lot of figs; but the person who prepared them was not an expert, or, instead of having inserted the raw powdered arsenic into the figs, he would have steeped them in a solution of the poison.

They again failed to murder him, and as soon as he told the prison keepers and inspectors that an attempt was made to poison him, they got very indignant and locked him up as tight as wax, and treated him awfully mean, which proved that at least some of them belonged to the bloody clique.

Dr. Juno soliloquized as follows:

"I cannot see why these people should be so determined to murder me; I have never done anything that would injure or demoralize them or their children. If I had kept a bawdy house, rum shop, gambling room, low concert saloon, political swindling house, or followed the thousand-and-one injurious, criminal and fashionable pursuits extant, I would have been esteemed as a good fellow; but, as I have opposed all these, and other unhealthy and unphysiological customs, and have proved, by the religion that Jesus Christ established, that my course was scientific and right, they have given me a *mock* trial in open court, and in the face of a republican country have cast me into this prison for serving God, Nature and Mankind. God forgive these degraded, wicked wretches, for really they know not what they are doing."

When Dr. Juno was pardoned, he at once returned to his old work of lecturing, preaching and practising his profession, and, to his astonishment, he did more business and had more intelligent audiences than he ever had before; this was a consolation to him, but a terrible disappointment to the saintly crowd, who now instituted more and worse plans of operation. And whilst Dr. Juno pursued the even tenor of his course, as if nothing had ever happened to him, the conspirators, in one combined effort, appealed to the State Legislature to pass a law which would suppress religious liberty, and which movement broke their camel's back.

CHAPTER XXXIII.

DOCTOR JUNO'S FIRST SHARP-SHOOTING SERMON ON MINISTERS AND DOCTORS.

(NOTE. *If the reader wants to fully understand the plot of this story, he must carefully peruse every discourse by Dr. Juno, or, when he arrives at the most interesting part of it, he cannot comprehend what made him the hero of our story. The following discourse was delivered in his own hall, to a crowded house, immediately after his pardon. This is not fiction.—S. M. L.*)

ELOVED FRIENDS:—We live in a progressive age—everything around us moves and appears to keep pace with time, except the doctrines of our own bodily and spiritual functions.

The true *Laws of Life*, or *Laws of Soul* (life and soul meaning the same thing—for He "breathed the breath of life into man's nostrils, and he became a living soul"), have not yet been reduced to a popular, practical and scientific stand-point. Truly, the platform upon which mankind stands at present, in relation to human health and perfection of body and soul, is as far from being on an equality with the material *arts and sciences* as Satan is from attaining celestial glory; or, as the honorable (?) Judge Sanctiblower is from a follower of decent judgment.

Thousands, nay, millions have speculated and theorized over these dogmas for more than three thousand years, and they are apparently no wiser or better now; indeed, if as wise and good as they were when they commenced. Ministers and doctors have been on a wild goose chase for fully seventeen hundred and fifty years, having perverted the simple though scientific teachings and practices of Jesus Christ, who healed both bodily and spiritual ills, and that without drug-medicines—these teachings harmonized with a *true* physiology, or, in other words, the scientific doctrines of the *Laws of Life*.

Before medicines were introduced as healing agencies, the cure of human ills was entrusted to the power of the inherent recuperative vital spark, or inner-man; and the high priests, by recommending *fasting and prayer*, *holy faith*, cleanliness, ventilation, bathing, quietude, exercise; including the use of symbols, charms, beads, etc., to pacify the mind, restored the sick with wonderful success, as compared and contrasted with the methods of cure which are now so fashionable, but destructive to body, soul and comfort by our numerous *blind leaders of blind*, who lead the millions into the broad road to hell.

Very few were the wants, and fewer the diseases, that existed before medicines were introduced; but, as soon as Paracelsus and others introduced mercury and a host of other medicinal nostrums, so soon did diseases increase in number and the vital principle of life become vitiated; also the imaginary wants of the race multiplied; and it seems ever since, man has lived by art, instead of nature; has doctored by art, and he is trying to fly to heavenly glory on golden wings. It is to the sorrow and fate of our bodily constitutions that medicinal poisons, that are non-usable by a naturally healthy organism, have been swallowed ever since, in the delusive hope that the healing power lies in the material agency instead of the inner-man or nature. No wonder that the most eminent lights of the medical world have denounced the whole materia medica and the concomitant practices of their profession.

The celebrated Dr. Rush said: "As long as medicinal agencies increase in number, so long will diseases multiply."

Sir Astley Cooper said, speaking of the medical profession as a whole: "It is founded on conjecture and improved by murder."

Dr. Franke said: "Thousands are slaughtered in the quiet sick room."

Long established customs seem to make law, and hence the popular blind belief, that medicines are really needed to assist nature in curing the ills flesh is heir to, instead of being always poisonous, totally incompatible to and non-usable by nature; although they may excite the inner-life or nature as a whip stimulates a horse, but to say that either the medicine or whip aids the life of man or horse is absurd. At the best, medicines only thwart the recuperative process of nature; galvanize or pickle the tissues; patch up the breach of the law of life, or at once burn out the vital spark.

Beloved friends, having shown you plainly the error into which drug-doctors have fallen, I will now open your eyes to the blasphemies and anti-natural doctrines of the sectarian ministers, who advocate *praying* for everything they want, instead of learning and living out the fixed laws of God, and thereby letting their *light shine in good works*, by returning to truth and nature, and scientifically saving *themselves* and their children from the sins, diseases and crimes that abound everywhere, notwithstanding their *much speaking, blind faith,* and *long,* sanctimonious *prayers.*

Jesus Christ says of such: "*They think that they shall be*

heard for their much speaking;" and on numerous occasions commands us all not to pray as the hypocrites do: "*For they love to pray in the synagogues, that they may be seen of men,*" etc.

We have therefore two kinds of institutions that are anti-Christ and anti-natural, which cause also two kinds of poverty, both of which need immediate attention, if the human race is to be benefited, elevated and Christianized. But I am sorry to be compelled to state, that from the acts of doctors and preachers it appears the human species can continue to degenerate without any scientific voice crying aloud: improve the blood of your species, as the farmer improves his stock of cattle—for the fixed laws of *generation* and *regeneration* are at hand, and the spirit of the Immaculate Son of Man knocketh at the door of the heart, but its hinges are rusted, therefore it cannot open to let in the monitor of grace and power divine; hence, we have *first*, poverty in health of body and soul, which is produced by ignorant, wilful or accidental violation of the fixed *Laws of Life;* and *secondly* comes poverty in purse, over which millions are made to moan and groan, which is caused by unphysiological domestic habits, such as expensive cookery, mixing and mincing messes of animal food, vegetables, spices, relishes, condiments, sugar in overdoses, teas, coffees and a host of other drugs too numerous to mention, thereby producing more appetite than health would furnish, hence, eating and drinking thrice as much as nature requires. Truly, each social gathering, religious or secular, must wind up with a feast; and at every corner of the street, in our boasted civilized and Christianized cities, we find several grog shops and as many eating houses, and each being filled with the most vicious qualities of aliment, plainly showing that saint and sinner look upon the stomach as a receptacle to hold all sorts of hash, trash, poison and swill.

Few of our clergy, as well as saint and sinner, miss laying in a good supply as often as an opportunity affords, not because the body or soul needs it; but to tickle a depraved appetite, to get a little pleasure from swallowing; thus they swallow the devil (evil) by piece-meal, but withal claim a saintly name.

Moreover, the ladies have their dining-room cupboards well loaded with game, rich cake and sundry other unhealthy dainties, unfitted for the stomach of a Hottentot, and the poor stomach is made a laboratory for everything that is palatable to the gustatory propensities; the consequence is, depraved digestion, which, according to popular Christianity and fashionable customs, must be aided by wines, tobacco, spirituous liquors, medicines, lager, ale and schnapps.

Immediately following these un-Christ-like and unnatural domestic habits, we find sickness, ugliness, peevishness, irritability, scrawniness, flabby muscles, morbid longings, perverted judgments, false ambitions, spurious modesty, riot, gluttony, drunkenness, sensuality, envy, avarice, malice, debility, disease, bloodless cheeks, etc., which are, in a measure, remedied by expensive dress, paddings, laces, braces, paints, powders, rouges, perfumes (to overcome *bad* odors) and the like, to imitate nature; but, alas! what is this make-up as compared with pristine beauty, symmetrical contour of muscle, rounded form, elastic step, the natural, healthful rose-leaf blooming on the cheek, coral lip and the soul-enchanting eye, with naturally acute senses, and a sound mind in a sound body! These are settled truths. May I ask, with St. Paul, "*Am I therefore become your enemy, because I tell you the truth?*"

Good friends, for uttering, publishing and advocating such truths, I have been sent to prison; cast into a felon's cell, to appease the appetites of scribes, pharisees and hypocrites. And will you stand by and allow these vipers and bloody conspirators, in this age of science, to persecute the man who, knowing the truth, dare maintain it, in spite of ministers and doctors, who neither comprehend nor care to learn or live-out the fixed laws of God; but who do their best to inveigle *you* into their heinous sophistries and perfidious practices? Arise, or be forever lost!

CHAPTER XXXIV.

PAT O'CONNER SAVES HARRY GOSSIMER FROM DROWNING, BUT ARE BOTH ARRESTED.

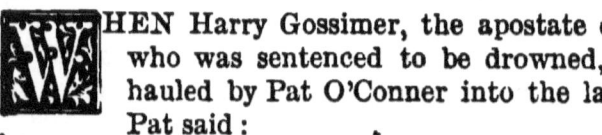HEN Harry Gossimer, the apostate conspirator, who was sentenced to be drowned, was being hauled by Pat O'Conner into the latter's boat, Pat said:

"Be me sowl, but ye are a quare fish; who air ye?"

"I am the victim of a most foul plot; but who are you, that you have arrived at such an opportune moment, like an angel dropped from heaven, specially to save my miserable life?" responded Harry Gossimer.

"Be jabers, I'm naither an angel dropt from heaven, nor an idle specalator "—

"No, sir; you are a Christian," interrupted Harry Gossimer, "for coming to my rescue, for which you have my never-failing thanks "—

"Plaze, don't blarney me wid yer smooth tongue; naither do ye owe me any tanks, sir, becase I was afishin' fur a bait what I may use som day fur to catch a few cunnin' grate fish wid," said Pat, laughing.

"You are merry; but tell me, do you know how I came here at this time of night?" replied Harry Gossimer.

"Know!" responded Pat. "Bedad, an' I tink I out to know, whin I watched them squally curmudgons this many a day."

"Watched them many a day?" said Harry Gossimer. "What do you mean by them?"

"Och! howly murdher, don't ye tink I knows them bluddy conspirators; an' do ye tink I does not owe them a grudge?" spitefully exclaimed Pat.

"I see that you have evidently been injured by these people, who brought me here bound, sacked and boxed to drown me, and who now think I am dead, and food for fishes," said Harry Gossimer.

"Och! they dirty divils; but what mane ye by sayin' that ye were 'bound, sacked and boxed?'" asked Pat O'Conner.

"Well, please let me tell you. They sentenced me to be hanged or drowned; I was permitted the consoling privilege to choose which death I preferred, when I chose drowning, for I thought *may be* I might be saved"—

"Be jabers, an' yer '*may be*' has comed tru," laughingly interrupted Pat.

"Yes, ten thousand thanks to your noble self," continued Harry Gossimer, "and after I had decided to prefer drowning, they bound me hand and foot, and also gagged me with a strong rope; then they put me into a large salt sack, and after that they boxed me up in a dry goods box, nailing it tightly shut, and brought me here in that manner to drown me; I suppose you know the means by which they conveyed me here, for I don't."

"An' shure I knows all aboot how they brot ye here, but, be me sowl, I cannot know how ye comed out ov bein' 'bound, sacked an' boxed;' ye air not a god, that ye could tare all them tings away from yer body; how, thin, did ye git loose?" asked Pat.

"Yes, truly, my dear sir, it would seem curious to be capacitated to extricate one's self from being '*bound, sacked and boxed;*' but, when they came to this spot where they sent me overboard, they first took me out of the dry goods box, and dropped me in the sack, which had heavy weights in its bottom, but by good luck I got my hand loose, and, when I was removed from the box, I opened my pocket knife with my teeth, and the moment they threw me into the water, I commenced to cut the sack and ropes to pieces, and lastly I cut the gag from my mouth; but you will see that my feet are bound yet," responded the poor victim.

"Howly Moses!" ejaculated Pat, "an' so they air; but, begorrah, ye made a narrow 'scape."

"You are right, but thank you and the Lord for this deliverance; and now, as I am safe, what had we better do, for these *bloody conspirators* are dreadful people, who would go to any trouble to kill me?" responded Harry Gossimer.

"May I be so bould as to axe ye, fur what they were akillin' ye?" asked Pat.

"Certainly, with pleasure; I was fool enough to join what they call the 'Sacredly Secret Conclave,' and whilst they were congregated at Tabernacle Hall this very night, for the purpose of contriving the most hellish work, I objected to co-operate with them, when they sentenced me to death for violating their iron-clad oath," said Harry Gossimer.

"Tanks, fur atellin' me all aboot it, an' I now undershtand; an' I was atinkin' what we better be adoin, fur ye knows them bluddy varmint so well as I could tell ye"—

"But, sir, I cannot understand how you know anything about them, for you are an Irishman, and very likely a Roman Catholic, and therefore cannot be, or ever have been, a member of the bloody clique," interrupted Harry Gossimer.

"An' shure, I bees an Irish Catholic, an' niver belonged to thim divils; but, hav I not bin a sarvant wid Gineral Washington Armington, an' has not Dr. Victor Juno an' Miss Lucinda Armington bin abdoocted an' throwed into them insane asylum dungons by them murdherin' curmudgon; an' haven't I an' me Judy darlin' seen anough to know what divils them varmint air?" excitedly and angrily said Pat O'Conner.

"I see, I see, you know more than I thought any mortal knew outside of their clique. But, my dear, good saviour, do these people know that you are so well posted on these topics?" asked Harry Gossimer.

"No, be Sant Patrick, they do not, an' I niver mane

they shall know, until I bees reddy fur 'em," ejaculated Pat O'Conner.

"But you speak of this so freely to me, a stranger; are you not afraid that I might inform them of your knowledge, and that by so doing they would murder you"—

"Yis, as they did ye," interposed Pat, laughing, and continued, "be jabers, do ye tak me fur a stewpid blackgard; becase, do I not know that ye dare not lit 'em know that ye bees alive; how the divil could ye tell on me, if ye would?"

"You are truly a philosopher, and anything but a fool, and as you have saved my life, I will trust it to you; therefore, where had I better go?" responded Harry Gossimer.

"I have tought ov a plan; ye go wid me to Gineral Armington's house"—

"I am afraid of being detected there; will you please give me your name?" interrupted Harry Gossimer.

"Yis, sir; me name bees Pat O'Conner, an' Judy McCrea is me fathful ——, now what air ye laughin' at?" said Pat, sheepishly.

"I was only smiling, when you could not say what Judy McCrea was to you; but I know she is your faithful darling," responded Gossimer.

"An' shurely ye hav sthruck they nail on they hed that time; an' no one am at they house but she an' meself; an' she bees as wide awak as meself, an' ye could trust yer life a tousand times wid Judy darlin'," earnestly said Pat.

They now rowed toward home; but it was getting daylight, therefore they had to spend their time along the banks of the Delaware until the following night. They landed at an obscure grove, and cautiously made their way to a hut and got some refreshments, when they returned to the boat, and sitting talking over all the matters with which the reader is already familiar, the day passed hurriedly away, and, when right dark, they pushed up to the boatman's wharf, and just as they landed, Pat O'Conner was patted on the shoulder by an officer, who said:

"I believe you are Pat O'Conner?"

"Yis, sir," responded Pat.

"I have a warrant for you," said the officer, and continued: "Who is this with you, I'll arrest him also?"

CHAPTER XXXV.

DR. JUNO'S SECOND STARTLING SERMON ON DOCTORS AND MINISTERS.

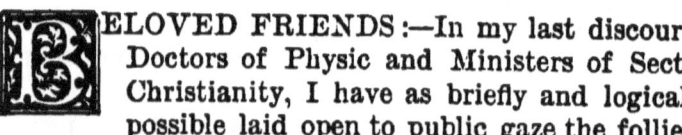ELOVED FRIENDS:—In my last discourse on Doctors of Physic and Ministers of Sectarian Christianity, I have as briefly and logically as possible laid open to public gaze the follies and fallacies that are taught and practised by these misled ink-suckers; pardon the common parlance that I am often compelled to use in chastising the haughty vipers' who sit in Moses' seat.

Heaven forbid that *the people*—who are the bone and sinew of the land—should any longer be kept in ignorance of the fixed laws of their own beings; should be made believe in false prophets, false Christs, and false leaders; that thereby they can be made the easier dupes for those who possess more money than brains, or craft than wisdom.

Jesus Christ lived a natural, normal life, and all his precepts and examples were in strict conformity with the fixed *Laws of Life;* but where do either the medical doctors or sectarian ministers follow the teachings and example of Jesus? Again, every one has duties resting upon him, which he cannot dodge without a train of the most deplorable evils following close upon his heels, and no one can mend a broken law by swallowing poisons, or by *vain repetitions* and *long prayers*, for such conditions he must do penance and return to truth and nature, if he wishes to be crowned with the laurels of pristine beauty, health and salvation

Two wrongs never can make a right. Departure from nature's law is one wrong, whose penalty generally is sickness; and to take medicines is another wrong, because all medicines are poisonous to a healthy person, therefore cannot make right what departure from nature's fixed law has made wrong. Neither did Jesus ever attempt to heal the sick by poisoning the springs of life, nor by long dictatorial prayers; but he did it by the sick being willing to make themselves passive or penitent, trusting to the god-principle within, which he was then capacitated and willing to magnify by animal-magnetic and soul-arousing powers. Thus, he *healed the sick, cleansed the lepers, raised the dead, cast out devils;* and as freely as he received this power, so freely he gave it to all who were willing to do penance and believe in him, who was the representative of the fixed Laws of Life, both of body and soul.

If we go back to "*the origin of life,*" and take a meagre view at the popular customs of raising and educating children, we shall find a wonderful amount of barbarity and atheism practised even at this progressive and boasted scientific age. Stuffed with unhealthy food and drink, and dosed with physic, as our infants are, is an outrage that cries aloud to heaven for reformation and enlightenment on this topic. "*Am I therefore become your enemy, because I tell you the truth?*" (St. Paul to the Galatians iv. 16.)

When the babe grows to childhood, he is forced to attend your badly managed school-rooms, where foul air and taxations of brain predominate over good sense, and thus the child's constitution is blasted before his bones are one-fourth matured, before the frame-work is half completed, and before the soul has established even the outline of a character, or moulded the faculty of thought, the precious casket is shattered and shriveled, unfitting it for the indwelling of the Holy Spirit.

The youngster, at once in school, must study letters and figures, which, when concocted together, teach him of brooks, rivers, lands, islands, seas, sun, moon and stars;

of arts and sciences ; of wars, seats and rumors of war ; of capitals, states, cities and empires ; of valleys, hills and mountains ; of mathematical problems, and, indeed, of everything else, except the rules, laws and injunctions which concern his own bodily growth and mental development. The latter are looked upon, by our artificial and ungodly doctors and ministers, as improper studies ; yea, even as vulgar and obscene subjects, which these over-learned professors hold as irrelevant to the enthronement of the "*Image of God*," or salvation of mankind ; therefore, such matters as the *Science of Life*, and functions of generation and regeneration, must not be discussed or taught, either by man or the Holy Spirit ; which shows that they prefer the people to go blind through the world, probably, that the latter may be the more readily gulled and led by their noses by these *blind leaders of the blind.*

If what I have just spoken be not true, why, then, do these bigots conspire to imprison and murder your humble servant ? They may endeavor to impress the popular mind, time and again, that God takes care of the body, if its mind is only prayerful, and watching Him so that He makes no blunders ; but, the propounders of this impious onslaught upon an infinite and beneficent Creator shall not go unchastized as long as I have breath to gainsay these infidel and heretical doctrines. I tell you, dear friends, that God never takes care of anything wherein his plans and immutable laws are frustrated and violated— in these matters, like in the material sciences, "*lip-service*" will not answer ; but, religion must become a science, in which we pray with wise heads, loving hearts, clean hands and supple feet, if aught is to be accomplished.

If, through ignorance, recklessness or hypocrisy in the onset of life, the growth, replenishment and physiological recuperation of the human frame are thwarted, how can we become sound, good and holy? It is thus no wonder that, with all the church wealth and multitudinous doctors and preachers, this world is so full of loafers, drunkards, politicians, sectarian bigots, vagabonds and cut-throats! *"Am I therefore become your enemy, because I tell you the truth?"*

Truly, this people run away from natural laws and commence to depend upon "*art*" and *human* government before they get their eye-teeth cut; and no sooner do they depend upon "*art*" than nature deserts them, and leaves them to rely altogether upon "*art;*" and this is the reason that they suffer from early old age, premature death and from all the ills flesh is heir to. Moreover, they become homely, miserable and degraded. Under these perverted trainings, they too often blame their Maker for the manifold sufferings which they are compelled to endure, and which they would escape were they to take an equal amount of interest in health and its laws, as they do in *filthy lucre* matters.

Whilst they have healthy brains and bodies is the proper time to secure it for future enjoyment. A wise rich man secures his money by safe investments, according to the laws of finance; equally so does a good, wise healthy man study, heed and obey the laws of life and health whilst he possesses the heavenly treasure. Whilst he has powers of discretion, he secures it, not only for his own selfishness, but for the purpose of transferring it to his children and grand-children, which, let me tell you, is the richest and most glorious legacy that a parent can bequeath unto his children. But, as I glance around, where do I find our good, wise men, according to this interpretation of wisdom? Looking at the negligence of the Laws of Life, at the smoking, chewing and snuffing poisonous tobacco (loving this filth more than God, Son or Spirit), at the rum-sipping and at the rage for worldly gain; for wealth in the extremes of fantastic fashion in dress, houses, churches, equipages and the silly lavish expenditure in efforts to outdo or outshine one's foolish friends, will any one, verily, can any decent person, blame me if I ask the question: Are we an enlightened and Christian community; or, do we *"go it blind!"* Are we even half civilized or moralized? Do we exhibit common sense? Certainly not good sound sense, for this is the growth of judgment founded upon scientific knowledge, and too few care to learn the path they should walk in.

Alas! alas! the errors and follies of the fathers are copied by the children, and the stultified ignorance of the ancestors is perpetuated in the descendants, and in a physiological and Christian sense, we are all on the broad way to destruction of body, soul and spirit.

Indeed few, if any, ask themselves the question, Do I live aright? Are my habits of life in consonance with God's fixed laws of life and health? Such queries would indicate practical thought—causing the reasoning faculties to bestir the befuddled brains—which at this age of pharisaism, sectarian piety and drug-medication, are carried in the stomach instead of the head; hence, saint and worldling reason that their stomachs want and actually *need* rum, teas, coffee, grease, oysters, spices, relishes, fermented, concentrated, seasoned and refined fixings. Thus, our so-called civilized people do not reason through the medium of, or from, their brains, nor from data or sound principle; else they would conclude that they should eat, drink, breathe, exercise, rest, sleep, dress, act, feel and think solely for health purposes, and thereby obtain Christ's pure blood and body, when the gratification of one perverted propensity would be esteemed no more legitimate than another; gluttony and licentiousness would be found to be twin-brothers whose monitions smatter of the devil and his imps.

Dear friends, notwithstanding all this perverseness of manner and digression from natural laws, many sincere followers of the false prophets, who claim to possess wisdom and Christian virtues, profane the divine "*Laws of Life*," by ridiculing and spurning simple food and natural drink (water), and call *their* pernicious and serpent-like appetites the voice of profound wisdom and learnedness;

and whilst becoming kin to all the ills, sins, flesh and lust of the devil; and with all this wickedness upon their heads (like my prosecutors and persecutors who sent me to prison), and even without a struggle for the right path, often cry aloud for blessings from the divine Creator, whom they have so shamefully disregarded, and I might most appropriately exclaim: "*Oh! ye generation of vipers, how can ye escape the damnation of hell?*"

However, with all the forenamed violations of God's laws, we boast of this ingenious and enlightened nineteenth century; the general education of the people; the spread of knowledge among the millions; of steam engines; of railroads and telegraphs; of destructive war implements; of the triumphs of chemistry; of the wonders of the photographic art; but the highest of all arts — the "art" of living a natural, Christ-like life — what can we boast?

Oh! for a praying, church-going, Christian community to take so little care in the "*art of living*" is a most shameful sin, a wretched blasphemy, and a gross infidelity to God's never-changing laws of life and health. Money and fleshly lusts, that war against the soul, seem to rule and control this whole machine of humanity, whilst sensualists and cut-throats, like Judge Sanctiblower, sit on the judiciary bench to deal out damnation to those who vindicate the cause of God and mankind.

Once more, in conclusion, permit me to ask you: Who are the sovereigns of America? Shall these misled doctors and ministers tutor your minds in such a manner that you dare not protect him who has suffered already the severest persecution for the welfare of humanity? Have you a spark of the milk of human kindness left in your bones that will not exert itself to the utmost to aid me in subduing these vile conspirators, who claim to be licensed from on high to carry out their hell-born desires?

Arise, O sons of earth, and strike for your inalienable rights, for your religious liberty, for your benefactors, for your health, for Jesus Christ, God and Mankind! Do this, and His will be done here in earth as it is there in heaven, and the Millennium will indeed be established!

CHAPTER XXXVI.

THE BLOODY CONSPIRATORS IN FEAR, AND FIGHT AMONGST THEMSELVES.

THE *bloody conspirators* almost ran their movements into the ground, breaking their camel's back, by causing the State Legislature to make several offensive laws, which, however, were only intended for Victor Juno; and when a certain newspaper was printing sentiments in its columns that came within these laws, and the friends of Dr. Juno arrested the publisher of this sectarian newspaper, they saw the blunder they made, as their instigated enactments were nauseating to their own saints.

They called a very special meeting of the sacredly secret conclave to meet at Tabernacle Hall, sharp at eight P. M. The president, Rev. Joe Pier, as usual called the saints to order, and after the minutes of the preceding meeting were read, a hot discussion took place about the reckless manner in which business is oftentimes transacted.

Brother Savage Ragtag took the floor and said: That he was arrested by some audacious scoundrel who is friendly to Dr. Juno, because he had published an advertisement of a certain celebrated patent medicine doctor, which came within the law that the brotherhood had recently enacted for the special benefit of Dr. Juno. Now, then, this law was so recklessly drawn up as to injure the business of many of the saints, if enforced on them; and there are enough rascals amongst us who make no scruples to spring our own trap on us, which truly is breaking our camel's back. Influence must be brought to bear upon the prosecuting officers to drop this charge of an *Obscene Libel*, now pending against him, for doing what *all* the other newspapers publish; yes, even the *Oracle* prints this same patent medicine advertisement, and in a measure it would serve Brother Generous right if they should arrest him also, because he had been the leader in having this reckless law framed and enacted.

"Remember, brethren, I have no objections to any kind of a law that will catch the renegade Dr. Juno, but I want it so cautiously framed as only to include quacks like him, without touching decent people's business," said Savage Ragtag.

To this onslaught, by Brother Savage Ragtag, on Goldeagle Generous, Colonel McStuckup pounced upon the floor and said:

"Mr. President and holy saints, I am not going to sit here and allow the libellous Ragtag insult the memory of my noble employer, whilst he is absent in Europe. Brother Generous is a Christian and gentleman of the first water, and he would give more money toward any of the saints' good work, as is often seen in the newspapers, than this growling libeller can raise in a lifetime "—

Here Deacon Rob Stew intervened and said:

"Mr. President, I ask you to call these green brethren to order at once, because we cannot, and *shall not*, lose time in fighting over irrelevant matters for which this special meeting was called."

"The brethren are out of order, and Brother Stew must be heard," responded the president.

"The devil he must," said Savage Ragtag, and was going to continue speaking, when a blow on his mouth sent him reeling like a top, after which he crawled into a back seat and shut pan.

Deacon Rob Stew now arose and said:

"Beloved saints, if you are wise, you will be silent and attentive whilst I will endeavor to show you where great danger is breeding; yes, danger that may bring every one of us speedily to the gallows, unless we plan and work like brave fellows "—

"O Brother Stew, please let us pray," responded Rev. Joe Pier, " for I am scared already out of a year's growth. Bring every one of us speedily to the gallows !—great Mars, I feel choked already! O beloved brethren and sisters, let us pray God to unite us in sentiment and action, so that we shall escape the hangman's ignominious rope ; because I despise hemp when it comes too nigh to a saint's swallowing organs."

"Brother Pier is right," continued Rob Stew, "and it must be self-evident to all of you that Dr. Juno, the accursed innovator, is gaining ground on us, notwithstanding our endeavors to disgrace him by convicting and imprisoning him for publishing an ' *Obscene Libel.*' Why the dare-devil is actually making capital of his imprisonment, by crying persecution, and I have a report at home of two sermons that he has lately delivered to large intelligent audiences, on Ministers and Doctors, in which he shows without cavil that he is right and that we are all in the wrong. His hearers, I understand from the reporter, whom I sent to get his speeches, were perfectly carried away by his logic and eloquent manner ; even my faithful saintly reporter esteems Juno the greatest man living, and if such loyal brethren as reporter Sanctiblower, son of Judge Sanctiblower, are being carried away, who is safe that is really intelligent, provided Dr. Juno is permitted to go on in his determined way ? The intelligent, temperate classes of the people, who are the most useful and respectable, will soon join this innovator. They respect him greatly, and before long he will make a move to crush us by rebellion, see if he don't, unless we can remove him from our midst "—

"Lord! O Lord! help, help us!" sighed out Rev. Joe Pier, with uplifted hands, and, interrupting the deacon, continued : "I feel it, O brethren, I feel it ; Dr. Juno, Dr. Juno is arousing the best people and carrying them away from us, and we'll surely be hung as common murderers. Oh! Oh!! Oh!!!"

"Do not be such a coward, Mr. President," angrily cried out Dr. Toy Pancy. "I also know that a certain class of people will join Dr. Juno, but these are few compared with all those who are his bitter opponents. Now, listen for a moment, Brother Pier, and don't be a fool; both you and the deacon forget that we can swell our crowd to an immense army by calling all the medicine doctors, medicine swallowers, tobacco dealers, rum dealers, and the users of these articles; also the jealous, selfish, miserly crowd will come to our side, if we should ask them to do so, and the *public press* is our slave already; therefore take comfort, and feel safe and sound."

"O dear, good, wise Brother Pancy, you really are a doctor, who can cure the weakness of the flesh by your deep thought, and I now feel I am myself again," ejaculated the saintly Rev. Joe Pier.

"Mr. President, I am not a public speaker, but I have a few words to say; and that is, that I am opposed to accept the services, or be thrown into communion with unregenerate people like the dissipated worldlings who indulge in rum, tobacco, profanity, Sabbath breaking and so forth," responded a sanctimonious brother.

"Silence!" interposed Deacon Rob Stew, "and hear *me*. We do not want your silly scruples on the habits of the worldlings, or on any one else; first, because such nonsense comes too near the accursed teachings of Dr. Juno; and, secondly, because we shall need all the help that we can get from all quarters; furthermore, I call upon the president to order all such rebellious stuff as being irrelevant, when we meet as a sacredly secret conclave; and remind all who belong here that I say our solemn oath cannot be violated with impunity. Remember the fate of the apostate, Harry Gossimer!"

"Yes, brothers and sisters, remember the fate of the apostate, Harry Gossimer, whose death, for dissenting with the profound wisdom of Deacon Rob Stew, should be a terrible lesson to all of you who are within reach of my humble voice," exclaimed the Rev. Joe Pier.

"I rise to request that Brother Rob Stew shall finish his speech. I want to hear his plans, and if they do not agree with mine, I shall take the opportunity to urge what I claim to be rational and will prove successful," said Sister Nancy Clover.

"O precious, holy and profoundly wise Sister Clover, your angelic voice always charms my soul and calms my fears; and I now order that the floor belongs to Brother Stew until he has finished his speech," exclaimed the saintly president, with a countenance quite serene, as he threw an affectionate glance at Sister Nancy Clover.

"Brethren, I know that we have only one way left us to carry us safely through Israel," said Deacon Rob Stew; "and that is by working in unison with the politicians and worldlings generally. We have reached that dangerous point when we cannot choose our company; in fact, we have not started right in the beginning, but we cannot go back, and do over what is already done; therefore, as our religion sanctions the *moderate* use of those things which physiological science totally rejects, and as we have always indulged in the same worldly habits as those do who make no professions of piety, why should we now, at this eleventh hour, object to cast our fortunes with dram-drinkers, tobacco-indulgers, money-seekers, gluttons, sensualists, warriors, politicians and people of that kidney? I boldly admit, before this sacredly secret conclave, that Dr. Juno is right in the sight of God and science; but, in the sight of the people, he is wrong; and we cannot change the people's tastes without sacrificing millions, and beginning with the unborn generations, by starting communities, as Dr. Juno says, and in those communities train the young to lead natural physiological lives, and grow them sound in body and mind, before they *increase and multiply and replenish* this wicked earth. These sentiments I have learned recently from a sermon, that I had reported, which Dr. Juno delivered in his own hall; and, whilst I must admit the soundness of his doctrines, I say that such views do not suit the elect; nay, such work does not become an old established sainthood, which has always called upon God for all its wants and blessings; why, brethren and sisters, such teachings would ruin us body and soul; therefore, I say we require to be a unit in carrying our old established work fearlessly ahead, and to prevent a crisis; a war that will cause our downfall with the only source we can look to for succor. I mean *the people*. We must remove this Dr. Juno; this vile agitator of a cause that would have been worthy our best efforts had we understood it as this innovator does."

"May I ask the brother a question?" said Dr. Toy Pancy.

"Certainly," responded the deacon.

"Well, sir, if what you have just said be *really* true, would it not be better and wiser for us to cease our erroneous work, and, instead of prosecuting long established ungodly usages, join Dr. Juno, and work with him; he is very generous, most benevolent, and would forgive any injury, if asked to do so; what say the saints?"

This reckless speech of Deacon Rob Stew, and the proposition by Dr. Toy Pancy, caused a terrible hubbub amongst the brotherhood, which resulted in a furious fight with fists, chairs and knives.

CHAPTER XXXVII.

DR. JUNO AGAIN IN THE INSANE ASYLUM.

INSIDE of the insane asylum blood was frequently shed by those who were made victims by the actions of the sectarian practices. When the physician-in-chief entered the cell of General Washington Armington, the general was talking to himself for several minutes before he took notice that the doctor was present; but the moment the crazy man saw his keeper, or doctor, he sprang upon him like an infuriated fiend, and cried aloud :

" You are one of them," which fairly unhinged the brave physician's nerves, and caused him to lose his presence of mind, when the general tore the flesh from his face, and caused the blood to fly in streams. The physician-in-chief screamed terribly, but in insane asylums there is so much noise made by the inmates that no one who was close at hand took any notice of it; until the unlucky doctor cried in a very boisterous voice:

"George, come here, quick; I am being murdered by General Armington." George was the keeper of the ward, and he was only a short distance from the general's cell, therefore heard and knew the doctor's voice, which caused him to make for the place; and when he reached the cell door, behold the physician-in-chief had bolted the same and let the key remain in the inside, which prevented George from unlocking or opening the only passage of access to the place where the crazy general was sitting astride the physician-in-chief, and with one hand and his weighty body the general held the hands of the doctor, and with the other hand he was pounding the bleeding physician in the face with fiendish fury, whilst the crazy general continually cried out :

"Give me my daughter! give me my daughter! you fiend! you fiend!"

What to do George did not know for an instant; but he quickly ran toward the office and screamed :

"Bring help; bring hammers and cold chisels, for my master is being murdered by General Armington!"

Instantly dozens of the help, and besides innocent lunatics, rushed to the spot of danger, and in thirty minutes they succeeded in forcing the stronghold open; all this time the crazy man continued pounding the doctor, who was nearly exhausted from the loss of blood and the terrible bruises which he received.

They grasped the general and ironed him, and carried the almost murdered doctor to his office. Medical attendance was bestowed upon him, but all hope of restoration was well nigh abandoned. He sank into an unconsious state, and remained so for three days, when he seemed to improve very rapidly, and in several weeks he was able to be about his business; but he always gave the crazy general a wide berth, and was very cautious to keep him securely locked up.

Dr. Juno learned that General Washington Armington was confined in this model asylum, and he was very anxious to visit him; but every attempt that Dr. Juno made to get access to the asylum was thwarted; until, finally, he got acquainted with some influential public men, and through their instrumentality he was granted permission to visit the general.

The moment the latter saw Dr. Juno, he began to weep and moan in the most heart-rending manner, and mumbled:

"O my dear son! where—where—where is my daughter?"

Dr. Juno said: "Noble father, I have done my utmost to find her; still, I have failed to learn even the least traces of her; but, I have some suspicion that she is not very far from here."

To this reply the general made no answer, but repeated the above sentence without cessation. Dr. Juno saw that the man was really insane, therefore he got ready to leave the asylum, but as he moved toward the door of exit, suddenly he was seized, blindfolded and gagged.

CHAPTER XXXVIII.

DEACON STEW FRANTIC WITH DELIRIUM.

THE riot amongst the bloody conspirators in Tabernacle Hall lasted for nearly one hour, before anything like order was established. The principal party that was being assaulted was Deacon Rob Stew and Rev. Joe Pier, because the majority were over-awed time and again by these two great leaders; and Deacon Stew had just a moment previous summarily chastised a brother for uttering similar, but less offensive, language. The deacon even threatened that brother, and all the saints, without compassion, with the penalty of the solemn oath and fate of Harry Gossimer, the apostate; and then spoke himself in the most reckless, silly and apostatic manner; when the Rev. Joe Pier confirmed the same by permitting the deacon to go on, until Dr. Toy Pancy asked him a question, which so opened the deacon's eyes as to almost cause them to start from their sockets.

Deacon Rob Stew evidently had forgotten himself at the time he uttered those words, approving the course and teachings of Dr. Juno, which so enraged the balance of the brothers, who were always snubbed and chastised by his deaconship if they made the least slip of the tongue, that they almost killed both the saintly deacon and cowardly Reverend President Joe Pier.

Had it not been for the wise and dignified Nancy Clover, these two tyrants would have surely had their beating hearts torn out by their roots; but Sister Nancy Clover evidently considered it wisdom to permit the snubbed saints to thoroughly beat these domineering twain, who became rather too overbearing; and when she thought they had enough, she mounted the President's rostrum, and, springing into the chair, cried with a loud but dignified voice:

"Hold, fellow saints, you have done enough of this for the present. I wish you all to comprehend that neither of us can be benefited by fighting, for assuredly '*a house divided against itself must fall*,' and great will be our fall; you are all sure of that. Then, why beat and abuse these zealous, hard-working brethren, who have devoted more time, money and mind to this holy work of sustaining the cause of the elect than this whole community combined? I say justly, therefore, that they have a perfect right to express themselves more freely in this conclave than the rest of you. Although I think myself that Brother Rob Stew made some foolish remarks; but I want you, and him also, to understand that I do not say this because he is almost dead by the thrashing which you gave him and Rev. Brother Joe Pier, for I am not afraid to speak my sentiments on any occasion.

"As Brothers Stew and Pier will not be able to transact any more business for a short season, I propose to take the floor, if Dr. Toy Pancy will take the chair, after the sick brethren are removed to the anti-chamber, their wounds dressed by the doctor and each made comfortable."

They were at once carefully carried into the handsomely furnished anti-chamber and placed on separate lounges. Deacon Stew was beaten so badly about the head that his mind wandered and his face and head swelled awfully. Rev. Joe Pier was not so much hurt on the head, but he complained greatly of his side, and lamented as follows, lest he should die:

"O Lord! O Lord! save my miserable life only this time, and I will be a better man in the future! Indeed, indeed I will; therefore save, O save my life!"

Sister Nancy Clover made a slight examination of the sufferers after the doctor had dressed their wounds—and when Rev. Joe Pier spied his beloved Sister Nancy, he said:

"O holy sister! pray for me; and dear, dear, sweet sister, tell me, b—o!—b—o—o! do you think I will die from this bruise—God save me?"

"No, Brother Pier, you won't die; be more manly, and you will soon be well again," responded Nancy Clover.

"Ten thousand thanks, angel sister; your charming voice and enchanting words always thrill my heart with joy, and cause my whole physical nature to warm and strengthen. I am much better already by your ethereal power; do stay by my side, won't you, angel of my soul?" sadly said the awfully pious Rev. Joe Pier.

"No, sir, I cannot remain with you, for I must go to pacify the saints, or they may get to quarrelling again, and in the heat of passion come in here and beat you worse than before," exclaimed Nancy Clover.

"O the Lord help me! go quick and prevent them from assaulting me again," said he.

"I will do so, after I ask the deacon how he is. Brother Stew, how do you feel; are you conscious of what is going on?" asked Nancy Clover; but the deacon made no answer, when the queenly saint passed into the hall, and after Dr. Toy Pancy was seated in the chair, she spoke as follows:

"Beloved saints, whilst I regret very much that this war amongst God's elect has taken place, I nevertheless do not doubt but what He so willed it; for everything is preordained, and the elect may anger and sin not; this has been the case with some of us this evening, and as our worthy president and more worthy deacon are lying probably on their death-beds, we should pour out our hearts to God in humble supplication to strengthen us in love and charity for the saints.

"And now, as I feel and see that you are all grieved at heart at what has occurred, I am free to say that we can confide in one another, and go on as if nothing had happened. It will take several weeks' careful nursing to restore our brethren, and in the meantime I propose that we unanimously arouse the worldlings, by telling them of the great danger that hangs now over them on account of Dr. Juno preaching and spreading forth energetically his vulgar natural doctrines. We all know that by nature we are defiled and abased; therefore, to me his teaching of natural things is repugnant to my maiden feelings and inherent saintly modesty."

At this moment Deacon Rob Stew staggered into the hall in a demoniacal manner, and proclaimed damnation to apostates and usurpers, which caused a furious rush toward him.

CHAPTER XXXIX.

NANCY CLOVER MAKES A MASTER SPEECH TO THE CONSPIRATORS.

HAD it not happened that Sister Nancy Clover had been lecturing the belligerent saints, the deacon undoubtedly would have been killed then and there; but the royal sister was still on the floor when the delirious deacon came into the hall, and she simply waved them back with her hand, and ordered the sentinel to remove him to his lounge, which was more, however, than one man could do; because, delirious people are always stronger when in this state than when calm; it took six men to carry him back to his chamber. Doctor Pancy was compelled to leave the chair and attend to the deacon; Nancy Clover, therefore, asked a meek brother to act as president for the balance of the evening, when she continued:

"I reiterate that it is vulgar; in fact, bordering on the worst form of obscenity for a man to be continually preaching, lecturing and writing on natural religion, natural laws, natural improvement of the race. The only way in which the race can be improved is by conversion, by faith in the atoning blood and by the grace of God. The elect saints receive all the grace that God designed for his chosen people, and as we are so blessed, as we are the elect who cannot sin, therefore in our hands all things are purified.

"We have a right from on high, through the grace of Christ, to use everything that we see, and use it as we please. But, what right have the non-elect to the kingdom of God, and to the rights and privileges that are only vouchsafed unto us? We, as the chosen people of the Lord, have a perfect right to use these people to our liking; hence, I say, why not conspire with, or solicit our enemies, or slaves—I mean the giddy worldlings, such as tipplers, rogues, politicians, or whoever or whatever they are—to join us; because, they were born for our use; they and their everything belong to us; then, what scruples can we have to get them to fight as our allies, to subdue and annihilate all innovators? And this Dr. Juno is the only dangerous man that lives; because he endeavors to give a new and scientific explanation of the Holy Bible, and by that new interpretation he proves to his hearers and readers that the Bible and science agree, a thing that cannot be; or, if such would be the case, then *our* holy religion surely could not be sound.

"We need not dread any innovators who denounce the Holy Bible as being a fallible work; because they can easily be cried down by us; but this audacious Juno takes our own instrument of salvation, and endeavors to explain every portion of it upon fixed natural principles; upon principles that the natural man and carnal mind can understand, as people comprehend the multiplication table.

"Now, brethren and sisters, I want your vote upon this question: do you not think that, if Dr. Juno can make the natural man understand that the teachings of the Divine Master are only the teachings of nature, or the teachings of a natural law, that our holy cause will be esteemed as a bogus one? All those who believe in the affirmative please rise to their feet and say '*I*.'

"The entire sainthood unanimously agree with me. Then, again, does not our sainthood suffer more from such a man as Dr. Juno than from all the balance of infidels, atheists, heretics, worldlings and agitators of isms and schisms combined ? Those who think so, please rise and say 'I,' as before. Again unanimous," continued she; "and as such we shall set ourselves individually and collectively to work, to-morrow, to urge all classes to aid us in subduing Dr. Juno."

Voices rang out vociferously from *all* parts of the hall : "Hear! hear!"

The physician-in-chief of the insane asylum rose and said :

"I did not expect to make any remarks this evening, but things have taken such a peculiar turn that I wish to express my views on the appropriate remarks of our excellent Sister Nancy Clover. Should her counsel be rigidly heeded by every individual of this brotherhood, I am *sure* victory would crown our efforts.

"I see a great deal of danger breeding, and although those who are now in high offices, as well as the evangelical ministers and standard medical doctors, are our friends; but these are nothing compared with the masses of *the people ;* and once let a *furore* be made in favor of Dr. Juno, and you will see what one man can do, who is bad, bold and indomitable like he.

"It has always been one mind that moved the masses. Look at Napoleon I., and from time immemorial the fearless agitator of reform or deform, by perseverance, gained his end ; because a lie often repeated becomes a truth in the estimation of the masses of the people. And we certainly should not be blind to the fact that it was a bad move to have given Dr. Juno an open trial in the Court of Sessions, and permit his friends to publish the same in pamphlet form to the world ; because the people are always crazy to read sensational matters ; therefore, the sale of his book on the '*Physiology of Marriage*' has been greatly increased, and the masses of the *people* say it is just the book they need and want to enlighten them how to prevent the various domestic ailments, which injures both the business of our medical profession and that of the ministers; because he reasons in that book that man must and can become his own saviour, by learning and returning to the laws of nature—a thing that is very absurd; but, nevertheless, such heresy suits the non-elect, who are very greatly in the majority, and whose attention has been riveted to the name of Dr. Juno, through that open trial, conviction and imprisonment of the innovator.

"Our people have made a martyr of him, is the cry everywhere, except among the elect and a few others. Now, I have closely watched all the plans that have been laid and discussed to disgrace, ruin and kill him; but there is one excellent method, of branding him as an *abortionist*, that no one has thought of; and it must be known that even the masses of the non-elect despise and detest abortionists; in sooth, they are murderers.

"Here is my plan: The druggists who can be trusted will manufacture specific pills for producing abortion, and label them, *Dr. Juno's Female Regulating Pills;* and if these druggists do not desire to sell them to the people themselves, they can introduce them to the patent medicine trade, and then get up a talk that Dr. Juno is manufacturing and selling specific abortion pills, which are sold publicly by that class of druggists who deal in patent medicines.

"Three birds will be killed by one stone in so doing:— *First*, the manufacturers will make a great deal of money on these pills at Dr. Juno's expense, and through his notoriety; *secondly*, the patent medicine dealers, who are none of the standard bearers, will be despised and disreputably touched up; and, *thirdly*, the celebrated (?) Dr. Juno will get a fame as the great abortionist, which will be as good as stabbing him to the heart in the estimation of the millions, who he might chain and charm without this stigma."

"Noble thoughts, brother; worthy the esteem of the whole sainthood, and I hope that several of our faithful druggists will be selected instantly, who are here present, as a committee of operation; because the plan is excellent, and if brothers Stew and Pier were well enough to comprehend it, they would cheerfully cry yea and amen to this most cunning little game. Brother, you have my heartfelt thanks for these holy thoughts. I move then that the president pro tem. will appoint the three brother druggists, whom I see in the hall, as a committee to manufacture and motion these pills into circulation," said Sister Nancy Clover.

"I second that motion," responded a brother.

"All right!" exclaimed several voices; and, just as the president pro tem. had announced the names of this committee, Dr. Toy Pancy entered the hall with a downcast expression, and said, solemnly:

"I fear Deacon Stew, the beloved, is expiring."

CHAPTER XL.

DR. JUNO, PAT O'CONNER AND JUDY M'CREA IN PRIVATE COUNCIL.

IN the insane asylum, after Dr. Juno was seized and gagged, a consultation of the managers was held to devise plans what to do with him; some wanted him confined again in his old dungeon, but the physician-in-chief said:

"Since Deacon Rob Stew and Rev. Joe Pier are lying at the point of death, and from the fact that an influential person caused Juno's permission to visit General Armington, I esteem it highly imprudent to retain him, or even harm him in any manner."

"But what can we do with him, now that we have had him thus summarily seized and gagged?" said another.

"That may be bad for us, because he may go out and expose us," responded a third party.

"Yes, and I heard him say to General Armington that

he suspicioned that Miss Armington was confined not far from the general's cell," said another.

"I wonder if he really believes her to be in our possession; if he does, I dread the consequences should we let him off now; any way, we dare not retain him in custody; but, I have it—some of the keepers can free Dr. Juno from his present shackles, and feign great anger and surprise at discovering this assault on him, stating that it was the innocent lunatics who did it, that are permitted to run loose in that ward, and who were very grievously annoyed when, a short time since, General Armington assaulted and almost killed the physician-in-chief. They evidently concluded that Dr. Juno was a friend to the general, and therefore took it into their heads to grab him—this will explain the matter satisfactory to Dr. Juno, especially if caution is exercised and great innocence assumed. Go then and do this instantly, for every moment will aggravate the matter; and should he say, 'Why did the officers not then and there stop them from this outrage?' say that the latter were afraid to do so without assistance, which they now come to offer," said the physician-in-chief.

Dr. Juno was at once relieved, and the foregoing explanation was made; but he said:

"That is curious," and looked as if he had great doubts about the matter. He did not say anything more, but he thought: "How is this; I cannot understand exactly why they should seize and gag me one moment and free me the next? That apology about the innocent lunatics was a lame one, which will not go down with me. I think they had fully intended to again cast me into that cell, or probably murder me, but they are commencing to fear my influence. Wait, boys, a little longer, and provided I live, if I do not bring your shanty down, I am a fool, and thereby free my darling Lucinda, who, I am *now* more than ever convinced, is incarcerated in some secret cell in this hell-hole!

"If I only knew some one that was acquainted with this

place, or who knows any of the servants in this asylum. The Armingtons are all in this place, but there is Pat O'Conner and Judy McCrea, who may know what I want to know; I will instantly go to Pat O'Conner and question him; however, he seemed to shun me on previous occasions; but that evidently was through fear of the bloody conspirators; however, I can try him. I will see him privately, and, if he only fears exposure, and has no other feelings against me, he will aid and enlighten me all he can."

He went in disguise that very night, about ten o'clock, to Pat O'Conner's residence and asked to see him; Judy came to the door and said that Pat would be in in a few minutes, "would he take a sate an' wate?"

"Yes, ma'am," said the doctor, and asked, "Are you Judy McCrea?"

"I bees that lady," she replied.

"Do you and Pat O'Conner live alone in this large house since the general is in the insane asylum?" asked the doctor.

"Yis, sir, we do; an' is thare anyting morer that ye lik to know?" interposed Judy, rather angrily.

"There is something more, Judy; I love your lost Mistress Lucinda, and I have news for you, and I came here to ask you and Pat to assist me, if you can, to relieve her from her cruel imprisonment"—

"Och, howly Moses! an' who be ye; fur what I knows ye may be atryin' to git meself an' Pat darlin' into trouble?" interrupted Judy.

"I am Dr. Juno, your friend, in disguise," said he, and removing his disguise proved to Judy the truth of his assertion.

"Tanks to the Lord! fur acomin' to sea us, fur Pat wanted to sea ye badly; but he was afeard to go where ye was, fur he was adreadin' them bluddy divils!" responded Judy, overcome with such vehement joy that she laughed and cried at once.

At this moment Pat O'Conner entered the house, when Judy called to him:

"Pat, darlin', air ye be yerself alone?"

"Yis, Judy, me darlin'," said Pat.

"Thin, com in, som one ye know bees here," she ejaculated.

"God bless ye, good Dochter Juno, but I'se glad to see ye; an' do ye know anyting ov our mishtress an' mashter?" choking with delight, said Pat.

"Yes, sir, faithful Pat, I have been to see the general in the insane asylum, and found him really insane, but I could not learn anything of Miss Lucinda Armington; however, I sincerely believe that she also is imprisoned in that place, not for insanity, but for having been my friend. I came to see you particularly to inquire, if you can give me any information in any way of the dark deeds of these bloody people?" exclaimed Dr. Juno.

"An' shure, yer noble sir, I kin give ye sich infurmation, ef ye kin manage not tow tell on me," said Pat.

"Certainly, good Pat, I would not expose you," said he, "because that would ruin everything; we must work in secret as well as they, or we cannot save our dear friends and benefactors; I mean Miss Lucinda and her father"—

"An' shure, ye air right," interrupted Pat, "an' I will tell ye, that I knows this many a day that ye were confined in that divil ov a dunjon, an' that our mishtress be caged in one ov them tird story cells ov that plaze."

"Pat, you say you *know* it; but, can you inform me *how* you know this?" asked he.

"Yis, sir, I'll tell ye how I knows it; Jemmy, me frind, what is now in the Penitentiary, was a overseer widin that asylum, an' Judy and meself tould Jemmy to hunt fur ye an' our mishtress, an' he did so an' found ye both; an' he tould me that he would let ye both out, ef he could, an' I tink he was cought adoin' they work, an' that is why these divils put him into the prison," said Pat, very much distressed.

"O Lord! O Lord! Pat, I have it all now in my mind. Jemmy opened my cell and was the sole cause of my escape from that hell-hole."

"Was he, bedad? I tould Judy I belaved he had to do wid yer escape," said Pat, half crazy with joy. "But will ye not do somethin' quickerer than lightnin' to git my swate mishtress outer ov that divil ov a plaze?"

"Yes, sir, I will do that just as soon as I can gather sufficient people and influence around me to do it successfully; but it would be foolish to try sooner and fail; much better keep everything quiet until I am strong enough to strike a fatal blow. I will get a permit from the Governor of the Commonwealth to visit Jemmy in the Penitentiary, and will learn particulars," said Dr. Juno.

"Och, murdher! an' ye knows how to work them curmudgon. An' I have morer to tell ye, ov tings I knows," responded Pat.

"Well, sir, now is your time to speak; and it is very necessary for me to get all the information instantly that it is possible for me to receive," said he.

"I'll tell ye; I saved a man's life what was agoin' to be drowned in the deep sea by these bluddy divils; an' jist as we, Mishter Harry Gossimer an' meself, rached the warf, begorrah, we were both arrested—Judy, darlin', I hears a knock on the doore; dochtor, plaze git into this closet," ejaculated Pat.

CHAPTER XLI.

DR. JUNO'S STUNNING SERMON ON THE IMPROVEMENT OF CHURCH AND STATE.

BELOVED FRIENDS:—Until church and state (in my sense of what the church is) become one, and an indivisible institution, there can be no perpetually natural or Christian government established, where God's will "will be done in earth as it is in heaven;" nor can peace and good will reign between the children of His footstool. Before being able to elucidate this subject scientifically, it behooves me to show you that Church and State simply aim at government—the government of mankind; but before mankind can be governed aright, each one must first learn to understand God's fixed law, that was ordained for man's government, and he must then be able to govern himself, and that fixed law is his king, which he must obey, or suffer the penalties that are sure to follow all violations of the Creator's immutable injunctions.

Now, then, look at Church and State as they are conducted at this age, whether in this or any other country, and you will see that both are anti-Christ and anti-natural institutions. They are like a perfect fruit tree that has been split in two, and each half hacked to pieces by the woodman; and whilst nothing but God's fixed law can sustain and again heal the tree; it therefore behooves the governor of treehood to return to this unchangeable scientific law of the Creator, and thereby bring into existence a new stock, stem, blossom and fruit, the latter of which will contain good seed, which, when planted in new earth, produces a new heaven on *terra firma*, when love to God and love to man would be the only statute that would be necessary for the government of all peoples and all nations; and thus, indeed, the millennium would be established, and stupid sects and wicked political parties would be esteemed by the sons and daughters of earth as mean, low and vulgar.

Thus, Parliament, Congress and State Legislatures would be useless institutions, and the ruinous business of continually, much and often voting, by a people who know not a whit of the fixed law of a Christ-like government, would cease to exist, whilst love to God and man should drive selfishness from the heart of mankind, and the infallibility and beneficence of God would be recognized by every human mind; and the following divine mandates would be heeded: That He allows the sun to shine and rain fall upon all alike, and that no one brings anything into the world, nor takes anything out of it that is carnal. On the contrary, let me briefly picture to you the heathen barbarity that the people practise upon one another as Church and State move now, or have done since the fall of man, or since "money" and "voting" have been the cardinal virtues of the government of this whole machine of human affairs.

The Church as now conducted (including all sects) is an institution that throws all the responsibility of mismanaged government of body, soul or spirit, upon the blessed and immutable Creator of all things; an institution that recognizes no unalterable science of life in its tenets; an institution that, in its short-sightedness, has inscribed upon its banner, "*believe and be saved*," whilst it overlooks the multitudinous injunctions of God, Nature and Jesus Christ, that point with the finger of science to "good works," by which all are to let their "light shine before men." These "good works" consist in the government of thinking beings, so that they understand, appreciate and live the natural life that Christ himself led, showing that although one has "no place where to lay his head," still he would continue faithful to the end.

An institution that builds brick-and-mortar houses, and dedicates or devotes them to God, instead of its devotees devoting *themselves*—body, soul and spirit—to God, as Jesus did; and instead of establishing one universal Catholic Church, which is composed of all the fixed laws and wonderful works of God, it splits *the Church of Christ* into hundreds of contemptible, ignorant, bigoted, narrow-minded sects, whose dupes make excellent fodder for politicians, legislators, governors and petty office-seekers, who contrive to run the State or States to suit their opinions, tastes and feelings.

An institution whose ministers or apostles sell out to the highest *lucre* bidders, like all the voters in State; hence, love the "uppermost seats at feasts," and who do not despise to be called of men "Rabbi;" who do not "first seek the kingdom of God," in the fixed laws and wonderful works of God; because their prayer-hearing master is as changeable and fickle as their opinions and perverted propensities are variable; thus, there is no one king, but each can be saved by "believing" and dictating to his sectarian, money and voting god what he wants or needs in the shape of grace, and the little trifles that each peculiar sect approves.

An institution that inculcates nothing whereby the blood and body of mankind would be improved in physiological quality, thereby resembling the pure blood and body of Jesus Christ; but, their sectarian, lucre and voting god rectifies all these little physical matters, if faith and prayer are kept agoing.

An institution that spurns the fixed laws of generation and regeneration; because its devotees love all sorts of good, palatable things, wherewith a little physical pleasure can be drawn out of these palaces of the believers, and by blarneying their god a little he purifies the blood by washing it in the pool of faith, prayer and voting.

An institution whose devotees need not make any change in their habits that pertain to physical perfection; because faith, prayer and voting changes the heart and purifies the soul, even if the body is rotten.

An institution that spits God in the face, mocks Jesus Christ, defies natural fixed law and crucifies and martyrs the benefactors of the human race. Look at my persecutors, the midnight cut-throats, the bloody conspirators, the companions of the right-hand imps of the devil. These are parents of the sectarian Church.

An institution whose cunning leaders laugh into their sleeves when they can dupe and mislead millions of sincere people, who, if they had an opportunity to learn the laws that govern God's kingdom in heaven and earth, would freely embrace the hallowed, immutable and beneficent gifts of the Creator, and become the followers of Jesus Christ in word and in deed.

An institution whose members and hangers-on are moved by some kind of gain ; yes, gain that has no significance to the attainment of heavenly glory ; but, gain in wealth, influence, sensuality, fashion, folly, domineering and the dainty deviltries that are pleasingly hid under a sanctimonious and hypocritical exterior ; and which so adorn the elect for the more effectual dispensation of nonsense to their gulled hearers. From all such pharisaical and anti-Christ acts, good Lord deliver us.

CHAPTER XLII.

DR. JUNO'S SCATHING SERMON CONTINUED.

THE State, as now conducted, is an institution where cunning men mislead and make drunk, with rum and flowery, meaningless logic, the masses of the voters, who are esteemed by the wily scoundrels good fellows when voting is to be done to elevate them to positions which they yearn to usurp, that they may rob the children of earth of *lucre* and of their inalienable religious or natural liberties.

An institution that places haughty cut-throats and wholesale thieves into the offices of trust of the government ; who love *filthy lucre*, *Moses' seat*, the *uppermost seats at feasts* and prejudice more than God, Nature, Man or Jesus Christ.

An institution that can place a Judge Sanctiblower on the judicial bench, whose prejudice and malice far excel his virtue and wisdom ; and who can be pompous and elated over those who honestly, and by hard labor, earn the money which he steals unmeritoriously from the coffers of the state treasury.

An institution that bribes its Legislators to enact laws to suit the pharisees and wholesale thieves, that they may continue to control the filthy lucre, and domineer and enslave the innocent, poor and confiding.

An institution that drives thousands into the broad road that leads to hell; impoverishes the millions at the glory of the few; drives many, thereby, to commit crime, who are compelled to steal or starve; and builds prisons, penitentiaries, insane asylums and poor houses, for which the poor are taxed to pay for the erection and sustenance of these hell-holes, into which they are cast for acts and conditions over which they had no control, and there to ache out a more miserable existence; whilst the popular cut-throats and wholesale thieves revel in wealth and power.

An institution that spurns those whom the beloved Jesus came to heal and save, and in the government of which institution Christ himself, should he return to earth, could not get a voice or position, unless he would denounce all his former teachings and turn scribe, pharisee, hypocrite and robber of men's rights to live, breathe, feel, think and act as nature and nature's God demand.

An institution that is founded upon error, and improved by the votes of the drunken rabble, who will sell their birthright for a mess of pottage, or a drink of rum.

An institution that sustains its paramour—the sectarian church—as long as the latter plays into the former's coffers, and breeds enough dupes to fill the field of state with deteriorated voters. That the majority may rule, although Christ says: "Narrow is the way which leadeth unto life, and few there be that find it;" whilst, "Wide is the gate, and broad is the way, that leadeth to destruction, and many there be who go in thereat."

Therefore, gainsay my doctrines, if you dare, by scanning the subject from any standpoint.

Again, I assert, and defy contradiction, by theory or practice, that a republican government that divides Church and State, and permits the pharisees, wilful and ignorant sinners, to rule it, is a *perfect* failure. As an example, look at our own American Republic; is it not the meanest monarchy, *filthy lucre* monarchy and most thieving and profligate tyranny on the globe? Certainly, it is not a government of an Eden nor Paradise, where clear-headed, clean-blooded and graceful people govern themselves and one another according to the injunctions of Christ, God or Nature. However, I cannot ask this sectarian and political people to jump from their anti-Christ, anti-natural, drunken, money-grabbing and hoarding condition into a state of Eden gladness; because, to ask this would be throwing "pearls before swine," and they would trample them under foot and turn around and rend me, as the *bloody conspirators* have already tried their best to do.

But I shall propose, as the first and foremost thing to be done to bring about the day of the Millennium, is to so change the Constitution of our Government as to make it a crime for any person to own more than ten thousand dollars.

That the nation shall have a treasury, into which all monies over and above ten thousand dollars of each owner shall be placed, without interest; but that for all sums of *lucre* that any person shall put into the treasury, he or she shall receive a deed for such amount or amounts, and, if he or she should at any time have an increase of family, or be unfortunate in life, he or she, or his or her heirs, may draw out again the principal of all that he or she has placed into the treasury. The treasury shall provide necessary labor for each man and woman who is not able to take care of himself or herself; that no one shall fail to do his or her share of work who is not independent; and idling and vagrancy shall be punished by incarceration in the physiological institution, where farming and all the necessary trades shall be carried on on healthful principles.

After the machine of a Christ-like government will be carried on in this way for one or two centuries, the Holy Ghost will find such an abundant room in the temples of God that *filthy lucre* and an artificial or political constitution will be considered entirely obsolete, and the Millennium will be established, when love to God and man will constitute the only constitution which each person will carry within this palace of the soul.

Thus, diseases, crime, avarice, penury and all the multitudinous ills and vices of human nature would vanish; when pettifoggers, quacks (in the healing art), law-makers, judges, hireling ministers, misers, wholesale thieves, tyrants, blind leaders of the blind and bloody conspirators would be the very ones who should fill the cells of the prisons, houses of correction, etc., which they now erect and fill with those whom they manufacture by their pharisaical charlatanism.

These governors of Church and State make men-traps, and then generate victims to fill them; therefore, they do nothing to prevent disease and crime, but they are experts at punishing those who were bred, born, circumstanced and in every way hewn out for criminals, congenital criminals. Thus, the sectarian ministers have employment to pray for them; the drug-doctors a lucrative trade to dose and drug them to make a business; the lawyers and legislators, seeing the fallacy of their leaders, or fathers in professions, make an excellent living at grab-game, by framing laws, and enforcing them or not, as it best suits their pockets and feelings.

Good people, awake to a sense of duty, and shuffle off these miserable blood-suckers in your anti-Christ and anti-natural church and state.

"Look through nature up to nature's God,"

and learn to know that

"Virtue is nothing but voluntary obedience to truth."

CHAPTER XLIII.

THE BLOODY CONSPIRATORS MOBBED.

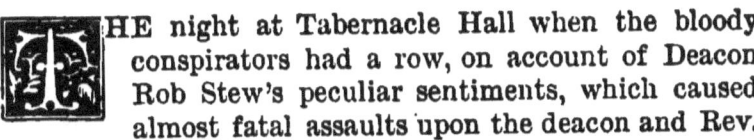HE night at Tabernacle Hall when the bloody conspirators had a row, on account of Deacon Rob Stew's peculiar sentiments, which caused almost fatal assaults upon the deacon and Rev. Joe Pier, it seemed that they could not finish all their plans; and at that part of their proceedings when Dr. Toy Pancy announced that he believed the deacon was expiring, another hubbub arose that nearly amounted to a terrific fight amongst the holy saints; but the dignified and influential Sister Nancy Clover nipped the thing in the bud by her cool and determined eloquence.

The cause of this hubbub was the various expressions of the saints, upon learning from Dr. Toy Pancy that Deacon Rob Stew was dying. Several downtrodden brothers, who despised the usurping deacon, cried out:

"Thank the Lord, he is dying!"

Which immediately aroused the friends of the deacon, who mourned and lamented heartily the dying state of the heroic man of the elect, and who shouted:

"Silence, apostates!"

Instantly the latter moved to assault the former, when Sister Nancy Clover cried out vehemently:

"Shame! shame! brothers; be men, not brutes! If these dissensions are permitted to continue, I feel assured that we shall be our own destroyers, which will prove that we are Dr. Juno's best friends. I have, therefore, one single question to put to you, which I wish you to answer as soon as you understand it:—Who do you love best, Dr. Juno or Deacon Rob Stew, and for which of the two will you work as a unit, for you are compelled to choose between the two antagonistic causes which these two heroes advocate? I ask, emphatically, for which will you work as a unit until you die?"

Like lightning a tremendous unanimous cry rent the air:
" For Deacon Rob Stew ! "

" So I thought," said Nancy Clover, soberly; " therefore, be silent until I go to the deacon's side, with Brother Pancy, and learn the state of our beloved brother's health."

Whilst Sister Nancy Clover and Dr. Pancy were examining the deacon, the saints were exchanging words on their favorite topic of destroying Dr. Juno's influence. They esteemed it impolitic to make attempts upon his life, because he has too many friends amongst even some of the religious denominations; besides, too many people believe, since he was sent to the county prison for publishing an " obscene book," that we were instrumental in sending him there; moreover, many believe that we had him incarcerated in the lunatic asylum, and have tried to murder him; therefore, we must not be too bold in our work, but there are plenty of ways to ruin his reputation; the physician-in-chief has given us a capital plan, and we may get additional new ideas that will do the work.

Whilst the saints were thus engaged in the pleasant anticipation of seeing this vile innovator ruined, Sister Nancy Clover returned to the hall and said :

" Beloved saints, our worthy deacon is dangerously ill, but I have hopes that he will recover; and there is one thing for us to take into serious consideration, and decide the matter before we adjourn. That is, what excuse shall we make to the outside world, and the uninitiated saints, for the absence from society of both the deacon and Rev. Joe Pier; because we dare not let them go home, where their friends and saints, who do not know of our sacredly secret conclave, will have an opportunity to visit them, as they would ask too many questions about the where and the how they received such awful blows ? It would be impossible to lie out of the matter, and therefore it would assuredly leak out that something most mysterious and incomprehensible was on the tapis, which some of these prying religious brethren and sisters would be determined to ferret out. It is our duty to keep our private matters entirely hid under a bushel, thereby keep the members of the sacredly secret conclave above suspicion."

"Beloved sister, you are a trump at all times," responded Mr. Grumbler.

"I do not know if I am a 'trump' or not, Brother Grumbler; but I can assure you that I can prophesy what will come of us all if we are careless. Our only salvation lies in shrewdness and vigorous business tact. Prayers to God, asking Him to do our work, will not answer in such cases; that does well enough to hoodwink zealots and drones, but it cannot answer practical saints like us, who have work, responsible work, to perform," said she.

"I think the best way to manage this matter will be to spread a report that the brethren were called suddenly away from home. A report like this can be started without letting any one know that it came from any of us who are of the conclave," responded a brother.

"Probably that is the best that we can do; at any rate, should we remove them to their homes, and they would not expose the matter when in their right minds, it is still unsafe to trust them as long as they are delirious betimes; moreover, I am not sure but what Brother Pier will go back on the conclave; he is such a coward, and therefore may never come to the hall again, or should he see danger breeding on our side, and behold safety on the side of even Dr. Juno, he would fly to him for succor, and expose and have us forthwith arrested. Therefore, beloved saints, you see into what great danger this fight amongst the saints of the conclave has brought us. I do not want you to think that I am cowardly, but duty compels me to be prudent and wise. lest our holy cause will be lost forever. I am, then, in favor of keeping brothers Stew and Pier closely confined, guarded and carefully nursed in this place until they are well, and promise to continue their allegiance; and spread a report, as the brother proposed, that they left home on an important mission. Brother Pier raves frequently in a delirious state, and threatens exposure and vengeance to those who have assaulted him. I move then that we adjourn to meet to-morrow evening, and in the meantime one of the faithful sisters, Dr. Toy Pancy and myself will provide comfortable beds and nursing for the sick," said Sister Nancy Clover.

The conclave adjourned, all feeling gloomy over the work of the night. They had their eyes opened wide to the danger of quarrels amongst themselves. Nancy Clover had no fears of either of the sick brothers that they would desert the cause, or expose anything in their delirium; really, Brother Pier was never yet delirious, but she wanted to completely subdue the spirit of rebellion and quarrelling, and now was the opportunity to work effectually. She was a long-headed woman, who would not stop at anything to gain her end. The sacredly secret conclave met regularly every evening for a week, which aroused the suspicion of Pat O'Conner, who was sure that some new "diviltry was abreedin'," and Pat connived with some of his friends to oust them from their hiding places.

There was great anxiety in the religious world, asking where Deacon Rob Stew and Rev. Joe Pier were; and whilst the saints of the conclave spread *their* report, as already known by the reader, Pat O'Conner and his friends started an opposite report, which was, however, not made too public, but was only talked about among those who were suspicious of the sanctimonious, who assisted in convicting and imprisoning Dr. Juno, and who could not see any crime in the latter; therefore, on the evening previous to a great religious celebration, the conclave were in session, having much business before them, when the sentinel stepped into the hall, and said:

"A stranger is insisting to be admitted; what can I do to pacify him, for he will not go away from the outside door?"

The president pro tem. said:

"Take two or three brethren with you and go out to him, and ask him to leave, and if he will not leave, go for a policeman and have him arrested."

As they opened the outside door a crowd of policemen and citizens rushed in and overpowered the sentinel and his companions.

CHAPTER XLIV.

DR. JUNO INFORMED WHERE LUCINDA IS IMPRISONED.

THE time Pat O'Conner ordered Dr. Juno into a closet, at General Armington's residence, when some one knocked at the door, at a very unusual hour of the evening, it proved that the *bloody conspirators* had kept a sharp eye on Dr. Juno after the mistake they made in the insane asylum, when the latter, by permission, visited the insane General Armington—the circumstances are familiar to the reader; and when the person who knocked for admission was admitted, Pat O'Conner recklessly asked him:

"Yer honor; an' what kin I do to sarve ye?" The visitor, being no one long or short of Mr. Grumbler of the conclave, stammered, and hesitatingly said:

"I—I—called here for Dr. Juno, a friend of mine is sick, and I was told that he was seen coming to this house. I am to bring him quick as possible to the sick man."

"Yer frend bees sick, bees he? an' ye wer towld that Dochtor Juno was seed acomin' here? Bedad, the cratur what seed him acomin' here must have seed his gost, fur I tell ye, Dochtor Juno an' meself bees mortal enemies, do ye mind that? Ye better go to his office, an' not be ahuntin' around here fur the dirty divil," angrily said Pat O'Conner.

"So, so," responded Mr. Grumbler; "you then are no friend of this man?"

"Begorrah! how kin ye axe me sich a ting agin, whin I towld ye? I hate the seducer of dacent damsils. Ef this Dochtor Juno should com tow this house now, while I have the honor tow be boss, I'd murhder him. Do ye mind that? Yis; an' I wish ye would tell him so; an' ef ye want nothin' morer, I tank ye tow hunt this fine dochtor, whare ye may find they divil," sarcastically said Pat.

This cool language and defiant air of an ignorant Irishman threw Brother Grumbler entirely off his guard, and convinced him that Pat was an enemy to Dr. Juno; who gave him (Grumbler) the cold shoulder, because Pat believed him to be the doctor's friend; and if Juno's patrons would receive such severe treatment from Pat O'Conner, what would Dr. Juno himself get, should he call on Pat? Thus, Mr. Grumbler departed in a serene and satisfied state of mind, reporting his convictions to the saints in whose service he was operating, and they also felt easy on that topic; still, they knew that Jemmy and Pat O'Conner were chums, and therefore Pat had better be watched.

When Mr. Grumbler had gone, Pat and Judy closed the house thoroughly, and set their prisoner free, who was locked up in the closet, when Pat asked him:

"Good dochtor, an' did ye hear me blarneying that bluddy curmudgon?"

"Yes, Pat; you are a trump; surely, your ready answers and deliberately cool deportment, if the tone of your voice proves anything, were excellent; and you threw that guilty scoundrel entirely off his guard. Now, then, Pat, I am ready and very anxious to learn more about my dear Lucinda, about Jemmy and the man that was to be drowned," said the doctor.

"All right, I'll tell ye; an' I'll begin at the beginnin' Jemmy bees Judy darlin's cousin, an' he towld us that he seed our swate Mishtress Lucinda"—here Pat and Judy snivelled like innocent children—"that he—he—see—d her locked up in a tird story cell, an' this bees all meself an' Judy knows ov it."

"Jemmy, then, I suppose was caught at his work of aiding us? He spoke to me on several occasions, but he said nothing of dear Lucinda. O God, comfort and save her until I am ready to free her!" ejaculated Dr. Juno.

"Och! good dochter, Jemmy did not wish to hurt yer feelin's, an' that bees why he did not tell ye," said Judy McCrea, modestly, but still snivelling.

"Undoubtedly you are right," responded Dr. Juno.

"I knows Judy darlin' bees right, becase Jemmy tould us both that he did not wish ye to be made feel so bad," said Pat, and, wiping his eyes, added: "O, Jemmy bees a good man, ef he bees a strong Roman Catholic."

"God bless Jemmy, and also bless you both; but I want to disabuse your minds about my ideas of the Roman Catholic Church; the Catholic is the only *true* Church, when in its pristine state; I am a Catholic in every sense of the word," responded Dr. Juno, whose eyes were filling with huge drops of tears whilst he was uttering these words. He was thinking of his beloved Lucinda, and as he was now satisfied that she was in that third story, closely confined in a cell, he could not think of anything else but to free her at once.

Faint heart never won fair lady, and a cowardly knave was not worthy of so excellent a creature; still, a voice cried: Prudence, prudence!

These three distressed souls sat, like innocent children, for some minutes, weeping and meditating on the same subject. They were evidently in this one place with one accord, which caused them to be inspired with the Holy Spirit, when all at once Dr. Juno exclaimed:

"Good, *most faithful* friends, God and right are on our side, and who can be against us when He is for us? We shall trust confidingly in His holy laws, but shall rigidly work with all our might to free every one of our friends as speedily as possible."

"Och! Dochtor Juno, may the Lord bless ye fur that word," sighed Pat; "fur poor Jemmy must be a sufferin' much, an' so do our swate lady an' mashter; an' mesel! an' Judy darlin' would giv our lives tow sea thim every one free."

"Pat, your great heart is full of the milk of genuine Christian kindness, and God will guide us, provided we shall cautiously use our inwrought faculties, which we shall assuredly do," said the doctor.

Ten thousand ideas flashed through Dr. Juno's brain at that moment, and he at once tried to arrange things, which he knew to be true, so that instant relief might come to his precious Lucinda. Thought he:

"What insults may that angel not have suffered, and all on my account! O Lord! fill her soul with hope and joy, for the hour of her deliverance is not far distant. Let me see; Jemmy is in the Penitentiary. I must at once seek our noble-minded Governor of this Commonwealth, and ask him to pardon Jemmy, who will be of great service to me. I will do this secretly, if I can. Then I must organize a *secret society* for the purpose of matching these bloody conspirators; and as soon as I can get sufficient men together to free my beloved Lucinda, I will make a dash into that hell-hole of an insane asylum; but, would it not be better to sue out a habeas corpus, and compel the physician-in-chief to produce her in court?

"No, no; there is no judge now upon the bench who dares to insist to search for her in this hell-hole, if the bloody clique say that no such person is there. Truly, they have made the impression that I seduced, carried away and deserted the beloved of my soul. Oh, they would make a laughing stock of me for the presumption of asking for a writ of habeas corpus."

CHAPTER XLV.

DR. JUNO ORGANIZES THE "SECRET ORDER OF NATURALISTS."

AT; please tell me now about the man of whom you spoke of being drowned, or something to that effect; may be he will be of some use to us in freeing our friends, and overcoming these bloody conspirators," said Dr. Juno.

"Cartainly, he'll be ov use, fur he bees very rich an' influatiell," responded Pat.

"The very man we want to use, if he is alive and ready to expose these dastardly scoundrels. Do you think he will aid us?" asked Dr. Juno.

"Cartainly will he, an' he bees wide-alive, fur I draw'd him out ov they sea akickin' like a big fesh," said Pat.

"Go on and tell me how this happened," demanded Dr. Juno.

Pat O'Conner told him the whole story about Harry Gossimer, with which the reader is already familiar, and said:

"Mishter Gossimer has gone West, to git away from these bluddy curmudgon; howsomever, he will be alookin' out fur they dirty divils. These hypecrets tink he bees drown'd dead, an' he bees agoin' to let 'em tink so until he git a chance to e'spose 'em," said Pat.

"Do you think he would write to me if I would first write to him and ask him to co-operate with me?" asked Dr. Juno.

"Yis, sir; but he bees not agoin' be his own name, an' ef ye wish tow write tow him, I will say a word, so he know all bees right. His name now bees John Williams Jordan," said Pat.

"Pat, will you assist me in organizing a secret society, where we can lay plots to entrap these demons? I know now of several true and fearless men who will aid me to the death," responded Dr. Juno.

"Yis, sir; I'll hilp all that, an' ef I die wid ye all," earnestly said Pat.

Dr. Juno cautiously left the house of the General by the side door, and reached his office without molestation. He retired, but his brain was so active that he could not sleep for thinking of his darling Lucinda.

He planned how he should organize the "Order of Naturalists," and as soon as they had enough men indoctrinated into the order they would free his dear Lucinda.

At his next physiological lecture to men alone he proposed to organize a beneficial society at the close of the discourse; but only those who comprehended, appreciated and were willing to carry out the teachings of nature could become members, and such he invited to remain in their seats after the audience was dismissed.

Forty remained, and after stating to these what was to be the motive and work of the proposed "Secret Order of Naturalists," ten of them left, and thirty remained to be initiated into the Order. The inner workings of this secret body of apt, able and heroic sons of toil were completely and conscientiously practicable, which always strengthens men's determination, hence fear or favor for mere gain did not belong to their articles of faith; but they steered straight ahead as one man, who, knowing God's holy truth, dared maintain it in spite of any and every power that human invention could bring to bear against it!

The membership increased rapidly, and after all their plans and operations were matured, Dr. Juno proposed to have Jemmy pardoned and Miss Lucinda Armington delivered from her unjust incarceration! He said:

"I have been to the Eastern Penitentiary, to see Jemmy, the former overseer of the help at the West Philadelphia Insane Asylum, and he avows that Miss Lucinda Armington is confined in the third story of this Lunatic Asylum! He further says that he was convicted on *suspicion*, that he was instrumental in exposing this foul outrage upon her, as well as my incarceration therein; but, that it was simply suspicion, not one particle of proof was produced against him, but Deacon Rob Stew made up his mind that he (Jemmy) was a dangerous person, hence had him arrested, indicted and convicted; and, although Jemmy was guilty in aiding my escape, as also in the exposure of Miss Armington's imprisonment, still they could not prove it on him; therefore, if at any time these same bloody conspirators, or their leader, Rob Stew, should become suspicious of any other man, they would dispatch him, as they did myself, Miss Armington, Jemmy or Mr. Harry Gossimer.

"With the sad story of the latter, and his miraculous rescue from drowning by the cunning and noble Pat O'Conner, you must all be familiar; hence we should make a move in the right direction by freeing the beloved daughter of General Washington Armington, who has been driven to real insanity by the villanous abduction and concealment of Miss Armington!

"I have thought this matter carefully over, and I have come to the conclusion that we can go boldly to this hell-hole Asylum, where Miss Armington is confined, some evening about nine o'clock, and by all being armed to the teeth, more for show than deathly work, and one man asking permission at the outside gate, and upon the keeper opening it, we all rush in, gagging and binding him and every one else as we go along, leaving several to guard them and the gate, whilst the rest march straight for the third story to release Miss Armington, knocking down, gagging and binding or imprisoning all who have a voice in the Asylum, or who interfere with our work; and after having freed Miss Armington, hinting boldly to the physician-in-chief and managers who may be about that we charge them to be very cautious how they move against us by way of exposing this work of liberating an abducted citizen!

"I am convinced that such a course will be successful;

because they dare not arrest me, nor any of you for having made the assault upon the accursed institution for fear of an exposure and speedy downfall of the bloody clique."

"Surely, Dr. Juno is a deep-sighted brother, whose course of action in this direction is beyond a doubt the best, and will be attended with the pleasing results of releasing the distressed young Lady Armington, as well as give these bloody hounds a taste of a mysterious and deeply strategic movement by a rival organization, which would almost scare the life out of the whole bloody clique; because they know they are guilty of numerous foul deeds, and therefore the members, like cut-throats and thieves, would fear each bush to be an officer, or an avenger of the wrong these innocent parties have suffered at their hands!" said a member of the order.

"Yes, sir, brother," replied Dr. Juno, "you are perfectly right, and I propose that we meet here next Thursday evening sharp at 8 o'clock, each member bringing a revolver, dirk, black-jack and any other weapon of death that he may possess, for I mean work, fight, death, or freedom. I have been long enough stigmatized and branded by these bloody conspirators and their followers as being cruel, low, vile and criminal; therefore the hour has arrived when it behooves me to accept the game of the name they gave me, and I shall be indefatigable, fight, and, if necessary, show the black flag, by striking the vipers dead without mercy or quarters. Think for one moment what I have endured whilst thrown into that loathsome felon's cell, in the county prison, for publishing a useful and truthful scientific physiological book. Think of the many wily plans that were laid for my ruination and destruction by these human fiends, and then ask me to be any longer merciful. As well ask God or the devil to yield their fixed intentions, as ask me to change the even tenor of my course.

"I therefore ask you to join me on the evening of next Thursday, when I will general you for the first time through these devils' ground."

CHAPTER XLVI.

LUCINDA SHOOTS DEACON STEW IN HER CELL, AND ESCAPES.

MISS LUCINDA ARMINGTON had received numerous visits from Deacon Rob Stew during her confinement, beside those which we have already described. Two or three of these visits may be worth mentioning, which come near excelling the first and second ones that he made the helpless lady.

On one rainy afternoon the deacon suddenly entered Miss Armington's cell, through one of the secret doors, which startled the poor girl terribly.

"How is my darling young lady?" said he. "I have been wanting to visit you last week, but business of great importance kept me so busily employed that I could not possibly find time. The last visit I made you was not as pleasant as either of us might have desired it, but I hope you will by this time know me and my intentions fully; therefore, yield to my wishes like a wise, obedient child."

"Indeed, sir," said she; "what are your intentions?"

"My intentions, my darling girl, are to make you my wife," said the deacon.

"Well, and how do you propose to do this little business, by fair or foul means?" very sarcastically responded Miss Armington.

"Haughty lady, I'll tell you; by fair means, if you prefer it; and by foul, if the former don't suit you," defiantly ejaculated he.

"Ha! ha! ha! you must think that I am a fool or a baby," she said. "Do you forget the tutorage I gave you when you visited me on a previous occasion?" And, rising to her feet, continued: "Deacon Stew, you had better be careful, or I'll murder you before you can leave this cell "—

"Not so fast, my sweet (?) young lady; do you see

this?" drawing a six shooter from his pocket and pointing it toward her breast, "now stand back, or I will shoot you," interrupted the deacon.

"Shoot, you cowardly villain!" she exclaimed; and as quick as lightning knocked the pistol from his hand, and, grasping it in her own, pointed it toward his holy breast, when he winced like a cur, and begged her:

"Oh! do not shoot; the pistol is loaded," and tried to back out of a secret door, when she said, commandingly:

"Stand still, and do not move one step, or I'll blow out your cowardly and villanous brains; do you hear me? Remember, I am as good as my word." He stood like a statue, almost petrified with fear and horror, when she began to laugh at him, and said:

"You are a fine fellow, a nice saint, a model deacon, who dares to insult a helpless woman by all sorts of proposals and assaults. Now, I want you to listen to me sharply, and swear by the God that is above us that you will do as I wish you to do, or I will shoot you as dead as a mouse. Do you hear me?"

"Yes, ma'am, I do," humbly responded the bold (?) deacon.

"In the first place, I want you to swear that you will never more harm Victor Juno, by word or deed, and will make immediate reparation for all the injury you have done him in the past. Swear it!" she commanded.

"I cannot do that; anything but that," he responded.

She cocked the pistol, and fired one shot into his right arm, the bullet penetrating the centre of the forearm and lodging in the plastered wall of the cell, when she said:

"This is shot number one, to disable your right arm; the next will be your black heart," furiously said Miss Armington.

"O Lord, help me, help me!" ejaculated the pious deacon.

"No, sir; the Lord won't help you, but I will," and raising her pistol towards his heart, continued: "Will you swear, or die in your sin and shame?"

"I'll swear to anything," ejaculated he; "propose the oath."

"I will. Repeat after me without mental reservation or prevarication," she said; and continued, "I, Rob Stew, do solemnly swear, without mental reservation, that I will never injure by word or deed Victor Juno, and that I will make immediate reparation for all the injury I have done to Victor Juno in the past, so help me God."

"Now, Miss Armington, I have done it; will you, therefore, put that pistol down, and let me go in peace?" said his deaconship.

"No, sir; not by a long ways; but you shall now give me your keys to this prison cell, and I will lock *you* up, and leave this place in your stead "—

"Holy Lord God," meditated the deacon, and, turning deathly pale, stammered:

"Miss A—r—mington, would you be so cruel as to demand all this of me?"

"Yes, sir, and more; for fear that the demons and lunatics in the place below should re-capture me, I'll demand you to take off your coat, vest, pants and hat, and give them to me, for a disguise, that I may represent your holy self for once in my life. This may seem immodest, but a desperate woman knows no frivolous modesty that she would not sacrifice for an honorable deliverance from a fiend like yourself. Do you hear, take off your clothes?" resolutely responded she.

"You certainly would not compel me to strip off my garments before you "—

"Off," interrupted Miss Armington, "or die, coward," and cocking her pistol, which made him speedily tear open, take off and deliver the same to her; but she did not attempt to put them on herself until she requested the deacon to tear a sheet into pieces, wherewith she made him firmly tie his own feet together, then ordered him to make a loop of another strip of sheet, and place his hands behind his back into the loop, which she drew tight with her left hand, whilst she held the pistol in her right hand for a shot should he fail to obey; as soon as his hands were secured by her left hand, she laid down the pistol and bound them securely; then she threw him on the floor and cast a lot of bedding on him; to this he objected, and was inclined to scream, when she commanded him to open his mouth, and she stuffed a large rag into it, and bound a strip of the torn sheet over it and his eyes. Thus, his deaconship secured, she removed her heavy skirts, then donned the saintly deacon's pants, vest, coat and hat; but all were too large, which made her look dilapidated; however, after getting the keys of her cell, and pistol in hand, the desperate young heroine started on her way toward freedom.

After leaving her cell and alighting upon the corridor of the second floor of the asylum, she met several keepers, who approached her, staring with amazement at her, without saying a word, when she asked them:

"Which is the best way to leave the asylum?"

To which a surly fellow said: "I don't think that a crazy lunatic like you will leave it any way."

"Why not, sir?" she said; "I am no lunatic, I want you to know."

"I am not so sure o' that," responded the surly fellow; and added: "John, go for the superintendent, and tell him a strange creature is in our ward; and ask him what we shall do with the queer thing?"

Miss Armington trembled at this state of affairs, but she made up her mind to fight her way out, if she had to shoot a dozen.

The physician-in-chief and the superintendent both arrived at the spot where she had the conversation with the keepers, and seeing that they might surround her, she backed into a corner of the corridor near a door; and when the physician-in-chief ordered the men to secure her, she drew her revolver and cocked it, and said, defiantly:

"I'll shoot the first man that lays a finger on me; open the door and let me depart in peace."

"Who are you?" demanded the physician-in-chief.

"I am a sane person, who wishes to be let out of this place," she said.

"Seize the ruffian!" commanded the physician-in-chief, when the surly fellow made for her, but she shot him through his right arm, which scared the whole batch of them; and the trouble was how to get the stranger out of that corner.

"I have it," said the superintendent, silently, to the physician-in-chief; "I will go and cause that door by him to be opened, and make him believe that he may escape that way, when either you or I will grasp him from behind."

"All right," replied the physician-in-chief.

The door was opened, and Miss Armington saw what they were after, but she thought that very likely she could make her escape; therefore, she would go through the open door; but as she moved the keepers were upon her back, when she turned upon them and fired at the breast of the leader, but at that moment some one grasped her elbows behind her from the outside of the open door.

CHAPTER XLVII.

LUCINDA IS RE-ARRESTED BEFORE SHE ESCAPES.

THE superintendent's plan of opening the door proved a success; and as Miss Armington turned to fire, he grasped both her elbows from behind, which raised the pistol the moment it went off, and thereby missed hitting any one.

The superintendent at once took the revolver from her hand, and rather roughly handled the poor girl, when she said:

"You have gained the victory, and I will therefore yield honorably, like a whipped enemy; be so kind then as to let me rise."

By this time the physician-in-chief and the rest of the keepers, help and innocent lunatics gathered around her. The physician-in-chief at once recognized her face, when he ordered her to be removed to his private office, and directed the rest, except the superintendent and two managers, to attend to their business. After these four men and Miss Armington were locked into his private office, the physician-in-chief said:

"Well, young lady; how do you come by this male garb and pistol? I know you, Miss Armington."

"Miss Armington!" exclaimed one of the managers.

"Yes, Miss Armington in disguise," said the doctor; and added: "What do I see? Deacon Rob Stew's coat, hat and vest, or I mistake myself."

"Well, yes; I acknowledge they are his garments, which may give you some idea how I came by this graceful (?) disguise," said Miss Armington, with contempt.

"What! the deacon did not aid you to escape by disguising yourself in his clothes?" ejaculated the physician-in-chief, looking amazed as well as his comrades.

"No, sir; not exactly 'aid,' your excellency," tauntingly replied she.

"How, then, did you get his clothes and that pistol? Who gave you the pistol?" said the physician-in-chief.

"I do not know that I choose to be so closely catechised, unless you promise to give me my freedom, which I think I deserve after having gone to all this trouble," she said.

"You ask too much"—

"How so?" interrupted Miss Armington; "what have I ever done to deserve this confinement, and to be compelled to be continually insulted by that rascally old Deacon Stew?"

"What! you call him 'rascally,' when he has favored you with this disguise"—

"He has not 'favored' me," interposed she.

"Girl, you confound me," said the physician-in-chief; "did you not say that these were the deacon's garments, and that he gave them to you?"

"Yes, they were his garments, and he gave them to me; but now they are mine, for I have earned them by hard labor, and at the risk of womanly modesty," said she.

"Explain yourself," said he; "for instead of understanding you, I become more bewildered by your remarks."

"Do you?" tantalizingly responded Miss Armington.

"Yes, miss, you are a puzzle to me," said the physician-in-chief.

"Doctor, I am astonished at you," exclaimed the superintendent; "don't you see with half an eye that the creature is as crazy as a loon can be; come, let us lock her up, and attend to better business than trifling with her."

"Indeed, bah! you are a pretty fellow to be so wise as to pronounce me a lunatic. If I am crazy I'll wager my life against a dozen soft heads like yours, that I can outrival you in anything," haughtily replied Miss Armington; and continued: "You must not think, because you are clad with a little authority, that your august position raises you to manhood, a thing you do not possess."

"Come, come, this is more idle talking than if Miss Armington were insane, and we would amuse ourselves over her wanderings; and, therefore, I ask the superintendent to go and attend to better business," responded the physician-in-chief; and so saying he unlocked the office, when the superintendent left; but the other continued:

"Come, now, Miss Armington, please tell me where you got that pistol"—

"I got it also from Deacon Rob Stew," interrupted Miss Armington.

"When did you get it from him?" said he.

"Not an hour since," said she.

"Really, Miss Armington, you must be crazy," said the physician-in-chief.

"Ah, indeed; you, too, doubt my sanity. Do you want me to prove my soundness of mind and purpose to you in the presence of these strangers?" said she.

"Well, you astound me; but you have the deacon's

clothes, and I do not see how you got the pistol, unless he gave it to you; yet, I cannot understand whether he has proved false to you or us," said he.

"You did not answer my question; I said, 'did you want me to prove my soundness of mind and purpose to you in the presence of these strangers?' But, perhaps, they are familiar with the doings of this place," said Miss Armington.

"No, miss; it is useless for you to make that attempt, for we all know why you are in this institution; and as I cannot understand you, and you will not explain, I shall be compelled to return you to your old quarters," responded the physician-in-chief.

"I can assure you that I expected nothing better from *you*, and as these gentlemen are co-conspirators of yours and the holy deacon's, I cannot call upon them for succor or sympathy," haughtily said she.

"Madam," responded one of the managers, "you have my heartfelt sympathy."

"Then assist me to escape, or use your influence to have me released," she pled.

He dropped his head, and, with tears in his eyes, said:

"As cheerfully as I would do so of my own accord; yet am I powerless to aid you, unless you consent to become the deacon's wife."

"*Ah!* indeed; you too desire that; well, gentlemen, if such I may call you, I am ready to be conducted to my cell, where I will show you a fine specimen of a deacon," sneeringly said she.

"What! you did not murder him?" asked the physician-in-chief, terror-stricken.

"Oh! no, he is too mean, low and cowardly a thing to kill. He and his likes"—looking at them with a contemptuous frown—"better live a while yet, that they may see the glory of the noble hero, through whose instrumentality I am incarcerated and insulted; but, mark me, I feel it in my inmost soul that the tables will shortly turn, and then I may laugh at you, when you get your deserved reward," said she.

They conducted the disguised heroine back to her cell, but, lo, the horrible looking deacon, with blood-shot eyes, swollen head and almost suffocated, lying in one corner of the cell, dumbfounded the gentlemen, who at once relieved him of his effectual gag and shackles, and the physician-in-chief asked:

"How came this so?"

But there was no reply; because the deacon fainted, whilst Miss Armington smiled, and really seemed to enjoy the joke.

This enraged the physician-in-chief, and for the first time he threatened violence to Miss Armington, who coolly said:

"He only got his dues."

"He is dying," exclaimed the physician-in-chief, "and you are his murderer, young woman."

"Yes, in self-defence I subdued him, as any one would, and as I would do again," heedlessly said Miss Armington. Suddenly the saintly and hypocritical, opossum-acting deacon came to, and seeing the pistol in the hand of the physician-in-chief, he grasped it, and, rising to his knees, raised it and fired at Miss Armington, ejaculating furiously:

"You she-devil, die!"

CHAPTER XLVIII.

THE BLOODY CONSPIRATORS IN TERRIBLE FEAR OF DR. JUNO.

DEACON ROB STEW had two serious assaults made upon him close together, for almost as soon as he had recovered from his gunshot wound, which, however, was kept perfectly secret, he received the beating at Tabernacle Hall. The night when the sentinel and two or three brethren attempted to remove the annoying man at the outside of the door of the hall, and were overpowered by policemen and citizens, the sacredly secret conclave were thunderstruck when they saw the intruders, and Sister Nancy Clover, who had the floor, thought the world was coming to an end; but upon seeing that it was only a crowd of police officers and private citizens, she exclaimed in a loud and dignified voice:

"Gentlemen, and should-be guardians of the peace, what means this tumultuous intrusion upon the holy meditations of a docile and law-abiding religious people? By whose authority do you force your way into our sacred hall this hour of the night? I pause for an answer."

This womanly speech rather took the policemen back; but the citizens, it seemed, were not to be so easily silenced, when one of them said:

"Miss Nancy Clover, we have come here by the authority of one of the religious denominations, whose most prominent members know some of the black deeds that are transacted in this place, and who have suspicion that Deacon Rob Stew and Rev. Joe Pier have been foully dealt with by those who belong to this institution."

"Sir! do you know that these are serious charges, and that before you intrude yourselves in such a peculiar manner you should have proof to sustain yourselves? And now I ask you to produce your warrant and proofs for the purpose of sustaining this assault upon our sacred rights; and, if you cannot produce them, I order the brethren to use all the means in their power to eject you from this hall, if you go not voluntarily, as, I hesitate not, you came here. I again wait for an answer," said Nancy Clover, with authority and vim.

Silence reigned for several minutes, when the heroic sister continued:

"I am compelled to conclude that you were not lawfully authorized to intrude yourselves into this hall; therefore, I order you to depart instantly, or take the consequences."

"As we have no proof at hand"—

"Nor a warrant to arrest any one," interrupted Nancy Clover; "therefore, you would better leave instantly, and thank God and this brotherhood if you do not get your deserts for this breach of the peace."

"Never mind that, Miss Clover," continued the citizens' spokesman, "we may astonish you with proof some day very soon that will not be any too palatable to any of your bloody clique."

"Leave this instant, you miserable rioters; and, as for these policemen, they shall learn, through us, that it is not their duty to join a cut-throat mob like you to break the peace. Now, brethren, I order you to go to the armory and produce sufficient weapons to shoot these ruffians down like dogs, if they don't instantly go away and leave us in peace," said Nancy Clover.

In a moment twenty or thirty brethren were armed with rifles and bayonets, who waited for their orders from Sister Nancy Clover to fire or charge with bayonets upon the intruders. She said:

"Prepare to fire."

Like lightning the brethren aimed at the intruders, who now scampered away much faster than they came; and the bloody conspirators were master of their own ground, who felt gleeful over the victory they obtained. Sister Nancy Clover spoke as follows:

"Beloved saints, don't you see what unanimity of action, a bold face and undaunted courage do? These villains were evidently meaning mischief; but, what or how they happened to come here I cannot contrive. They were evidently suspicious that we had something to do with brothers Pier's and Stew's absence from the religious celebration; because nothing but sickness or death could keep these faithful saints from such a religious gathering.

"But, how did they know all about our secret work, for that man actually spoke as though he knew more than he ought to know. Can this demoniacal Dr. Juno have fathomed our brotherhood, and have spies on our track?

"It is a good thing that the deacon, as well as Brother Pier, is improving very rapidly, and will both soon be well, when this matter may be brought before the Court of Sessions ; however, it may be wiser not to agitate anything of this kind, but time will tell best what we would better do. I shall be too happy to have brothers Stew and Pier again with us, for counsel, and to aid our noble cause, which seems to be assailed in several new quarters."

At this part of the proceedings, the physician-in-chief of the insane asylum took the floor, and said :

"Mr. President and beloved saints, I am fully persuaded in my own mind, from what I have lately seen, that our enemies, through the instrumentality of Dr. Juno, are gaining ground upon us rapidly; and unless we fortify ourselves by renewed efforts in all directions, we shall surely be overpowered. I do not speak thus to discourage the brotherhood, but to rivet them closer together in thought, feeling and action, so that we will not have any more quarrels and fights amongst ourselves, which is like a house divided against itself, by depriving us of a power that we most need just now. It would astonish you to know how much trouble we have had with Miss Armington at the asylum, and the indomitable energy this young lady possesses; why, she has almost turned the head, the other week, of one of our most loyal managers ; and if she has that much influence with *our* best people, what a mighty auxiliary she would be to the cause of Dr. Juno, should she by any chance escape us !"

"Nonsense ; you certainly do not think it possible for her to escape, do you ?" asked Nancy Clover.

"Well, no ; but it is hard to tell what influence this innovator may bring to bear against us," said the physician-in-chief.

"But does he know that Miss Armington is in the asylum ?" ejaculated Sister Clover. "How could he know it ?"

"He knows more than some of us think," said he ; "but

I do not think he knows it, still I think he suspicions it; because he has been there himself."

"Dunner und blitzen, I tinks you bis a sed o' fools, to bis so skeert; mine Cot, I yust winch unzer decon whash bin vell," exclaimed Honson Teafel, for the first time.

CHAPTER XLIX.

LUCINDA DOFFS THE DEACON'S CLOTHES, AND THREATENS TO SHOOT THE CONSPIRATORS.

WHEN Miss Lucinda Armington was fired at by Deacon Rob Stew, when they returned her to her cell, he missed her; on account of his wounded arm he could not guide the revolver, therefore the bullet barely escaped the hip of the physician-in-chief, who was frightened out of a year's strength, and who exclaimed:

"I am confounded and confused at the state of things. What *is* the matter between you two, will either of you explain?"

Neither felt disposed to do so. The deacon felt ashamed and a little conscience-stricken, although one might suppose that his conscience was so perfectly seared that nothing could touch it; and Miss Armington was too dignified and insulted to gratify them by explaining what the reader already knows.

At last the old lover of this heroic damsel said:

"If you wish to know how all this came, I will tell you, after you restore to me my wearing apparel."

"What! have you given your clothes to her for the purpose of allowing her to escape in this disguise?" asked the physician-in-chief.

"No, indeed, I did not give them to her"—

"Yes, you did, coward," interrupted she.

"We—ll, yes, I did give them to her, but not voluntarily," stammered the deacon.

"I see now how it was," said one of the managers.

"Will you please darken this cell, and then compel her to give me my clothes? and after I am dressed, and ready to leave, I will tell you all about it," responded the deacon.

The cell was now darkened, and Miss Armington was requested to dismantle and convey her disguise to the owner of it. She said:

"Oh, gentlemen, do not fret yourselves about it, here are his trappings; and now I ask him to make a hasty retreat from my presence, or I'll make the old villain sweat before he gets away."

In a moment these militant lovers had their wardrobes arranged to a degree of chastity in the dark cell, when the deacon said:

"I am ready, give us light; but, O Lord, how my arm aches."

"Your arm?" responded the physician-in-chief, "what causes it to ache?"

"Why, this she-devil of a woman shot me through it," said he.

"How did she get the pistol?" asked one of the managers.

"Well, brothers, I am now ready to tell you all about it. I have been in the habit of visiting her, and she treated me so savagely that I feared she would do me personal violence sometime"—the men laughed at this, which displeased him.—"You may laugh, but I would as lief be housed up with a mad bull as with an infuriated she-devil like her." He gave her a fiendish look at this moment, which was responded with a glare from her eyes that *he* knew meant mischief. "Brothers, let us leave this cell, I will tell you all about this matter elsewhere," timidly said the deacon.

"I would rather you would tell us all in the presence of Miss Armington, as we should like to hear what she has to say to it," ejaculated the physician-in-chief.

"Will you then keep her safely away from me, for my arm is painful, and she may make an assault upon me, when I tell you all?" said he.

The men laughed again, and Miss Armington could scarcely keep from doing the same, but she wanted to frighten the old deacon, and cure him from venturing in the future into her cell.

"Go on, Brother Stew, we will warrant that she shall not touch you," replied the physician-in-chief.

"I have been to visit this woman occasionally on errands of real charity; in fact, I loved the girl, and would have taken her from this place and made her my own wife; therefore, you may know that I intended no harm," said the deacon; "but she abused me awfully, and the last visit preceding this one, she actually threatened my life"—

"Cowardly cut-throat, tell the whole of it," interrupted Miss Armington.

"Who has a right to speak?" continued the deacon, savagely. "Well, brothers, I made up my mind that hereafter, when I would visit this modest virgin, I would carry weapons of defence; therefore, I brought that revolver with me to-day"—

"How came she to possess it," interrupted one of the men.

"She took it from me as I was about to defend myself against a furious assault upon me. I should have shot her, undoubtedly, had she not knocked it from my hand, in less than the sparkle of an eye, and as quickly picked it up, and presented the muzzle of it to my breast, and vowed she would shoot me dead if I hesitated to obey her orders. I saw that she meant what she said, but still I thought she would not shoot so freely as she once used her fists upon me; but I misplaced confidence in her, which is proved by her firing a bullet through my right arm, on the least prevarication on my part to comply with her august orders. She vowed, after sending that bullet through my arm, that the next time I hesitated, when she asked me to do a thing, she would shoot me through the heart. Now, I am not a coward, but discretion "—

"Ha! ha! ha!" laughed Miss Armington, whilst she interrupted him, and gave him a terribly defiant look.

"Yes, laugh, you miserable she-devil; but the next time I have business with you, I will fix you so you cannot do any harm to me or any one else, mind that," said he. "I was going to say that, under certain circumstances, discretion was the better part of valor; therefore, I obeyed the fiend and ingrate, and trusted to Providence, and you see He has favored me "—here he gave her a look that meant victory—" as He always does the elect "—

"You will see whom 'He favors,' if you live a little longer," interrupted Miss Armington, considerably embittered and chopfallen.

"Never mind, my lady, I will be even with you yet," ejaculated the deacon; and continued: "But this she-devil was not satisfied with shooting through this arm, but ordered me immodestly to take off my coat, pants, vest and hat, and give them to her ladyship. I even hesitated a moment, when she raised the pistol to my breast, and, undoubtedly, would have fired had I not quickly obeyed; then she ordered me to tear a sheet to fragments and tie my own feet together, and make a loop and place my hands into it, when she had me secured as you have found me."

Miss Armington kept her eye upon the pistol, after the physician-in-chief took it from the deacon, and with a bound she grasped it, and jumped into the corner of her cell, and said, pointing the pistol toward the deacon's head:

"Now, leave speedily, all of you, or I will rid this world of a lot of the vilest cut-throats that ever breathed the breath of life."

CHAPTER L.

THE LEADING BLOODY CONSPIRATORS AT LOGGERHEADS.

QUICKLY the deacon moved toward the door and said:

"I will go; please put that pistol away!"

The physician-in-chief stepped forward toward Miss Armington and exclaimed:

"You certainly would not fire so imprudently?"

"Wouldn't I, then," she interrupted him, and instantly pointed the pistol at his face, when he dodged, and the party of conspirators left precipitately and bolted the doors behind, then repaired to the medical office, where the deacon asked the physician-in-chief to examine and dress his arm.

Afterwards they argued as follows:

"What will we do with this woman; she has that loaded revolver, and no one is safe to go to her cell whilst she has it?" said one of the managers.

"Ah!" responded the deacon; "you do not think it so funny to have a loaded pistol pointed at *your* heads; but, when I related my perilous adventure with this desperate girl, you thought it an excellent joke! I cannot see what has come over her; when she lived home with her father, she was a perfect lady; quiet, chaste, modest, kind and very polite, but now see what she is."

"You need not wonder at the change, for she has the general's blood in her, that never knew fear or favor in time of war, and our treatment toward the poor girl is desperate war," ejaculated the physician-in-chief. "How many loads does that revolver hold?"

"Six," replied the deacon, "but I only had five loaded."

"Let me see; how many shots have been fired since she took it from you?" asked one of the men.

"She fired three down stairs, one at the deacon, and the deacon one at her; that makes the five," said the physician-in-chief.

"Surely, if you are certain that she fired three times down stairs, the pistol must now be empty; therefore her threats were barren, but she as little knew that as we did," responded the deacon. "I am glad that I am safely away from where she is, and I do not know that I will ever risk my life in her presence again, unless I first chain her securely."

"Oh! Brother Stew, you would certainly not be so cruel as to do that," angrily interposed the sympathetic manager.

"Wouldn't I, then?" continued the deacon. "Well, I am not so sure but that I should be tempted to do anything to revenge myself on her, for the humiliation to which she has subjected me. She is a perfect devil! I never could have believed that the female lived who dared do as she did. I am astonished, angered and pleased with her heroism. Ye gods, what would not such a woman be worth as a wife! If I only *could* by some means gain her affections."

"Dear brother, never dream of gaining that lady's affections; because such stock as she would never forget the injury you have done her. Moreover, she is fired to redoubled energy by the love she bears that Dr. Juno. She is your life-long foe, and would send you to glory, rather than be happy with you, or even see you happy," ejaculated the physician-in-chief.

"I don't believe all you say; because if she had desired my death, she could have taken my life after she had me bound and gagged," said the pious Deacon Stew.

"She had other fish to fry; to escape was her ambition, and not to kill you; moreover, she believes that your conscience will prevent you from being happy, and she may have thought far enough to have doubted if she could escape, and she wants you to live, she said, to see you suffer by the vengeance that her lover will visit upon you," said the physician-in-chief.

"Bah!" responded the deacon; "the vengeance that her lover, the heretic Juno, will visit upon me I do not fear. Far distant is the day when he will have that satisfactory opportunity to wreak vengeance on me."

"Do not be too sure of that, dear brother," responded the sympathetic manager, "for Dr. Juno is making rapid strides toward gaining immense popularity."

"What! are you one of his sympathizers? Do you doubt our success in finally overcoming this innovator, and how dare you connive with him?" ejaculated the deacon.

"O my brave (?) deacon, who skulks from a little woman, you should not be quite so pompous and self-conceited; you do not now have me in Tabernacle Hall, where you are monarch of all you survey; but even there, some of these days you will get yourself taken down, mark my words," said the sympathetic manager, who was in love with Miss Armington.

"May the curse of the Almighty strike you deaf and dumb for this secession! You are a very dangerous man to be trusted with the secrets of our sacredly secret conclave, and I will see that your case will receive early attention; remember Harry Gossimer, the apostate!" furiously interposed Deacon Stew.

"Gentlemen, or brothers, this is neither the time nor place to discuss and quarrel over matters that are part and parcel of our conclave and holy cause; therefore I charge you, be silent and do not fight amongst yourselves, or surely the downfall of our house is not far in the distant," responded the physician-in-chief.

"It is my duty to chastize any renegade brother who has taken our solemn oath and is familiar with all the inner workings of our cause; and this sympathizer of the Juno crowd must be summarily handled, or surely the sainthood will suffer through his apostasy," exclaimed the deacon.

"Better be moderate, Brother Stew," said the physician-in-chief, which aggravated the domineering deacon, when he said:

"Well, I shall require an explanation at our next meeting at Tabernacle Hall, concerning the peculiar conduct of both of you; and as for Miss Armington, I will pay her another visit before long, and show her my power; there is something going on that I cannot comprehend," said the deacon.

"I should not wonder but you could not comprehend the brow-beating and personal chastisement that the little lady up stairs gave you. You want something similar some of these days, by the brethren, to show you your proper place, you cowardly tyrant," ejaculated the sympathetic manager.

The deacon was fairly foaming at his mouth with rage; but what could he do with his lame arm, except grin and bear the insults that he received in this asylum? It will be remembered that at the following meeting, as already described, the deacon and Rev. Joe Pier got a solid beating, which was partly caused by the sympathetic manager, and which nearly cost the pious deacon's life for his temerity.

These brethren parted with rather conflicting sentiments and bitter feelings toward each other, a thing that must have pleased the guardian angels of Dr. Juno and company.

CHAPTER LI.

NANCY CLOVER LECTURING DEACON STEW.

DEACON ROB STEW and Rev. Joe Pier were confined three weeks in the secret chamber of Tabernacle Hall, suffering from the terrible beating that the saintly brethren dealt them so generously, without money and without price.

The deacon suffered immensely; was delirious and in agony for several days, and when he came to his senses again Sister Nancy Clover had several quiet discussions with him, in which she counselled him to be more moderate and cautious in his deportment toward the saints, otherwise he would prove the worst enemy to the cause, by being over-zealous and too severe.

He did not feel disposed to agree with his beloved Sister Nancy Clover, and said:

"You are like all the rest, giving me advice that is not sought for; therefore, I do not value it; hence, shall not heed it. If you folks had our holy cause as much at heart as I have, you would be equally zealous in promulgating its advancement, and quite as severe on delinquents, backsliders and apostates as I am."

"Brother Stew," said the sister, "you are mistaken in your logic and the course you are pursuing. You cannot drive intelligent and heroic minds as you can the lower classes of the sainthood. You should be old enough to know that, in a project like ours, a great deal of policy, in the shape of a little flattery, is necessary to cause an energetic unanimous action. Cannot you see that this beating, that you and Brother Pier received, was caused by the spite the brethren had against you, for being so terribly rigid with them? Had you used a little more soft soap instead, neither you nor Joe Pier would have had any need to suffer from the terrible bruises you have received."

"If your logic is correct," said he, "why did they strike Brother Pier, he never was severe on any of them, but as mild as mush and milk, and as easily scared as a child of five years?"

"But on account of being afraid of you, he invariably enforced your commands, contrary to his own convictions, which caused them to despise him, instead of hating him as they did you. Since you have been lying sick in this place, I have lectured to the brethren in such a manner as to cause them to be a unit again, and they are now all friendly toward both you and Brother Pier. I therefore pray *you* to take my advice; and when you come before them again be resolute and determined, but more conciliatory than you were before, when you will strengthen the bonds of sainthood, and cause a powerful unanimous co-operation with the whole religious world," said Nancy Clover.

"My beloved sister," said he, "I must acknowledge that you are the best and wisest strategist living; therefore, I will most heartily and thankfully carry out your excellent advice. You must have labored hard and suffered much since that night of the fight."

"You are right, I have done all that, but I never find it hard to conciliate the sainthood; however, I use policy, and by shrewd flattery and common sense appeals to the disturbed minds, I am always capable of exercising an influence that works favorably in carrying out the plans in anticipation. Probably you have noticed this on several occasions," responded Nancy Clover.

"Yes, beloved saint, I have seen it, and had it not been for you and your wise counsel our sacredly secret conclave would have gone to ruin long before this time. You really are an angel, worth ten thousand butterflies like the modest, fashionable women of our age. I admire a woman that can act her part dauntlessly in life's great conflict. There are only two females on this earth, that I am acquainted with, whom I admire. You are the one, and Miss Lucinda Armington is the other," seriously said the deacon.

"Bah!" exclaimed Sister Nancy Clover, with a contemptuous sneer on her countenance, "what do you see in her to admire? She is a poor, weak, silly fool of a chit, and I am astonished at you to admire the one that despises you, and is your mortal enemy."

"I cannot help admiring and loving the little imp," said the deacon; "because she has the mettle of a heroine, and fire of an infuriated tigress; noble qualities in a woman, if she knows how to use them, as Miss Armington does."

"Indeed," ejaculated Nancy Clover; "and when and where did you detect all these excellent qualities in that despicable creature? It must have been since we had her carried to the asylum."

"Certainly; it has been since she is confined in the asylum," said the deacon.

He now related his adventures with Miss Armington, with which the reader is familiar, when Sister Nancy said:

"So you admire and love the character of a woman who can work her own way through calm and storm? Well, brother, I admire *you* for having so much good sense, for it would be better for the race of mankind if women would learn to stand upon their own legs—I mean their own inalienable rights—and although I hate Miss Armington, because she is our enemy, yet I nevertheless think more of her for having thrashed you, and also for that most ludicrous exchange of apparel. Really, beloved brother, the latter incident seems very ludicrous to me, although it may have been almost death to you; yet, as you admire the heroine, for such she is, in spite of everything, you must look upon it in the same light that I do."

"Truly, dear sister," responded the deacon, "I often laugh to myself about the ridiculous picture I must have made. If any one could have seen the whole affair, he would, undoubtedly, have enjoyed it amazingly at my expense, as the boys did at the bull-frogs."

"How was that?" said she.

"Did you never hear that story? Several boys were throwing stones at the frogs, which was fun for them, but death to the frogs."

"Surely, your case was not unlike the frogs, and you were a lucky frog to have gotten off so easily," said Sister Clover.

"Yes, dear sister; but you know that the Lord always favors His elect; and, although I have received several assaults recently, you can readily see the finger of Jehovah each time pointing to my side, which saved my life in the most perilous conflicts, and I have unbounded faith that God will protect me on any occasion," exclaimed the deacon.

"Do not be too sure of all that, good brother; for although my faith in God and in our holy cause is equal to anybody's, yet there are certain fixed laws which He has made, and which we are ordained to learn and obey, else we cannot stand erect and safe in life or death," said she.

"Hut-tut! dear sister, do you know that you are advocating Dr. Juno's cause when you speak that way? I hope you are unlike one of the managers of the insane asylum, who was a great admirer of Miss Armington, and is evidently in sympathy with this heretic," ejaculated the deacon.

"Truth is mighty, Brother Stew," said she, "but I will not commit myself in public or before the sainthood, as you did, to receive a furious pummeling," laughed she.

"Really, you are a trump; say or do what I will, you always catch me in some corner, which plainly shows that you are the better man of us two; therefore, I shall heed your excellent advice now and in the future," exclaimed the deacon.

Brother Joe Pier came into the room, when the conversation was changed.

CHAPTER LII.

LUCINDA BITES DEACON STEW'S EAR NEARLY OFF.

WHEN Deacon Rob Stew, the physician-in-chief and managers were suddenly driven out of Miss Armington's cell, by the handsome manœuvre of the young heroine with the empty pistol, the deacon was determined to pay her a visit as soon as convenient, some evening, when he could bribe a few of the keepers to handcuff her for him, then *surely* he would be master over the proud and fearless girl, however, he did not expect that he would be so roughly handled by his own people before he would have the pleasure of treating himself to a coercive interview with Miss Armington.

As soon as he was right well again, he made his evening visit to the asylum, and bribed George and William to join him at eight o'clock that evening, to go with him to her cell ; and said he to them :

"I have a pair of excellent handcuffs here, which I want you to put securely on her wrists, joining her hands behind her back, so that she cannot strike me with them ; and be sure that you graduate them so she cannot slip them off ; by this screw you can make them larger or smaller, and when you have done it, come out, and I will go in to her, and when I have done with her, I will come out and let you go in and remove the cuffs again. I also want you to turn the gas on her cell, and light a glimmer, so I can have light, should I desire it ; now go in, seize and handcuff her."

"But, should she scream, and we be detected ?" responded one of them.

"Never mind," said his deaconship, "she will not scream, she is not of that sort ; but she may fight you like an infuriated demon ; therefore, do not give her an idea of your intentions until you have an opportunity to grasp her hands."

"Oh, never fear," said George ; "we understand how to handle *strong* lunatics ; why should we hesitate or fail to manage a weak lady like her ?" laughing at the absurdity of such caution by the deacon.

"All right," interposed the deacon, "only you secure her before you come out of her cell. One thing more ; she has that revolver in her possession, with which she shot at some of you several weeks since ; but it is empty, of this I assure you, therefore, should she threaten to shoot you with it, be not afraid of that."

"Enough," ejaculated they simultaneously, and made their ingress to her presence.

The pure and innocent maiden was sitting by her table, with her elbows resting upon it, and her hands to her face, whilst her eyes were turned toward the skylight overhead, from which the light of day still caused a glimmer to descend into her cell. Suddenly she heard the presence of George and William, when she sprang to her feet and ejaculated:

"Who's there? and what do you want at this unseasonable hour of the day?"

They advanced toward her without saying a word, when she said, fiercely:

"Stop, or I'll shoot you!"

"Your threats are barren, for your pistol is empty; we know what we are about," exclaimed George, and fearlessly advanced, when she dealt him a blow with the heavy revolver that sent him spinning like a wheel; William now tried his hand, when he also received a dangerous blow on the top of his head, which struck him dumb to the floor. Having thus disabled her enemies, she boldly stood still, preparing herself for a second blow, should they advance again; in a few moments George scrambled up and said:

"Miss Armington, we do not wish to harm you, nor did we come here of our own accord to insult you; but we were ordered here"—

"Who ordered you, and what to do?" interrupted the heroine in a defiant air.

Silence reigned for several minutes, when a deep groan came from the place where William lay, when George said:

"You have killed him!"

"What is that to me? and I kindly tell you, unless you leave me, I *will* kill you both, mark me!" said she.

The deacon heard that a terrible scuffle was going on inside of the cell, when he opened the outside door, however, carefully allowing the inner-gate to remain locked; he saw William sitting on the floor in a position as though he was going to rise to his feet, but was unable to do so; George was standing in front of William, parleying with Miss Armington, whose back was turned toward the door.

The deacon now made a noise as if he was going to come in, which caused Miss Armington to turn partly around, and when she saw some one coming she felt lost, as she could not guard before and behind herself; therefore, she expected to be overpowered, but she made up her mind to warm the monsters before they should secure her. As she turned toward the door, George grasped both her arms from behind, which made her almost powerless; still, she tussled a good while with him before he succeeded in handcuffing her.

She knocked his handcuffs twice to the floor, and had not William been able to put the first one on, he probably never would have gotten them on. William was still stupefied, and it was all he could do to fasten the cuff on her delicate wrist; of course, when this first arm was secured, George had an easy time to fasten the second one, which, when done, he let go of the young lady's person. When the deacon saw this he asked:

"Have you handcuffed her securely?"

"Yes," replied George.

"Then I will come in," said he.

"Oh! you most miserable coward, I thought it was your pusillanimous work," ejaculated the persecuted young lady.

"Truly, miss, I made up my mind to be even with you," said the deacon, and giving the boys orders to leave, he closed the door, whilst all this time Miss Armington was very docile, acting as though she would submit to anything almost. She thought:

"I'll throw the pious coward off his guard, until I see an opportunity to punish him."

The saintly deacon now began to abuse her; he blackguarded her; said that he thought he would get her in a position that he could easily manage her, as he now had her; that he intended to often visit her this hour of the night, when he could have the services of the men to handcuff her for him, and, continued he:

"I mean to use you just as I please, since you refuse to become my wife; however, I will again say that if you will voluntarily marry me, I will not force you to become as good as my wife; now choose between the two, for I shall conquer you."

"Do you think so?" said she.

"I *know* so," interposed his holiness, "for the Lord is always on the side of His elect."

At this moment he placed his arm around her waist and pulled her to his breast, she submitting gracefully, only she turned her face aside, when he kissed her on the cheek; suddenly she took his long ear into her mouth, and bit it until the deacon fairly yelled, "Murder! murder!"

CHAPTER LIII

DR. JUNO'S STIRRING SPEECH TO THE "SECRET ORDER OF NATURALISTS."

R. VICTOR JUNO promised to lead his men through these devils' ground, and on the night of meeting for that purpose, he spoke to the brothers of the "Order of Naturalists," as follows:

"DEAR BROTHERS:—You all know what is incumbent upon every one of us in these troublous times. When the leaders of piety meet in secret conclave continually, for the purpose of subjugating those who behold God in Nature, and who recognize Nature to be the language through and by which an Infinite, Beneficent and Immutable Creator speaks to us in scientific 'arts,' it is time that we gird on the armor, not only of defence, but of aggression.

"We have been stigmatized by these *bloody conspirators*

as heretics, infidels, obscene libellists, seducers of innocent women, cheats, profaners of the 'temple of God,' and, in sooth, epithets and acts have been heaped upon us in public, private, by pen, tongue, muscle and the knife; yea, dungeons and their concomitants were made the recipients of our bodies, whilst we were robbed of every right that is inalienable to man and beast; therefore, as we have never taught nor practised anything that would injure or defile body, soul or spirit of friend or foe, young or old, male or female, the time has arrived for us to act bravely in the aggressive, until we strike terror to the hearts of these vile leaders of the blind, whom these comparatively few demons lead on to the work of dividing and subdividing the holy Church of God, until hosts of mean, bigoted sectarians claim to be the elect of God, when they are the followers of *false prophets, false Christs, blind leaders*, and by deceiving themselves, are made the tools of the veriest cutthroats that ever disgraced God's footstool.

"I ask each one of you then: Do we love *our* scientific, progressive, teachings and an infallible Creator as much as these vile *vipers* do their master—the devil—and his work? Do we fear them who can destroy the body, but cannot harm the soul of the just? Do we assume to be men, whilst we permit these serfs of the devil to usurp all power on earth, or will we strike for our rights, our homes, God and fixed law?

"These few leading conspirators misguide and jeopardize the lives of the millions, who believe them to be the oracles of heaven, when they are the very ones who rob them of the knowledge of God's fixed laws, deprive them of natural, Christian freedom, and use them as the veriest dupes to carry out their own hellish work, whilst they have no more love for them than imps have for angels.

"I have thousands of times lain in my bed wondering how it was possible for these pharisaical leaders to hold the sincerely inclined religious people in such ignorance of God's hallowed laws, and in bondage to sectarian monopoly. God is generous. Jesus was generous. Nature is bountiful, and by uniting all the sound sense that is contained in the Bible, we must conclude as rational creatures that salvation must be the acme of all the 'arts and sciences;' but, yet, the examples and precepts of Christ, who was the alpha and omega of obedience to fixed natural law, are as nothing to the sectarian Christians.

"Let us worship God as much as possible as Jesus did, by 'good works,' which centre in the improvement of the race, the amelioration of those whom we are commanded to love as ourselves; and let us comprehend that we cannot carry out that holy injunction until we make natural the habits of the whole people; yes, physiology must become the catechism of the nations.

"Brothers, there were three kinds of slavery, two of which still exist, that must be abolished before our cause can have free scope:

"*First*,—and least, was Negro Slavery.

"*Second*,—Social—including Marital and Sectarian Slavery; and

"*Third*,—and worst, Slavery to the Eating, Drinking, Sexual and *Filthy Lucre* Propensities.

"The least of these three slaveries has been abolished by the sword, the next to the least is the slavery of the wife to her husband, who must bear his embraces, children, obey him, but does not belong to herself nor own the property that she earns with her own hands, yet she must nourish his children at her own breast and feed them, whilst the man may be slave to rum, tobacco, licentiousness, etc.; but the same selfish sectarian spirit that sanctions this social serfdom also enthrals its misled victim; but the slavery that the 'Order of Naturalists' aim to abolish is the king of slavery, because it undermines the constitutions of the race so gradually that few can be made believe that it defiles the 'temple of God;' deteriorates the blood, rots or petrifies the bodily tissues, thereby scientifically hardening the heart, causing the spirit of selfishness, and the propensities of men, women and children to master the moral nature of the race, whose love is so cold on account of this worst kind of slavery!

"Therefore, our cause, which is so offensive to the *bloody conspirators* and their followers, strikes at the root of all evil, which, when understood and adhered to, will abandon, of its own free accord, the lesser evils, and give each person capacity to master his own spirit, when he and she will become *bona fide* legislators or voters, and through love to God and mankind will govern everything with an eye single to God's glory; thus, the Millennial dawn will appear, and the *Image of God* will be substituted for the image of the devil, or image of ugliness and disease; and love will be free amongst the inhabitants of the earth, who will be

> "'Slave to no sect, that takes no private road,
> But looks through nature up to nature's God;
> Pursues that chain which links th' immense design,
> Joins heaven and earth, and mortal and divine;
> And knows where faith, law, morals all *began*,
> All *end* in love to God, and love to man!'

"In conclusion, brethren, let me reiterate that with these Christ-like sentiments and right on our side, we are clad in the armor of heaven; hence, knowing that we are right, we can fight to the hilt, if it be necessary to do so, to abolish the worst of slavery! The genuine Christian will always sacrifice the good of the few for the many; will sacrifice himself, if necessary, for the cause of God and his wonderful works and fixed laws; therefore, when we meet the foe to-night, and danger stares us in the face, remember that 'our cause it is just, and this be our motto, in God is our trust?' and the banner of freedom in triumph shall wave when our work is completed through God's power in the brave; then, onward and upward, let your prayer of might be a bugbear of death to the *bloody conspirators* until they are ousted from their lofty (?) reign of terror, and are *made* to respect God's fixed law of nature, or are degraded and banished from the field of human life!"

CHAPTER LIV.

DR. JUNO MOBS THE INSANE ASYLUM AND FREES LUCINDA.

PRECISELY at nine o'clock Dr. Juno started with his one hundred drilled men, who were armed to their teeth, in squads, for the Insane Asylum. He told them that he would stay with the leading company, and after one of them would gain access to the outer gate of the asylum he would march his squad speedily into the yard, bind and gag the gate-keeper, or whoever else would be there; a signal would be given to the rest to follow, afterwards he would general them as he thought it best!

They reached the outer gate at half-past nine, and entered it easily, and after securing the keeper at that post, and the whole regiment was admitted, Dr. Juno ordered six men to guard that place, when he marched with his company or squad toward the principal door of the main building; the same had already been locked for the night; the bell was rung gently, which caused an old drowsy fellow to open it abruptly, and asked:

"Who rings the bell this time of night? This is not the door to receive insane folks."

"Is it not?" said Dr. Juno, and added, "Seize him," which also meant gag and bind him. This door was guarded by two men, and after twenty-five active brethren were inside, the doctor ordered a captain to take the balance of the men and guard the outside building, permitting no one to enter or escape short of the penalty of death, and to be ready, should a signal be given, for their attendance inside!

The doctor now said to his men:

"I think we had better secure the officers of the asylum *first*, and imprison them by bolting them securely in cells, or use ropes on them ; where is Thomas, who is acquainted with this whole establishment ?"

"Here I am, brother," said he.

"Show us to the officers' apartments," responded Dr. Juno.

In an instant they stood before the physician-in-chief's office, which was lit up, and upon a knock on the door, a sharp voice asked:

"Who is there?"

"I am here," replied Thomas, who imitated the voice of one of the keepers, whom he knew.

"Wait a moment until I unbolt the door," said the physician-in-chief.

In a moment the office was filled with soldiers, when the physician-in-chief reached for a bell-pull and asked:

"Who are you, and what means this intrusion?"

"Not so fast, sir," said Dr. Juno ; "it is not necessary for you to pull that bell, neither is it necessary to tell you who I am. I am no ways disguised, like some of my enemies, when they are on errands of deviltry. We are here on an errand of justice and mercy. Not to harm any one, if we can obtain what we came for voluntarily; but if resistance is made, we shall kill those who come in our path like vermin ; mark me!" authoritatively spoke Dr. Juno.

"You are Dr. Juno," said the prisoner ; "but what is your pleasure?"

"We want Miss Lucinda Armington!" commanded Dr. Juno.

"Miss Lucinda Armington!" ejaculated the prisoner, feigning surprise. "I cannot give you what I have not got *to* give."

"Here, old viper, none of that," said Dr. Juno ; "gag and bind the villain, and see that you handle him rigidly, for the old rogue shall learn how it feels to be a prisoner, for his lying."

"Murder! mur—" cried he, but before he got it out the second time, a piece of an old rag was jammed into his gustatory apartment. They let him lie on the floor of his office, left it and locked the door and took the key.

"Lead on, Thomas, in the direction of the rest of the officers," commanded Dr. Juno. Soon they arrived at the general office, where the business of the asylum is issued from, and there they met four of the night officials, who were always on the alert for danger.

Dr. Juno spoke in a commanding manner:

"Gentlemen, we want you to surrender yourselves peaceably as prisoners of war, when no harm shall befall you."

"We are not so sure of that, my brave hero," said an impudent voice, who jerked the alarm bell immensely, which was as quickly replied to by Dr. Juno, who said to his men:

"The half of you will take care of the outsiders, and the balance charge upon these men !"

The man that sounded the alarm and spoke, opened a table drawer, and took a revolver therefrom, which he levelled at Dr. Juno's heart; but, before he could fire, Dr. Juno gave him a terrific blow with his huge fist on the temple, which levelled *him*, and in a minute every man was securely done up, as was the fashion.

The outside men, however, did not succeed so well, as their numbers were in the minority as compared with the keepers and general help of the place; but as soon as Dr. Juno made his appearance on the spot, he said:

"Soldiers, fire upon any one who makes any advances !"

This caused an inclination to create a stampede. When Dr. Juno saw this, he again ordered:

"Any man that moves to leave the place, shoot him dead also !"

All stood still and trembled with terror; Dr. Juno saw this, and said:

"You are the hired servants of this hell-hole, and I want you to understand that we will not harm you, if you obey my orders; but if you refuse, you may meet your

God quickly for disobeying me, for I am hard-hearted and will be observed."

"What do you wish us to do?" asked one.

"I want you all to surrender yourselves," said Dr. Juno, "and show us an apartment wherein we can securely imprison you for a short period."

"Take us to the main cell, which is empty," said the same prisoner.

They were all conducted into that cell, which was first inspected by Dr. Juno as to its security. After they had entered, Dr. Juno asked them :

"Have you got the key to Miss Armington's cell, in the third story?"

Silence reigned, and no one seemed to answer, when he continued :

"Do you refuse to speak? I want you to understand that I will not show you any quarters, provided you resist me by word or deed; therefore, answer instantly, who has that key?"

"I have," exclaimed a burly fellow; "here it is."

CHAPTER LV.

MEETING OF VICTOR AND LUCINDA IN HER CELL.

IT was George who had the key, and who gave it to Dr. Juno, when they bolted the cell doors and left three soldiers to guard the prisoners.

One of the keepers escaped the vigilance of Dr. Juno, and passed around through another corridor to the physician-in-chief's office, with the intention of arousing an alarm; but when he got to the office door, he found it locked; he then called, knocked and listened betimes, when he heard a muffled voice saying: .

"I am locked in; get a key and come in."

He tried his keys, and found that one of them unlocked the door; he rushed to the spot where the prisoner lay, and, removing his shackles, said:

"Heaven! doctor, all the keepers and help are arrested and imprisoned in the *main cell;* what shall *we* do?"

"You leave the asylum by the rear gate, and arouse the neighborhood, and be sure you do it quickly; in the meantime I will see what I can do," said the physician-in-chief.

Very foolishly the guards, who were left to protect all the bound, gagged and locked-up prisoners, paid no attention to the doctor's office, esteeming the physician-in-chief safe enough for as long as they cared for his incarceration; but they missed it a little in this conclusion.

Dr. Juno, after receiving the key to Miss Armington's cell, asked Thomas to lead the way to it; and when the lover speedily threw the doors, four in number, open, and appeared in Miss Armington's presence, what should he see but a demon inclining over the poor girl, who was all bloody; Dr. Juno hurled him aside as though he were a flea, and picked the prostrate prisoner and beloved of his soul up from the floor and laid her gently on the bed, thinking that she was dead; but he soon saw signs of life reappearing, and in a few minutes she asked:

"O God, where am I?" and screaming with all her might: "Go away, you fiend, or I'll murder you yet!"

Dr. Juno kissed her on the forehead, and exclaimed:

"My precious darling, your own betrothed is by your side; fear nothing."

She opened her eyes with amazement, and hysterically stammered:

"Great God, is i—t y—o—u? O let this not be a dream! I pray, I pray, great Father, let this not be a dream that will vanish with the awakening of my slumbers!"

"No, no, my precious one, it is not a dream, but a *bona fide* reality," ejaculated Dr. Juno, with immense tears in his eyes, whilst he dropped his face upon her neck and wept like a child, until he shook from head to foot. Miss

Armington came to realize that her own beloved Victor was holding her in his own dear arms, when she exclaimed:

"Where is Deacon Stew?"

"What!" thundered Dr. Juno, whilst he sprang away from the young lady, and grasped the bloody deacon in his hands, and dashed him upon the floor like a dog, whilst he was just going to jump upon his face with his heels, when Miss Armington said:

"O Victor, come here."

When he went to her, she replied:

"Do not murder him, my dear Victor, leave him to heaven, and the wrath of his Maker."

"Darling, your opportune words have saved his miserable life; but what has he done to you that you are so bloody?"

"The blood that you see on me came from *his* body, not from mine," said she. "He had me handcuffed, and then he insulted me"—

"What! handcuffed you?" interrupted he.

"Yes, and they hurt my wrists severely; please remove them, dear Victor."

"Great heaven! you handcuffed, and I not see it; what a stupid fellow I am," said Victor; "but I will murder this foul demon; soldiers, bind him like a felon, place his hands uncomfortably behind his back; look, like this poor young lady's are, only make them tighter, so he may receive his reward."

"Have you the keys to these handcuffs, old hypocrite?" asked Dr. Juno of the deacon.

"No, sir, I—I h—a—v—e not," stammered he.

"Who, then, has got them? Be quick, or you'll die on the spot," exclaimed Dr. Juno.

"George has got them," responded the deacon.

"George is the man who gave you the cell keys," said Thomas to Dr. Juno.

"Oh, yes; he gave me a bunch of keys; I guess he was wise enough to have added the cuff keys; let me see; here they are, I think; yes, all right my darling, free once more from the shackles of these *bloody conspirators*, who shall be tortured nigh unto death, but shall yet live to feel their degradation, whilst they writhe in agony," ejaculated Dr. Juno.

"Mercy, O mercy! be merciful!" prayed the deacon.

"Merciful! ha! ha! ha! merciful to you; to you, a fiend, a carrion monster, a cut-throat, a ravisher of innocent helpless women; you dare to ask for mercy at my hands again, and I will cut you to pieces by slow degrees, and cauterize every incision, you infamous dare-devil, or rather leprous coward. May the double curse of God fall on your pestiferous head," exclaimed Dr. Juno, with terrific emphasis.

A noise was heard down stairs, when Dr. Juno continued:

"We will away from this place. Soldiers, take this scab on decent people—the deacon (?)—to my office, but gag him before you remove him"—

"I pray you, do not gag me; I will keep silent, come what will or may, if you do not gag me," stammered the deacon.

"Silence, old ruffian; men of your stamp are never to be trusted; I know you too well. I know of too many foul deeds that you were ringleader or commander of, so gag the fine (?) deacon (?), and load him on the express wagon, and haul him direct to my office, and six of you guard him there until I come. Here, take these handcuffs with you, I shall use them on him as a memory-strengthening plaster for the pious (?) deacon," responded Dr. Juno.

At this moment a soldier came up stairs, and said to Dr. Juno:

"General Juno, the physician-in-chief, whom you had gagged and bound, has disappeared, and another man escaped from the asylum by a back entrance; I am afraid they may arouse the neighborhood, and give us trouble."

CHAPTER LVI.

DR. JUNO OFFERS AMNESTY TO THE CONSPIRATORS.

DOCTOR JUNO and his regiment left the asylum about one o'clock A. M., without any trouble, with the exception that he did not get to see the physician-in-chief, to whom he intended to give some sound advice before he would free him; however, he gave it to the four night managers, who still continued in fetters, with the exception of the gags. They were removed for the purpose of taking the oath that Dr. Juno proposed. He spoke to them as follows:

"You belong to this fine orthodox hell-hole, and undoubtedly are members of the *sacredly secret conclave* of the *bloody conspirators*, and therefore I hold you as my mortal enemies; hence, expect no mercy from me, but instantly answer me such questions as I shall ask you;" pointing to each separately, he continued: "Are *you* a member of that *secret conclave?*"

"I am," said one.

"Are you one also?" asked Dr. Juno of another.

"I shall not answer that question," said the one now addressed.

"You will not answer, indeed! But I think you will, and I will give you half a minute to do so by my watch," responded Dr. Juno, holding his watch in his hand: "No answer, the half a minute is up; soldiers, use the tormentors on this scoundrel until he is ready to answer."

The soldiers applied three tormentors to him, which consisted of thin ropes with handles to the ends; the ropes were put around a limb, and then twisted by the handles until the victim cried enough or died. Whilst the soldiers were torturing the stubborn man, the doctor asked the remaining two whether they belonged to the said conclave, who freely answered in the affirmative. The torments acted like a charm upon the stubborn man, who said that he did *not* belong to said conclave.

"I do not believe you!" said Dr. Juno, "and I tell you now, for once only, that I will brook no lying from any man, friend or foe; for if you lie, in saying that you do not belong to said conclave, and after I ascertain from these men that you *do* belong, I will torture you worse than for anything else."

"Then I'll speak the truth; I *do* belong to the conclave," said he.

"So I thought," responded Dr. Juno. "Remove the tormentors; and now let me warn each one of you not to be rebellious, but answer me in everything truthfully, for I shall ask you many questions only to try your veracity; questions that I know, if true or not; also, do as I command. As you are ready to hear my advice, I charge you to be attentive, that you may hear and understand what I say to you, else your own lives may be made to pay the penalty of your recklessness.

"This advice is for your *own* good, and is nothing of a secret order, therefore be not alarmed; but act like men of honor, and turn from error. You are undoubtedly aware that both myself and Miss Lucinda Armington have been abducted, some time since, and were cast into this charnel-house by your bloody clique; and you must also know that Miss Armington was still confined within these walls until this present moment.

"I came here to liberate her, not to injure you, nor for the purpose of revenging myself; but to serve God and my fellow-creatures; to save even your own souls and bodies from further degradation and despair; and whilst I am compelled to be cruel to the perverse and prejudiced, I am nevertheless ready to receive the vilest penitent sinner to my ranks, and would rejoice were I capable to save every *bloody conspirator;* however, such men as Deacon Rob Stew and your physician-in-chief are very self-righteous and hardened sectarian blasphemers, who must be severely dealt with to bring them to their true sense of understanding things ; but I may say to you that whilst my summary punishment of yourselves is severe, and may seem no better than that which was heaped upon myself, Miss Armington, Harry Gossimer, Jemmy and others by your clique; still, the object is different.

"I visit chastisement upon you and my enemies, not from jealousy, malice, selfishness or worldly power, but for the purpose of abolishing a crying evil! For the purpose of saving mankind from the yoke of partisan and sectarian bondage ; that love to God and mankind may rule his kingdom in accordance with the generous teachings of Jesus and the infallibility of nature's laws; therefore I offer you, even you, my bitter enemies and prisoners, the same boon of salvation that I claim for myself, and if you will repent of what is past, and turn from the error of your ways, and join God's rational Christians, we will welcome you with open hearts and hands, as our precious Master, Christ Jesus, pardoned and accepted sinners who forsook their evil ways, and took up their cross and followed him!

"To me it makes no difference whether you and your bloody clique publish to the world what has this night transpired in this place or not; because, if you do so, it will cause a speedy *exposé* of your own deviltry, and prove to the world that I have been the friend to humanity, whilst you persecuted me to your utmost capacity for serving God and mankind!

"I now ask you to repeat the following oath, which you dare not violate ; but before I will propose it I am willing to pause for a moment, for the purpose of learning from you if either or all of you have made up your minds to forsake these bloody conspirators ; therefore, speak ?"

"I would be willing to do so, but I was compelled to take the *solemn oath* of the said conclave, which is awful, and it would be dangerous for any member to violate it, independent of the hereafter," responded the man who first said he belonged to said conclave.

"You must bear in mind that God will forgive anything that the penitent man will ask by returning to '*good works;*' by ceasing to do evil and learning to do right; and as for the danger to your own life, I would also have you to know it is tenfold greater in the place you stand now than it would be were you to discard the shackles of demoniacal serfdom and become a free man!" ejaculated Dr. Juno.

"Will you give me time to think over this matter?" asked he.

"Yes, sir, your own time; but I shall now ask each of you to separately pronounce the oath after me: 'I, ———— ————, solemnly swear, without mental reservation, that I will never more conspire against the followers of Dr. Juno, nor against him personally, so help me God! And further, should I ever be found to do so, I will not ask for mercy, but receive my reward according to the deeds committed in the body, and this I solemnly swear by my body, soul and spirit! May the Lord help me to keep this vow! Amen.'

"Now, misled brothers, farewell; but be kind enough to acquaint your leaders of what has transpired, and tell them that this advice is also meant for each of them!"

CHAPTER LVII.

LUCINDA FREE AND AT HER OWN HOME AGAIN.

AFTER Dr. Juno had finished his lecture to the four prisoners, he conveyed Miss Lucinda Armington to a carriage in waiting for this purpose, and carried her to her own old home, which was still in possession of Pat O'Conner and Judy McCrea; and when he reached the house he ordered the footman to ring the bell and arouse the servants. Shortly after causing several strong pulls upon the door-bell, Pat O'Conner ran his head out at a second-story window and exclaimed:

"Who bees thare? An' what do ye want this time o'night?"

"Pat, come down, and call Judy also to be with you. I have your mistress here; you certainly know me, 'square'!" said Dr. Juno. "Square" was a secret word by which Pat and the doctor were to know each other if ever found in danger where they could not recognize each other.

"Och! be Sant Patrick, it bees Dochtor Juno," ejaculated Pat to himself, and he donned his garb in a moment, and aroused his Judy darlin', shouting gleefully:

"Judy, darlin'! Judy! Och! Judy, begorrah! Dochtor Juno bees down sthairs wid our Mishtress Lucinda, cum, cum queek!"

Judy sprang to her feet like lightning and exclaimed:

"Pat, ye air adreamin', an' shure thare bees no trooth in it; but ye'll git into trooble ef ye ain't kereful; mind that for a warnin'."

"Judy, darlin', cum, an' don't be afoolin' wid yer batrothed an' mishtress, ye slapy goose; cum, I say"—

"Yis, Pat, I'm acumin' strate," interrupted Judy.

Pat opened the front door courageously, for he knew for a certainty that it was Dr. Juno; but Judy was scared and suspicious until she saw Miss Armington and Dr. Juno, when she bellowed forth in terrific hysterics of delight, grasping Miss Armington around the neck:

"They Lord! they Lord! they Lord! Och! me swate lady! O-O-O-c-h! me swate lady! am I awake! O-O-ch, me swate lady cum back, an' for shure! But ye look so thin an' pale. Och! me swate lady!"

"Judy, an' ye mak a fool ov yerself," snivelled Pat O'Conner, whilst Dr. Juno and Miss Armington both wept with joy and gratitude! It was a happy moment all around, and for once servant, mistress and master felt as one family, without distinction. The bravery of Pat and Judy, and their lasting fidelity to the welfare of their employers, supported by their faith in God's justice and in the virtue of the persecuted, made them the beloved creatures of the household.

Dr. Juno broke the ice by saying in a cheerful manner:

"Well, my faithful friends, I have kept my promise"—

"An' shure ye hav," interrupted Pat, still weeping as if his Irish heart would burst; "an' ye bees the gratest man livin', an' be me sowl I'd giv me life fur ye inny time, so I would!"

"Thank you, Pat; I fully appreciate your worth and valor; but now let Judy get something to eat and drink for her mistress whilst she reclines on this easy lounge," said Dr. Juno.

"Yis, sir," responded Judy and Pat simultaneously.

Miss Armington was so overcome with the joy that she experienced by the surrounding circumstances; the great delight her restoration gave to these humble and faithful servants, was to her almost too much to bear without fainting dead away! She could still not yet fully realize that it was a settled truth, that she was delivered from her persecutors, and was once more in her own home, surrounded by her beloved Victor, the faithful servants and her most affectionate father; therefore the first word she uttered, after Pat and Judy left her presence to procure a repast, was:

"Father! Where is dear father?"

To this question Dr. Juno was nonplussed; what could he, or what would he say quickly? He did not desire to tell her that he really was insane, nor should he tell a falsehood, so he said:

"Your father, beloved Lucinda, is not at home at present; but we hope soon will be; in fact, the dear soul has been mourning your loss until he could not rest here, at home, where he had your smiling company"—

"Dear Victor, there is something not right about poor father, do tell me, is he dead?" she interrupted. "I see it in your countenance that something is wrong."

Dr. Juno hung his head in deep grief, when she continued, "Oh! speak, beloved Victor! Do not keep me in suspense, say the worst that has befallen him. Is he dead?"

"Sweet angel! he is *not* dead," sighed he, mournfully.

"Thank God for that!" she exclaimed; "but where is he?"

"He went to Europe to seek you"—

"Is he then still in Europe?" she interposed.

"No, my precious love, he is not," said he.

"I see, my beloved Victor, that you try to hide from me the real state of affairs about dear father," responded she; "but do not hold a thing back"—

"You love me, do you not?" asked he.

"Of course I do, precious dear; but you cannot be jealous of an affectionate parent's love"—

"No, my darling, not jealous; but grieved to tell you that he is insane"—

"O God, O God! my dear, desolate father insane, and on my account; but not through any act of mine, as heaven knows," said the distressed child, weeping and mourning until she could no more. Dr. Juno went and cast his arms around her slender and half-worn out form and sent his animal magnetism into her body, whilst his love and prayer baptized her nervous centre with renewed life, and soon she beheld the misery of her betrothed lover, when she said:

"O my long lost darling! you are everything to me, and I should rejoice and praise God for having you with me; but it seems so cruel, so very hard, that my beloved, good, noble father should suffer through us"—

"Yes, it is *my* fault," he interrupted. "Had accident not thrown you in my path on that seemingly fatal day when Pat O'Conner's horses ran away neither, you nor your father would have had occasion to suffer this martyrdom." Here he ceased to speak, and wept and shook like a leaf when the wind blows it. She at once saw that he misunderstood her, when she was aroused and exclaimed:

"My dearly beloved Victor, you did not understand me! I did not mean that *you* are to blame; no, never, never. O, I beseech you, do not take this matter so much to heart!"

CHAPTER LVIII.

PATHETIC INTERVIEW BETWEEN LUCINDA AND VICTOR!

DR. JUNO raised his head and wiped away his great tears, and said:

"Oh! what can I do for having brought so much misery upon you, my dear, my most precious Lucinda? My love for you is beyond the power of language to express it; but my love for God and his cause is equal to it; therefore, I cannot see how I could have acted to have kept possession of the two things or creatures that I love far better than my own life, namely, yourself and my cause"—

"Noble, brave, herculean hero, I love you a million times more for that righteous expression," interposed she.

"But I have really been the cause of all the misery that you and your excellent father had to undergo; and you, dear saint, who have always had all you wanted or needed have been taken away from everything that was delightful, and have been cast into a dungeon, been insulted, abused and tortured on *my* account!" ejaculated he, in great distress and earnestness.

"But listen, my precious one, I have found *you* by the loss you speak of; yes, for a brief period of suffering and loss of imaginary wants, I have gained a jewel that is worth more to me than kingdoms and worlds combined! Do not deem me a poor, weak chit of a thing, but look upon me as a woman, who knowing the right dare also maintain it, and if the firmament overhead falls! I have loved my father; but as long as there is life there is also hope, and I feel now almost certain that you and I, with the help of the fixed law of a just God, will be able to calm his frenzied brain and heal him of his disease!" said she.

"Holy angel! you speak like an inspired oracle from heaven"—

"Yes, and who made me such but your noble self?" interposed she, smiling and touching him tenderly under the chin, whilst she kissed his brow.

"Heaven be glorified for giving me this 'help-meet;' now am I blessed, now am I crowned with glory, and I feel that ten thousand deaths would be painless with you by my side; you, whom I looked upon as a tenderly bred and lavishly raised child of affluence, have grown an inspired seraph, who can vitalize the dormant faculties of sage and sire; you, whose talismanic power and expansive mentality can teach me what I thought no woman could know or do; you, who are worthy to become the wife of a throned monarch, how can I ever repay you for this intrinsic heroism?" said he.

"Precious dear, you can repay me fully by continuing to love me, and no woman is happier than to see her lover act like a man of principle and man of honor, who would suffer and die for the right, as I am convinced you would, for you have already suffered the most cruel martyrdom; have gone through many dangers, but have been saved by a higher power than man can wield for me; for me alone! Is this not so?" asked Miss Armington.

"Yes, sweet saint, I am yours body and soul, and yours alone forever. So help me God!" responded he, whilst he pressed her to his heart.

A knock at the door, when Judy announced that she had prepared such edibles as they had in the house, which they were invited to partake of. Dr. Juno conducted the young millionairess to the table, where they found everything that was healthy, palatable and fine, and whilst they satiated the inner being, they spoke to Pat and Judy, who were as lively as bees, waiting upon their long lost hosts; and when they had finished their meal, the persecuted lovers returned to the drawing room, where Miss Armington, by request of her lover, told him how she was abducted, and the general treatment she had received at the asylum.

She related everything to her beloved except the last interview with the deacon, with all of which the reader is already familiar; when she had finished her recital of the exciting incidents, he said:

"The deacon is a vile reptile; but you, my exquisite angel, are truly a heroine and saint of the first water."

"Do you think so, darling?" she said, giving him one of those seraphic smiles which a perfect woman alone can give.

"I am sorry, dear saint, but really, I must repair to my home; I have much to tell you that will astonish you, but I must leave it for the next time we meet," said he.

"When will that be, beloved Victor?" asked she.

"Whenever my darling desires it," said he; "but I must not monopolize too much of your time, for you require rest from excitement."

"Do not say that, for I only rest when I am in your precious presence; come to-morrow; but, before you leave me, tell me only one thing. Where were you when father was first attacked with insanity?" asked she.

"I was in my own office, where your noble father visited me, to ascertain of the whereabouts of your precious self," said he.

"Did you know where I was?" exclaimed she.

"No, my love, I did not; but I had some strong suspicion that you were somewhere in that hell-hole," said he.

"What made you suspicion that?" asked she.

"Well, to tell you the truth, I was abducted the very same night, and almost the same hour, that you were, and was gagged, bound and carried to a horrible basement dungeon, that was damp, dark and unhealthy, in that same asylum," ejaculated he.

"O how horrible! most horrible! But how did you escape?" asked she.

"Through an honest Irishman's assistance, who was a friend of Pat and Judy, by the name of Jemmy," said he.

"Jemmy! the honorable fellow; I know him, he was an overseer, was he not, at the asylum?" asked she.

"That is how I was aided, my love," said he.

"Then it was through Pat O'Conner and Judy McCrea that we got our freedom," replied she.

"Yes, darling, primarily it was," said he.

"Oh! beloved Victor, how you must have suffered; but I do not ask you to give me a full statement of everything that transpired since we were abducted, just now, as you wish to go to your office, but I long to hear it all very soon. One word more, and I have done for the present, my precious Victor. Where is father?" asked she.

"I am grieved to tell you that he is a lawful prisoner in that same asylum, but they treat him very kindly; I have been to see him once," said he, softly.

"Poor, dear father!" she sighed.

"Do not mourn, my precious love, we will get him well," said he; "but now I must go to my office, and punish the villanous old deacon."

CHAPTER LIX.

DOCTOR JUNO PERFORMS A SERIOUS OPERATION ON DEACON STEW.

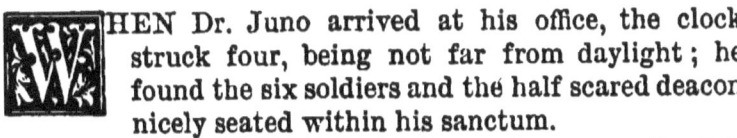HEN Dr. Juno arrived at his office, the clock struck four, being not far from daylight; he found the six soldiers and the half scared deacon nicely seated within his sanctum.

He immediately ordered the soldiers to remove the fetters from the deacon; then he handed the handcuffs to them which his holy (?) deaconship had put on Miss Armington, to be shown him, when the doctor said:

"Scoundrel, do you know those little bracelets?"

"Yes, sir, I do," responded the chopfallen deacon.

"Did you order them to be put on Miss Armington, so that you might carry out your infernal designs?" ejaculated Dr. Juno, flushed with holy indignation. "Answer me squarely, or you may infuriate me so terribly that I will slay you before you have time to reply; speak, instantly!"

"Yes, sir, I had them placed on her; but"—

"No 'buts,' sir," interrupted Dr. Juno.

"We-ll, I was go-i-n-g to say that I did it only to prevent her from assaulting me," stammered the pious deacon.

"Liar, that you are," exclaimed Dr. Juno, and now addressing his men, continued: "Soldiers, put them on his beautiful wrists, joining his hands behind his back, as he did to the innocent and helpless young lady, for the purpose of ravishing her; and as soon as you have done that, place him on this large centre table, on his back, and secure his legs backward and upward, for I shall 'make him a eunuch for the kingdom of heaven's sake,' so he cannot become a breeder of sanctified criminals, nor make any more attempts to ravish innocent females!"

"Oh! have mercy! mercy! mercy! I pray you; I ask, humbly, a thousand pardons, and will make reparation for all the insults, danger, injury and wrong that I have done to the young lady, if you only will grant me the privilege of escaping your just wrath! By the God above me, I swear it!" ejaculated the helpless deacon, in terrible despair, whilst Dr. Juno stood silent for a moment, staring the deacon in the face, half smiling. Then he said:

"Well, sir, you acknowledge more than I thought a saintly scoundrel could be guilty of, and then you coolly ask me to let you off, and you appeal to God and swear to a lie, thinking that I am a fool or a chicken-hearted dunce; but I will show you how coolly I can cut you; how easily, slowly and torturingly I can ply my professional skill; and again, I will not harm you, but, to the contrary, benefit you so much that you may yet repent of your bloody deeds, and be converted to a sound piety before you die! This would be a Christian charity, holy deacon (?), elect saint (?), would it not?" said Dr. Juno firmly, sharpening his scalpel as calmly as if he was going to carve an apple.

"Oh! doctor, you do not know what drove me to do those acts, with which you are undoubtedly familiar by this time! It was love, pure love, which was refused me, that drove me to those desperate acts," exclaimed the deacon, and continued, "and as you also know what that is, I hope you will be merciful to a disappointed man, whilst you have gained a glorious victory over me."

"Indeed! you reason like a philosopher, or like a wicked fool. Does love, 'pure love,' torture and ravish, or attempt to ravish its idol? and do you look upon a man like me to be such a contracted minded being as to be duped by such sophistry, whilst you are securely in my power? Soldiers, gag him now, when I will to work," said Dr. Juno.

It took him twenty-five minutes to finish his operation, when he had the deacon freed from all his shackles; but, before he permitted him to depart in peace, Dr. Juno said:

"I shall be compelled to ask you to make an oath, before you leave my office, to the effect that you will never, by word or deed, aid or abet any one, or do any act, that will injure either of the Armington family, myself, my followers or my cause."

"You might as well murder me at once," responded the deacon, indignantly and haughtily.

"No, sir, I will not become your executioner as yet a while; but I can torture you quite a little more, and shall do it, too, if you are not *very* careful," ejaculated Dr. Juno.

"I don't think you can, for I am suffering a thousand deaths at present, physically and mentally," exclaimed the deacon.

"I am delighted to think that I am able to chastise you

thoroughly, by having done to you what will save you from damnation, if anything can do so ; in the long run, you will say so yourself, noble, pious deacon," said Dr. Juno.

"Never, but I shall hate you"—

"Be careful, old fellow," interposed Dr. Juno ; "you are not yet out of my power. From your present remarks, I guess you do not feel inclined to make the oath for the purpose I have proposed it."

"I shall not interfere with any of you in the future, because I know it would not benefit me any ; therefore, rather than be further harassed and tortured by a hardhearted creature, like yourself, I will swear to anything that you may propose," replied the deacon, looking more reconciled to his altered condition.

"Then repeat after me, in the presence of these witnesses, repeating your own name as you know such things are done, assuming my position :

"I, Deacon Rob Stew, solemnly swear to never more, by word or deed, injure Dr. Victor Juno or any of his followers or friends, and should I do so, I agree to have my upraised (left) hand burned into cinders ; my right hand, which now clasps my beating heart, cut into fragments, and my heart torn out by its roots ; moreover, should I fail to do as before stated, I hope to have my soul cast into outer darkness, where there shall be weeping, wailing and gnashing of teeth forever and ever, and where the devil and his boon associates shall hiss at me, and pour pestiferous reptiles, with envenomed darts, upon my sensibilities, lashing and torturing me beyond the expression of language. This do I *voluntarily* swear, and hope for no other destiny should I fail in the fulfilment of such promises as I have herein made. So help me God !"

"That will suffice, holy deacon ; how do you like my style of an oath ?" asked Dr. Juno. "You are free to leave."

The deacon was dumbfounded ; he could not utter a

word; but amazement stood upon his countenance. He left the house with the utterance:

"Accursed be your mystery!"

CHAPTER LX.

THE BLOODY CONSPIRATORS BOTHERED AND ARRESTED.

THE last meeting that the sacredly secret conclave held at Tabernacle Hall was on the night when Honson Teafel said:

"Dunner und blitzen, I tinks you bis a sed o' fools, to bis so skeert; mine cot, I yust winch unzer decon whash bin vell."

Never before since the organization of the bloody conclave were they so long without calling a meeting; but as soon as the deacon was well he had other matters to attend to, and then his unfortunate visit to the asylum, and the results that took place in Dr. Juno's office, hindered the call of a meeting until Deacon Rob Stew and Rev. Joe Pier were ready to be present.

The Rev. Joe Pier was well pleased with the nursing he received at Tabernable sick-room, at the hands of his beloved Nancy Clover; therefore he was not anxious to hurry his convalescence; at any rate he was slower in recuperating than the deacon, who, however, had his love-stimulant in that third-story cell in the asylum; therefore, it can be seen what a powerful panacea love is!

Neither of their affection was reciprocated by the ladies of their choice; but the saintly deacon got the worst dose of it, whilst the reverend lover received more kindly attention from Sister Nancy Clover, because her idol, General Washington Armington, was a lunatic, and beyond her holiest reach!

After Deacon Rob Stew had recovered from his wounds that were inflicted upon him by Miss Armington's bite in his ear, which the young heroine nearly bit off, as also from the surgical operation performed by Dr. Juno, he called a meeting of the secret conclave for Saturday evening, sharp at 8 o'clock, requesting a full attendance, as he had many important matters to discuss.

On the night above mentioned Rev. Joe Pier took the chair, as of old, and Deacon Rob Stew made the opening address, who, however, seemed to be, in many respects, an altered man since he last met with them. Some conjectured that his altered condition was owing to the beating that he had received on that eventful night, when he and Rev. Joe Pier were nearly killed; others thought that his long confinement in a sick-room caused the change; at any rate the deacon spoke gently as follows:

"Brothers and Sisters of the Sacredly Secret Conclave:—I rise to say that I have seen much that was disagreeable and mysterious since I have met with you in this hall. I am not splenetic and rash, but yet I have that within me, which goads me on to victory in the work which was instituted through my instrumentality! We are besieged on all sides by those heretics who believe in and follow the teachings of Dr. Juno; and unless we can exercise a powerful, unanimous influence with the orthodox religious classes, and also with those who deal in the merchandise to which Dr. Juno is opposed, we are lost; yes, I say this for the benefit of every member of the conclave, lost!

"Just think, I have been compelled to listen to the recital of '*our solemn oath*' by Dr. Juno himself, and, after he had finished its recital, he had the audacity to ask me:

"'Deacon, how do you like my style of an oath?'

"And he looked at me with an eye that said·

"'Don't I have your oath verbatim?'"

"What did you answer him?" asked Rev. Joe Pier, and continued, "for I am actually feeling weak in my loins to be compelled to listen to this dangerous story of Brother Stew."

"I said nothing, because I was struck with amazement," replied the deacon.

"How does it come that you were found in company with this vile innovator?" said Nancy Clover.

"Do you not know that Dr. Juno mobbed the Insane Asylum one night a few weeks since and liberated Miss Lucinda Armington?" responded the deacon, looking distressed.

"Why, certainly, this is news to me, and I think it is so to the balance of the saints," said Nancy Clover. "Further, I cannot understand why he has not been arrested for so doing, and why this matter should be kept quiet; if he is not summarily punished for breaking the peace, and for intruding himself upon our holy institutions, he will grow bolder and become a more dangerous rival in the field of conflict!"

"Noble Sister Clover, you argue well," said Rev. Joe Pier; "and I tremble, fairly shake in my boots, at this awfully perilous state of affairs."

"Friends, will you hear me out before you come to such conclusions, or before you censure any of the saints for keeping this matter quiet?" asked Deacon Rob Stew.

"Of course we will," responded Nancy Clover.

"Well, then, the reason for treating this outrage with perfect silence is self-evident, namely, should we expose Dr. Juno, as he dared us to do, *he* would profit by it, at *our* peril; because Miss Armington is now at liberty, whilst Dr. Juno is surrounded by a numerous and determined army of soldiers, who obey his commands without prevarication or hesitation; in fact, it is said that his men are ready to invade even this sacred hall and arrest us all, which would be an end of us," said Deacon Rob Stew.

"Holy Ghost! look down from above and shield me! Oh! O Lord, I feel that we are lost! lost! lost! I have always been fearful that we would make some awful blunders, and would be hung some day! Oh! Lord, I feel a choking sensation already," exclaimed Rev. Joe Pier, who was interrupted by Sister Nancy Clover:

"You have always been a contemptible coward, and I order you to shut pan. If you cannot *en*courage the saints, do not *dis*courage them ; but I want to hear our noble deacon finish what he has to say, when I will show you a plan to save our cause, and that will explode Dr. Juno's movements."

"Noble, holy, immaculate Sister Clover," said Joe Pier; "you do so comfort me and calm my fears, for I have never found you to fail in anything."

"Silence," ejaculated Nancy Clover, "and let the deacon finish." The deacon continued :

"Dr. Juno knows all our secrets, but how he has obtained them I am puzzled to know ; because I cannot believe that we have one brother or sister who would be wicked enough to violate our solemn oath, knowing what would be the result "—

"Yes, let them remember Harry Gossimer's fate," interposed Rev. Joe Pier.

"I am not a coward," continued the deacon ; "but since Miss Armington is at liberty, whilst Dr. Juno is surrounded by good and influential men, I must say that great danger is hanging over the sainthood. Still, I am in favor of rallying the friends of the elect all over the country ; but I am myself a prisoner of war, being under parole, and should I be found to aid or abet in this movement I would be mobbed and shot or hung !"

"I cannot think it," exclaimed Nancy Clover ; "nor can I see why you lay so much stress upon the freedom of Miss Armington. She is nothing but a chit of a thing, who has always depended upon her father, who is a confirmed lunatic "—

"Do not deceive yourself, noble Sister Clover," interrupted Deacon Stew, "about Miss Armington, for she is anything but a 'chit of a thing.' She is a perfect demon, a tigress, a strategist and a cunning, fierce and deep woman, who will wield more influence by half than any living man if she gets a chance !"

"She shall not get a chance, then," responded Nancy Clover.

"Then she will *make* a chance, for she has outwitted and outgeneraled me on every occasion," said the deacon. At this instant a furious knock was made upon the outside door, and like lightning the same was burst open, when Dr. Juno stepped into the hall and said:

"I arrest you all!"

CHAPTER LXI.

LOVE SCENE BETWEEN VICTOR AND LUCINDA.

MISS LUCINDA ARMINGTON felt too happy after Dr. Juno left her. She thought:

"Can it be possible that I am free from bondage, free to go and come when I please? Can it last? Will not these bloody conspirators again try to abduct me? Surely I shall keep myself secluded for a time, when probably they will not disturb me; but should the deacon come to my home I think I should kill him; let him come. I am no more the little, confiding, harmless child that I was before that fatal night, when I was carried off by those ruffians.

"I have an indistinct recollection of all that transpired that night; at least I do now remember it for the first time. Let me trace the hours that I was seemingly unconscious. I walked into the lawn, deeply thinking of my own, my dearly-beloved Victor. I was worried about him, when suddenly something was thrown over my head, and I was grasped by a rude man and carried into a carriage, but beyond that I cannot recollect what happened until I found myself in that cell; and, oh! the horror that came over me, and the anxiety I felt about precious Victor, was too, too awful.

"I have learned much since then that may be useful to my dear Victor. I know how to take my own part, how to chastise a villian, and I really would undertake to general an army of soldiers, if by so doing I could assist precious Victor. Victor, Victor! you are my life, my soul, my joy, my all! Without you I could not live, and should you be overcome by your enemies, I would take your place and fight like an 'infuriated fiend,' as the wicked deacon called me.

"I am anxious to learn something more of what has occurred since I have been absent, so I will ring for Pat and Judy."

"At yer sarvice, me dear mishtress," responded Pat.

"Yis, me luvly mishtress, we longs tow sarve ye, an' we tank the Lord fur bein' wid us agin," said Judy.

"Tell me all you know about what has happened since I have been away; about poor, dear father, and how you suspicioned that I was confined in the asylum, for dear Victor told me that it was you, my noble, brave and faithful saints, who discovered my and dear Victor's whereabouts," exclaimed Miss Armington.

"Och! me lady, an' I blarneyed the ould deacon, an' he tould me anuff tow gav me tow know that ye were in thare," said Pat, looking as huge as a mountain, and continued, "they nixt time thim divils would try such doin's shure they'd find hogus pocus trown in ther way, let 'em mind that!"

Miss Armington listened for two hours to Pat and Judy, when they had time to repeat all they knew of the whole affair, with which the reader is familiar; but on several occasions they all three burst into tears, as the incidents and accidents that befell her poor deceived father and beloved Victor caused the affectionate and heroic girl terrible pain.

When they were through with their story, Miss Armington asked to be conducted to her bed-chamber by Judy. She retired much fatigued, and in a few moments fell into a sound sleep, and slept until daylight, when she rose and dressed herself, as she expected her idol, Victor, to come early that day. At nine that morning he arrived, when the parlor had been thrown open for the first time since Miss Armington was abducted. She received Dr. Juno in the parlor, and after saluting each other with pleasing sentiments, embraces and kisses, such as betrothed and persecuted lovers were alone able to bestow upon each other, Lucinda said to him:

"My precious Victor, please tell me now all about your trials, privations, and sufferings, as well as what you have done toward promulgating the cause which is so near and dear to your manly heart."

"It will give me exceeding great joy to do so; but I am equally anxious to learn your story, all that has happened to you since we were torn away from home," said he.

"Yes, my beloved Victor, you shall know all; but I have told you the most that has transpired whilst I was a prisoner, and as I have been away much longer than yourself, for Pat and Judy told me all they knew about it, you know more to tell than I do," exclaimed she.

"That is so," said Victor, "and I have a great deal to say to my precious love; therefore, before *I* commence, be frank and tell me first what the vile old deacon did to you last night? Did he accomplish his evil designs?"

"No, sir, dear Victor, he did not," ejaculated she, indignantly; "but after he had me handcuffed he thought I was an easy victim, and I let him think that I felt as though resistance was useless, when he approached me, threw his arms around my waist, and pressed me to his body, whilst he attempted to kiss me on my mouth. I did not resist in the least, on purpose to throw him off his guard, and when he attempted to kiss me on my mouth, I turned my face aside and permitted him to kiss me on my cheek, and instantly I took his nasty ear in my mouth—you know I had to do it, disgusting as it was—and I then laid all my strength into my jaws, and my sharp, solid teeth sank nearly through his big ear, which caused him to scream murder; and although I felt his nasty, hot blood upon my breath and on my face, neck and breast, I still hung unto the ear, until I must have fainted away, and the rest you saw yourself."

"Thank God! dear angel, that you had the courage of a lioness and the wisdom of a sage. You are a *woman*, a *genuine* woman, one whom the gods would do homage to, one whose noble and heroic deeds swell the soul of man, and cause him to idolize and worship you as a goddess; in sooth, you are one in my esteem, and my life is magnified to ten thousand times its former size on account of being the possessor of such a treasure as yourself and your lasting love!" exclaimed Victor.

"Do you, then, love me so much?" said she, tenderly looking into his heaven sparkling eyes. "But I am not worthy so good and great a man's affections"—

"Love you so much! Yes, truly, I love you more than pen, tongue, eye or God could express," interposed he, whilst he sealed it by gently pressing a kiss upon her lips, which was re-electrified by the response she gave to it; and he continued: "Most exquisite seraph, this is heaven on earth! this is love to God and man! love in its normal sphere! love that could not permit a wrong thought to enter the purified temple of God!"

"My heaven-born Victor, you overwhelm me with exquisite sparks of delight; you magnify my womanly heart, until its innermost recesses become thrilled and electrified with oceans of bliss, and I am carried away to the realms of the blessed on the wings of celestial love! I pray it may continue to bind us together," said she.

"Amen! So be it!" responded he. .

CHAPTER LXII.

THE FIGHT BETWEEN THE NATURALISTS AND CONSPIRATORS.

THE time was approaching when bloody war seemed to scent the air; because either side was determined to win. The *bloody conspirators* had recently met with an opposition that they never thought could be brought to bear against the elect; but it only shows that truth and righteousness are more powerful and influential, when rightly presented to all classes of people, than all other things combined.

Dr. Juno fully understands how to swing "the flaming sword" skilfully around the heads of saints and sinners, and with his great mind, he can fairly carry conviction to the heart of any one. Yes, he can make it seem that even his most cruel treatment of his enemies is a Christian charity. Take, as an example, Deacon Rob Stew's case, which undoubtedly will prove a benefit to the deacon.

Then, again, behold Dr. Juno's noble and Christ-like amnesty and invitation to his persecutors; what an act of charity, and how much more humane such conduct is, to that which is shown the world by the sectarian people, who are the children of the bloody clique!

The sacredly secret conclave has been broken up at their last meeting at Tabernacle Hall, when Dr. Juno and his men took all the members of the conclave prisoners of war. As Dr. Juno stepped into their hall and said:

"I arrest you all," he found his old prisoner of war—Deacon Rob Stew—on the floor making a speech, which was a breach of his parole; and when the latter beheld Dr. Juno, he almost fainted, which caused the whole sainthood to remain silent as the tomb. Whilst these two heroes gazed at each other, Nancy Clover rose to her feet, and in a most solemn and dignified manner said:

"Dr. Juno, sir: What cause have you to make an assault upon our private meditations? Do we not live in a free country, where all have an inalienable right to serve God according to the dictates of conscience"—

"Truly," interrupted Dr. Juno; "but conspiring to rob others of this very right that you have just spoken of, is not serving God nor man, and it illy becomes you to argue in favor of republican liberties, whilst you individually and collectively have used every foul means to crush those who claim that very right, but which this sacredly secret conclave of bloody conspirators has prosecuted without just cause, has persecuted with a determination that has at last, thank heaven! aroused the loyal heart of American freedom, and I am here as the champion of that cause and people, for the purpose of dispersing, disposing and forever subduing this bloody clique!

"Do you comprehend me now, and dare any man or woman in this place resist my orders? If there is any one here who dare do so, whilst I have my army of soldiers within and without, let him do so at his or her peril; however, I am willing to hear what this ingrate and perjured villain—Deacon Stew—who is your spokesman, has to say for being found again amongst you, evidently urging you on in the treasonable work of deviltry. I pause for an explanation."

The deacon stood still and silent, casting his eyes upon Nancy Clover and Rev. Joe Pier, when Sister Nancy Clover said:

"Brother Stew, speak up to this man, and do not be brow-beaten by a rude innovator and public rioter like this Juno"—

"Better be a little cautious how you address your satellites in my presence, or you may fare unpleasantly, if you *are* the feminine planet star of this conclave; be assured of that, my brave heroine in a bad cause!" interposed Dr. Juno.

"Sir, you impudent scoundrel! how dare you insult me

THE CONSPIRATORS AND LOVERS.   257

in this manner! I order the brothers to repair instantly to the armory for weapons, and, if you won't leave, shoot you down like dogs!" responded Nancy Clover in a terrific rage.

"Arrest that woman, and convey her to the background," commanded Dr. Juno.

In a moment she was seized, but she struggled terribly, and called out:

"Brothers, shoot these rioters!"

"Ha! my lady, two can play at that little game," said Dr. Juno, and commanded: "Soldiers, make a charge upon all the conspirators who resist, and if any are found with arms in their hands, shoot them dead! Show them no quarters; they gave me none when I was in their power!"

By this time the conspirators made a desperate struggle to arm themselves, several having returned from the armory with rifles; but Dr. Juno had the advantage, therefore he said again:

"Soldiers, slay and bind every one who dares to resist, and carry that woman out of this hall."

To which Nancy Clover replied, as she was being secured and carried away:

"Fire! brothers, fire! and yield not one inch of ground!"

Just then a Naturalist put a stopper of tow into Miss Nancy Clover's chatterbox, when the saintly heroine gave the ungentlemanly fellow a blow with her fist that caused him to seek the floor, and she shouted:

"Brothers, victory or death! Make a bayonet charge; shoot, cut and kill these cut-throats!"

By this time Sister Nancy was ruthlessly dragged from the scene by the hand of Dr. Juno, who said:

"You are a dare-devil and will cause the spilling of blood, therefore you shall feel my power," when he threw her to the ground and gagged and bound her with his own hands, and ordered his men to remove her to the wagon and guard her. Then he returned to the hall, where he found a terrific fight. Shooting, bayoneting and striking with chairs were freely in operation; he urged his men on, and, raising his own revolver, levelled it at the face of Rev. Joe Pier, who had skulked behind a post; when the skulker saw Dr. Juno's movements, he screamed vehemently:

"Brothers, stop, oh! stop this fighting; and, O Lord! Brother Juno, don't shoot, don't, I pray you! I pray you!"

This had a wonderful effect on the conspirators, each one lowering his weapon; and when Dr. Juno saw it, he also said:

"Soldiers, cease your assaults; but if any conspirator makes an attempt to renew the fight, shoot him! Watch them, whilst they have those loaded rifles in their hands. Conspirators, hear me. I order you not to stir or shoot, for the first man that does, will see a bullet from this pistol kill this man, Joe Pier!"

To which Rev. Joe Pier fairly yelled:

"Brothers, drop your arms. Lord! drop them instantly! And Brother Juno, remove that pistol, for God's sake! I fear, oh! I fear pistols, and let us make peace; I am a peace man, yes, the Lord knows, a peace man!"

To which Dr. Juno replied:

"I see you are not a very fierce warrior; but I do not fancy the idea of being called a brother by you. I am no brother of yours, neither in bloody conniving nor cowardice."

"I know that, O Lord! I know that, to my sorrow and dread; but you are a noble, brave and great hero," gasped Rev. Joe Pier.

"Come, come, Reverend President Pier, do not attempt to soft-soap me, or I may wipe your hypocritical life from that cowardly body of yours," said Dr. Juno, again raising his pistol to his heart, when he winced and stammered:

"Oh! s-a-ve, save my life only this once, and I will tell you a-ll!"

CHAPTER LXIII.

DR. JUNO'S CONCILIATORY AND BLACK FLAG SPEECH TO THE CONSPIRATORS.

DOCTOR JUNO now addressed the conspirators as follows:

"FELLOW CITIZENS: I suppose you appreciate the condition in which you are now placed. Your leaders are in my hands and powerless; if you value their lives, do each of you as I command, or they shall suffer for it, and you shall have the Black Flag held over your own heads.

"I have a large army of soldiers without; you are besieged on all sides, and your hero—Deacon Rob Stew—is already my paroled prisoner of war, who I am *sure* has violated his parole, and for which he shall pay heavily. I have no malice against you, either individually or collectively, but stern duty to my cause and my fellow creatures demands rigorous action, and I am either tender or hard-hearted, altogether according to the circumstances and behavior of those with whom I am compelled to deal.

"In the first place, then, I ask you to surrender your arms cheerfully to my soldiers, when you will be safe until you rebel again. Soldiers, do your duty. Take possession of all the arms of the conspirators wherever found in this building. Also, remove the dead and wounded to appropriate quarters, and guard all the conspirators, not allowing one to escape.

"Now, then, I will lay before you what my intentions are, by what authority and power I appear before you as dictator:

"It must be self-evident to all thinking minds, that the spirit of selfishness is the same anti-natural and anti-Christ one that sustains sectarian and partisan movements.

"You, the *bloody conspirators*, are the quintessence of

sectarianism and selfishness; you have been jealous of every one who has entertained different views to your own narrow-minded ones ; you have persecuted every one who has served his Creator as *his* conscience dictated, without having given him an opportunity to promulgate his views ; and neither have you been able nor willing to show him the soundness and philosophy of your own tenets; but you have usurped every right of the sovereigns of free, noble America !

"By your anti-Christ doctrines you have made mammon your God, and therefore you have made yourselves rich in filthy lucre by your selfish, penurious and bigoted teachings and practices ! You have had laws made to exempt your property from taxation, claiming that your brick-and-mortar temples of fashion were the churches of God, when they are houses wherein nonsense is dealt out to the sincere and unsuspicious ; where the Bible is falsely interpreted, and where Jesus Christ is misrepresented, and by your sanctimonious seemings have cheated the millions of the sovereign people out of their rights ; rights to be equal possessors of all the real wants of the human temple ; rights to know the fixed laws of God, and opportunities and conditions for all the people to fulfil the measure of their manhood by rigid obedience to His hallowed laws, thereby giving them a vivid appreciation of His wonderful works !

"You have created circumstances throughout the world that make the rich richer and the poor poorer; you have had laws made to protect the selfish sectarian and partisan in his illy-gotten lucre and position, whilst the poor, starving people, (whose duty it is, to themselves and to their God, not to commit suicide by starvation,) are imprisoned for taking a loaf of bread or ear of corn. You own all the land, and claim to own heaven, earth, air, men's, women's and children's souls, or you would 'feed the hungry' with healthy food, and 'clothe the naked' with the habiliments of heavenly knowledge ; a knowledge of the fixed, natural laws of God, created and vouchsafed to all mankind alike ;

a knowledge of the precepts, example and teachings of Jesus Christ, as contained in his sermons on the mount; a knowledge that, when promulgated throughout the world, will prove that sect, party and self belong to the devil's kingdom!

"You therefore have my intentions, when I tell you that all sects and parties shall be abolished, and the law of love to God and man shall become the Alpha and Omega of this nation; and to bring about this heavenly condition, we the sovereign people must make it our business to vanquish every one who advocates such doctrines; and I am authorized by the Workingmen's Platform, by the rights of the sovereign people, and these people themselves, to subdue you, kindly if I can; but if you are not willing to abandon your heinous work, then I shall wave the black flag over your heads, and the power which lies in the people who revere God's laws gives me sovereign sway and masterdom!

"I hope I have been understood by all of you; but for fear that some of you are too dull to comprehend plain Christianity, I will reiterate that the money power and its father —sectarianism—shall be levelled summarily by the sovereign people of America, and I have the honor to be the leader in carrying out that holy movement; therefore, I will ask you to repent of the past, and by surrendering your property to the Treasury of the Nation and becoming one of us, you shall have a perpetual, equal membership in our brotherhood! You shall receive the same that we do, so long as you are faithful to fixed law and order; but, on the contrary, if you refuse to voluntarily join us in spirit and truth, we must place you in such a position that you cannot harm our cause any more.

"I pause for a reply, or I will hear remarks from any of the conspirators."

"Dr. Juno," responded Rev. Joe Pier, "I have only to say that we may have been imprudent; but it never was any will of mine to deprive any one of his freedom, and whilst I have been president of this conclave, I have never instituted any retrogressive movement. Still, I have been urged and *compelled* to enforce many things that were repulsive to my better nature, and I, for one, am penitent, and will join the most righteous cause, which I really cannot help seeing you espouse!"

"I am happy to learn that the president of this 'conclave' is ready to do penance and become a progressive Christian; but before I can confide in such promises and in the man who makes them, I would like to know how Mr. Pier was '*compelled* to enforce many things that were repulsive to his better nature?' Who compelled you? You were the president, hence the leader of this conclave," said Dr. Juno.

"It w-a-a-as the d-e-acon," stammered Rev. Joe Pier, whilst the deacon eyed him ferociously, which caused the hypocritical coward to stutter, but being pressed by Dr. Juno, who interposed:

"Go on; never mind the deacon's threatening countenance; he is my prisoner, and death hangs over his perjured head."

"Well, sir," continued Joe Pier, without fear, seeming to feel relieved by Dr. Juno's assurance that his deaconship cannot harm him any more, "I will speak to the point, and without fear, as I know *you* are a man of your word, and will protect me from the injury which this most diabolical Deacon Rob Stew would inflict upon me, if he had it in his power, for divulging any of his infamous conduct"—at this point the deacon involuntarily made a grab for the Rev. Joe Pier, who fairly screamed—"Oh! Lord, keep him from me, dear Dr. Juno!"

"Stand back, or die!" ejaculated Dr. Juno, levelling his pistol at the deacon's breast; but the latter did not care for pistols or anything else, hence grasped Rev. Joe Pier by the throat!

CHAPTER LXIV.

CONFERENCE BETWEEN DR. JUNO AND CONSPIRATORS.

DR. JUNO saw that Deacon Stew was fairly frantic, and would strangle Rev. Joe Pier if a speedy act would not tear him away from the cowardly reverend gentleman; therefore he ran up to him and gave him a stunning blow with his fist on the temple, which sprawled the savage deacon like a dead frog, when he ordered his soldiers to bind him. The Rev. Joe Pier sprang to his feet and ejaculated :

"Noble Dr. Juno, the Lord bless! Oh! the Lord bless you! Oh! I am so scared I do not know what to do! What shall I do? What must I do to be saved?"

"Do what is right, as you always should have done," replied Dr. Juno; "then you would not be found in such dangerous company."

"Noble sir, you are right," exclaimed Rev. Joe Pier; "but will I be safe? O Lord, will I be safe when the deacon gets his liberty again? I wish I had never seen these *bloody* people. O Lord! Lord! save and succor the elect!"

"Nonsense," exclaimed Dr. Juno, emphatically; "do not talk to the Lord, in my presence, of the elect."

"No, sir! Lord! no, sir! I won't!" said Joe Pier, scared almost to death; "but what, O what *can* I say or do to please you?"

"Do what is natural and right," responded Dr. Juno.

"Yes, sir, I will, if you will only tell me what and how that is, for I am so anxious to be a good man," coweringly said he.

"You cowardly dog," growled Deacon Rob Stew at his Brother Pier, "you are a fine fellow to do what is right. You will do anything that is mean to save your contemptible life. Dr. Juno, permit me to say to you, although you hate me, and that hatred is reciprocated, that you had better not trust this hypocritical Reverend Doctor Pier, for the moment he finds out that your party becomes the weakest, he will turn and join the strongest; he is a dirty coward, and I am sorry now that I have not slain the ingrate before this late hour."

"Great Lord! Dr. Juno, do not believe him, he is the most domineering, tyrannical and hard-hearted wretch that ever lived. He will covenant with the devil himself to gain his point," ejaculated Joe Pier, in the most excitable manner.

"Indeed, boys, I see that neither of you are to be trusted," said Dr. Juno, smiling.

"Oh, yes, dear doctor, you can trust me. I am only cowardly when I am in the wrong, for I fear the devil, and to die whilst laboring in a bad cause, such as we conspirators have done, should make any conscientious man fear and tremble," exclaimed Rev. Joe Pier.

"Really, you both astonish me," said Dr. Juno, "and I see good in each of you. You might become most useful members of society if you would desert your bloody comrades, and join the Progressive or Natural Christians. I would cheerfully take you both and all these, your brother and sister conspirators, on probation, under parole and secure guardianship. What say you two leaders?"

"I'll do it, and may the Lord bless the attempt," exclaimed Joe Pier.

"I won't do it," responded Deacon Stew, "and Dr. Juno knows why I will not."

"Surely, you do not forget the altered state of circumstances, lovely deacon?" said Dr. Juno, laughing quite freely.

"Accursed be the ground you tread upon," silently mumbled the deacon.

"Well, soldiers, we must to work and away; therefore, prepare to parole those of the prisoners who will be willing to take the iron-clad oath, and those who are arbitrary conduct to our secret prison."

"I will give those a chance to step to the right side of the hall who wish to be paroled, the others remain where they are," said a captain of the Naturalists.

The entire sainthood, brothers and sisters, stepped to the right side of the hall to be paroled.

When Deacon Rob Stew saw this, he said:

"Cowards! would you all desert me and our beloved cause?"

As he made this remark he caught the eyes of the physician-in-chief and Dr. Toy Pancy, who looked sufficiently defiant to satisfy his deaconship that they would care as little for their parole as the deacon did himself. This greatly pacified him, for he had great hope that the dead and wounded (which numbered ten conspirators killed and six wounded, whilst only a few Naturalists received trifling wounds) would cost Dr. Juno's life, or at least his liberty, for the deacon little dreamt what a deep and extensive under current existed throughout the nation.

Dr. Juno, also, watched and saw the eyes of these two physicians, and he therefore permitted his captain to administer the oath to all the conspirators, except to these two physicians; when they were reached Juno said:

"Captain, I will attend to them, finish the rest first."

"I have finished all but the deacon and two physicians," said the captain.

"Bring Nancy Clover into the hall," commanded Dr. Juno, when he brought the five leading conspirators together, namely: Clover, Stew, Pier, Pancy and physician-in-chief, and after dismissing all the paroled prisoners, he addressed them as follows, and swore them on an extra oath:

"I have it in my power to shoot you"—

"Oh, don't; I pray you, Lord!" interrupted Joe Pier.

"Silence!" ejaculated Dr. Juno, "I will have no more interruptions. I will not kill you now, but shall demand an extra oath from you; and whilst I administer it, an officer has gone for a warrant for your arrest, for conspiring against the working people and myself"—

"Oh! Holy Ghost!" mumbled Rev. Joe Pier, audibly.

"You have committed sufficient crime to be convicted and hung; at least I shall ask ten thousand dollars bail for your appearance at Court, to answer the charges as above stated."

The officer and magistrate, also a Naturalist, made their appearance in the hall, and each of these parties were asked to give ten thousand dollars security for their appearance at Court; failing to procure said surety, they were locked up in a station house, and the following morning were bailed out; but the newspapers were full of it, there having a great change taken place in the opinions of even the editors of those papers that used to libel Dr. Juno. But it only shows, as I have stated in the first part of this story, that newspaper men have few, if any, prejudices beyond their pockets; and whenever they see that the party which they have formerly libelled is likely to become the most popular and influential, they drop all others and espouse the cause of the one that has the heaviest purse. When the prisoners were asked by the magistrate what they had to say, Rev. Joe Pier exclaimed, in agony:

"I acknowledge my shortcomings and imperfections; but I am not guilty of sufficient crime to be either imprisoned or hung, bless the Lord!"

"Mr. Pier," interposed Nancy Clover, "I consider you the greatest scoundrel in the country "—

"Oh! holy sister, how can you! O Lord! how *can* you say that!" exclaimed Joe Pier. "I shall lose all my faith in you for saying that."

"No matter to me; but you shall suffer for all your apostasy," said Nancy Clover.

"Great Lord! Oh! but I am a heartbroken and fearful man!" ejaculated Rev. Joe Pier. "You would surely not harm me, dear sister?"

"Away, to the lockup, with these bloody conspirators," said Dr. Juno.

CHAPTER LXV.

A PLEASING INTERVIEW BETWEEN VICTOR AND LUCINDA.

DOCTOR JUNO visited his beloved Lucinda very often, and she had so much to say and ask that she generally missed getting full satisfaction about her dear old father; but getting an opportunity this evening, she said:

"My faithful and precious Victor, I have on several previous occasions desired to converse with you about dear father, and I hope you will pardon me for making this topic the subject of our interview."

"Certainly, exquisite angel," said he; "but I had determined to give you my ideas about your excellent father this very night."

"Surely, my love, we must have been of one mind; I hope our whole lives will be as congenial and delightful as the present causes them to be. My love for you is of that ardent character that my whole body thrills with joy the day long. I feel as though my life was a charmed one, and if we should be able to have poor father restored to us, I would be the happiest girl that ever lived."

"My seraph, you warm my heart with upheaving currents of passionate and effervescent love! Love that cannot be experienced and expressed by common minds. An uncommon, holy, immaculate love that stimulates every fibre of the organic domain, whilst it magnifies the soul to the dimensions of a god. In sooth, language fails to express the deliciousness of the cupid darts that penetrate even the most minute vascular tissues of my entire system. Sweetest angel, such love is worth living for, and I cannot help thanking God intuitively for having made us so fearfully and wonderfully, that we are the strongest and most apt when love prompts the mind to perform the duties of life. Yes, truly, under such circumstances everything is easy; that which would be drudgery under other conditions, becomes delightful recreation. And the most stormy hours pass gently away and promise renewed joys so long as such love as ours exists. I pray and I will cheerfully labor for its continuance in all time to come. You will join me in that, won't you, exquisite saint?" said Victor.

"Yes, indeed, my darling, I will; and it is no effort, neither, precious Victor," said she, smiling and pressing her lips upon his hand, when he said:

"Oh! holy angel, here"—holding out his lips—"is better metal for kissing than my hand."

"But I love every spot of you," she modestly replied, and kissed his lips.

"That is right, all is right, and we are blessed, quadruply blessed," said he. "But now let us speak and plan of your dear father. I think if I should take you to the asylum to see him, it might prove a great benefit to him."

"Darling, I would be afraid to enter that wicked neighborhood; they might seize and imprison us again," responded she.

"No, no, my precious seraph; they would not attempt that at this late hour of the day. Of course, you know that I had them arrested last night!" said he.

"Arrested! Who?" asked she.

"The bloody conspirators, of course, all of them, and had them paroled, and the leaders bound over in ten thousand dollars to appear at court for conspiracy," said Dr. Juno, smiling.

"Why, darling, how dare you be so bold and dauntless? Are you not afraid of the religious world? You know the influence these people have over the most wealthy; and nearly every religious sect will stand by them, as well as many worldly persons," responded Lucinda.

"Be not so sure of that, nor fear anything, precious saint; but remember that there are thousands upon thousands of the working classes, who are the only reliable, solid stuff, ready to fight to the hilt for our cause and their rights; yes, these people have felt the oppression that sectarians and partisans have cast upon the whole country, and they are ready for a terrible vengeance," said Victor.

"O precious Victor, do not risk your life for these bloody conspirators," replied she.

"You would not have me be a coward, would you, my darling?" said he. "But we must now make our arrangement to visit your noble father to-morrow afternoon. I will get a permit from Judge Freelove to visit him, and if we can arouse him, and he seems well enough to leave the asylum, we shall bring him home with us."

"Oh! bless you, my excellent Victor; but how would you get a chance to bring father home?" asked she.

"Judge Freelove knows me; he is a Naturalist, and if I promise him to take care of your father, he will grant me a permit to take him home," said he.

"I would be entirely too happy if God would grant us this favor," ejaculated Lucinda.

"I feel it in my bones, precious love, that this favor *will* be granted unto us. I shall give you some instructions how to assist me in restoring him to sanity; and with your health and love for him, and my magnetic will cast into the scales of his mentality, we can right the polarity of his nervous system," said he.

"O love, tell me how or what I shall do to aid you, and I will so gladly do it," exclaimed she, zealously.

"When we go into the presence of your father to-morrow, I want you to centre all your strength into your fingers, and by pressing one hand upon his forehead and the other upon his pulse at his wrist, and determinately willing him at the same moment to get well, you will aid him and me psychologically to cure him. I will give you further instructions then, if necessary," said he.

"My beloved Victor, I feel as though we should succeed in restoring him, because I have unbounded confidence in your skill and in animal magnetism, and I see you understand the science of psychology as well as physiology; in fact, I think what you do not know is not worth knowing," she exclaimed.

"Thanks! my angel, for the compliment; but whilst I am not vain, and hope I am not so soft as to take to flattery, yet I have sufficient self-confidence to know when I understand myself and when I do not. It were well, if men, and women too, would know a little more about these human manifestations and natural functions, and have the courage to stand by actual knowledge, than to believe so much that is foolish and injurious, if harbored and followed," said he.

"Verily, my darling, you are a genuine philosopher, whose equal does not live," said she, "and I long for to-morrow's sun, that we may see dear father, and restore him, if possible."

"So do I, precious one," said he, "for I want him in the army to wipe out the pharisees and swindlers of the age."

CHAPTER LXVI.

VICTOR AND LUCINDA VISIT AND RESTORE GENERAL ARMINGTON.

THE day was a clear one, a rain at sunrise having settled the dust and rarified the atmosphere, which was very favorable for a powerful psychological manifestation. Dr. Juno and Miss Lucinda Armington reached General Armington's cell in the Insane Asylum at three o'clock in the afternoon, and as good luck would have it, the general was fast asleep when they entered his presence. When Dr. Juno saw this, he cautioned the keeper not to wake him, which he had already attempted to do.

"I want him to remain in a passive condition for a while," said Dr. Juno, "and if you will close the doors of his cell quietly and leave us here until I knock at the door, I will be very much obliged to you."

"Certainly," answered the keeper, and did as he was directed by Dr. Juno.

Dr. Juno now said to his beloved Lucinda, who began to weep:

"My precious dear, please collect yourself as soon as possible, because I want your physical and mental equilibrium to assist me, and by giving thus away to your feelings you spoil the conditions, provided you carry it too far or too long."

"Certainly, dear Victor, I do not wish to do that," she responded, and instantly ceased weeping.

"We must endeavor to impress his mind whilst asleep," said he; "and if we can get him under mesmeric influence and wake him shedding tears, we have restored him to sanity! Therefore, you take his left hand into your right one, and with your left hand gently press upon the nape of his neck, whilst I will take his right hand into my left and manipulate his thinking brain with my right hand, and then we must unite our breathing, and, when united, catch up with his respiration; and the moment we have him that way we must centre our entire wills and unflinching determinations upon him, desiring his sanity, when success must come!

"Ignorant people, who do not understand the laws of psychology, nor the laws of vitality, would laugh at this treatment; but it is generally the case that people cry superstition, and laugh at things to which they are blind! Will you do as I directed, and do you understand me thoroughly, my precious love?"

"I will, and fully understand you, and I am strong in my faith," said she.

"I will wake him at the proper time, and then if you feel like weeping with him it will be all right," said Dr. Juno.

They operated as proposed, and in about fifteen minutes Victor called aloud to him:

"General Armington, awake to glory, your daughter is by your side, and all is well!" And, truly, the general awoke and wept like a child. Lucinda wept, and Victor followed the fashion, and after a few moments of tearful joy, Miss Armington said:

"Dear pa, we have come to take you home with us; how do you feel?"

"O my dear, long lost child, have I really found you? And is this not a delusion?" exclaimed the general.

"No, precious father, it is no delusion," said she; "but it was my dear Victor who has saved and restored both of us. Come, father, and thank him for it."

"God bless you, my son," responded he. "I have accused you wrongly the other day, and I once more ask your pardon. Will you, *can* you forgive me for the accusation?"

Dr. Juno fell upon his knees before the general and said, in tears of grief and joy:

"Dear general, you were not to blame, and as I told you then, 'had you done less' than you did, 'I could not respect and love you as I now do.'"

"Those were the words you repeated, after I shot at you; but, as it is all over, and since my dear daughter is safe in my arms, I am delighted to meet you again; but why are we here?" said the general, looking around, seeming thunderstruck, for it must be remembered that when the mind returns to sanity, it can only remember what happened when in its last moments of sanity previous to getting insane.

"Well, dear father, if such I may call you," said Dr. Juno, "I will tell you all about it; you turned insane in my office, where you last recollect of seeing me, and the pious people placed you here"—

"Pious people! But where is this?" interposed he.

"It is the West Philadelphia Insane Asylum," responded Dr. Juno; "but your lovely daughter and myself were determined to restore you to health, if possible, and by the aid of God's natural laws we have accomplished our task, and, thank God, are rewarded; moreover, I have a permit from Judge Freelove to take you home with us."

"Heaven bless you, my son, my son!" ejaculated the general, and began to weep and shake like a child, which caused a triune weeping respiration; because the pulses of these three souls beat as one, and it seemed the Holy Spirit baptized them, as were the apostles of old. Soon they composed themselves, when Dr. Juno knocked at the cell door, and the three passed out of the asylum, entered Dr. Juno's carriage and drove home to the general's residence.

When they arrived at the homestead, Pat O'Conner was busily engaged doing some work in front of the house; but when he spied Dr. Juno's coach, he dropped everything and ran to the house and called Judy McCrea, when they came together to receive their mistress; but when they saw the pale, careworn general, they leaped for joy, but kept perfectly silent; because they did not know that he was restored to sanity. The moment the general saw them, he exclaimed:

"My excellent servants, you are still faithfully at your post. God bless you, as I wish my own children blessed, noble souls!"

Pat and Judy gazed at each other, then at the general, then at Dr. Juno and Miss Armington, then at each other again, when they fairly bellowed and blubbered forth:

"Och! they Lord, they Lord, they Lord!"

18

CHAPTER LXVII.

DOCTOR JUNO'S PLANS LAID BEFORE THE "SECRET ORDER OF NATURALISTS."

BELOVED NATURALISTS:—I have need this evening to lay before you my plans, which I have already in operation throughout the West, and I propose to have them as speedily inaugurated in the East and South as possible. Harry Gossimer, the man whom the bloody conspirators are still under the impression is dead in the sea, has been my right hand man throughout the West. He goes under an assumed name. His wealth has given him power to reach what are called the better classes of thinking people, as well as the less apt or less cunning classes of the working men, and I can call any day upon the West for an immense army.

I have also *Jemmy*, the former overseer of the insane asylum, whom I had pardoned, working amongst the Irish and other Catholics through the Northwest; and further, as you know, we have vanquished the sacredly secret conclave, and I have General Washington Armington restored to manhood, and he is ready to go into the field when the trumpet of the Naturalists shall sound; therefore, we are having a public of our own, but still, I will give you my plans for a thorough overthrow of money and sectarian monopoly.

Jesus Christ advocated doing things in secret that cannot be appreciated by "dogs" and "swine," and as he is our exemplar, we shall heed his teachings; therefore, here, East and South, as in the West, I shall propose to introduce our doctrines and plans, for the purpose of overpowering the spirit of anti-Christ, into all the now-existing secret societies in which the working men are members.

In the West, Harry Gossimer has been perfectly successful with all the secret beneficial societies—the Free Masons,

Knight Templars, and a few other aristocratic organizations were skipped—and whilst the members of these secret societies are "Naturalists," according to our "Secret Order of Naturalists," they are not known as such, as they go by their old names. It is important to let our enemies think that we are feeble in means and numbers, whilst they claim to be strong and numerous; moreover, they really think that the people have faith in their teachings, hence, do not fear to war with us; and when the strife will begin, we will astonish them, by not only mustering an immense army of drilled and secretly equipped soldiers; but when the thousands of their own cowardly dupes, who are still their followers for gain of some kind, will desert their ranks and step into our field, which will be blooming with more natural and congenial fruit.

These are my plans, and when our views are ably presented to the working people, who always should have been the rulers of America, but who have been ruled by scoundrels in the various sectarian, political and *lucre*-grubbing rings, and who care no more for the poor "bone and sinew" of the land than a monkey cares for the multiplication table.

Show me any Christ-like love for the race of mankind, as emanating from our opponents' side of the house. Show me where the fallen, the poor, the misled, the debauched are taken by the hand, as Christ so humanely and beautifully inculcates, and are raised to manhood, are elevated, are invited to reform, to repent, and are blessed with favorable conditions, by which they would be made to grow sound, and finally would become partakers of the kingdom of God.

I might go on and cite innumerable instances where the race could be improved; but degenerative circumstances are increasing with the increasing wealth of individuals and corporations, whilst the spirit of sect and party hoodwinks those who would govern Church and State aright, and the grand aim and end of this whole fabric of the bloody conspirators is to become the owners of everything, and the result is apparent in the signs of the times.

If this machine of human affairs fails to work aright, it is no fault of the Creator, no fault of Jesus Christ, no fault of the Holy Spirit, no fault of the Science of Life, no fault of a sound Physiology; but it is the fault of those who are breeders of sinners, those who "increase and multiply" their own species under deteriorating circumstances, thereby bringing imperfect, sickly, criminally organized children into existence, who cannot act otherwise than their congenital defects direct them to do; and such pitiable creatures are easily gulled, are driven to the wall, and when they cannot help committing petty crimes, are imprisoned in dungeons, or punished for the sins which their generators have thrust upon them; whilst the wholesale thieves, cut-throats and sensual propagators of imbeciles are the honored and feted of this land, where milk and honey should flow.

Are we then blind also to the multitudinous grievances that continually embroil our country, and rob the children of earth of their inalienable rights? Or, are we ready to proclaim salvation to the fallen, the poor, the humble, the congenital or hereditary criminal, by using the means that God ordained for this purpose, or will we lie calmly quiet and permit those "scribes, pharisees and hypocrites," whom Christ has condemned with eight of the most terrible woes, as recorded in the twenty-third chapter of St. Matthew, to proclaim salvation by tongue and lip, when their "hearts" and "good works" are far from the work that was ordained for its *bona fide* fulfilment?

We need eloquent apostles in the lecturing field, men and women, who can proclaim with demosthenic and cloven tongues, whilst those who know the right will use their *bone and sinews* in striking terror to the souls of the tyrants who now usurp the rights of God, angels and mankind generally. I am not splenetic and rash, but I have that *within* me which would make the ocean one vast sheet of human gore, if it were necessary to save the fallen, the enthralled and the misled.

Brothers and sisters, can you appreciate my feelings, my motives, my zeal in the work before us ? Can you realize the duty that rests upon each of us, who knows the right and sees the wrong ? Can you let days and years pass away whilst understanding your duty, making it not your individual and collective business to strike the fatal blow at the national serpent that has crawled over generation after generation, simply because what is everybody's business has so far proven to be nobody's business, until this hydra-headed monster has so snugly and tightly encoiled itself around your necks that you fear to strike the first blow for its disentanglement ?

In conclusion, I implore and entreat each of you to work in this cause as you do in your workshops to build scientific machinery, when this immense machine of human government will bequeath to you and your children the kingdom of heaven.

CHAPTER LXVIII.

EFFORTS TO ARREST DR. JUNO FOR RIOT AND MURDER.

ALTHOUGH Dr. Juno disbanded the bloody conclave, and had the leaders arrested and under heavy bonds to appear at Court, they, the latter, still endeavored to have Dr. Juno arrested and tried for riot and murder; but it seemed that the tables were being completely turned; verily, it is a long lane that has no turn.

Dr. Juno told Deacon Rob Stew: "If I ever catch you in public conflict, I shall order you to be shot on the instant, for violating your parole; you must not think, because I permitted you to go free this time, that you will be permitted to go on in your lawlessness."

To this the deacon made no reply, but he soliloquized:

"I'll have your neck surrounded with hemp before you will get that chance, you infernal innovator and rioter. I shall influence the religious people to arrest you forthwith. Who shall I get to swear out the warrant? I dare not do that myself, because it would look malicious in the estimation of the saints; moreover, this Juno would be demoniacal enough to slay me for it. I will consult some of the members of the conclave, even if it is broken up; they will not observe their parole; no, sir, not any of those who have taken our solemn oath. I will see Brother Grumbler, Nancy Clover, Dr. Toy Pancy and physician-in-chief, either of them will issue the warrant, I'll bet!"

The deacon went straight for Mr. Grumbler's house, for the purpose of requesting him to go before an alderman to swear out a warrant for Dr. Juno's arrest for riot and murder, having caused the death of ten conspirators. Mr. Grumbler was at home, but did not receive the deacon very kindly, he said:

"Good evening, Brother Grumbler, I have come to ask you to do a little work for the saints." Mr. Grumbler savagely spied him all over, and exclaimed:

"I should like to know into what other trouble you would drag me? Have I not suffered enough for the bloody clique, and do you forget your own parole, and expect that I am fool enough to walk with open eyes into the lion's mouth? You may do your own dirty work hereafter; I am no more under your control."

"Great heavens! you false, too, as well as that cowardly Joe Pier," ejaculated the deacon.

"No, old tyrant, not false, but true to my honorable oath, made for a just cause, a thing that I have long since wished for. I am going to join the Naturalists, and so are all the conspirators who have been your tools! Whom you have cuffed and ordered around like cattle, and considered to be your mere dupes, having used us to carry out your infamous plans; and I tell you now, unless you cease your plottings against Dr. Juno, I will expose you in these very efforts at renewed conspiracy, whilst doubly under parole, and besides under bonds for conspiracy; moreover, I will have *you* arrested and locked up for having murdered Harry Gossimer, as well as the several other heinous deeds that you are guilty of," said Mr. Grumbler, in great earnest.

"And this from you," responded the deacon, looking chop-fallen and humbled.

"Yes, sir, from me," exclaimed Mr. Grumbler; "and more, I want you and all your associates in crime to keep a very respectable distance away from me, and if you have done, there is the door!"

"You would not dare to turn me away in this rude manner?" said the deacon.

"Dare!" exclaimed Mr. Grumbler, in holy wrath. "Yes, by my soul, I'll kick you out of my house in the twinkling of an eye if you come any of your presumption over me. I am your equal in any way, and in honorable manhood, your superior, but in dastardly, criminal plotting certainly your inferior. Now, quit my premises."

"I will leave you, as you request it; but "—

"No 'buts,' sir," interrupted Mr. Grumbler, and caught the saintly deacon by the neck and bottom of his pantaloons and pitched him headlong into the street, and slammed the door shut and bolted it, and grumbled:

"I guess that will cool his ardor and humble his conceit. This villian has always professed to be better than we, the working people, but we shall let him and his clique know very soon who is boss in America."

The deacon left Mr. Grumbler's premises a wiser, if not a better, man, and he meditated:

"My God! has it come to this?. Have really our followers and co-laborers deserted us? Well, I shall not be bluffed off in this manner, but I will at once visit Sister Nancy Clover, who will not desert us, nor treat me in such a rude manner. I will warrant she desires to see me as bad as I want to consult her. However, I cannot ask a woman to swear out a warrant for the arrest of Dr. Juno, and I want him jugged to-morrow morning."

He reached Nancy Clover's residence at eight o'clock, and was invited into her handsome parlor; but when Nancy learned that it was Deacon Rob Stew she directed the servant to conduct him to the library, where they met in affectionate delight; still, the deacon was less passionate in manifesting love than Sister Nancy Clover, who fairly embraced him, and said:

"O dear deacon, I am too happy to meet you; but what do you think of Joe Pier? Did you ever think that we had one single member in our conclave who was so cowardly and treacherous?"

"Truly, noble sister, I am taken back considerably; but you know Joe Pier was always a coward, and a mere catspaw to scratch others for us. Still, he is not the only apostate that we harbored as loyal and trustworthy brothers; I have just come from Mr. Grumbler's house"—

"Well, surely, he is a staunch and faithful brother until death," interrupted she.

"Alas! good sister!" sighed the deacon, "I am heartily grieved to say that you are very much mistaken, for he has joined the Naturalists, and has literally kicked me out of his house not twenty minutes since!"

"Great Jehovah!" exclaimed Nancy Clover; "kicked you out of his house and has joined the Naturalists! You stun my sensibilities, you set me wild! Brother Grumbler deserted our cause!. Could soul of woman think it? Could any man be loyal until death?"

"Yes, brave sister, here is one," ejaculated the deacon; "and if all the world prove false, I alone would continue loyal to my cause until death would stop me from further promulgating it!"

"Deacon, dear deacon, I honor and love you for that expression," said she, whilst she threw her arms around his neck and wept, and continued: "You have my respect, my love, my all; will you, can you reciprocate this feeling?"

"We-ll, I do n-not know that I can," sadly replied the deacon, and looking the disappointed elderly heroine and maiden lady in the face, and continued: "I have suffered entirely too much through the villanous acts of that Juno. Curse his filthy soul! But I respect you, and honor the ground you walk on "—

"Truly, you must know that Miss Armington is forever lost to you, and the general is lost to me, so we may as well link our fortunes and affections together," said she, very affectionately.

CHAPTER LXIX.

DESPERATE EFFORTS OF DEACON STEW AND NANCY CLOVER.

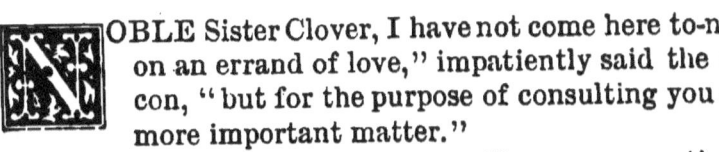

"NOBLE Sister Clover, I have not come here to-night on an errand of love," impatiently said the deacon, "but for the purpose of consulting you on a more important matter."

"Indeed!" exclaimed Nancy Clover, sarcastically, "what then *is* this *more important matter?*"

"I want some one to swear out a warrant against Dr. Juno, charging him with riot and murder, which will send him to prison at once. You know murder cases are not bailable, and we can then go ahead again. We can postpone his trial for several months, and in that time may be able to gain on him and his crazy followers," said Deacon Rob Stew.

"You are a shrewd fellow, Brother Stew," replied Nancy, much changed in her feelings, "and you need not delay in that matter, but any advice that I can give, I will freely proffer."

"Tell me, then," said he, "who do you think would swear out the warrant?"

"Do it yourself," ejaculated she.

"No, good sister, it would not be wise or quite safe," responded he, "because—well, I have several reasons."

"Because what?" asked she, "and what are these 'several reasons?'"

"Well, because I am already the second time under parole, beside under bail, as you know," said he; "then, again, I have been threatened by Mr. Grumbler; he said, if I would annoy this Juno any more, he (Grumbler) would expose us, and have me, and you too, arrested for murdering Harry Gossimer, and for other deeds that were instituted and carried into execution by the sacredly secret conclave"—

"Lord! did he not help to execute all these deeds?" interrupted she, indignantly; "and would he be fool enough to get his own neck into the halter? No, never; you need never fear his threats, they are futile, and I mean to tell him so to-morrow."

"You have always been wise and discreet," said he; "but I am afraid that you would do an imprudent thing to say anything to Mr. Grumbler; because he told me to-night that if he should learn of any more conspiring on our part, he would at once inform on us, and cause our arrest; and as we are now under bonds to appear at court for conspiracy, it would injure us to violate the law again; therefore I advise you to give up the idea of saying anything to Mr. Grumbler."

"Under those perilous circumstances, I shall consider discretion the better part of valor; but this riles me dreadfully," said she, "and I shall find some way of revenging myself upon all apostates and innovators; mind, I am not to be subdued so easily."

"What is your opinion we had better do?" asked he.

"Do! great Lord! Arouse the religious community, by telling the leaders plainly that their freedom and rights will have to take back seats, if this vile heretic is not summarily punished for his audacity," ejaculated she, furiously.

"You are right," said he, "this is our only hope; but we dare not let them know that we have been carrying on a sharp game in secret conclave, whereby we have duped them. The masses of the people are too great idiots to understand that the religion of the various sects is only a make-believe, a mockery, and if they have been so easily duped for so many years, it will be no trouble to gull them further."

"You are right, dear deacon," replied she. "But if our own lives were not in danger, I would as lief join you in the holy bands of wedlock and leave this harassing life; what say you?"

"I do not feel like marrying; I am an altered man in many of my views; and since this Juno has fallen across my path, I have not the least desire to marry; I have no taste that way!" said Deacon Stew.

"I see, dear brother, you do not love me," said she, despondingly; "but you are not to blame."

"No, indeed, I am not," responded he; "but Dr. Juno is, the low scoundrel!"

"There is Joe Pier, who has always loved me to distraction; in fact, he was crazy to marry me; but he has turned Naturalist, therefore I despise him more than ever."

"Well, you better prove true to your parole, and also join the heretics, when you can marry the dastardly and contemptible Joe Pier," said the deacon, with a sneer on his countenance.

"Never!" she ejaculated; "but I have no one left me to love and respect except your noble self."

"I am grieved at that," said he; "but had not things taken such a peculiar turn, I might have married you, for I used to think more of you and Miss Armington than of all the world combined."

"Say that again, beloved deacon," she exclaimed, affectionately and hopefully, "which gives me real joy, for I cannot see, then, what objection you have to marrying me, since all hope is gone with that hateful girl Armington!"

"I am not a marrying man," said he, impatiently. "I cannot marry, I am ruined as a man!"

"Ruined as a man!" interposed she. "How can you be ruined; I have wealth, and everything else to make us happy?"

"No, you have not; I wish to God you had," exclaimed he. "But now let us talk of business. How shall we jug Juno? Who will swear out a warrant?"

"Try Dr. Toy Pancy," exclaimed she, considerably depressed in spirit; "and if he will not do it, I *will*, for I do not care whether I live or die, if I am to spend my life in single blessedness; I despise single life."

"God bless you! noble heroine," said he.

"Conquer or die is my motto," exclaimed she.

CHAPTER LXX.

WHAT THE NEWSPAPERS SAID OF THE RIOT.

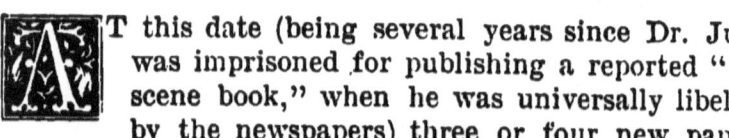AT this date (being several years since Dr. Juno was imprisoned for publishing a reported "obscene book," when he was universally libelled by the newspapers) three or four new papers have been in successful operation, which were started upon the principles of the workingmen's platform, and Dr. Juno's plans were all approved and promulgated by these reformatory organs; in fact, Dr. Juno edited the leading one himself for several years.

The "Oracle" was the oldest advertising sheet, which was purchased by a monied clique, and was conducted by a hypocritical sap-head, who was, with all his little heart and contemptible soul, in league with the sectarian and lucre-grubbing people; and of course, as this "Oracle" was looked up to by all the dastardly picayune papers of their sort, they followed in the steps of their lofty "Oracle."

The following articles appeared in the various daily papers of Philadelphia, after the arrest of the conspirators by Dr. Juno, which the sectarian press entitled a "Riot," whilst the advocates of the Naturalists called it by more exalted names, as will be seen:

Editorial from The Oracle.

"*An Infamous Riot — Dr. (?) Juno the Ringleader — Ten killed and six wounded.*—Night before last one of the most infamous and dastardly riots took place at Tabernacle Hall that was ever recorded in the annals of history. Never until such lectures, and such books as his were thrust into the faces of all who were bad enough to hear and read this ignorant charlatan's harangues and obscene publications, was Philadelphia disgraced by such crimes as midnight mobs and cut-throat riots; and not until the mayor and his detectives will summarily arrest this dangerous culprit, and the honorable court convict him for murder, and the sundry other acts that he has been guilty of, will the peace of citizens and safety of life be vouchsafed to the Christian community.

"It is fully twelve years since we refused him any access to the advertising columns of the *Oracle*. During all that time he has been going on in his infamous course. And now we hope and pray that the authorities and religious community will attend to him and his deluded followers without compunction of conscience."

Editorial from The Evening Moon.

(NOTE.—This murder-reporting little sheet is the tiny cur that swallows the bark of the "Oracle," and re-barks the latter's sentiments, aping after its godfather in everything.)

"Dr. (?) VICTOR JUNO has again shown himself in a new infamous phase of criminal action. This bold bad man will never have his just dues until the gallows ends his demoniacal life.

"Night before last he and a lot of his deluded comrades armed themselves and went to Tabernacle Hall, and there not only disturbed the inoffensive meditations of our best class of Christians, but actually killed ten and wounded six; besides, arrested our noble Deacon Rob Stew, Rev. Joe Pier, Miss Nancy Clover, Dr. Toy Pancy and the physician-in-chief of the Insane Asylum, upon a charge of conspiracy; conspiracy of what, we cannot solve; but when the trial comes off, if it ever will, we shall see where the shoe pinches.

"Will the authorities forthwith arrest this infamous Dr. (?) and Reverend (?) gentleman and his chums in riot and murder, or will he again be allowed to go scot free, or be pardoned by our generous Governor? We will see and report."

Editorial from The Evening Telltale.

(Note.—Of all the contemptible and dastardly cut-throat liars and hypocrites, the white eyelashed editor of this sectarian knuckling sheet beats it. He is one of Jesus Christ's genuine vipers.)

"An Old Offender in the Field Again.—Victor Juno, not content with the just conviction and imprisonment he received several years ago, has made riot and bloodshed his present game, and that upon our most respectable inoffensive religious people. The other night, as sacred worship was held in Tabernacle Hall, Juno and his co-conspirators in crime went to the hall, broke the doors open and killed ten and wounded six Christians; now, unless our present Governor interferes and pardons Juno, as his friend Governor Golden did on a former occasion, it is likely the Penitentiary or gallows will closely embrace him for the infamous and cold blooded riot and murder of innocent people.

"When Juno was convicted and sentenced to the Penitentiary, it was sincerely hoped by the decent part of this community that he would be kept securely under lock and key for as long a period as the law allowed. For a number of years past he has been an unmitigated nuisance in this city, and he should have been suppressed long ago.

"We hope and pray, for the peace, comfort and safety of our religious classes, that he will be speedily convicted and put where the law finds he belongs. We proffer our services free for its consummation."

Editorial from The Morning Workman.

(NOTE.—This is a new journal of large circulation and influence amongst the "bone and sinew" of the State.)

"THE BALL STARTED TO ROLL—*The Bloody Conspirators Ousted and Arrested.*—Our valiant and heroic fellow townsman, Dr. Victor Juno, did last night what he long since ought to have done. He equipped his regiment of picked soldiers, and marched direct for the old haunt of the bloody conspirators; as he marched his men into the hall, himself at the head, the irate and brazen-faced saintly Nancy Clover ordered the bloody hounds to repair to their armory for weapons, a third story room, where these Christian (?) lambs keep a finely equipped outfit of military trappings, and she ordered them to shoot down Dr. Juno and his soldiers, which, of course, caused a furious fight, that wound up by killing ten and wounding six conspirators, whilst only two or three of Dr. Juno's men were slightly bruised.

"The leaders of this bloody clique were very pugnacious, and would not promise to desist from their heinous work when the doctor had them arrested for conspiracy; but before he sent for a magistrate they unanimously agreed to be paroled. This was granted to all of them, but the leaders were bound over in ten thousand dollars to appear at court.

"Thus bad begins, and much worse remains behind. The 'Oracle' and his satellites, in malicious falsifying, will swell their saintly columns with praise for their pious

(?) people, and holy (?) invective is in store for our heroic leader—Dr. Juno.

"We confidentially whisper a word of caution to our deluded contemporaries, as we have often done before, for we pity these misled zealots. The hour is close at hand when their *lucre*, sectarian and political power must yield to the sword of the working people, who are rapidly being indoctrinated into the work of *bona fide* popular sovereignty!

"Long prayers, either to God or man, will avail them nothing; but they have been exhorted and reminded often and long enough to heed the voice of wisdom, which fell upon their self-righteous ears with contempt; therefore mercy cannot be exercised until the last foe expires. Mark our admonition, haughty vipers, your hour is drawing nigh; therefore, repent while it is to-day, or take the consequences.

"Dr. Juno, who has suffered the most barbarous martyrdom at the hands of these self-styled 'elect,' is not a man to be trifled with at this eleventh hour of the downfall of the blasphemers; they ought to know him by this time, and they also should know that the people have looked on patiently for many years, and are heartily tired of these canonical usurpations and corrupt administrations in church and state. The era of the new radical, scientific departure is rife, and the trumpet may sound any day."

Editorial from The Evening Communist.

"The Hour of Retributive Justice has Come.—Dr. Juno made a raid upon the vilest set of cut-throats last night that ever disgraced a decent nation. We can fairly worship the wise, the brave, the genuine Christian man, who has labored with indomitable energy for the cause of God and humanity for a quarter of a century, and who in his hour of prosperity can forego the pleasures of a life of affluence to do justice to his poorer fellow-creatures.

"The malignity that the editors of the would-be 'Public

Press' of Philadelphia have heaped upon this genuine reformer for many years will now have an opportunity to see the beginning of the end of their nefarious usurpation and malicious lying! They have duped the people for many years by making them believe that Dr. Juno was the scoundrel which they said he was; but, thank God, Dr. Juno persevered in the right until he has convinced seven-eighths of the entire community of the righteousness of his cause and the course he has pursued during his entire public and private life.

"We prophesy that these domineering saints (?), who love money, self and position more than truth, principle or God, will soon have cause to open their deceived eyes when they find the feelings of the masses of the people that they have engendered by trying to misrepresent this benefactor!

"'Lay on MacDuff, and damned be he who first cries hold, enough!' And let all of them know the deep-dyed rascality that has for centuries been practised against the Christian rights of the people! Look out, scribes, pharisees and hypocrites, for a just Providence exercises vengeance through His instruments—the faithful people—on you! Wait a little while longer and see!"

EDITORIAL FROM DR. JUNO'S WEEKLY.

"We have had occasion to silence the Bloody Conclave at last, and we counsel repentance and a return to God and Nature, or a doomed existence for those who persist in the error of their ways. We pity the misled and haughty people, but duty calls for terrible work!"

CHAPTER LXXI.

THE EDITORS OF THE CONSPIRATORS' NEWSPAPERS RECEIVE DOCUMENTS ASKING THEM TO LEAVE THE COUNTRY.

THE newspapers having had their say, the "Secret Order of Naturalists" held a business meeting that was attended by nearly every male and female member in the county of Philadelphia, and the editorial remarks of the "Oracle," "Evening Moon" and "Evening Telltale" were discussed, when Dr. Juno said:

"Beloved Naturalists, you have before you the sentiments of that instrument which greatly moulds public opinion; and as these organs have always been governed by men who were after *lucre* and glory of men, and who cared not, nor do now care, whether they benefit the *people*, or even their own followers and believers who support them, I think it is fully time that we should give each of these scribes twenty-four hours' notice to leave the country, or take them and hang them by mob law upon the first poles that can be reached, with this motto upon them: *Sic semper tyrannis.*"

"I am delighted to see our Father so decided to mete out a just reward to these demoralizing newspaper men, who have cried thief and cut-throat long enough, whilst they themselves were the veriest ones," responded a brother Naturalist; "and I move that we draw up a legal document, and seal it with our official seal, and have it signed by the secretary."

"That is right," said another; "I second the motion, and I would call upon Dr. Juno—our Father—to compose the document in his usual dignified style."

"All those in favor please say ———," spoke the president, and added, "It is unanimously carried."

BANISHMENT DOCUMENT.

"We, the Sovereign People, known as the *Naturalists*, having congregated together for rigorous work, do unanimously agree that you the editor, J—— G——, and proprietor, L—— C——, of the newspaper entitled the O——, who having recently written and published articles in your columns derogatory to the character of Dr. Victor Juno and his followers, are hereby positively ordered, without hesitation, to leave this country—the United States of America—in twenty-four hours from this hour, and that you do not return again until such time as we choose to permit you to come back; and this we order under the penalty of death by the law that is inherent in the Sovereign People!

"We hereunto affix our legal seal of the 'Secret Order of Naturalists,' which gives you *bona fide* evidence of our determined intention to execute what we have herein expressed. May God have mercy on your sinful souls!

{SEAL} "Given under the hand and seal of the 'Secret Order of Naturalists.'

"——— ———, *Secretary.*

"——— ———, *President.*"

The above legal form of a document was made out for each of the editors and proprietors of those three newspapers, and a committee of three fine looking men served them in company upon each editor and proprietor; and that selfsame hour each of these cowardly howlers scrambled to get ready for a hasty exit from the land where they had their own way in everything for many years.

They did not let it be *even* hinted what caused them to leave home so abruptly. The baldeagle managing proprietor of the "Oracle," and his man Friday, steered hastily for Europe, the former's favorite place of resort; being an Englishman by birth, as well as his editor—man Friday—they fled to the bosom of their mothers' home, evidently singing "Sweet Home" as they journeyed away from their illy gotten lucre and falsely earned reputation as liberal

Christian benefactors and generous right-hand donators of the working people's money. The lambs in despair left their noble pile! Yea, the wolves in sheep's raiment "skedaddled" like whipped curs, but dared not let it be known what caused this sudden departure.

These papers had nothing more to say about any transactions that referred to Dr. Juno or the working people. The bag of wind exploded, and the cowards slunk into silence in a foreign land. Thus were the conspirators deprived of their most useful instruments for arousing their own people, and the worldlings who had not yet become indoctrinated into the new scientific departure; however, these zealots and their various sects, who stuck by them, had not the least suspicion that so few continued faithful to the orthodox powers. They consoled themselves that their holy religions would cause the great majority to take sides with them in the hour of conflict, provided an internal war should be commenced, a thing which they expected, and hence prepared for it.

CHAPTER LXXII.

FUTILE EFFORTS TO ARREST DR. JUNO—HIS WEDDING INSTEAD.

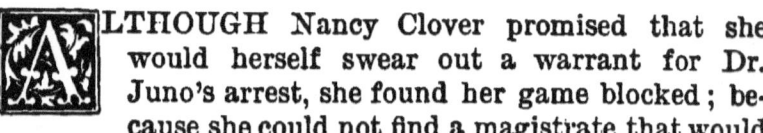

ALTHOUGH Nancy Clover promised that she would herself swear out a warrant for Dr. Juno's arrest, she found her game blocked; because she could not find a magistrate that would issue a warrant against the man who was wielding more influence than even Napoleon I. She at last went to the mayor of the city, but although he was a sectarian bigot and lucre-worshipper, still he smelled a huge rat; having been secretly informed that if he would take any steps against Juno, that he might get his walking papers, like the editors and proprietors of the rascally orthodox newspapers; and he was not so ambitious to knuckle and prance around European aristocrats as was the baldeagle manager of the "Oracle," who has continually sought for communion and recognition amongst the European potentates for many years; therefore his honor told his beloved Sister Clover that circumstances had materially changed within a few years, and that he would have to have a large army of soldiers at his elbow before he would dare to comply with her request, to issue such a warrant.

This from the honorable mayor was an awful knockdown argument, and a damper upon the high spirits of Sister Nancy Clover. She therefore soliloquized:

"Great Lord! no one dare to grant me law. I cannot get a warrant; even the mayor refuses, on account of the powerful influence that this impudent Dr. (?) Juno—Rev. Dr. Juno, M. D., D. D.—bah! This is most disgusting and revolting to my womanly nature; and there remains but one thing for me to do, to clear the track, and thereby remove this great obstacle that blocks the game of the '*elect;*' and that is, to shoot him through the heart and send him to his long account.

"I shall to work, and revive the practice of shooting; and I understand Miss Lucinda Armington and this superb (?) Rev. Dr. Juno are to be married next Thursday evening at General Washington Armington's residence; yes, they are going to have a good time, having invited several hundred of all sorts of people; even common working people and poor trash are to commingle with the rich. Lord, O Lord! what is this world coming to! Before *I* would permit my servants and the dirty working people to come into my parlors on even a common occasion, much less on a festive period like a wedding, I would die in despair; but, then, these lower classes are Juno's strength.

"Oh, how I long to continue in communion with the '*elect;*' yes, the *élite* and refined, where real piety and chaste civilization predominate over vulgar and obscene nature! Naturalists! truly vulgar trash! But then these devils are making the rich even fall in love with their natural doctrines; and, in sooth, uncouth country looking lasses and coarsely formed men are looked upon as the loveliest and best creatures! Oh, horror! this is poison to *my* refined and fastidious tastes and habits.

"No doubt at all but that when Miss Armington and her crazy father, the once refined and beloved idol of my soul, were brought to their home by this great Naturalist —Rev. Dr. (?) Juno—they embraced those illiterate, low, rough Irish servants, Pat O'Conner and Judy McCrea, the deceitful Catholic devils. How I long to choke the whole set of them. I am fairly spoiling to serve the whole batch of them an irreparable injury, and if it costs me my life, or worse. Next Thursday evening the brave lover of Miss Armington will die at my hands, before the minister shall say Amen to the nuptial ceremony. Mark me, or I am none of God's elect."

What a brave and useful woman this Nancy Clover would have made had she been engaged in a good cause. She had learned that Dr. Juno and Miss Armington were to be wedded, and that all the members of the "Secret Order of Naturalists" were invited guests, who were the people that Dr. Juno converted to his doctrines, and whom he taught to live together as "*one family*," having a common interest, a common love, and a common treasury, out of which all would be sustained. Even Pat and Judy, who were formerly Roman Catholics, joined this reformed body of Natural Christians, who believed in *living* a life, as nearly as possible, as Jesus did himself, and as he directed all should do, regardless of color, position, condition or birth. All were God's children, in a general sense, and, therefore, all who were faithful to fixed injunctions had an equal right to have their real wants supplied; but those who voluntarily led infidel or unfaithful lives, could not expect to be blessed with freedom on earth, nor obtain salvation.

Instead of Dr. Juno being under arrest for riot and murder, he was at liberty to plan his varied work. He practised healing of the sick and preached the genuine Gospel, made all the arrangements for his marriage, and superintended the rapid equipment of the Naturalists throughout the country, for the purpose of snatching the reins of government, of what is known as "Church and State," from those who have usurped every right of man, and even of beast.

He was convinced that God gives his human species the power to hold dominion over everything; provided, no *false prophets* and *blind guides* are allowed to mislead and hoodwink the confiding and sincere people; and he esteemed money, and its concomitant matters, as *filthy lucre*, as trash, as compared with that knowledge of God's fixed laws and wonderful works. In other words, what will it profit a man if he should gain all the wealth that money can buy, and thereby lose his *own happiness*, his own beautiful manhood, his own health of body and soul, and thereby claim a fame and name that would cause the spirit of Christ to weep, the angels to mourn, and God to frown?

CHAPTER LXXIII.

NIGHT OF THE WEDDING—DR. JUNO SHOT.

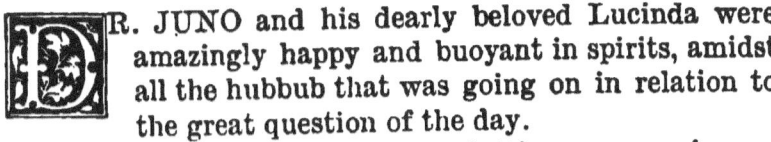R. JUNO and his dearly beloved Lucinda were amazingly happy and buoyant in spirits, amidst all the hubbub that was going on in relation to the great question of the day.

He was fully aware that great plottings were going on with his enemies, and although he had banished some of the vile agitators—the newspaper scribes—and had the leading bloody conspirators under bonds, still the beginning of the terrible work had not even yet been fairly commenced; therefore, he kept a vigilant eye on his enemies, and the night of the wedding he had ordered a company of picked soldiers to bring their weapons and deposit them in the general's mansion, as a little safeguard against contingencies, for he has been accustomed, for a quarter of a century, to be annoyed or arrested when he made any manifestation that had a tendency to excite favorable public attention.

The night was a beautiful one, the moon dimly illuminating the eastern horizon, and being in the fall of the year, when the gentle draughts of exhilarating air were gratefully quaffed through open doors and windows, which made the festive scenes a most normal and delightful manifestation of a united and affectionate people, leaving nothing to mar the pleasures of joyous hilarity, merry-making and Christian love.

After all the guests had arrived, and everything was being prepared for the nuptial ceremony, a woman could have been observed amongst the numerous guests that congregated around the large parlor windows, which opened to the floor, who was disguised as an humble working girl, and who kept herself in the midst of the female visitors. She watched every movement of the happy bridegroom, and she worked her way to the side of a window, where she had a clear look of the entire parlor; and when the guests formed a circle for the commencement of the ceremony, and as the minister began to ask Dr. Juno:

"Wilt thou have this woman"—

Nancy Clover, having aimed unbeknown to any one for Dr. Juno's heart, fired a bullet, and the bridegroom fell to the floor bleeding immensely, which caused a tremendous commotion!

General Armington sprang in the direction from which the pistol was fired, and cried out:

"Arrest the culprit that fired that pistol, no matter who did it, bring him into the parlor."

The Naturalists at once formed into a line, at the request of a captain, who said:

"Friends and soldiers, do not permit any one, man, woman or child, to escape at the peril of his or her own life; we shall learn who fired that fatal shot."

Nancy Clover had, of course, no chance to escape as yet, and what to do puzzled her awfully. She meditated as follows:

"If I remain amongst this crowd I will be detected. Still, I have less chance to escape through this line of people, who seem to be armed and ready for action. I look like an humble woman, and I shall act as innocent as a lamb; but I must get rid of this pistol. If I could only slip it into the pocket of one of these servant girls, it might be that no one could vouch for her honor, and whilst they would accuse *her*, I should go free.

"I will feign to be sick, and thereby cast myself upon some of these women, when I may find a chance to slip the pistol into some one's pocket. It was glorious that I was standing entirely amongst these females, who, like poor geese, all shut their eyes when the pistol went off, hence did not detect *me*, and they already have their eyes on another person, which relieves me vastly. I shall tell them that the blood of the poor doctor made me sick, which will gull them, and give me a chance to escape, if all goes as I anticipate."

She played her part well, got ill, put the pistol into an old woman's dress pocket, and fainted dead away! A rush was made towards her, when the old lady said:

"Please do not crowd so this way, but make room so that the air can pass this way, and bring some cold water, this lady has fainted from seeing the blood."

"Is that all," responded several.

"I'll soon be better," sighed the innocent (?) murderess, and verily such was the case, for she felt quadruply better on account of having nothing about her person that could betray her.

Dr. Juno was instantly removed to the drawing-room and laid on an easy lounge, whilst three physicians, who were present—Naturalists—waited upon him, in connection with the faithful bride, who was as pale as a ghost, but uttered not a word, until the general asked, addressing the physicians:

"Gentlemen, what are your diagnosis? Does he live yet, and is there any possibility of his recovery?"

"He revives," responded one. "Yes, he seems to be coming to," said another, when Miss Armington grasped his right hand in her left, and placed her right hand upon his forehead, and forcing her life into him, said:

"My beloved! you are better!" This caused him to say:

"Yes, darling! I only fainted! But who struck me?"

"No one, my love," said she.

"Please do not deceive me, precious one; I even now feel it here," exclaimed he, pointing to the left side of his chest.

"Some one shot you," said the general; "but I thank God you are alive, and devoutly pray that you will soon be well."

"Thank you, dear father," said Dr. Juno, and added, "Doctor, see if the bullet, or whatever struck me, entered into my thorax."

The physicians probed the bullet-hole, but found it had struck a rib and glanced off, making merely a bad flesh wound.

CHAPTER LXXIV.

ALL THE GUESTS EXAMINED AND THE ASSASSIN DETECTED.

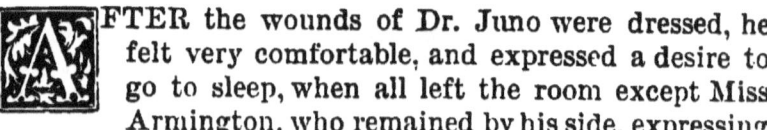FTER the wounds of Dr. Juno were dressed, he felt very comfortable, and expressed a desire to go to sleep, when all left the room except Miss Armington, who remained by his side, expressing her great affection and grief at the sad termination of the ceremony, when he said:

"Darling Lucinda, do you remember the dream I once told you I dreamt three times concerning our nuptials, and each time being interrupted by deep, designing enemies?"

"Indeed I do," replied she.

"This seems like a fulfilment of that dreadful dream; but now will you sit by me a while, until I compose myself, for I feel it is necessary for me to keep quiet and go to sleep, if I can?"

"Certainly, my beloved; with joy I will remain with you, and pet you to sleep," responded she.

When General Armington and the three physicians returned to the parlor, he said to the officers of the regiment:

"Gentlemen, order your men to guard well the outside, preventing any one from escaping, whilst you order, first, all the men in single file to pass into the parlor from the right hand window there, and after we shall examine each one, and finding him not guilty, we will pass him out by the left door, separating them until all the men are examined; and if we do not find the murderer amongst the males, we shall then do the same to each lady; now begin."

The line was formed, and every man was vouched for as a good, loyal Naturalist; all cheerfully permitted to have themselves thoroughly examined, because they were as anxious to find the criminal as the general himself, and all were of the opinion that it was a woman who fired the pistol; the floors and surrounding grounds were examined, but no weapon was found; then the females' turn came, and nearly one-half of them were being vouched for as being loyal Naturalists, upon whose persons no weapon was found, which seemed to appear very curious, and some even suspicioned that a traitor or traitoress was amongst the members of the Naturalists; but at this moment the made-up, disguised Nancy Clover's turn came; no one could vouch for her, she was a stranger; not a single person even knew her; she was examined without the least objections being made on her part; she seemed innocent, but General Armington said:

"As this woman is a stranger, and cannot be vouched for, although she seems innocent, it cannot be esteemed improper to retain her as a prisoner until we find the true culprit; and if we do not find him or her, we shall be compelled to make this lady give a full account of herself, who invited her, and how she happened to be here."

The heroic and determined Nancy Clover was asked to "stand aside," and was guarded by two soldiers, whilst the balance of the women were vouched for and examined, until the third to the last made her appearance, who had the pistol in her dress pocket, and as the examiner at once got his hand upon the pistol, and took it from her pocket, he said:

"Here is the weapon."

"Great God!" was an exclamation that was heard all over the room.

"Maria! O Sister Maria! what have you done?" exclaimed a gentleman, and the entire brother and sisterhood of Naturalists were amazed. Some exclaimed:

"It cannot be possible that our most faithful sister is guilty!"

"No, never! I have done nothing"—

"But how came that pistol in your pocket?" interrupted General Armington, gently. "I do not charge you with the crime, but cannot you tell us how you came to have this pistol in your pocket?"

"I do not know," continued sister Maria.

Nancy Clover's nerves were wrought up to a high pitch of excitement at this state of affairs, and she soliloquized:

"The old fool is being vouched for as one of their most popular and loyal sister Naturalists, which makes it seem dark for me; but I will be calm."

"Think for a moment," said the general, "if you recollect that some one was close enough by you, who might have slipped it into your pocket."

"Curse that old crazy scoundrel," thought Nancy Clover.

"Yes, I do remember!" exclaimed Sister Maria; and, turning toward Nancy Clover, continued: "This woman fainted and threw herself into my arms, and I now remember that she was fumbling about my dress, but then I did not suspicion her; I am sure she is guilty."

The general said: "So I thought," and a groan went through the large crowd. "Sister Maria, you also stand aside," continued the general, "until we finish the balance of the ladies."

In a few moments the rest were examined and vouched for, when the general ordered:

"Captain Thomas, please order your soldiers into the parlor, and form a circle with them, and six of us and these two ladies will go into the centre, and complete our search."

This done, the general questioned Maria as follows:

"You are *sure*, Maria Wilson, that this woman," pointing to Nancy Clover, "was the person that fainted in your arms?"

"I am *most positive* of it," said Maria; "I know by that mark on her forehead."

"Do you think she really fainted?" asked he.

"No; but I can now easily understand why she recovered so quickly after she was done fumbling about my dress," said she; "she evidently only feigned to faint, to deceive me."

"What have *you* to say to this, stranger?" asked the general of Nancy Clover.

"I have never touched this woman, to my recollection," answered Nancy.

"Who are you? What is your name?" questioned the general.

"I cannot see why I should be suspicioned," she ejaculated, waxing indignant; "neither do I see that it is any of your affairs what my name is."

"I will show very soon whether it is or not," responded the general, angrily.

"Look here, general," said the captain, whilst pulling a wig from the chaste stranger's scalpology, "this woman is in disguise; she is evidently a bloody conspirator, fixed up for assassination."

The general took a piercing look at her face and form, when he exclaimed, with holy indignation:

"It is Miss Nancy Clover, the prime minister of the bloody clique, by the gods! How dare you, miserable wretch, come to my house to assassinate my son-in-law?"

Here a tremendous rush was made for the would-be assassin by the Naturalists.

CHAPTER LXXV.

THE ATTEMPTED ASSASSINATION OF DR. JUNO, BY NANCY CLOVER, CAUSED A TERRIBLE PUBLIC WRATH.

HAD General Armington not interfered, the Naturalists would have lynched the indomitable Nancy Clover; but he exclaimed:

"Do not harm the poor wretch, but let her receive an ordinary trial by court martial, which will give her all she deserves; in the mean while, we will send her to prison, until we see the result of the wounds which she has inflicted on Dr. Juno."

"Sir, you are a gentleman, even if you are my enemy, and I thank you for this courtesy to one who would scarcely have done as much for you," said Nancy Clover, really looking grateful at the general; "and, if it is not asking too much, may I be permitted to say a few words in my own behalf?"

"I have no objections; but, to be candid with you, I must assert that you had better not enrage these people too much, as I might not be able to control their just indignation, when you might fare much worse than if you had remained silent. They all consider you guilty, therefore, any denial of, or excuse for, this dastardly act would surely add flame to the fire; but use your own discretion," kindly said the general.

"Well, general, I will speak to you in the presence of all that are here assembled, and say, that I am not guilty of the crime with which I am accused"—

"Silence! impudent, ignorant ingrate," shouted two stentorian voices, which interrupted her speech, and one of them added: "You serpent, liar and assassin, how can you have the audacity to make such remarks in our presence, when you were just told by our kind hearted general to be cautious how you insult us? Do you take us to be fools, or cowards, thinking that you can throw dust into our eyes, because the noble Christian of the house has been lenient with you, and on account of respect to him we have desisted from summarily dispatching you?"

A dash for her was made by men, who almost tore her limb from limb, when she screamed vehemently:

"General! O general! save me!"

"Please desist for a moment," exclaimed the general, which they did at once, when he continued, addressing the assassin:

"Have I not told you to be cautious; why did you not heed me?" and, turning toward his guests, added: "I really would rather not see violence used upon this woman in my house; not that I think she does not deserve instant death, but I dislike to have my residence made a scene of even just shedding of blood!"

"Then, let us take her away from your premises, far enough away, and there do our sworn and imperative duty," ejaculated an indignant Naturalist, whose cry was sanctioned by a general "Amen!" To which General Armington said:

"Still, the principle would be the same as if you acted

so in this house; permit an escort of our brave soldiers to conduct the doomed woman to prison"—

"Then she will be let out on bail," interposed a herculean voice, to which several said:

"That's so."

"I move," said Maria Wilson, into whose pocket the assassin put the pistol, "that we send her to prison, and leave her to the just indignation and scorn of the whole people; and that the whole truth be published in our daily papers to-morrow."

"You are right," said General Armington, and this seemed to pacify the entire company present, and Nancy Clover was conducted to Moyamensing Prison and closely locked up.

The newspapers had a correct statement of what had occurred largely displayed in their local columns, and the reformatory journals had made scathing editorial remarks, whilst the orthodox "press" simply published the local report, as handed to them by the Naturalists.

The spirit of furious war was now infesting the atmosphere, and large groups of all sorts of people were found to congregate in the streets, who discussed both sides of the question; a few made reckless remarks to the effect that "it served him right," meaning Dr. Juno, which were immediately resented by fist, knock-down arguments, which made the sympathizers with the conspirators rather more cautious in their public expressions.

The followers and friends of the bloody conspirators, who had been domineering for many centuries, and claimed licence almost from heaven to usurp every power on earth, were sorely chagrined at the onslaught that was being made upon their kind in successive successful attacks, that they now came to a sense of positive danger to their whole fabric of sectarianism, hence they were being unanimously aroused throughout the country. Telegrams were sent all over the States, requesting the equipment of the saints, politicians and worldlings who agreed with orthodox and unphysiological customs and doctrines, which was the only panacea for the subjugation of the poor, the working trash, who were led on by this Victor Juno, and who were infatuated with the teachings that this bold innovator presented to the masses.

When the "bone and sinew" of the land—the sovereign people—saw that the bigoted sectarian and rotten political spirit was running rampant, they, too, laid their heads together; and the various secret societies throughout the United States held special business meetings, where all the arrangements for a civil war were made, without a single sectarian or politician knowing anything about it; hence the conspirators all over the land were of the opinion that when *they* once commenced to resist the Naturalists by war the latter would be soon subdued and forever silenced! But alas! what a great mistake this presumption of the "elect" proved to be!

CHAPTER LXXVI.

DR. JUNO AND LUCINDA ARMINGTON MAKING LOVE.

"DEAR, precious Victor, although our nuptials were interrupted last night, and your dear life was in great danger, but, as the old saying is, 'a miss is as good as a mile,' I am so thankful to God that your great and noble heart was missed.

"If we had no trials and deprivations we might not appreciate the gifts of heaven as much as you and I do under the various perilous circumstances through which we have passed. Don't you think so?" said Lucinda, with her heaven-blue eyes full of animated love and fire.

"My darling angel, in one sense you are right, but in another wrong," replied Victor; "for instance, if we were perfect, entirely perfect Naturalists, and were surrounded by similar creatures, it would not enhance our joy to be persecuted, tortured and libelled; but as long as we are far from being perfect Naturalists, and are neither surrounded by such, we have not the capacity of appreciating God's last and noblest piece of mechanism, without being stimulated by the undulations in life's great battle.

"Therefore, precious Lucinda, we sinful creatures are benefited by great contrasts; but if we really were the purified 'temples of God' we would love Him with all our strength, and one another as ourselves, which was the hallowed rule that the blessed, loving and beloved Naturalist —Jesus Christ—laid down for us! Love, immaculate love, unalloyed by self, should be the only law that real Naturalists or Christians should learn to understand, possess and obey; but as the means are not used to gain this end, we as a nation can never fully appreciate God's goodness toward the highest type of His mechanism."

"But, dear Victor, do you not love me more than a perfect Naturalist would 'love his neighbor,' as Jesus says?" asked she.

"Do you suppose, my most precious darling, that I could love you more than, or even as much, as Christ loved the world? Not that He loved the *evil ways* of sinners, but He loved sinners, because they were part and parcel of the Creator; and although He denounced the selfish, self-righteous, self-willed and haughty viper, who had only a whit of God's vitality in him, Christ did not turn away from those who were born and bred under morbid circumstances, visiting thereby upon the human species, weaknesses over which they had no control.

"By looking over all the teachings, acts and life of Christ, you will behold what powerful love He possessed for the passive sinner, for the sinner who was penitent, who was willing to learn and live out God's fixed laws, and by love (as we claim to heed the many admonitions that God alone is just), we can appreciate His highest law the more, namely, 'Love.' Do you not think so?"

"Indeed, indeed I do, and I love you so much *more* when I see that your noble mind is fairly wrapt up in the great science of human life, and in the herculean effort of perpetuating it everlastingly. What a crown you will have laid up in heaven for yourself by this noble and godlike work in which you have been engaged all your life, through calm and storm, in spite of opposition, persecution and martyrdom!

"Who, that possessed any good sense, could fail to love you, to almost revere and idolize you, as I do?" ejaculated Lucinda, with a serenity of expression that almost excelled the archangels.

"I devoutly praise the Lord for your appreciation of my love, which you have so tenderly, earnestly, ardently and innocently expressed. It vitalizes every fibre that has been wounded by that assassin, and it makes me almost love the hand that brought me to this sick-bed, where I have learned to love whatever partakes of God's vitality," said Victor.

"O Victor! most glorious Victor! I cannot help realizing that you possess a Christ-like heart," interposed she "for you would pardon this person, I believe, who has within a hair's breadth taken your precious life, if she would ask for forgiveness."

"She!" said he; "what do you mean by 'she?' It is not possible that a woman fired that bullet at me?"

"Yes, dearest love, it was a woman," responded she.

"God forgive the woman," sighed he.

"I am not so sure that He will forgive her, unless she changes her course of conduct," responded Lucinda.

"Who was she? What is her name?" asked he.

"It was Miss Nancy Clover," said she.

"Nancy Clover!" ejaculated he.

"Yes; that fiend," said Lucinda.

"Well, well; these bloody conspirators are becoming desperate," said he; "but let us not discuss disagreeable things, but let me tell you of my love for you, my saint."

"Oh, do; exquisite Victor," interposed she.

"I love you with a love that passes not away with man's

passion; but a love that is registered in the *book of life;* a treasure in heaven, where my heart is also; hence, it can never fail, can never lose its ardor; and when once legitimately centered upon the normal propensities, I hope will magnetize the physical organism to perfection, that will cause the elements of human life to flow with the extremest mental joys and physical pleasures, in the consummation of the command to 'increase and multiply,' in the blessed 'Image of God.'"

"Darling, you speak beautifully; but I cannot say that I comprehend you exactly," modestly exclaimed she.

"Oh, never mind; you will understand all in due time, and be blessed, I think, with those blessed gifts of which Christ says: '*For of such is the kingdom of heaven,*'" said Victor, when she laid her head on his breast, and their souls bled with joy.

These lovers were continually together until Dr. Juno was able to go about his business. They postponed their wedding day for a month, and in the meantime were in good spirits; but Miss Armington was convinced in her own mind that war would break out before their wedding day would arrive, when a further postponement would be necessary.

She did not look upon the dark side of the picture; neither did she desire to put gloomy feelings before the mind of her beloved Victor, who needed encouragement just then to assist his cure; but she saw war, cruel, terrible war; a civil war which would subjugate the sovereign people of America, and give the spirit of selfishness and anti-Christ sole control of Church and State.

CHAPTER LXXVII.

CONGRESS MOBBED FOR RECOGNIZING GOD IN THE CONSTITUTION.

WHEN the religious people found that Miss Nancy Clover was cast into prison, they went unanimously to work to have her freed on bail; and as Dr. Juno improved *very* rapidly, having actually not at any time been in danger of losing his life by the pistol wound, on account of having had too healthy blood and solid bodily tissues, therefore nothing but the penetration of a vital organ could have caused his death, she was allowed to enter twenty thousand dollars security for her appearance at Court; and when she was again at liberty, she created a terrific stir throughout the orthodox community; hence, a feeler was thrown out by the saints.

They petitioned the United States Congress, which was in session, in the strongest terms, demanding that God should be recognized in the Constitution of the United States. The following were the leading points, which fairly broke the camel's back:

"We, the evangelical, religious denominations of the United States, hereby petition to the sixty ——— Congress to enact a law whereby the Constitution of the United States be instantly amended, as follows:

"WHEREAS, Numerous blasphemous and Sabbath-breaking organizations are regularly holding secret meetings, throughout the country, for the purpose of desecrating the Lord's Day, and subverting the holy religion of the Lord Jesus Christ, and,

"WHEREAS, A certain innovator has violated the most sacred institutions and holy rights of God's elect, by riot and bloodshed, and,

"WHEREAS, This outlaw threatens to mob the holy saints, and is already so great a terror to the nation that public officials everywhere dare not enforce the laws against him; therefore, be it

"*Resolved*, That the holy religion of the Lord Jesus Christ be acknowledged in the Constitution of the United States, and it is hereby enacted and ratified by the majority of the members in Congress assembled, that,

"FIRSTLY—No one shall be allowed to preach the Gospel of Christ who has not been regularly ordained in some orthodox evangelical denomination; and,

"SECONDLY—That no ordained preacher shall be allowed to preach, as a minister of the Gospel, or perform similar functions, who is not in good standing in a regular evangelical church organization; and,

"THIRDLY—That the Sabbath day shall be kept as the Lord's day, in which no secular or worldly work, business or recreation shall be allowed to be performed; and,

"FOURTHLY—That every citizen shall attend once on each Lord's day (unless too ill to go) some evangelical church that is in good standing; and,

"FIFTHLY—That each and every evangelical denomination shall have to undergo, annually, an examination by a Board of Censors; which '*Board of Censors*' shall be composed of one or more of the leading officers (bishop, priest, elder, deacon, etc.,) of each evangelical denomination; and,

"SIXTHLY—That all children, as soon as old enough to understand their paternal dialect, shall each Sabbath day attend some evangelical Sabbath school, where the Holy Bible is read and taught; and,

"SEVENTHLY—That all other worship, claiming to be religion, shall be suppressed, and its leaders shall be tried by a jury of twelve evangelical Christians, who are of good standing in some evangelical church of good repute; and if found guilty of violating one or all of said ordinances herein expressed, shall suffer the penalty of death by hanging; and,

"EIGHTHLY—That this Amendment shall instantly

take effect, and that each informer on an innovator and violator of said Constitutional Amendment shall receive from the treasury of the United States as reward one thousand dollars, one half of which he shall donate to the church of which he is a member, and the same shall be so recorded on the church book, and shall be accounted, '*Reward laid up in heaven.*'"

The foregoing Amendment scheme was a "feeler," which met with favor at the capital of the United States, where inksucking scoundrels had two-thirds of a majority, and who were ready for anything that placed *filthy lucre* into their pockets; this the evangelical amendors knew; hence instantly raised one hundred millions of dollars, which was divided between the *lucre*-seeking Legislators, and which gave the sovereign working people (who were taxed in the long run for every cent of this money) a loathing for the whole batch of usurpers and cut-throats; and as soon as the Amendment was announced as having passed, an army of Naturalists were found surrounding the capitol at Washington, D. C., who opened a terrific fire, with shot and shell, upon the building wherein Congress sat, which caused the bribed scoundrels to scatter, some endeavoring to escape through the lines of the soldiers, who were shot down like brutes, whilst others hid in the cellar, in niches and corners of the great marble structure; but all this availed them nothing, because every man who voted for the Amendment was killed in less than ten hours.

The President telegraphed to the Governor of each State to send on all the militia that could be mustered, as a furious war had commenced, which required every available means to subdue; but only three Governors responded to this call.

CHAPTER LXXVIII.

Dr. Juno's First Great War Proclamation.

WHEN the newspapers all over the Union had published this unconstitutional Amendment, it aroused the masses amazingly; even those who formerly had no sympathy with Dr. Juno, nor love for his doctrines, now freely investigated his teachings, and almost like magic he became the accepted heroic reformer of the close of the nineteenth century.

In fact, the orthodox "public press" all over the country disapproved the course which Congress had taken; because this usurpation came too close home to many, who were willing to ride on the backs of sectarians and politicians, so long as it paid them and *their* precious rights were not too closely clipped; but this Amendment their own "Scribes" stigmatized as "a dangerous usurpation, that cannot be tolerated in this nation!"

This was throwing fuel upon Dr. Juno's hearth, and he was wise enough to see it, and made capital of it by issuing the following:

Proclamation.

"Fellow Citizens:—From the condition of things in general, I am constrained to issue this, my *first*, Proclamation to the people of the United States of America.

"Firstly—I ask each one, male and female, of all colors and nations, who reside within the jurisdiction of the United States, to join the Naturalists, who inculcate the observance of all natural laws, and have but one faith, one God, and are members of one family, whose *highest law* is love to God and man, whose *aim* is happiness, whose *end* is universal salvation by a return to, and obedience of, the Creator's fixed natural injunctions.

"Secondly—I offer protection to all people who are

opposed to the power that money and *lucre*-gained positions wield; who are opposed to sectarian and political cliques and rings, that have recently shown to the world, by a Constitutional Amendment, what I have always said they would do, if permitted ; and you, the sovereign people, '*the bone and sinew*' of America, have, by your unconcerned silence and forbearance, given them permission to place scoundrels into all the high positions in Church and State, which was giving them the power to cut down your 'Inalienable rights to serve God according to the dictates of conscience,' and to keep science from the field of human life.

"THIRDLY—I also offer succor to all the people who will, in this hour of war, aid us in slaying and subjugating these criminals, who have stolen the livery of heaven to serve the devil in, no matter whether such people are Jews, Gentiles, Protestants, Catholics or Worldlings; and if, after they are vanquished, and peace is declared, the said Jews, Gentiles, Protestants, Catholics or Worldlings cannot conscientiously join the Naturalists, they shall not be molested in thinking and acting as they choose, so long as they do *not* become a nuisance, an injury and meddlers in our affairs.

"FOURTHLY—I proclaim that no more dishonest men or women shall hold any office in the United States so long as I have influence enough to prevent it ; but I claim that if my doctrines (as laid down in the forty-second chapter of this truthful novel), were observed, by making an amendment to the Constitution of the United States that no man shall become a millionaire whilst thereby hundreds are made paupers, dishonest officials would naturally become obsolete ; when a healthier state of affairs would reign, and plenty of time would be afforded every one to devote himself and herself to pleasant and rational enjoyment, which would make earth heavenly, a thing that these vipers and constitutional usurpers would deprive every person from doing, by their selfish anti-Christ and anti-natural dictations.

"FIFTHLY—I would kindly hint that there is now left only *one* of two things : first, join us in conquering the usurpers and bloody conspirators, and remain free to serve God according to the dictation of conscience ; or, second, remain passive or neutral in this conflict, and thereby, without action, aid those who would rob us all of our property, of our natural rights, of our salvation, and call it the piety of the '*elect*,' from which, great Lord, deliver us !

"I appeal, in conclusion, to all the people, to seriously pause before they cast their lot with the destroyers of every liberty and comfort that God and a sound physiology have vouchsafed unto every human soul. I pray, all the people, for their children's and grandchildren's sake ; and for the sake of God and the angels, to assist us in subjugating our enemies ; when war, rumors of war, famine, pestilence and hard times would come no more ; when all sorts of slavery, all sorts of selfishness, usurpation and anarchy would take wings and fly to the infernal realms of damnation !

{SEAL} "In the name of God and man, I hereunto set my hand and seal, this —— day of ——, 1900.

"VICTOR JUNO."

It was astonishing to see the effect this proclamation had upon the masses of the people. And it was still *more* astounding to see that every newspaper, daily, weekly and monthly, published it. Some of the most bitter orthodox papers published it as a presumptuous and wrath-exciting document, hoping by so doing they would rile and arouse the people in their favor ; whilst others inserted it, for fear its omission might create an onslaught upon them. Many of these people, pharisee-like—*à la* Rev. Joe Pier—were afraid to die in their hardened sectarian sinfulness ; therefore they would do, on such occasions, as they were taught, by precept and example, by their *blind leaders* to do all their lives, namely : act the hypocrite. If they were experts in nothing else, they were in hypocrisy. A poor wind that does not blow some one good, is an old saying, and I might apply it to the traitors of all countries and nations, who betrayed either party for gain of some kind, and to gain an extended lease of life was a sweet balm of Gilead to treacherous cowards, knaves and hypocrites!

CHAPTER LXXIX.

DR. JUNO'S TERRIBLE ARMY ORDERS.

NOW, cruel war was fairly in operation when the wedding day of Victor and Lucinda had to be again postponed, as Dr. Victor Juno was the Chief General, and in fact Father of the Naturalists, who instituted this revolution that now called him into the field of terror.

General Washington Armington, who was a powerful and eminently popular tactician, having earned a world renowned fame in the War of Mexico and in the more recent Rebellion with the Southern Confederacy, was second in command to Dr. Juno; and as the former was the intended father-in-law of the latter, they were sworn friends, who wielded a talismanic influence at home, where they were best known.

Harry Gossimer—the was-to-be drowned conspirator—who labored in the West under an assumed name (but for convenience' sake we call him by his own name—General Harry Gossimer), led a Western army into Washington, where the war was commenced, and generaled that successful attack upon the bribed and cowardly Congressmen; but who was driven speedily westward by the militia, who obeyed the President's call.

Dr. Juno now took the field, and moved instantly in the rear of the conspirators' army that drove General Gossimer westward, and on reaching the country through which the armies had passed, Dr. Juno issued the following:

Army Order Number One of the Naturalists.

"*To the Sovereign, God-fearing and loving People I issue this Order, with a determination to carry it out to the letter:*

"First—All persons who aid the army of the conspirators shall be considered as the allies of the enemies of the working people.

"Second—All the enemies to the working classes and Naturalists shall be shot, unless they were forced to take up arms, and, when taken prisoners, must at once be sworn into the army of the Naturalists, and enter their ranks, or be shot on the spot.

"Third—The sick and wounded of the enemy shall be humanely cared for until well enough to take our oath of allegiance; and, when sufficiently recovered, shall take the field against the conspirators, or be shot.

"Fourth—No distinction shall be made between the sexes, so far as our enemies are concerned; but little children alone shall be kindly and tenderly guarded and protected, no matter who are the parents, for they have had no choice in the conflict, have no voice; hence, must be cared for; this is peremptory. Females are not compelled to take up arms, but they must take positive sides, and be treated as friends or enemies; and if enemies, must be shot the same as men for their disloyalty to the natural cause of the producers.

"Fifth—This war was not our production, but we were compelled to strike for God and mankind, or suffer the devil to swallow us and our descendants up in victory; therefore, we are in favor of being as cruel as we can be to our enemies, for the purpose of giving them the sooner a surfeit of rebellion to God and mankind.

"Sixth—We await with open arms the return of the prodigals, or we shall wave the black flag over their heads. War knows nothing but cruelty and death to the foe; and on these principles has this strife been inaugurated by the bloody conspirators, and on the same platform it shall be carried on and ended.

"My soldiers will promptly execute every part of my *first* proclamation, and this my first army order.

"Given at Headquarters of the Army of the Naturalists, this sixth day of ———, 19—, by

"VICTOR JUNO."

When this army order was published, many said that General Juno could never raise an army under such discipline that would be able to cope with the army of the orthodox people; moreover, that thousands would not join his cause that would have done so had he accepted the customary course that is pursued in time of war; but Dr. Juno was an original man, and knew what he was doing.

It was a grand mistake on the part of the sectarian conspirators to flatter themselves that any such cruelly stringent orders from Dr. Juno would prevent him from having a sufficiently numerous army and navy to enforce his commands; but his enemies did not know that all the *secret beneficial societies* throughout the United States, and even Canada, were a unit in fighting for the working people's cause, which Dr. Juno espoused; therefore, when the "tyrant"—Juno—as he was called, wanted more men, all he had to do was to say so, and on all occasions, and in every part of the country, they came forth equipped and drilled soldiers.

This amazed the orthodox advocates, whilst it frightened thousands so badly that they esteemed General Juno as a man of talismanic powers, whose will and orders dared not be opposed with impunity; still, the orthodoxy had the most money; hence, could buy enough drunken and daredevil men to make up an immensely numerous army and navy, far outnumbering the Naturalists' soldiers; but the purchased men fought for gain, and not for principle, and constituted a dissipated and drunken army and navy, whose leading officers often were dead drunk when the most fierce battles raged.

On the other hand, General Juno's army and navy was

composed of men who fought for principle, and who had been the "bone and sinew" of the nation from their birth; therefore, the following:

Army Order Number Two of the Naturalists.

"*To the Soldiers and Marines of the Naturalists:*—I have simply to say that they shall be fed on the best fruits, grains, vegetables and lean herbivorous meat that the country can afford. Those who remain at home, except the little children, *shall* live on the poorest food, whilst you will have the very best, which is necessary to carry you through the war with safety.

"Water and pure liquors are the only admissible beverages, and the latter shall only be used as stimulants and medicines by those who have been in the habit of the vice of stimulating. The physicians will see who needs the pure liquors.

"Clothing, blankets and general equipments shall also be of the best in the land; but no fashionable and useless display shall be tolerated.

"Tobacco, spices, drugs and other delicacies shall not be admissible under any pretext; and our hygienic medical and surgical treatment will furnish better remedies. Every secret beneficial society has had several men and women educated as physicians and surgeons, who understand the law of cure or law of growth; therefore, our soldiers and marines shall be killed in battle only, and not in hospitals by charlatans.

"By treating our soldiers and marines to food and drink that makes nothing but pure blood and solid nerves, flesh and bones, their wounds will heal like magic; hence, we have no dead weight on our hands, by having two-thirds of them in hospitals; nor will we have any prisoners of war to guard and feed, because we send them as sworn soldiers into our ranks, or shoot them charitably, ending their lives hastily.

"Given at headquarters of the Army of the Naturalists, this —— of ——, 19—, by   Victor Juno."

CHAPTER LXXX.

RETALIATORY MEASURES OF THE CONSPIRATORS' ARMY.

WHEN the army and navy of the conspirators became acquainted with the black-flag order by Dr. Juno, they appealed to their officers for the privilege of retaliating, by not giving any quarters to the Naturalists. To this the officers did not object in the least, but were rather pleased with the idea of summary retaliation, forgetting that such a course of licence to a drunken, paid and dare-devil army of men was a dangerous pretext, dangerous to their own safety, and the safety of their own people; because such privileged licence was only proper with men who fought for principle, fought for what they loved and knew was right.

This privilege of retaliation, granted to an army and navy of men that were not interested in the cause for which they fought for lucre, could easily be turned to advantage against their own employers, provided insults were offered these soldiers and marines, or if a chance for greater gain of money could be obtained, they would carry their retaliative measures as willingly against their own people as against any other; and as these hired soldiers hated the rich people, who had always made, and still make mere slaves and drudges of them, it was a great oversight in the officers of the orthodox army and navy to permit retaliation.

Dr. Juno having been a man of extensive foresight, who fully comprehended human nature in all its numerical phases, saw all these things in advance; hence, was prepared to take advantage of everything.

He told his men that their enemies should surely retaliate, and if they did it would be a great feather in his cap, because such a shiftless, dissipated and unprincipled set of hireling warriors, as they, would soon ravish their wealthy masters; yes, rob their leaders, slay them, and seduce their women, in retaliation for the wealth and power the rich have always had over them.

No one should be so big a fool as to think that the poor, the wretched, and even the most debauched, had no desire to possess large amounts of filthy lucre. These were the very people who saw the most value in the dirty stuff; therefore, they felt vindictive, and were inclined to retaliate on their employers even before they had received their bounty.

They looked upon the war, for which they were hired to shoot people, as a popular way of being paid for murdering innocent people in cold blood by the wholesale; hence, a single-handed murder, in all time to come, seemed to them a trifling offence, as compared with the wholesale butchery to which they were accessory.

To the wise, these conclusions are scientific; and the prophecy of these deductions may be seen, in time to come, to be fulfilled to the letter, as they have been in the past. Dr. Juno had all his officers instructed, before the war was known of, in all the important points that would be necessary to successfully consummate the work of the Reformation. He said, often, to his disciples:

"Beloved Naturalists, evils must often be exchanged for evils, when *false prophets* and *blind leaders* are recognized as the sovereigns of a nation or nations; because all the conditions surrounding the people are, under this state of affairs, unfavorable to the purification and elevation of the race; hence even the best men and women of such a nation are creatures of morbid circumstances; therefore cruel war, to speedily wipe out self-righteous and domineering leaders and their satellites, would be a charity, although a cruel momentary caustic to create a healthful granulation of a malignant indolent sore, which requires the most fiery escharotic to burn out the virus of such a detrimental disease!

"I am for peace and good will to man; but before the calm and balm of peace can come to such a wicked, Godforsaken, lucre-worshipping people, as this generation of the bloody conspirators are, we must thoroughly purge this terrestrial globe with fire, thunder and lightning, and wash the sins of hereditary diathesis from amongst the propagators of future generations!

"The quickest way to do this the easier and better the results; hence an internal war that will strike terror to the hearts of the self-righteous, Bible-hardened and reckless transgressors of fixed law, will be the only specific panacea for the thorough eradication of our national consumption.

"This, dear Naturalists, is my apology for instituting a rigorous and black-flag war, the cruelty and terror of which was never, and shall never be known. And if it pleases God that *I* shall be the greatest sufferer by it—as I have always suffered by adhering to these teachings—I am very willing to hold out faithful to the end, and thank the spirit that moved me to commence and consummate this work, which I am fully convinced will be finished by you if I should fall in the first battle; therefore strike with a glowing heart, and strike vehemently, and do not spare a foe any more than God Himself would save an impenitent soul from perdition! So help you God!"

With such teachings, tactics and management as Dr. Juno has for years labored to instil into and establish amongst his followers there was sufficient magical vitality and heavenly bounty bestowed upon them to satiate all with a never-ceasing love for God and mankind! Hence when they went into the field of battle with a hired foe they cared nothing for such retaliation as could be heaped upon them.

The first retaliation that transpired fell upon the innocent of the conspirators' own flesh and blood, which demoralized an already demoralized and debauched army; therefore, twenty of these soldiers were not equal to one Naturalist! This was proved by the first great battle, which was fought on the western shores of the State of Virginia.

General Gossimer had only two thousand men thoroughly equipped, who were being driven by an orthodox standing army of forty thousand regular soldiers, whilst Dr. Juno pursued the pursuers of General Gossimer with only five thousand picked Naturalists; and when Dr. Juno's brigade had reached the pursuing conspirators' army, he ordered an immediate assault, and General Armington directed the attack, whilst Dr. Juno ordered General Gossimer to turn upon the foe, when thirty thousand conspirators fell dead, besides the wounded; but only six hundred Naturalists were killed and wounded!

General Armington took the balance prisoners, and Dr. Juno immediately appeared upon the ground to swear into his own army those who were ready to side with the Naturalists, and those who refused were shot dead without compunction of conscience!

CHAPTER LXXXI.

CAPTURED CONSPIRATORS SHOT DEAD.

DR. JUNO addressed the prisoners, who were not too badly wounded to comprehend him, as follows:

"FELLOW-CITIZENS AND PRISONERS:— We do not war against men for gain, or for glory of men, but for the rights of all who were of woman born, for equal rights, for just rights, for the subjugation of those who possess more than their share of this world's goods, for the subversion of those who pay you with the money which belongs as much to you as to them to fight for them, so that they can continue to usurp every right of mankind, and thereby hold you in bondage to their heinous tyranny!

"But we are here as *your* friends, the friends of the whole people, who are willing to live and let live as freely as they themselves wish to live. I ask you to join us, and if you refuse you may know the consequences. Those who desire to join us will move in the direction of our soldiers."

Room was made for the prisoners who desired to join the Naturalists to walk within the lines of the latter, when all passed over except what remained of two regiments, when Dr. Juno continued:

"Do you, who remain in your old position, desire to continue rebellious? I will give you thirty minutes to consider the question of either joining our cause and our army or to be shot dead within that time!"

"You would not dare to shoot us," ejaculated a half-intoxicated and impudent colonel of one of the regiments.

"Do not be deceived, my misled man," said Dr. Juno; "but you will see that I shall do that very thing."

Dr. Juno now administered the oath of allegiance to those who were willing to join his army. The following is the oath:

"'You do solemnly swear that you will join the army and cause of the Naturalists, and will nevermore, by word or deed, aid or abet the orthodox or conspirators' army or navy; but will faithfully obey the commanders of the Naturalists.' All those of you who are willing to abide by this oath, or expect to be shot dead, if violating it, will signify it by raising their left hands toward heaven, and placing their right hands upon their hearts."

It only took a few minutes to administer this oath to a whole regiment, on account of being able to administer it to them all at once; because the answering it with their hands gave the officers a chance to see if all had taken it. When Dr. Juno had finished this task, he said to the rebellious prisoners:

"You have five minutes to decide between death and joining our army."

Which caused about two dozen more to take the oath; and when they had done so, the same colonel cried out:

"Cowards! you do not mean to fight for the heretics; I know you won't, but you are scared by the high-flowing language of this braggadocio; he dare not shoot us, and he knows it."

"Your time for repentance has expired; your hour of grace has gone by. Soldiers, prepare to fire," here a regiment of Naturalists formed into line, when he continued: "Aim, may God have mercy on your souls, fire." Bang! off went the rifles, and about one-half fell stone dead, when Dr. Juno repeated: "Soldiers, prepare to fire; aim, may God have mercy on your souls, fire!" when the balance were dispatched, without one prisoner failing to expire at once, except the impudent colonel, who was not yet aimed at. When Dr. Juno saw this, he said:

"Providence or chance has saved your miserable life, and before I will order you to be shot, I will permit you to say what you now think; whether I 'dare not shoot' you?"

"Sir," quite humbly said the colonel, who seemed fully sobered by this time, "you are a brave man; and if you will permit me, at this late hour, I will cheerfully fight desperately under so heroic a commander as yourself. I pray you, accept my offer."

"Certainly, sir," responded Dr. Juno; "come and take the oath, and you may be of great service to us, if for nothing else but to warn others, who in the future may be of your opinion. I do not desire to shoot men in this or any other manner; but war means surrender to the strongest or death, and this is the only way to strengthen and make an army victorious."

"If I may be so bold as to ask, are you not afraid that these compulsory deserters might turn upon you, when an opportunity affords?" said the colonel.

"Not at all," smilingly answered Dr. Juno; "we are guarded against that, and our remedy is specific, which you may see some day."

"I hope so, indeed, since I have become a Naturalist," said the colonel; "but your most generous and sound sense address to our men, previous to ordering any of us into your ranks, then touched my better nature; still, I felt ugly toward all of you, and I must say without a cause, for I am already convinced that your motives and teachings are misunderstood by the great majority of our soldiers."

"May God open the eyes of all before one more drop of blood is spilled," sadly responded Dr. Juno.

"Amen!" came from hundreds of the men, and some of them had large tears in their eyes, caused by the sincere, earnest and impressive manner in which Juno said:

"May God open the eyes of all before one more drop of blood is spilled."

Let the reader, for one moment, think of a man who had suffered for nearly half a century the most barbarous martyrdom, and when he had it in his power to speedily annihilate every one of his enemies and become dictator, he could utter the foregoing sentence and act upon it!

Was this not enough to cause the spirit of Christ to hover around the hearts of all who saw such an act by man? Could anything more noble, more Christ-like, more God-like be done by sinful mortal? And could any heart be so stony as to spurn such an achievement?

CHAPTER LXXXII.

THE RELIGIOUS CONSPIRATORS DUMBFOUNDED.

THE newspapers all over the country published the Proclamation and Army Orders of Dr. Juno, which, however, few but his own people believed he would execute; but after he did so the whole orthodox world was dumbfounded; in fact, they could not believe that the man lived who would assume such a responsibility as to inaugurate such black deeds as shooting dead prisoners of war! But such was the case, and many of the public journals denounced Juno as an infamous tyrant and dastardly usurper, whilst the liberal "Press" approved of this novel but effectual warfare!

The President ordered a draft to be made for five hundred thousand men, and issued a proclamation ordering the guarding of every arsenal in the Union; but he was too late, because seven-eighths of them had already been in secret possession of the Naturalists, and by the time the draft was fairly begun, over nine hundred thousand Naturalists were in the field equipped with the military trappings which were stored in said United States arsenals; even the war vessels had nearly all been in possession of the Naturalists, which was a dreadful state of affairs!

There was but one thing left for the orthodox people, and that was to offer immense bounties, amounting to five and six thousand dollars for good able-bodied soldiers, who were familiar with tactics, and half as much for green men; this was sufficient inducement to raise an immense army and navy, the President having by this time made an additional call, making altogether over one million of men!

But, alas! when the officials of the government that was, —the orthodoxy—went to the various arsenals for the implements of war, great Mars, they were apparently empty; the muskets, cannon and accoutrements had fled, and what to do with this immense army and navy, and not enough weapons to equip one-half of them, was a stunner!

This news was kept as secret as possible. The orthodoxy would not expose it, because the effect would be fatal to their cause; and the Naturalists would never divulge their secret operations, hoping, however, to astonish their enemies when the crisis of war would come!

There were many excellent generals in the orthodox army, who were on the field, and who mustered and marched all their equipped veterans toward the main army of Dr. Juno, hoping and expecting to out-general him and, if possible, take him prisoner and shoot him, as he shot their men.

A terrific battle was fought in the southern part of Ohio, where the army of the Naturalists lost ten thousand men in one day in killed and wounded, which made things look blue; but in less than twenty-four hours they were reinforced secretly, or unexpectedly to the orthodox army, when the wheels of fortune were immediately reversed, and over thirty thousand conspirators fell dead in six hours, ten thousand prisoners were taken, and the balance of them escaped the fire and wrath of Juno's men.

The same day the prisoners were again challenged, as before, when about two-thirds of them could not resist Dr. Juno's appeal, nor cared to be summarily sent beyond this shoal of tears; the persistent and rebellious ones were shot dead, except four orthodox generals, who, of course, would not join the Naturalists, and they felt certain Dr. Juno would not shoot them. He addressed them as follows, after he had the balance shot:

"Brave soldiers! You are the leaders of a misled and drunken people! You have deserved ten deaths, where these poor soldiers that have just fallen at our hands have scarcely deserved death. But my way of carrying on war is greatly different from old customs and usages, and all who are fools enough to join your army and navy cannot expect any better than death if caught in rebellion against the sovereign people's rights!

"Although you deserve instant death, I will still not have you shot until such time as I find it necessary for my own safety to shoot you. I do not believe in policy in times of peace, but in the terrible hour of war good management points me out the plan I am about to institute.

"I will retain you as hostages, and should any of my generals or myself ever be taken as prisoners of war by your people, I will now issue my order that if we are shot, or whatever ill usage we shall receive, shall instantly be given to you in return. If you have anything to say, now is your time; I make it a rule never to execute or imprison a foe without giving him an opportunity to fully vindicate himself by words, if he can do so, and I hope I shall in all future time be granted the same privilege, which, however, your people have denied me for nearly twenty-five years.

"Yes, they have closed the newspaper columns against me, have robbed me and mine of every right that God and a free Republic permit their subjects; and since you and yours have started the war, we mean to finish it in prime order. Now, I shall be happy to hear from the intelligent gentlemen who stand before me."

"Noble sir," said the eldest of the four, "we have never before been able to appreciate your excellent character, and although you have always done business in an original manner, we have not given you credit for being so great a philosopher and general as your novel tactics prove you to be. It is said that still waters run deep, and I have been of the opinion, a month ago, that you could not raise ten thousand soldiers, but I now see that, whilst you seemed to be apparently *still* of late years, you have been running deep, working most wisely in secret; and although I am your prisoner, I do not fear that any insult or injustice shall be visited upon us, whilst your hostages; therefore we shall cheerfully submit to whatever you dictate."

"You flatter me," responded Dr. Juno; "but whilst I harbor no malice, I am nevertheless not easily gulled by flattery. But I may never find it in my power to repay the debt I owe the leaders of the orthodox conspirators; still, I will assure you that *you* will never harm myself or my cause any more, and if I did not see the necessity of using a little policy in case of a mishap, I would shoot you with as little compunction of conscience as I would kill a snake. I mean this kindly, because duty cries aloud for such kindness to the little ones; and as long as the accursed doctrines of orthodoxy rule, human souls will be sprung into existence at haphazard, through lust and assumed chastity, whilst the land will be flooded with criminals to the manner born, who are reared with less science and care than farm brutes or vermin."

CHAPTER LXXXIII.

DR. JUNO WRITES TO HIS LUCINDA.

DOCTOR JUNO ordered that it should be kept a secret that these hostages—the four generals—were alive, until such time as he saw fit to permit its publication. He said:

"Let the enemy think that we have shot them as well as the common soldiers."

He now wrote the following letter to his beloved Lucinda:

"HEADQUARTERS OF THE ARMY OF THE NATURALISTS,
"*December* —, 19—.

"MY DEARLY BELOVED LUCINDA:—I have great cause to thank God and the working people for the advancement of our cause. I have just taken many prisoners, and amongst them four of the greatest generals that this country can produce. I did not shoot the latter, but wisely retained them, my darling, for hostages; because I may some day fall into the enemy's hands; and I will here say that I expect some immense fighting shortly, and whilst I have it kept a secret that I have not shot the generals, I wish you to keep posted in all that transpires; and should your father, myself, or other Naturalists be taken prisoners, I desire that you at once execute the plan that I have left to your hands; and should they kill me, do not despair, my most precious darling, but carry out my will, as you have it with you. The Secret Order of Naturalists will obey you to the letter in carrying it out.

"I do not wish to distress you, sweet angel, but you know I am amongst the army, and often in the thick of battle; but the angels guard the soul of man who proves faithful to God's cause. Should I never see you more, which, however, I hope to do, be assured that as my spirit liveth, it shall whisper comfort into your soul, and when you come home, where parting shall be no more, we will have cause to praise God with such delight that the supremest joys will quicken and eternally magnify our great love for Him and one another.

"We do not die (but simply go to our Father who is in heaven) when the spirit leaves this mortal coil; and I do not fear him who can destroy the body, but cannot harm soul or spirit!

"I dress like a common soldier when in battle, but on other occasions I wear my uniform as general. I am well and in excellent spirits. Be of good cheer, and give my love to all who may honor me sufficiently to enquire after my health; and, most *dear* angel, keep a mountain of my warmest gushing affection for your holy self. Farewell, and may heaven smile upon us all, and upon our enemies, and upon those *particularly* whom I am *compelled* to send hence so speedily.

"From your own Faithful   VICTOR."

"HEADQUARTERS OF THE ARMY OF THE NATURALISTS,
"*January* —, 19—.

"MY PRECIOUS DARLING:—I hastily take my pencil to write you particulars of the state of our position, and the intention of the enemy. I have just heard from three Naturalists, who are in the conspirators' army, and whilst we are never entrenching ourselves very strongly, we have on this occasion thrown up strong breastworks; but we shall to-morrow morning, at six o'clock sharp, go for the enemy, and your father, General Gossimer and myself shall be in the heat of battle until we win the day or die on the field.

"Our three spies say that the enemy is making its best effort to whip us, and if they fail this time, all is over with them: but if they win, they expect to retaliate and rout us, and speedily end the war. They do not know what we know; do they, precious dear? They have three men to one of ours, still, that is nothing; but if you hear that we lose, arouse the Naturalists all over the Union.

"Do it any way, as soon as you receive this letter. The orthodox army is awfully demoralized, and many of their officers are fashionable topers, who are setting a bad example to their men; but with us it is otherwise. Considering, then, that we are clear-headed, and they nearly all intoxicated, who can doubt what the result will be? Still, we may lose the battle; at any rate, this is to be the fiercest butchery that was ever fought on American soil.

"Arouse the Naturalists, and fear nothing, my sweet dear. Trust to God and the right, and all will be well. Farewell, darling.

"I remain until death, your own   VICTOR."

"TERRES GARDEN, *Jan.* 9, 1900.

"MY OWN DEAR VICTOR:—I received your last letter about an hour ago, and whilst I am no coward, still I am afraid that sooner or later you will fall into the enemies' hands, when they will shoot you in retaliation.

"I do not wish to lose you, and live myself. Should you be killed, I promise you that I will instantly take your place, and fight to the death. I am not revengeful, but I am *sure* that you are in the right; and as I love you, equally so do I love the cause for which you have jeopardized your precious life a thousand times; and when you are gone, what have I to love or live for but that which you loved, lived and died for?

"The orthodox community are fairly in a foam about your black-flag proclamation, and its execution on the field of conflict. They denounce you in the strongest terms that language can express, and if they were not afraid of the working people and Naturalists, they would set a reward of millions on your head.

"I assure you, most precious Victor, that I am, and have continually been, arousing the Naturalists in an effectual manner, and I am making hundreds of converts to our cause daily. If you are the head in the field of battle, I am the head in the field of conversion. Trust me with anything that may aid you, and I will at it with a vim.

"Precious Victor, please write to me as often as you can, for I am awfully anxious to hear from you personally, although I am very busy in arranging regiment after regiment, which I fill up by my secret workings, and by lecturing in public. I suppose you will feel astonished at this, but I cannot be idle and grieve, like too many women would do under similar circumstances, whilst I am capable of practically helping you and the great cause of mankind.

"I find a woman can do more than a man to arouse the sympathies of thinking minds, and although several attempts were made to insult me when I was addressing large audiences, your friends soon settled the unruly members. I am now being called for, therefore excuse my abrupt closing, but accept my warmest love, and believe me to be your own most affectionate LUCINDA."

CHAPTER LXXXIV.

THE FEAR AND DISTRESS OF THE CONSPIRATORS.

T is often astonishing how long it takes the masses of the people to accept, or before they are even willing to examine, anything that is novel. New ideas, and new discoveries or inventions are spurned, are the conjurations, in public esteem, of some brainless seeker after *lucre;* probably this conclusion is arrived at by the masses because they *themselves* are guilty of doing nothing that does not bring money or its equivalent; hence, the above-named conclusions. Oftentimes the most useful and logical matters must be kept floating before public gaze for years before any of the modern patterns of society will behold the grandeur and superiority

of such useful and logical matters. For instance, look at the *Public Press,* which should be, and is, the moulder of the public mind ; these men, who own and edit the newspapers, claim to stand at the head of the pile of moralists and humanitarians ; but whilst they look upon long-established unphysiological and abnormal usages as the legitimate institutions of the land, they overlook and even spurn the establishment where new ideas (new to them, but old as the world) are presented to the gaze of the people.

These journals will collect all the murders, rapes, thefts and other crimes that are committed over the world, and fill their columns, local and editorial, with these heinous and disgusting sins of criminals to the manner bred and born, and send this olla-podrida into all the Christian families, where innocent, dear little children are fed on it, which has the effect upon those undeveloped minds to cause a desire for the sumptuous dishes which come through criminal courts and crime-publishing newspapers ; whilst these heathen owners and editors of this public-mind-moulding press have looked for many years upon the science of "Sexual Physiology," "Secrets of Generation," and normal regeneration with a holy horror. They, nevertheless, professed to be the guardians of the public and private morals, whilst they were themselves besmeared with criminal slime from crown to toe. Consistency seems to be no part of such men's acts, as little as it is with the lethargic minds, who spurn new ideas, inventions and discoveries. But when the people once begin to see through such a criminal code of morals, they change like magic, and then the obsolete matters will be instantly forgotten, and will be treated as stupid and worthless. It has been so from time immemorial in all things, and it is equally so with the scientific teachings of Dr. Juno ; the whole people now applaud him, and those who, several years ago, have spurned and persecuted him, would now kiss the ground he walks on, if they were privileged to do so.

Many cannot even yet see the propriety and need of advocating the fixed laws of human *Generation* and *Regeneration;* but to the wise a hint on this subject will suffice. These are the two topics that have caused one continual round of distress to the orthodox conspirators, simply because if such practical, scientific piety were carried out by all who "increase and multiply," that false religion of the conspirators, which is founded upon conjecture, would receive a permanent death, and this bitter spirit of persecution of the man (Juno) who advocated the only *bona fide* piety, would not have taken place; consequently this war, and the terror that now prevails amongst the orthodox conspirators, would not exist.

These bigots and self-righteous drones are paying heavily for their folly. Very, *very* few respectable people stand by them, and they are all as much in fear of the working classes and Naturalists as they used to despise these sovereign people of America.

Who but sensualists, drunkards, gluttons, misers and selfish dupes are their satellites and hireling soldiers? Not an honorable, decent person would, even at the close of this nineteenth century, be counted as a partner of their religion or illy-gotten lucre, lucre that was unjustly wrung from the working people by all sorts of cunning and craft, as is too well known to their dullest followers.

To-day these people are in terrible fear and distress, from the fact that they see that the *bone and sinew* of the land are exacting their inalienable rights. Are demanding the long-standing account to be summarily settled, which was due to them many years ago, but was haughtily withheld from them by these political and sectarian usurpers.

These *false guides* would cheerfully, this moment, sell their birthrights for a mess of pottage, and join the cause of the Naturalists, if they would be *sure* that they would be accepted, and thought they could extricate themselves from their augean filth and stereotyped blasphemy.

They have by far the largest army, but their leaders lack courage, their soldiers are debauched, their women are downcast, and, in fact, the whole thing looks bad, viewing the matter from an internal standpoint; of course, the world at large is not acquainted with the true state of affairs, and it is now the time when the leading, but gloomy conspirators can practically and excusingly apply their hypocrisy, by keeping up the deception that their army and navy are by far the most numerous, which is their only salvation to this hour; for if their own people, throughout the sectarian world, would know the true state of affairs, seven-eighths of them would prove false to the bad cause of orthodoxy and leave it, joining the strong and safe side; because these people are awfully afraid to die.

You can hear them continually lament that "It is a serious thing to die!" If they were the saints they profess to be, they would rejoice when the hour of their departure for the blessed realms of angels would arrive.

In fear and trembling the orthodox conspirators are pushing the war with all their might, and the cry is:

"This coming battle will win for us; our army is immensely large; we have the very best generals; the navy is in a good state, but of little use in the coming fray. Hurrah for the orthodox army!"

CHAPTER LXXXV.

TERRIBLE BATTLE FOUGHT—DOCTOR JUNO SHOT AND LOST.

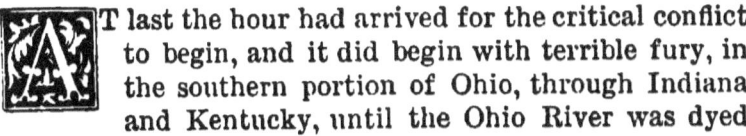T last the hour had arrived for the critical conflict to begin, and it did begin with terrible fury, in the southern portion of Ohio, through Indiana and Kentucky, until the Ohio River was dyed crimson with the gore of human beings.

At first the conspirators' army dashed into the field as though they were going to fairly swallow up the Naturalists; but the brave heroes did not fear them very much; at least, the manner in which they repulsed the right wing of the conspirators' army, proved that they were prepared and ready for the fray. This flank movement of the Naturalists fairly routed and ruined the conspirators, and in their flight they were shot and cut down like chaff; however, the conspirators were very heavily re-enforced, when they made a stand, which caused a considerable commotion amongst the Naturalists, whose time for a repulse came in turn; and they were driven back in good order for ten miles, but only seven hundred prisoners were taken by the conspirators; and what seemed very peculiar was, that only about two thousand Naturalists were killed and wounded, whilst over sixty thousand conspirators were crippled and slaughtered.

The latter seemed to fire too high; whether this was owing to drunkenness or mismanagement of the officers, was not known; still, they made a poor impression on the sober Naturalists. When the report spread that the latter were driven north into Ohio, a new uprising and influx of Naturalists took place, when the conspirators were again routed, and were driven, bloody and worn out, through the Ohio River in double quick, many having been taken prisoners; many were drowned who ran into the river, and finding it too deep to wade, and could not swim, sank to rise no more.

These scenes were heart-rending and revolting. It was Dr. Juno's black flag proclamation that caused the enemy to risk their lives in the river, rather than be taken prisoners, to be summarily shot down like dogs.

When the army of the Naturalists reached the Ohio River, and found that the enemy was demoralized, Dr. Juno ordered his men to pursue them, whilst he was at the head of a brigade, dashing forward like infuriated demons. Those who could swim, he ordered to wade and swim, whilst his immense cavalry force swam their horses, and the ammunition was carried across the water on flat boats, pontoons and over the old bridge, which the conspirators had not time to disturb.

Now, the climax of carnage and horror approached; both armies were heavily re-enforced from every available point, and in Kentucky the next to the last and worst battle was fought. Dr. Juno kept pursuing the enemy, until he could go no further, on account of the conspirators having received immense new supplies of men, who fought like envenomed veterans; and the Naturalists on the northern side, where Dr. Juno's division was so fiercely pursuing the conspirators, were repulsed furiously, and quite a great many Naturalists fell dead and wounded; they did not run, but fought until they reached the Ohio River again, when Dr. Juno was riddled with bullets, and the balance of his army had to surrender.

Over thirty thousand prisoners were taken, Dr. Juno included. But at the same time the army of Naturalists under General Gossimer, from Indiana, were pressing vehemently upon the left wing of the entire conspirators' forces; whilst General Armington had an immense fresh army marching from the East upon the right wing of the enemy; under these circumstances, the conspirators had no chance to either shoot or guard their prisoners, who were immediately rescued, and again joined their own army, when the conspirators were making tracks for their fortifications in the southwestern portion of Kentucky, where they were pursued and re-enforced.

Thus ended that terrific battle, but neither army had many prisoners, except the wounded, who were kindly treated by both parties until such time when the black flag was swung over those who refused to take their respective oath of allegiance.

One thing must be said to the credit of the conspirators, that they rescinded their order or permission of retaliation, and each Naturalist prisoner had to be tried by court martial before he could be punished. Their own people all over the Union demanded this in respect to their *old* customs and usages. However, there were other things pressing down against advocating or pursuing the course that Dr. Juno instituted; *first*, they found it too dangerous for their hired and demoralized army to be allowed to shoot prisoners in retaliation; and, *second*, their entire community could not bear to let their army do what all of them so severely denounced as barbarous and uncivilized.

It was this very cry against Dr. Juno's black-flag conduct that united the orthodox people; had it not been for this cruel course, which Dr. Juno inaugurated and carried out, not one-half the people that did unite themselves in active warfare would have taken any interest or part in this war.

Dr. Juno knew all these things in advance, and he also was aware that the conflict would be much more severe by the course he adopted, than it would have been had he followed the old usages. Still, his way proved to have been, after all, the wisest, most charitable and practical.

Dr. Juno could not be found by the Naturalists; but by mere chance a brother saw the conspirators carry him alive from the field dangerously wounded, which the Naturalists kept quiet; but this fact caused an immense stir amongst his people.

CHAPTER LXXXVI.

MISS ARMINGTON TAKES THE FIELD WHEN SHE FINDS THAT DR. JUNO IS GONE.

WHEN the news secretly spread amongst the secret societies that Dr. Juno was either dead or a prisoner of war, Miss Lucinda Armington issued a *Proclamation* through the newspapers, and also sent it far and near by telegraph to the workingmen and Naturalists, which was given in hieroglyphics, so that none could comprehend it except the members of the secret societies. It was to this effect:

TERRES GARDEN, ———, 19—.

The hour has come when our hero is no more with us.

He has been shot at the head of his brigade in the retreat on the 7th instant, and is now in the enemy's hands, either dead or alive. Probably they are not yet cognizant of it.

I need not say that this is a terribly distressing affair to me personally, as well as it must be to the brotherhood of the people, and it behooves us to make herculean efforts to rescue him, whether he is dead or living! If he is no more to be with us as a friend and benefactor, let us, nevertheless, obtain his body and finish the war for the people!

I have promised my beloved Victor, in our last interview, that if he fell on the battlefield, or was otherwise deprived from seeing this work completed, that I would take his place and fight and labor until I, too, followed him or gained the victory! This was his will, as expressed in a written document now in my possession.

I therefore proclaim to you, the loyal subjects of my devoted and betrothed husband, that I will take the field at the head of the army of Naturalists, and I hereby call for every available able-bodied man that can be secured to *instantly* join our army and navy, and by at once (in secret) attacking the enemy on all sides we may finish this cruel work of warfare by one united, gigantic blow, and thereby obtain the body of Dr. Juno.

General Gossimer will rally and control the western portion of the army, my father will take charge of the eastern divisions, and I will see to that part of it which can be centred upon the enemy from the North. One week from to-day, at eight o'clock in the evening, I have appointed for a united clandestine movement upon the conspirators.

In the meantime, the enemy shall be made believe that we are nearly used up, and cannot take the aggressive for months; this will cause them to relax their vigilance, when half of their officers will get drunk with bad liquors, and the men will imitate their masters and superiors, as is always the case.

Admiral Cunning I hereby order to advance his iron-clad navy up the Ohio river as fast as possible, and although he cannot do any particular harm to the enemy where he now is, still, when the land forces shall scatter the conspirators, he will be able to cause a river of blood to flow in horror!

The sisters of our Secret Order of Naturalists will co-operate with the soldiers, and each regiment will have a free supply of them with it to prepare food, do nursing, and attend to such duties as they feel disposed to voluntarily perform, and such as will be assigned them by the officers.

Remember the hour for the united assault, and be it *particularly* understood that I order that the *Proclamation* and *Army Orders* of my betrothed husband—Dr. Juno—shall be carried out in all cases as if he were upon the field!

Given by the successor of Dr. Juno, who will instantly repair to headquarters of the army of the Naturalists, by

LUCINDA ARMINGTON.

This proclamation of Miss Armington had a most salutary effect upon the entire country, and the workingmen and Naturalists rose as one man to slay the enemy. Every word of it fell upon holy ground, and mind, muscle and money were lavished in every conceivable manner to carry out this proclamation of the betrothed lady of the lamented and most beloved Dr. Juno.

The females were ready to shoulder arms all over the Union. At a public meeting that was held by the ladies the day after this loyal document was issued, the following resolutions were unanimously adopted:

Whereas, Our beloved benefactor and loyal master—Dr. Victor Juno—has won a great battle on the 7th instant; and,

Whereas, Several of our men have fallen into the hands of the enemy, who may execute them summarily; and,

Whereas, We, the female population of the United States, feeling a great interest in the cause of humanity, shall instantly co-operate with the army and navy of the Naturalists; and,

Whereas, We desire to see this war ended, that peace and good will may come unto all the working people; therefore,

Resolved, That we recognize the *Proclamation* just issued by Miss Lucinda Armington, the affianced wife of Dr. Victor Juno, who will preside at the head of the army of the people during the illness of Dr. Juno, and that we shall lend our assistance toward the subjugation of the enemy, and solicit the co-operation of our sisters throughout the Union. Mrs. S—— T——, *Pres't.*
Miss R—— K——, *Sec'y.*

HEADQUARTERS OF THE ARMY OF THE
NATURALISTS, ——, 19—.

I hereby order that my *Proclamation* be strictly observed, having this day learned that our beloved Victor is a prisoner of war in the hands of the enemy, having been penetrated with bullets without injuring a vital organ, and he is recovering very rapidly, as he always does; at any rate, I understand that he is to be tried by court-martial on the very day I have mentioned in my proclamation. You are all familiar with that, and I hereby enjoin vigilance and punctuality, giving extra dignity and power to the cause.

The rest remains to be seen on that auspicious day. Heaven grant that the right may conquer. LUCINDA.

This terse little order was published to the world, but no one but the Naturalists understood the whole of it, as the proclamation was not published to the world, but only to those who understood the hieroglyphics of the secret societies. It kindled a fire of fury and determination in every loyal breast.

"Dr. Juno a prisoner of war, and to be tried by court-martial! Great powers above," was the unanimous impression. "Surely he will be shot forthwith, unless the conspirators dread his followers."

The following sentiments were freely expressed by the sympathizers of Dr. Juno:

"The orthodox army dare not shoot Dr. Juno, we will make it too hot for them to do so in the next twenty-four hours." "Dr. Juno will make a speech before that court-martial that will magnetize his enemies with dreadful horror, and come away unharmed." "If Dr. Juno is allowed to speak before he is shot he will defy the enemy." "When the conspirators learn that Miss Lucinda Armington has taken Dr. Juno's place at headquarters, and has ordered the execution of his first proclamation, they will not find him guilty of crime." "If the court-martial will sentence Dr. Juno to be shot, they will find it entirely too dangerous to execute the sentence." "If Dr. Juno is shot by the conspirators it will cause a terribly revengeful feeling throughout the world, because his motives and movements have all been too unselfish and philanthropic to deserve death." "Beware! O Pharisees! how you insult and handle our heroic master."

CHAPTER LXXXVII.

THE TRIAL BY COURT MARTIAL OF DR. JUNO.

AFTER the orthodox conspirators had lost nearly one-half of their men in that dreadful battle just fought, they were very blue, although then their army was safely inside of their strong fortifications, until the news came that Dr. Juno had been shot and was their prisoner in one of their hospitals.

No one knew him until he had been carried, amongst other prisoners, to a hospital, and then not until the surgeon had dressed his gun-shot wounds, of which he had twenty, no one fatal, when one of the nurses recognized him, who at once went to the physician and said:

"Dr. Johnson, do you know that the man who has had twenty wounds, neither of which you said was dangerous, is Dr. Juno?"

"You are crazy!" ejaculated the doctor, and stared at the nurse as if he would devour him.

"No, sir!" emphatically exclaimed the nurse. "I am not crazy, but I am telling you the truth, for I know the doctor well."

"Pshaw!" interposed the doctor; "he was a private soldier, dressed in the commonest manner. He may resemble Juno, but never was it he."

"If it is not he you may shoot me," exclaimed the nurse, very much agitated, "for I have spoken with him, and I know his voice as well as my own, and it is not likely that I am deceived in his voice and personal identity. Please come with me and see for yourself."

"I don't know him, if I should fall over him," said the physician, angrily; "therefore my going to see him would not benefit anything"—

"We will ask him whether it is not he," interposed the nurse.

"Fool! do you think he would be big enough an idiot to tell the truth?" ejaculated he; "for if Juno has dressed in a private soldier's disguise, he will not acknowledge that it is he were we all to ask him, knowing that such an acknowledgment would prove his instant death."

"Yes he would," exclaimed the nurse. "I know him too well; he is no coward nor dissembler. Do, please come, and let us ask him; you know the reward that is offered for his capture; we may be entitled to it by this move."

"Sure enough," said he. "I will go with you."

They hurried to the bedside of Dr. Juno, who was sleeping as serenely as if he never had seen a care or had a trouble, when the physician said to the nurse, whilst they both gazed upon his manly face:

"Tom, this man has an uncommon face, and he sleeps as if he were in perfect health, and enjoyed a happy life. I hate to wake him, because he is recuperating like magic under the influence of such a sleep."

"Never mind all that," said the nurse; "he will soon sleep again."

"That may be so," exclaimed he. "Here it goes."

And he touched his shoulder and said·

"Dr. Juno, is that you?"

"Yes, sir," ejaculated Dr. Juno; "what do you want?"

This almost paralyzed the physician, when he asked again, seeing that the man was now fully awake:

"Sir, I wish to know if you are Dr. Victor Juno?"

"I am," very calmly said he.

"Do you know where you are, Dr. Juno?" continued the physician, still doubting.

"Of course I do," said he, and turning slightly in his couch, continued, "I am in my enemy's hospital; now please let me sleep, and when I am better I will gladly speak with you."

The two inquirers of the name of their patient now left the room together, and after they were beyond Dr. Juno's hearing, the physician said to the nurse:

"Tom, this man astonishes me. I am favorably disappointed with him. I always thought that he was an ugly tempered and rascally old fellow, without sense or conscience; but such a head as this man has shows talent and good qualities. I did not notice him when I dressed his wounds, or I would have seen by half a glance that noble countenance. I love and respect him."

"Is it possible that you are so violently taken with the man who has caused this most unjust and cruel war? and then, think how he shoots our soldiers when they are taken prisoners! I want to see him shot in return for his uncivilized and barbarous conduct," said Tom.

"I do not wish to see him shot; he is too noble a looking man to execute in that style. Have you read his masterly proclamation and army orders? They were sound in doctrine, and, if carried out, will soon end the war and prove a real charity," exclaimed the physician of the hospital.

"I shall at once repair to the office of General Orthod, and report what I have learned," said Tom.

When the officers of the conspirators had learned that Dr. Juno was their prisoner, they at once convened a *special* court martial, and in a few days, when he was able to sit up, they tried him. The day of trial, and other particulars, were published to the world in all the orthodox newspapers, in staring head-lines.

The orthodox people and army and navy were in high glee over this sudden downfall of the Naturalists; for they were certain, if Juno was no more, the war would instantly close on their own terms. In this they were very, *very* much mistaken, as this state of affairs caused an opposite effect.

They, at any rate, considered that the Naturalists were well nigh exhausted, and as soon as they found that their leader was taken prisoner, they would yield and sue for peace. From these conclusions, they considered that they would make haste slowly. They would recruit their army, and, after disposing of Dr. Juno, would offer terms of peace.

They found the celebrated prisoner recovering so rapidly that they thought, if they would not give him his trial and execute the sentence quickly, he might escape from their clutches. The leading members of the court martial agreed to visit Dr. Juno in the hospital, and ascertain from him if he was able to appear at court. Some of them thought that he would feign to be worse than he was, to cause a postponement of the trial. General Orthod asked him:

"Dr. Juno, we have convened a special court martial to try you, and I wish to know if you think that you are well enough to attend court to-morrow?"

"Well, sir," said he, "I have considerable pain in several of the wounds, but I am strong, and *very* well at heart; therefore I shall be delighted to appear at the 'special court' which you have had the kindness to convene for my benefit."

"All right, sir," responded General Orthod, and added: "Can we serve you in any way?"

"No, sir, I kindly thank you; I have all I need, and he who wants more in time of cruel war, is no Christian," responded Dr. Juno.

These remarks were very bold, decidedly cool, and to some of them seemed sarcastic. They caused the officers to discuss Dr. Juno's *sang froid* with deep anxiety; in sooth, they felt more fear and concern about the easy manners of the prisoner than the latter did himself of the trial and its results, which was a stickler. The following conversation took place concerning the matter:

"General Orthod, please tell us, what do you think of the self-composed and easy manner, and monstrously cool language of our prisoner?" asked a colonel.

"Indeed, indeed! I am more puzzled than I have ever been in my whole life!" responded the general, with a sigh, and remaining silent, stared, as it were, upon vacancy, which was an uncommon thing for him to do, and which caused the rest to feel very superstitious about the matter.

After exchanging several other remarks, they parted to meet in their court room the following day, at ten o'clock in the morning, to try Juno.

CHAPTER LXXXVIII.

THE COURT MARTIAL TRIES JUNO.

THE hour of ten in the morning had arrived, and the officers constituting the Juno Court Martial were all present, when General Orthod said, before the prisoner was in court:

"Gentlemen, I have had some very strange forebodings since we have had that interview with the heroic prisoner, who is about to be arraigned and tried before us this morning; and as I am the presiding judge in the case, it is my duty to act according to the usages in such cases; otherwise, I would much rather be excused in having a part or parcel in the case that we are called to pronounce upon. This man Juno is, to say the least, a brave enthusiast, and I believe that he feels that he is in the right; but that cannot save him from summary punishment at our hands."

"I agree with the general," said Colonel Sanctiblower, son of Judge Sanctiblower; "but I am determined not to falter in the rigid performance of duty."

The general then ordered the prisoner to be brought into Court, after which the doors were thrown open to spectators, who crowded the room to its utmost in a moment.

Dr. Juno was brought into Court by four officers, who assisted him to walk, having been too lame, from the wounds he received at the head of his army, to walk without considerable assistance. He was placed into an easy chair, which the sympathetic physician of the hospital had ordered to be provided for his august patient, whom he desired should be as comfortable as he could make him whilst he lived, even if he would be shot afterwards.

After everything was arranged, and the Court called to order, a lengthy silence ensued, which partook of the nature of a Quaker meeting, causing every one to feel as though a solemn hour was at hand, and more solemn work. At last General Orthod said, in a tremulous voice:

"The Court is ready to proceed with the trial of the prisoner; are counsel ready to proceed?"

The prosecuting attorney responded: "We are prepared to proceed."

Dr. Juno was asked to stand up, when the Clerk of the Court said:

"Victor Juno, you are charged with high treason and murder; how say you, guilty or not guilty?"

"*Not* guilty!" responded Dr. Juno, in a cool and composed manner.

"Dr. Juno, have you counsel engaged?" asked General Orthod; to which he replied:

"No, sir; I will be fully competent to act as my own counsel."

"The Court is ready to hear the case," said General Orthod. The prosecuting counsel rose and spoke as follows:

"*Your Honor, and Gentlemen of the Commission:*—It becomes my painful duty to charge the prisoner at the bar with felony of the highest grade.

"*Firstly*—This indictment charges you with high treason, and inciting to mob law.

"*Secondly*—It charges you with cold, premeditated murder of innocent persons, who have fallen into the hands of the rebel horde, which you claim to control.

"*Thirdly*—It charges you with riot, robbery and malfeasance of office.

"The line of prosecution, which I propose to pursue, is that of the *second* charge, '*cold, premeditated murder,*' which is ample to find a verdict for the States for murder in the first degree, the penalty of which, in times of rebellion, is death by shooting. I will not ask this commission to hear useless testimony, neither will I take up their precious time with the discussion of the minor charges as found in this bill; but content myself with proving that you, Victor Juno, the prisoner at the bar, are guilty of shooting men dead, contrary to the usages of civilized life.

"Will George Henry Adkinson take the witness' stand?"

After being sworn, this witness testified as follows:

"I was in the next to this last battle, which was fought in the southern part of the State of Ohio. Myself and several thousand other soldiers of the Union were taken prisoners, and after the fray was over, as Dr. Juno's officers marched us toward headquarters of the prisoner at this bar (Dr. Juno), I slipped away and returned by good luck to our own army. The rest were all shot by the order of Dr. Juno."

Prosecuting Attorney.—Were there any of our generals taken prisoners?

Witness.—Yes; four.

P. A.—Name them.

W.—Generals Cadwell, Stew, Pancy and Pierce.

P. A.—Were these four generals also shot?

W.—Yes, sir.

P. A.—Do you know whether our wounded men were kindly treated?

W.—Yes, sir; they were very kindly treated, and were very skilfully doctored; were very soon cured up, but were shot as soon as well enough to stand upright.

P. A.—Did this Dr. Juno, the prisoner at the bar, himself order them to be shot; and did he not give them a chance to defend themselves?

W.—He did himself order all to be shot; but he gave them only this chance of defence, that they should voluntarily take his oath of allegiance, and go into his army at once, if well enough to do so; if they refused, they were shot.

P. A.—Cross-examine.

Dr. Juno.—Did you see any one shot, with your own eyes, in the manner you have stated to this commission?

W.—No, sir; I did not see any one shot, but I was told so, and read your proclamation and army orders to that effect in the newspapers.

Dr. J.—You should not swear to what you *hear*, or what you have read in the newspapers; it is not a sound doctrine. That will do, I have no more questions to ask.

WILLIAM N. SNIGGLEFRITZ, sworn.

Prosecuting Attorney.—What do you know of this man—the prisoner at the bar?

W.—I know nothing but what I have heard and read in newspapers.

P. A.—That is not legal evidence. That will answer.

Gen. Orthod.—Mr. Snigglefritz, were you a soldier for the Union in this present conflict?

W.—No, sir; not exactly a soldier, but I have been with the army.

G. O.—What did you do with the army?

W.—I sold liquor and tobacco.

G. O.—To whom did you sell liquor and tobacco?

W.—To any one that would buy.

G. O.—If I catch you again at that work, I'll have you court-martialed; mind me.

W.—Yes, sir.

GUSTAVE FIERCE, sworn.

Prosecuting Attorney.—Where are you from, and what do you know of Dr. Juno, the prisoner at the bar; tell us all about it?

W.—I will. I was a spy in the army of the working men, and saw all your drunken soldiers shot in battle and after battle. Dr. Juno was always doing his duty, and he was always sober, too; a thing that I cannot say of the Union army—

P. A.—(Interrupting him.) Stop, Fierce; you talk entirely too fast, and too much that is irrelevant to the subject. Tell us, did you ever see or hear the prisoner shoot or order any one to be shot, who was a prisoner of a war?

W.—Yes, sir; I have seen the prisoners shot, and have heard the prisoner say to his men: Be sure you shoot well; aim well, shoot fair and quick. In fact, the prisoner is a practical, clear-headed and sober man, which is more than you can say—

P. A.—Stop, stop—

W.—Yes, sir, I'll stop, but—

Gen. O.—You must not speak any more than you are asked—

W.—I don't, for he told me to tell him all about this matter, and I simply complied with his request and told him what I knew to be a live fact, for, really, I consider Dr. Juno the best soldier and purest man living.

P. A.—Now stop, sir, or I'll send you to prison.

W.—Oh, goodness! do you think that you can scare me with prisons? No, sir; I am a native born Naturalist, although I do not belong to the Secret Order of Naturalists of which Dr. Juno is the founder and father.

P. A.—That will do; I have no more to ask.

W.—But I have not yet finished.

P. A.—Never mind that, but go; leave the stand.

W.—I won't do it.

Dr. Juno.—Your honor, may I be permitted to cross-examine this witness?

Gen. O.—Certainly, sir.

Dr. J.—Mr. Fierce, were you in our army when Generals Cadwell, Stew, Pancy and Pierce were taken prisoners?

W.—Yes, sir, indeed, I was at home at that hour.

Dr. J.—Do you know if these generals (Cadwell, Pancy and Pierce) are alive, or were they shot?

W.—They were alive three days ago. You know that you retained them as hostages.

Dr. J.—That will do.

This testimony of one of their own witnesses, a loyal saint, as they thought, and one of their own spies, who spied, however, more for Juno than for them, put a damper on their feelings; which caused the laying of heads together all around the court room, and the astounding exclamation could have been heard everywhere:

"Generals Cadwell, Stew, Pancy and Pierce held as hostages, and not shot! Great heavens!"

CHAPTER LXXXIX.

HON. BLUSTER GIBBONS' SPEECH BEFORE THE COURT MARTIAL.

HALF a dozen more witnesses were examined, but nothing positive could be proved that Dr. Juno had either himself shot, or ordered any prisoners of war to be shot; and, according to orthodox customs, no one can be convicted on such evidence; moreover, it was proved by what the orthodoxy considered her best witness (Mr. Fierce), that Generals Cadwell, Stew, Pancy and Pierce were alive to this day, and were held as hostages, which looked badly for the conspirators' court martial. Nevertheless, they had to carry the matter through, therefore the prosecuting attorney closed his remarks in the following speech, in which the spectators evinced little interest:

HON. BLUSTER GIBBONS'—PROSECUTING ATTORNEY'S— SPEECH.

Gentlemen of the Commission:—The duty is incumbent upon me, as a loyal man to my God, to the elect and to the country, to argue this case in such a manner as to do reverence to our holy cause.

Gentlemen, you have listened with great interest to the witnesses who were this morning examined. If we were not, each of us, fully assured that this Right Reverend (?), this Doctor of Divinity, and Doctor of Medicine and Psychology, was guilty of the crimes of riot, treason and cold-blooded murder, I should have more to say about the matter than I probably shall in the few remarks which I propose to submit to you in this case.

Gentlemen, you and I have no business to entertain any feeling about this case; we are simply here in the performance of a high public duty. Simply to vindicate and sustain the majesty of the laws under which we live. Simply to protect that most sacred right that any of us may claim as our home or constitutional right; the right to execute the invader of old established usages, the murderer of prisoners of war, such as the prisoner at the bar is.

Gentlemen of the commission, you have heard the testimony of the witnesses, and you know, without witnesses, that this man is guilty of murdering our brave soldiers, as if they were dogs; as if he had the right to trample upon the sacred usages of all civilized countries.

I hope this Progressive Christian, this Right Reverend Bishop Juno, is not to carry us back to the age of Mohammedanism, or to the dark ages. The assurance of an innovator like he, to dare to shoot our men as if they were mere cattle; not even giving them a chance to defend themselves, as you here permit him to be defended.

Why, gentlemen, he should have been immediately shot, as he shoots our men, whom he was taken on the field. Yes, we should not give him an opportunity to open his impudent mouth.

He has always been a perfect nuisance to decent Christian people; look, what has he *not done* to disturb the peace and comfort of the religious community. He has justly been arrested and imprisoned for publishing and circulating obscene books; books that were so lewd, filthy, wicked and infamous that the same were too offensive to go on the records of the Criminal Court, in which he was convicted, and that is bad enough, God knows!

Gentlemen, you are called upon to give a verdict of murder in the first degree, and by so doing, you will remove a stumbling-block to grace divine; a bugbear to the liberty of the saints; because you are all very well informed how this man at the bar has, for a quarter of a century, thrust himself impudently into the face of every decent man, woman and child.

His harangues to the sensual masses he has everywhere

delivered, until he has so agitated a bad cause as to proselyte thousands, and with these dupes he has instituted this most barbarous, gigantic and atrocious rebellion; and, unless you, gentlemen of the commission, find him guilty of the highest crime in the country, and forthwith sentence him to death, and order his execution instantly, this war will continue.

Once he is removed from *terra firma*, then farewell rebellion. I hope every person within the reach of my voice agrees with me in this view of the question. Why should we hesitate in doing, or delaying, our duty in this plain business transaction? Let us vindicate our cause whilst we have it in our power; whilst we have this malignant upstart, this reverend tyrant, this butcher of human beings, who has no more conscience and heart than a tiger, or an infuriated bull!

The testimony is ample to cause his speedy conviction and execution. Look at him; how cool, hardened, unconcerned and lost to shame he is. A man who is guilty of such crime, as this Right Bishop Juno is, should repent in sackcloth and ashes before the avenging hand of justice sends his impious soul, if he has any, into the presence of a wrathful Creator!

Of all the brazen-faced, egotistical and self-elated scoundrels this wicked wretch beats it; of all the calm-headed cut-throats and presumptuous braggadocios, I must assert he is the quintessence. If there were any symptoms of insanity; if he had any slight signs of *not* being *compos mentis*, we might have some sympathy for the creature; but a *non-compos mentis* could not wield the mighty influence for evil that this prisoner at the bar has done.

He is a self-made demon, who can speak so plausibly to the masses as to cause them to believe that he is the most learned and wise man, when he is moved by Satan, guided by imps and sustained by the cheek of all that is infernal and damnable! Who of you, my hearers, doubt this? Who of you doubt anything that I have said of this deliberate murderer?

I will wager all that is sacred to me that if this honorable Court will permit it he will make an attempt in a harangue to justify himself in every crime that he has figured. He is so lost to decency and good breeding that his conscience is seared, and it is only sport to the wretch to murder our innocent soldiers, and if he had *us* this moment in his power, as we have him, he would order us to be drawn into a line, and place a cannon at one end of the line and blow us to glory like dogs; yes, like he did our soldiers in every battle where any of our men fell into *his* dastardly hands!

In conclusion, gentlemen of the commission, I do not wish to insult your intelligence, nor continue to argue with you as though you were also conscience-void, like this beast at the bar! Although he looks self-satisfied and composed, but I assure you that he is almost scared to death! Yes, I can at times see an expression on his countenance that shows his dread of the result of this just trial.

Let us make an example of this leader of the greatest mob of ruffians that ever breathed breath! Who are his followers and rioters? I will tell you: the greasy, dirty mechanic, the common laborer, the off-scouring of the land, who are not good enough for us to wipe our feet upon; yes, these stinking workingmen make up his so-styled army and navy, who have stolen our war implements by a series of secret society movements, knowing well enough that by fair means they could not have given us so much trouble.

Gentlemen, I am not going to doubt your morality, your virtue, your Christian graces. I am not going to suppose for a moment that you mean to stand by and justify this flagrant violation of law by any further remarks upon this subject of these atrocious wholesale murders. I shall simply present the testimony to you under the charge of rigid justice, and will ask you to find a verdict of guilty of *murder in the first degree!*

CHAPTER XC.

DR. JUNO'S GREAT, DEFIANT DEFENCE.

R. *President and Gentlemen of the Commission :—*As I am privileged to defend myself, permit me, in the onset of my remarks, to say that I shall not appear before you as a whining coward, nor shall I seek favors at your hands.

You have not proved anything against me upon which, according to stereotyped orthodox usages, you could find a verdict of guilty against me for murder in any degree ; but I emphatically acknowledge that I have ordered all your men to be shot dead who were taken prisoners, and who would *not take our oath of allegiance and fight in our army and navy* against you, after I exhorted them to do so, and gave them an opportunity to defend themselves. [Hisses and groans.]

I am aware that this course of warfare is looked upon by all nations as *outrageous*, but I am not controlled or guided by the public opinion of this or any other nation, simply because this and every nation on the globe are governed by customs or habits.

Whatever is a custom or usage finally becomes a law—custom makes law—whether such custom is founded upon fixed law, God's law, or upon conjecture, and the result of this habit of allowing customs to create law for a nation proves to have been, and still is, the ruination of the people ; the working people, the poor people, the fallen people, for whose welfare and eternal salvation I have lived and labored, through calm and storm, for many long years, regardless of comfort, gain, glory of men, or the favor of the pharisees themselves.

To me *war* is always "outrageous," and therefore as we *must* have this outrageous evil as a necessity, the severer the blow the sooner will it be ended. It is quadruply outrageous to protract war, to make it a lingering cruelty, carrying it on for years, until a nation is ruined in every way, and finally closing the conflict without having established a sound public doctrine, or without having taught the belligerents that it was caused by unfaithfulness to God's hallowed injunctions; without teaching the nation or nations that Jesus Christ was a *Naturalist*, who taught us by precept and example that the poor man's soul is as near and dear to Him as the rich person's. Yea, He went farther and said:

"It is easier for a camel to go through the eye of a needle than for a rich man to enter into the kingdom of God."

Jesus meant what he said, for it is utterly impossible for a man to be happy in the hereafter, when this mortal coil returns to clay, and the spirit stands aloof and reflects upon the impiousness of having held as his own that which he neither brought into the world nor took out of it, and which God designed for the use of all alike, whilst they journeyed on His footstool, where the most talented, apt and wise should do, but do not, as Christ commanded:

"Preach, saying the kingdom of heaven is at hand," meaning all the fixed laws and wonderful works of God.

"Heal the sick, cleanse the lepers, raise the dead, cast out devils; freely ye have received, freely give. Provide neither gold, nor silver, nor brass in your purses."

I have by acts followed these natural teachings all my life; and you and your co-conspirators, who have worshipped God contrary to this scientific method, have persecuted me and mine for nearly half a century, until you became so cruel, tyrannical, overbearing, selfish and self-righteous that neither I nor my followers could exist in peace and comfort; therefore, we saw that it behooved us to teach you a terrible lesson, and by so doing save the unborn generations from falling into the same horrible pool of corruption that nations have waded in for hundreds of years.

Thus, I have instituted the most speedy, although cruel

plan to save the race from the thraldom that *filthy lucre* creates, and thereby give to the *poor* a chance to be honest, healthy and natural. [Great applause.]

Do I look like a man fond of war, who would delight in the misery of the people? I hope not. Do I look like the man that the Hon. Bluster Gibbons has made me out to be? [Cries of "No! no!"]

Do any of my sermons, lectures, orations or writings advocate cruelty to the people? Or, have I always advocated that the few should be sacrificed for the good of the many? [Cries of "Yes!"] What induced me to oppose the whole world but my unfeigned love for the people, and the practical reverence I had for God?

War is always cruel, and thousands of innocent ones must suffer for the guilty, in such outrageous times; but the right always conquers in the end. It was such men as yourselves; yes, you and your proselytes that have caused this barbarous conflict, and it is *I* who had shot, and intend to have all your rebellious men speedily shot, when taken as prisoners; and if I die at your hands, Generals Cadwell, Stew, Pancy and Pierce die also; such have been my orders.

However, I feel that it would be best for my cause if you should shoot me; therefore, I resolutely and fearlessly defy you to shoot me. [Cries of "Hear! hear!"] If I should fall at your hands, it would cause such a holy indignation throughout the Union, amongst the sovereign people, the working people, whom the Hon. Bluster Gibbons styles, "the offscouring of the land, who are not good enough for you to wipe your feet upon," that they would wipe you out like slate-pencil marks. Yes, I am fully convinced that I had better die at your hands; so find me guilty of anything, and vent your hypocritical spleen upon him who has been a "stumbling-block" in your unhallowed path, and then you will see the glory of God appear. [Tremendous applause.]

I speak this, gentlemen, with reverence and in great earnestness; and now, as I have given you a brief explanation of the motives that prompted me to shoot your men, I will add that I esteem you, gentlemen, and your boon associates (not these spectators, who are twin to our "offscouring of the land ") as the most impious, black-hearted and dastardly set of hypocrites and vipers that the world ever looked upon.

You have had your own way so long that you think it presumptuous in any man, or body of men, to throw you from your sacrilegious saddle, in which you have been riding to the devil on the double-quick, and have dragged the millions of sincere and confiding working people with you. Deny this if you can. And more, you have owned everything; have even stolen the livery of heaven to serve the devil in; have, by your selfishness, usurped every right of the people—when I say *the people*, I mean the working people, the producers, the "offscouring of the land," who are not good enough to wipe your pharisaical feet upon. [Tremendous applause.]

I, gentlemen, have the honor of having caused your little game to be permanently blocked, and even your own people, these your spectators, seem to approve of my course, if I may judge of the kindly applause that I have received since I have feebly spoken in defence of their rights at the sacrifice of your lofty positions; positions which you have obtained by cunning, craft and deception, which very much looks to me like legalized wholesale robbery, like selling principle and piety to the highest bidder, and which resembles the graphic picture, which is painted in the twenty-third chapter of St. Matthew, of the New Testament, in the language of the Son of Man, who likewise gave himself as a sacrifice or ransom for the cause of God and humanity, viz.:

"Wo unto you scribes and pharisees, hypocrites! for ye compass sea and land to make one proselyte; and when he is made, ye make him twofold more the child of hell than yourselves. Ye serpents, ye generation of vipers, how can ye escape the damnation of hell? Behold, your house is left unto you desolate!"

In conclusion, let me invoke you to repent, every one of you, and join our cause of God and humanity, that the Spirit of Christ, and the re-appearing or second coming of Christ, may be made manifest. [Uproarious applause.]

But, if you refuse to accept the *bona fide* boon of salvation, and persist in your haughty manner to usurp the power, which alone is vested in God and His faithful people, you will shortly receive your doom; mark the words of one who is *your friend*, however abrupt and cruel his language may seem. [Vociferous applause.]

I have done; and it remains for you to do as you see fit; in either way, *I* will be benefited. May God have mercy on your souls.

CHAPTER XCI.

THE VERDICT AND ITS EFFECT.

AFTER the close of Dr. Juno's speech, the spectators were all removed, as well as Dr. Juno, when the following wrangling discussion, between the "Gentlemen of the Commission," took place:

"Well, gentlemen," said the president, General Orthod, "I scarcely know what we had better do with this bold man; if we find him guilty of murder in the first degree, as we ought, and sentence him to be shot, we may prove to be our own worst enemies; for, assuredly, it will cause a mutiny in our ranks, which was plainly to be seen when Juno made that dare-devil speech. He is certainly a great, bold and heroic man, and I rather admire him. I feel that we had better acquit him, on the ground that the testimony was not sufficient to convict him; but I am ready to hear your opinions."

"Gentlemen, I am astonished, thunderstruck, at the remarks of our general, and president of this court martial," ejaculated Colonel Fury Stuckup. "We must strike a fearless blow now, or become the laughing stock of the whole civilized world. If mutiny, riot and internal rebellion are to come, *now is the time to let them come;* because the enemy is well nigh used up, and cannot take the aggressive for a long time; whilst we can easily subdue the few giddy-headed rioters who were psychologized by Juno's blustering sophistry, and who will as soon yield to our commands, as they applauded this arch fiend. Again, once Juno is dead, we will be master of the post, for his like does not exist; and as regards the testimony not being sufficient, is nonsense; did he not boldly plead guilty? And after his speech will reach the masses of our people, would they not spurn us, and denounce us as cowards and cut-throats, were we to acquit him? No, gentlemen, he *must* be sentenced to death, and to-morrow he should be shot."

"For my part," said Colonel Windy, "I agree with Colonel Stuckup; this man must die as soon as possible. I would myself feel disposed to assassinate him if he were acquitted; therefore, I am for speedy work, let the consequence be what it may. I call for the vote of the commission"—

"I second that motion," interposed Colonel Stuckup, who was terribly elated and stuck-up over the apparent victory his speech had over General Orthod's wise remarks.

"I would like to make a few remarks, before action is taken in this very important matter," responded Brigadier General Longhead. "I perfectly agree with our wise, experienced and eminent president, who can see farther than these young men, who probably are moved more by passion than discretion. This man—Dr. Juno—has made a wonderful and lasting impression upon our own fighting men, upon whom we must depend for victory, and if we sentence this fearless creature, they will murder us.

"I saw a phonographic reporter take down the whole proceedings, and a friend of mine whispered to me, during the time Juno was speaking, that compositors were then at work setting up the same for publication in pamphlets; and their distribution amongst the army, navy and the people, will be self-evident; the result you will see, if we convict this man. In sooth, we may be executed by our own men, before Juno, if we find him guilty. We have made a great blunder in having allowed the *people* to be present in the trial, and the Hon. Bluster Gibbons' remarks about the 'working people' were a stab into our own sides. I will vote against conviction."

"I now call for the vote," ejaculated Colonel Windy.

"No, sir, first give me a moment to answer General Longhead according to his folly," interrupted Colonel Stuckup. "You talk like a man who is about turning traitor, or like a scared boy, or a villain "—

"Sir! to whom do you address your ungentlemanly and illy timed remarks?" interrupted the president, General Orthod. "If you speak of General Longhead, you *yourself* are guilty of the charges with which you would brand this wise superior officer, and I emphatically command you to make an apology to him, or I shall order your arrest."

"I *did* speak of General Longhead," responded Colonel Stuckup; "but his foolish speech made me too indignant to hold my tongue, and I only make an apology by the order of our president and superior officer (?); under any other circumstances, I should resent the proposition and challenge discussion to the death!"

"Your apology is accepted, but in the future guard your stuckup tongue as becomes a subordinate young officer, when your words may be heeded," said General Orthod in a firm and polite manner. He knew that this was not the place and time for bantering words, but he wanted peace in his commission until this verdict was rendered.

There were twenty-four men in this commission; nearly all were rabid orthodox conspirators, except Generals Orthod and Longhead, therefore the wise remarks of these sages were not heeded; and as the votes were called for without any objections, twenty-one were cast for conviction, and three for acquittal.

It was now eight o'clock in the evening, and when the

verdict was made public, a rush by the people was made for the court room, where the commission had convened; but the members of the court martial had all left except Colonels Stuckup and Windy, who were addressing some of their friends on the fight and fuss they had with Generals Orthod and Longhead; the mob forced its way rudely into the midst of the room, and cried tumultuously:

"Where are the members of the commission?"

Colonel Stuckup jumped upon a table and violently called for attention, and said:

"*Fellow Citizens:*—Colonel Windy and myself are the only members in the house; the rest have left. [Groans.] We have worked hard to render a verdict of guilty. [Hisses.] Please permit me to acquaint you with a dastardly outrage. [Groans, and a move to lynch them.] Keep silent for only a moment, when you will hear who are your best friends and who your enemies. [Cries, go on, go on and hurry up.] Would you think it, Generals Orthod and Longhead did their best to acquit Juno. [Good! Go on, quick.] But the colonel, here, and myself made strong speeches for conviction, and the result you know."

No sooner had these remarks been made, when these two colonels were seized and dragged into the street, where ropes were furnished, and they were hung to the nearest trees; and their swords were taken from them by the rioters, who stabbed them dozens of times into their abdomens with deathly violence.

When the mob saw that their victims were dying, they pinned printed black cards upon their bodies, which were previously prepared, with these words upon them:

"The work of the '*Greasy, Dirty Mechanics, the Offscouring of the Land,*' and friends of Dr. Juno."

The mob now moved for the Hon. Bluster Gibbons' residence, but they were disbanded before they went a square, by the Regulars, who were ordered to fire upon and arrest them. Still, this did not remove the perturbed spirit that had invested the minds of the *working people*, the very people who fought against their *own* interest, which was indelibly inscribed upon their minds by that great speech of Dr. Juno, which even the entire army and navy of this people had read by this time, and which was fomenting the feelings of these hired soldiers and marines to a fever heat.

General Orthod was appealed to by the citizens to issue a proclamation, which would check this internal rebellion, this threatened mutiny: but he said:

"I have advised the two young men—Colonels Stuckup and Windy—who were lynched by the mob. I told them, and so did our prudent General Longhead, that our own people might become our executioners, if we should find Dr. Juno guilty; but they spurned our advice, and found him guilty, and what is still worse, is, they have sentenced him to be shot to-morrow, at ten o'clock in the morning, which will cause a terrible scene of bloodshed. I am fully persuaded that we are lost; utterly lost by following the programme of the commission. I have done my best; so has Generals Longhead and Wisdom, who were the only members that opposed conviction; all the rest were for it."

"But, general," responded a parson, "do you not suppose that a judiciously executed proclamation would put a stop to this fearful rioting? Offer them good will, if obedient, and summary death, if disobedient to your orders."

"I will do my duty," said he, when he speedily wrote the following:

PROCLAMATION.

It is my duty to issue this Proclamation, which grieves me to the heart:

FIRST—All rioters, or those who incite to riot, shall be shot on the spot.

SECONDLY—I will do everything, as I always have done, to benefit our cause and our people; but riot in our own family divides the house, when it may fall, which might encourage the prostrated foe sufficiently to rally his forces and continue the war after Juno is shot.

THIRDLY—The soldiers and citizens will heed and execute this proclamation.

Given at headquarters of the army of the Union, this ―――― day of ――――, 19―, by　　　　　　　ORTHOD.

―――◆―――

CHAPTER XCII.

THE SHOOTING OF DR. JUNO AND THE LAST BATTLE.

HE evening when the verdict against Dr. Juno was published to the conspirators' army, at precisely the same hour when the Naturalists' army began to move toward the enemy, the Naturalists received the news half an hour later, and this caused a vehement, double-quick march for the scene that was to take place the following morning at ten o'clock.

Lucinda telegraphed to her entire army, navy and people to make tremendous haste, and strike vehemently, as they —the conspirators—had internal trouble, which might postpone the execution of her beloved Victor.

The enemy was informed that the Naturalists were moving rapidly upon him, but this kind of news was not believed by the officers of the conspirators; hence they gave themselves no uneasiness in that direction. However, they feared their own people, and the only thing they cared about this report was that it might embolden their soldiers and encourage them in their mutiny.

General Orthod's proclamation was published in the morning papers and by circulars, which created a determination amongst the officers to execute it, and frighten the people, if possible; but the majority of the men of their army that was in that place were only waiting for a time to show their determination; and although their fortifications were very strong, and a few men could hold an immense force in abeyance, still all this could avail nothing on this momentous occasion. At eight o'clock in the morning the conspirators had to believe to their sorrow that the army of the Naturalists was approaching; because their pickets were driven in from all sides, who reported that an immense army was besieging them, when General Orthod ordered the men into the forts; but hundreds of them were intoxicated, even many of the officers had too much gas on their brains to attend to their duty.

They had their hands more than full, as Dr. Juno *must* be shot peremptorily at ten o'clock, which would be an hour of sore distress; because the enemy would be upon them, the execution of Juno might cause riot and mutiny in their own ranks, and what to do was a puzzle to the leading generals in command of the troops.

Time was brief, and the rattling of musketry and clattering of wagons and horses' hoofs were audibly heard in the distance. The fray was ready to begin, and the planting of huge cannon all around the conspirators' forts seemed to be the work of a minute, when shells and hot shot fairly rained upon the fortifications and camps of the conspirators, which made awful havoc; thousands were shattered to atoms by the fierceness of bursting shells, and truly the hour of terror had arrived, being now ten minutes of ten o'clock, when the officers who were ordered to execute Dr. Juno speedily selected fifty soldiers to prepare to shoot him.

Dr. Juno was brought into an open space of the main fort, and the men were commanded to aim and fire, which they did; but instead of hitting Juno they, from some cause or other, missed him, which amazed and almost paralyzed the officers, who were now becoming superstitious, believing that this man's life was a charmed one. This, however, was not the case; but the soldiers aimed two or three inches higher than his head. This was a settled matter amongst the soldiers, that whoever would be selected to shoot Dr. Juno should aim too high, and should any one of them prove false the rest should shoot him on the instant.

Dr. Juno saw that the officers were affrighted, whilst the soldiers seemed to evince a desire to have Juno command them, when he made one leap for the musket of a soldier, who had his piece ready loaded to fire, and cried aloud in a commanding manner:

"Soldiers, obey my orders, and shoot down every officer and man who fights any longer against the *working people!*"

In an instant every officer in that large fort fell dead, and the white flag was run up, when the Naturalists took possession of the strongest fortification.

General Armington commanded this division, and as he stepped into the fort who should he behold, with open arms, but Dr. Juno! The scene was a grand and impressive one! They embraced each other and wept for joy, and the soldiers of both armies, who beheld them, also shed tears like little children; even half-intoxicated men seemed to realize that a holier element was going to rule, and that scene of carnage was changed into a peaceful audience chamber. But the battle still raged most furiously in other quarters, men falling like drops of rain in a furious thunder-shower. However, the news soon spread that Fort Principle was taken, and that Dr. Juno was alive, which caused an instant surrender of the entire Union or conspirators' army!

General Orthod surrendered his sword to Dr. Juno, they being the chief commanders of both armies. The general said to Dr. Juno, as he handed his sword to him:

"Dr. Juno, I cheerfully surrender my sword to you, and hope that we may never more have need to take it up; my best wishes are for the advancement of your cause. I have never understood you until you made that bold and noble speech before the court martial, of which I was president. And, if you will permit me, I will state that myself and my excellent associate here, General Longhead, favored your acquittal, which act almost cost us our lives!

"The more rabid and inexperienced officers that were members of that court martial overruled us, but they are, every one, dead now, having been lynched and shot by the mob, by the *working people*, who saw in you their saviour; and my sympathies were, and forever shall be, with you and your cause. [Applause.]

"With these intrusive remarks, I submit myself to your charge, and pray to be accepted as a brother Naturalist!" [Tremendous applause and hurrahs fairly rend the firmament overhead.]

Dr. Juno modestly received the general's sword, and said tremulously, having been perfectly overcome with joyful emotions:

"This act of yours alone is sufficient joy!" Sobs and tears caused silence for a few minutes. "I say your generous sympathy overwhelms me with joy and gratitude. You, sir, upon whom I have always looked as having been one of the greatest generals and statesmen that America has ever produced, are doing reverence to me, and are ready to join our beloved *Order of Naturalists*. This, truly, is a conquest of which I am proud, and I thank God and my followers for this victory, for now little remains to be done to finish the work of reformation, because the 'camel's back is broken,' and the country will freely receive its new habiliments, which will bring good will to men, a thing that must be desirable to all rational minds.

"General Orthod, I hail the hour and worship the power that gave you into our hands, and brought our hearts to beat in unison on the religion of the Lord of hosts! The blessed Naturalist, Jesus Christ, is our exemplar and guardian, whose sympathies always were with the poor, the fallen and needy people. I represent him to the best of my ability, and I hope that the Millennium is not far distant!"

"Amen to all you have said, generous brother," responded the general, when quite a tumult was caused without the guards. Miss Lucinda Armington, the female general, had arrived, and desired to see Dr. Juno, which produced tremendous cheering and deafening applause.

CHAPTER XCIII.

PATHETIC MEETING OF VICTOR AND LUCINDA AFTER THE BATTLE.

HE interview between Victor and Lucinda was—what shall I say, heart-rending, or heart-bleeding; in sooth, thousands stood with quivering lips and tearful eyes. Remember, this was not by any means a common meeting of common lovers; but, when we reflect upon the numerous privations, sufferings and anxieties that these two lovers of God, lovers of humanity and lovers of each other, were compelled to go through, and at the close of these perilous adventures they meet again, safe and sound, it was really a touching scene.

Very few who have lived in affluence, or who led reckless lives, could appreciate the impulses that moved these lovers and their spectators. The latter had suffered in battle, had experienced the hand of the haughty *lucre*-king, the power of the inhuman tyrant and the misery that poverty and want caused in a land where, so to speak, milk and honey should abundantly flow unto all the children of earth alike.

When Dr. Juno heard that the people were exclaiming: "General Lucinda! Hurrah for General Lucinda! Hurrah! *Hurrah!!* HURRAH!!!"

He asked what this all meant, for he was not yet aware that his beloved affianced wife had taken his place in the field of battle; and after General Armington briefly told him, he cried aloud:

"Make way for my affianced wife!"

24

Then the people parted to permit the happy couple to meet. Dr. Juno stood like marble, with open arms, and exclaimed, when she flew into his arms:

"My beloved! my guardian angel!"

Silence and throbbing of hearts spoke the balance, until the lovers regained their equilibrium, when Dr. Juno raised his head and said:

"Friends, pardon a weak man's overflowing soul, which is an evidence of the love he bears for a good and *true* woman, such as this one, my Lucinda, is!"

When he repeated the last part of this sentence, he had his right arm around her waist, whilst he held her right hand in his left, and gazed most lovingly into her upraised eyes, which made a picture that was almost celestial to behold.

He now conducted her into an open coach, and Generals Armington and Orthod joined the couple, when they were driven through the immense crowd of the soldiers of both armies, besides citizens, who cheered vociferously, many rending their garments, throwing their hats into the air, and many novel expressions were made that indicated joy. However, several persons expressed themselves as displeased, who were literally torn into atoms by the infuriated concourse of *working people*.

The people had learned for the *first* time that they were the sovereigns of America, and they recognized Dr. Juno as the man who brought about this great reform, and they vowed to heed his counsel in all time to come, as he was the only man who thoroughly understood how to direct a sound government according to the new era.

After the four generals, namely: Lucinda, Dr. Juno, Armington and Orthod, had been driven through the large concourse of spectators, they went to the headquarters of General Orthod, where they had all their wants supplied, for they were all hungry; and Dr. Juno had his old, common army clothes on yet, which looked none too clean and sound; because he was taken prisoner in them, was wearing them ever since, and they were full of bullet holes, which gave them a ragged aspect.

After he exchanged these war worn rags for a new suit of black, he appeared before his beloved Lucinda, and the happy couple had a great deal of news to relate, that transpired since they last met. Dr. Juno told her how he defied the court martial, and Lucinda said to him:

"You are a most fearless hero; it is a miracle how you have escaped; but Providence seems to favor us, for which I pray and thank God without ceasing."

"You are an angel!" replied he; "but I knew what I was doing when I defied them. You know, my precious darling, I have always told you that I had unbounded confidence in *the people;* and when I saw that the court house was crowded with spectators, I felt secure, because I knew that I would be able to make firm friends of nearly every one of them. It was my speech that saved my life and won the battle so easily."

"How so, my love?" said she. "I cannot see that, because they found you guilty and ordered you to be shot at ten o'clock this morning!"

"Just so, my angel, but don't you see that the soldiers rebelled, and would not shoot me; and my speech caused a crowd to lynch every one of the court martial that voted for my conviction!" responded he.

"You are my great hero, and I can only thank God for again being with you, safe and sound," said she.

They sat for several hours in deep conversation concerning the things with which the reader is familiar.

The war was now literally at an end, and the officers and leaders of the conspirators made themselves very scarce; not that they dreaded the Naturalists so much, but they feared their *own* people more, who were just beginning to find out how they had been humbugged for so many, many years, by the false representations that were made by the conspirators.

These orthodox conspirators had always represented

Dr. Juno as one of the worst, lewd, low criminal men living, whilst the shoe was on the other foot. He was the very man who ought to have been brought forward by these professed saints, who took upon themselves to guard the welfare of the nation, when it is being proved by unimpeachable testimony that they were the very ones who bankrupted body, soul, spirit, church, state and finance.

Their house was founded upon the sand, and the rain of shot and shell, and the storm that the *working people* have produced, caused their infamous temple to fall, and *great* was the fall of it.

Dr. Juno published a brief order, stating that his generals would attend to the disposal of the armies that were at that place, whilst he would journey East, and when home in Philadelphia, he would issue his Proclamation of Peace.

He took two regiments of picked Naturalists as an escort with him; but he had something else in his mind's eye besides escort, which was to settle the long standing account with the lucre-tyrants and sanctimonious demons who had persecuted and robbed him of all his rights for years.

The axe shortly fell upon the necks of the guilty parties, as will be seen as we pass on.

CHAPTER XCIV.

DR. JUNO'S ASTOUNDING PEACE PROCLAMATION.

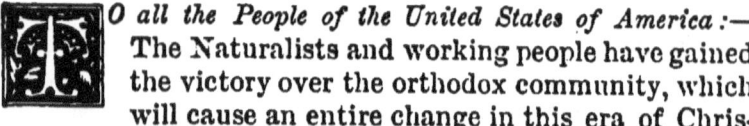O all the *People of the United States of America :*— The Naturalists and working people have gained the victory over the orthodox community, which will cause an entire change in this era of Christian Reformation. It behooves me, therefore, to issue this, my

PROCLAMATION OF PEACE:

Firstly—The enemy has surrendered his entire army and

navy, and thus the war is ended, and I pray that a permanent peace may speedily come; but this cannot be until every man and woman has complied with the demands which an outraged fixed law and an unchangeable Creator require; and therefore I proclaim and command that all the wealth in the land shall be placed into the treasury of the Naturalists. All persons *must* deposit all their money and valuables in the treasury, for which they will receive deeds, and after the new constitution is drawn up they will learn the workings of the new Christian government. This is peremptory, and failure to comply is death.

Secondly—As money-worshipping has been the great sin and ruination of nations, and as the owners of *filthy lucre*, or its equivalent, are compelled to give it all to the treasury, out of which they will be supplied with things as "they have need of;" and as these owners of valuables have sinned by so possessing what is for the good of all, so likewise you, the *poor people*, have sinned by indulging in unhealthy habits, such as rum, tobacco, medicines, profanity, licentiousness, and so forth; therefore, you are equally compelled to give up your sinning or die!

The debauched, however, will soon die from disease; famine and pestilence will wipe them away, which may save us the annoyance of shooting them, if stubborn and rebellious.

Thirdly—All the public buildings will hastily be turned into institutions of instruction, wherein the weak-minded ones will be placed and so treated and cared for as to give them sound sensibilities. Each person must now "earn his and her food by the sweat of the brow." Idleness shall be a felony, and determined and persistent stubbornness and rebellion against the new order of things shall be punished by shooting the miscreant.

Obedience and submission to fixed law or death is the edict, and I shall have this executed with as little compunction as I had when I shot the prisoners.

Fourthly—Let all comprehend that the old order of things

is no more. From the President of the United States down to the smallest public officer, they have all been removed with the close of the war, and must now be esteemed as *working people*.

Each man, woman and youth must do his or her share of work, which will be simply two or three hours' daily recreation, that is necessary for the development and preservation of a sound mind in a sound body!

Fifthly—The people at large have learned through this war that the Naturalists' soldiers were healed without medicines; therefore they may know that the Christian manner of "healing the sick" is the only right one; hence medicines, fashions and all artificial and useless things must be abolished instantly! The only fashion admissible shall be to learn and obey the fixed injunctions of the Creator, and grow and remain natural!

Sixthly—Self and selfishness for mere isolated gratification shall be treated as a virulent disease, and such invalids must instantly be placed into the institutions of instruction until healed, or remain there for life. I do not wish to be understood that you should not take care of yourself, —this you *must* do, no one can do it for you,—but you shall not be jealous, overbearing and hold usable things for yourself alone.

Seventhly—The deacons of the Secret Order of Naturalists understand all about the new order of government, and they are hereby authorized all over the Union to carry out our plans. Foreigners who may arrive on our shores must enter the institutions of instruction before they can live in the United States, and sojourners from abroad *must* comply with the new order of things to the letter, or they will be imprisoned in the institutions of instruction. They are *positively* forbidden to introduce, or themselves use, on our soil any agencies, or put themselves under influences, that are prohibited by this proclamation and the new constitution!

Eighthly—Upon these conditions alone can peace come

to the hearth and homes of the people of the United States.

Further, no one shall be permitted, under the penalty of death, to destroy or remove valuables from the United States. I argue that as long as this nation did not know how to take care of itself, it is necessary that it be taken care of by enforcing God's fixed laws, which shall be esteemed as monarch, and individuals shall only be permitted to be free and do as they please so long as they please to do right, which right is alone found to exist in leading natural, godly, Christ-like lives.

Ninthly—Those who do not understand how to act will be esteemed good citizens by instantly applying for information to any of the *Secret Order of Naturalists*, which are everywhere in operation, but which were not known heretofore; however, they will from this day display their banners and open their doors for giving information.

Tenthly—Provisions, clothing, tenements, and all necessary things shall from this day be supplied to each as they need, and no one shall usurp more than his or her necessities demand, under the penalty of being imprisoned in the institutions of instruction. Those who voluntarily apply for admission into said institutions of instruction shall be permitted to leave when they please; but those who are placed forcibly therein shall be esteemed as prisoners, who cannot leave until their cases are investigated, and are granted permission to leave.

Persons escaping from the institutions of instruction who were prisoners shall be punished by death.

In conclusion, I can but say that we shall prevent diseases and sins by rigid punishment of those who violate God's fixed laws, when fewer will suffer and die (except of old age) than by the barbarous old orthodox manner, where every one was free to violate God's law, and if that violator was mean and selfish enough to hoard up *lucre* could thereby create unnatural statute laws, build prisons and inflict insult upon injury, and all this to the subversion of the whole race of mankind. All the newspapers shall publish this proclamation, and shall cease to be published by any one except selected Naturalists.

Given this ———— day of ————, 19—, by
VICTOR JUNO.

N. B.—Be it known to all men that God is a dictator, and we who are His faithful children must likewise dictate to those who are in bondage to fashions, follies, vices and profligacies; but I hope and pray that the day is not far distant when every rational creature will worship God by voluntary obedience to His unalterable mandates, when indeed the Millennium will be established, a new Eden be created, where pristine beauty and innocence will reign supreme, and love to God and man become the only statute of the earth.
V. J.

CHAPTER XCV.

DR. JUNO WITH HIS PICKED SOLDIERS BRANDS THE PHARISEES.

IT is a long lane that has no turn, and whilst the proprietors of the daily Philadelphia newspapers have had everything their own way for many years, having maliciously libelled Dr. Juno and shut him out of the advertising columns of these public organs, to which all citizens have a right; in other words, they might as well have gone to his safe and robbed it as to rob him of the right of advertising his lawful business, whilst they could continually publish lies of the vilest character about him, but, at last the tables are turned.

Again, the Young Men's Association had him arrested and cast into prison, whilst those who were dependant upon him suffered agony; the judges and ring officials all chimed in with the newspaper and Sabbatarian conspirators; hence, he arrested every one of these people, male and female, and had them imprisoned in the same prison where they had him incarcerated years before, and as the tables were now being completely turned, he considered it his duty to disgrace them for their deep-dyed hypocrisy and low conduct; therefore, he did not shoot them, but after retaining them in prison for several months, until he had drawn up and published the new constitution, he took them out into the large park, and in presence of the multitude branded them on their foreheads in the following words:

"Bloody conspirator; shun him like a reptile, or die!"

Dr. Juno, previous to indelibly branding these *vipers*, made the following speech to *the people*, after forming a large circle by his soldiers, the *vipers* standing in a group in the centre, and the speaker in front of them on an elevated platform:

"*Friends and Fellow Citizens:*—I do not glory in the downfall of a sinner, or of an enemy; but, when we study God and His wonderful works and fixed laws, we can readily ascertain what is our duty, even though that duty may not be a pleasantry.

"I would much rather see a sinner and an enemy repent and turn from error to right than punish him myself; however, God punishes all transgressors, and if we are His children and are commanded to have dominion over the things of earth, we are compelled to punish those who would, if they could, lead the innocent and unsuspecting into the broad road to hell.

"It becomes us to exhort a straying fellow creature first; but, if he is haughty and self-righteous in his course of sinfulness, then it becomes our Christian duty, or call it a *natural* duty, if you prefer that expression, to punish or disgrace such scribe, pharisee and hypocrite.

"Here you behold a group of men and women to whom I have appealed for years, in the *strongest* language possible, to repent of their degrading and haughty sinfulness, but they spurned the law of God and the cause of mankind, which I have laid before them. They have robbed *us all* of that knowledge and those means by which *the people* might have regained their natural, godly, Christ-like state long ago; they have despised the *working people* [applause], whilst they have used every cunning device to rob them of their hard earned money; and in the lofty guise of being charitable, they gave thousands of dollars publicly, of the people's *lucre*, to their so-called charitable institutions, to show unto men that they gave alms liberally, and with this flourish of trumpets they advertised themselves in the most heinous manner, and thereby shut up your eyes, when they could with impunity steal millions of your hard earned money.

"Thus, they have made themselves lords of creation by robbing you and elevating themselves to Moses' seat, when they were the very *vipers* whom Jesus of Nazareth hath denounced with the most terrible curses! [Tremendous applause.] These vipers have not shown any sign of penitence; and if they had it *now* in their power, as they have had for nearly a quarter of a century, they would do the same acts, and glory in being the chosen *élite*, whilst the 'greasy mechanic, who is not good enough to wipe their fine feet upon,' as the Hon. (?) Bluster Gibbons said in his speech before the court in which I was tried and convicted. [Vociferous applause.] Look at them now, what a scared set of forlorn and crime distinguished set of sinners they are, when shown up to the '*illiterate, coarse, dirty working people!*' [Enthusiastic applause.] Should we pity them? Does God pity such arch fiends, when he sends them to their own orthodox hell, which they have pictured and laid out to you, for *your special benefit*, if you do not fall down and wince like curs and give them your everything, and worship them for being so generous, charitable and good as to give to the poor thousands? Their giving has only been a sham, a public bait, an anti-Christ manner of giving alms, yet these wretches usurped the name of saints, of being the chosen people; because they were wicked, apt, shrewd and niggardly enough to hoodwink you. [Terrific applause.] You who were good enough to pay the taxes which they saddled upon you, whilst they made you believe that *they*, indeed they (?), paid the heavy taxes.

"Cannot you now see with half sound senses that these monsters were your worst enemies; the enemies of God; the mockers of Jesus Christ—see the fifth, sixth, seventh, tenth and twenty-third chapters of St. Matthew in the New Testament—and the degenerators and murderers of pure, innocent, defenceless little children? Yes, they teach doctrines so unnatural and heinous, that cause the birth of innocents by haphazard, who inherit hereditary and congenital diatheses from the unhealthy state of the parents; and when millions of sickly little lambs are called to life, who should not have seen the light of day, they dose and drug them, and in one-thousand-and-one ways infringe upon God's fixed laws, and plaster it all over by prayers and rhapsodical speeches made by their canting preachers. [The applause at this point was deafening, and continued for minutes.]

"It would be too great a charity to send these most wicked wretches to their long account; so I propose to brand them indelibly on their foreheads and cheeks with this instrument, which I had prepared for all such sinners, and I shall order the execution of its decree.

"This shall be esteemed an everlasting and the greatest disgrace that can befall a creature. The decree is this: 'Bloody conspirator; shun him like a reptile, or die!'

"Should, in course of time, any of these wretches prove worthy to have this stigma removed, I will cause a countersign, which, when planted across this, will redeem them from the odium that this brands them with, when they shall be looked upon as *working people*.

"In conclusion, let all take warning how they disregard the voice of God and the Naturalists, and with heartfelt sympathy for each according to the deeds done in past days, I now order the officers to brand each one of these persons on this elevated stand so that all may see the work executed." [Great applause.]

The baldeagle proprietor of the "Oracle" was the first man who had the dose administered. He looked sheepish enough, and some of the spectators cried aloud:

"Dob him on his bald head!"—"Give him a double dose, there is sufficient room on that glossy and hardened scalp!"

These remarks caused immense mirth, which seemed to be a hard pill to take for the fellow who had lived like a nabob in a one hundred thousand dollar castle, every cent of which was wrung out of the *working people's* pockets. When they were all branded, Dr. Juno entered again upon the stand, and said:

"I order that these people will be taken back to prison, and kept there until I see how the new order of things works."

They were now marched to Moyamensing, the band following in their rear playing the "Rogues' March."

CHAPTER XCVI.

DISPOSAL OF NANCY CLOVER AND COMPANY, AND PREPARATION FOR THE MARRIAGE OF VICTOR AND LUCINDA.

IT will be remembered that Dr. Juno and Miss Lucinda Armington's wedding has been three times interrupted. The last time Nancy Clover shot Dr. Juno just as the minister was about to pronounce the ceremony; and in sooth, it was each time the work of the bloody conspirators, therefore, to make sure of it this time, Dr. Juno had Nancy Clover, Deacon Rob Stew, Dr. Toy Pancy and the physician-in-chief of the insane asylum hunted up and brought before him for trial.

Several of them were under heavy bonds when the war

broke out, but of course nothing could be done then; however, now came the hour of their discontent. The Rev. Joe Pier was formerly one of the associates of these leading conspirators, but he was not a bad man at heart. Circumstances, associations and the want of money to supply his material wants drove him into this work of the devil, and it is known to the reader that he repented and turned a Naturalist the first opportunity that convinced him of a surety of protection from these bloody conspirators.

When Dr. Juno had found the forenamed persons, he ordered their imprisonment until he could summon all the victims of these sweet saints (?), who proved to consist of General Harry Gossimer, Miss Lucinda Armington and father, Pat O'Conner, Judy McCrea, Jemmy, Mr. Grumbler, Rev. Joe Pier and Dr. Juno himself.

The day of trial was appointed, Dr. Victor Juno acting as judge, and when the holy elect, Nancy Clover, Deacon Rob Stew, Dr. Toy Pancy and the physician-in-chief were arraigned they were thunderstruck to behold Harry Gossimer!

The lovely Sister Nancy Clover fainted dead away when she was brought face to face with Harry Gossimer, and Deacon Rob Stew stood, with eyes and mouth wide open, looking as if he really thought the spirit or ghost of the drowned Harry Gossimer stood before him; so also thought Nancy Clover, who fainted three times in succession; the two physicians had more nerve, therefore could bear the sight of their victim.

When these elect sinners were restored to their senses, Dr. Juno said:

"Nancy Clover, Rob Stew, Toy Pancy and physician of the insane asylum, stand up. You are charged with conspiracy, murder and crime of all characters, what say you, guilty or not guilty?"

"Not guilty," responded each one of them.

The witnesses were now regularly examined and cross-examined by counsels on both sides. The testimony of

General Gossimer and Rev. Joe Pier was soul-stirring, but the rest was less to the point, although General Armington and his daughter Lucinda exposed some deep villany with which the reader is already familiar.

Gen. Harry Gossimer, sworn.

Dr. Juno.—General Gossimer, do you know the prisoners at the bar?

Answer.—Yes, sir, to my sorrow and to their disgrace.

Q.—Please state what you consider a few of the worst things that you know of them.

A.—I became a member of what was known to its members only as the Sacredly Secret Conclave in the month of January, 18—. Mr. Rob Stew and Nancy Clover were the leading conspirators. All the members had to take a terrible iron-clad oath, which was known as the *solemn oath*. [The reader is familiar with it.]

The object of this Sacredly Secret Conclave was to banish or murder everybody who would oppose the peculiar old school or orthodox religion. They styled themselves the "elect," and as such could not sin, but claimed to have a perfect licence to persecute everybody who entertained different views to them.

This conclave was nothing more or less than a bloody conspiracy, and was inaugurated for the special purpose of murdering our Father here,—Dr. Juno. I know this, because, on a certain meeting night, when all the prisoners were present and co-operated, I was constrained to object to a certain murdering plot, when this Deacon Stew, instantly ordered my arrest, and I was at once cast into a dungeon, and the same evening was convicted, without being present at the mock trial, and after they had concluded the same. (what happened the Rev. Joe Pier can tell you, who was then their president), I was ordered before them, when the president read me a lecture and sentenced me to be drowned or hung for my audacity in refusing to countenance the murder of Victor Juno, the honorable judge upon the bench.

I was taken to the river and was drowned, as they thought, but the noble Pat O'Conner saved my life, and I am here safe and sound. [The reader knows particulars.]

Cross-examine.

Counsel for Defendants.—Mr. Gossimer, are you certain that every one of the prisoners was present and countenanced what you have related?

A.—I am most positive.

Q.—Have you not been insane some years ago, and is this not one of your peculiar imaginings?

A.—Better let Rev. Joe Pier and Pat O'Conner answer, if they are "peculiar imaginings."

C. for D's.—That will do, that will do.

REV. JOE PIER, sworn.

Dr. Juno.—Mr. Pier, give us briefly what you know of the prisoners at the bar, and also state if what Gen. Gossimer said is false or true.

A.—It is scarcely necessary for me to make a long statement concerning the motives and acts of the Sacredly Secret Conclave. It is only necessary for me to say that *every word* that General Harry Gossimer has said is *true*, and a thousand worse things have I been compelled to hear and see; and Rob Stew invariably threatened me with a horrible death should I fail to carry out and enforce his heinous work! He and Nancy Clover have been too domineering and wicked, whilst these two doctors were always ready to execute their nefarious commands. All that Mr. Stew and Miss Clover had to do was to propose a criminal plot, when these prisoners were ready to act; thus was Dr. Juno to be poisoned on several occasions, and the villanies which they continually concocted were legion.

Cross-examine.

C. for D's.—Mr. Pier, did you not act in concert with the prisoners at the bar in the "legion of villanies," and are you guileless in having concocted any criminal plots?

A.—I am not on trial; but if it is any gratification to you or your clients, I will say that from fear of being assassinated by them, or being discovered and overpowered by others, I did connive with them, and did also my best to invent anything to save myself from being sent hence with all my sins upon my head! But the *first* opportunity I had I repented and joined the Naturalists; and our heroic Father—Dr. Juno—has several times offered the same opportunity and privilege to the prisoners at the bar. but they spurned his beneficent overtures. I hope, however, that he will yet permit your clients to repent, and if he does, I pray *them* to accept the hour of grace.

C. for D's.—I did not ask you to preach a sermon to my clients.

A.—But you cannot say that they don't need it, and it would not be the first one, nor the first time that I gave them good advice, which, however, they always spurned.

C. for D's.—I have no objections, should my clients wish to repent and join the Naturalists, for I am myself an advocate of Nature and Nature's God.

Dr. Juno.—I am willing and ready to hear from the prisoners themselves on this topic, and if they are *heartily* penitent, I may require only probationary training in the West Philadelphia Institution of Instruction.

Rob Stew said:

"I spurn any such propositions; I am no coward, and I will die by my faith."

"Ditto," ejaculated Nancy Clover.

The two physicians remained silent. After all the witnesses were heard, Dr. Juno said to the members of the Naturalists, who were all inside of the circle made for them:

"Brothers, how say you, are these prisoners at the bar guilty? All who feel that way will rise to their feet."

They all arose, when Dr. Juno said, in a firm voice:

"Friends, you behold before you my worst persecutors, a parcel of Satan's own band, who are hardened beyond expression. They deserve death without mercy; but, as war is over, and as we can make excellent use of them, I order that they be branded with our disgracing motto on their foreheads, cheeks, arms, legs, feet, trunk, and each one have the letters B and C cut through their ears; after this is done, they shall all four be imprisoned for life in one room, unless *I* pardon them, where they shall work four hours a day, and be kept as a free show to all the world."

When these prisoners were removed from free soil, Dr. Juno and Miss Armington appointed the day for the long and often postponed nuptials. This time nothing marred the consummation of the pleasing function.

CHAPTER XCVII.

THE WEDDING.

ON Friday (which was always the lucky day of Dr. Juno), the fourth day of ———, 19—, was set apart for the wedding day of Victor and Lucinda, and all the Naturalists, or working people (hereafter, the Naturalists and working people mean the same) were invited; but no others were permitted to be present.

This was done as a precautionary measure, because Dr. Juno had learned to guard himself more closely than of yore; moreover, just then there were many unconverted persons living everywhere who would have delighted to molest or kill either him or his betrothed wife.

Many people were of the opinion that this would be a grand carnival, because money was plenty with both General Armington and Dr. Juno; but this was not the case. Nothing unnatural or unnecessary was done or presented; still, every one was made happy and satisfied by the cordial welcome that all received at the hands of their hosts.

The best and plenty of healthy food was ready at all

hours, and everything that was pleasing and enjoyable to a natural person was to be had; but no artificial beverages, nor gross dishes, neither tobacco was seen there; in sooth, these things were not craved by the Naturalists, and although some of the new members of the novel order of things had been but recently inveterate habitual indulgers in riotous living—using tobacco, rum, condiments and so forth; but the famous teachings of Dr. Juno, and the peremptory orders to the people to desist totally from the use of such things, inspired them with higher joys and loftier ambitions than tippling, gluttony and money-getting.

The idea of getting money to purchase imaginary wants, unhealthy agencies and which cause diseases, had already been exchanged for love to God and mankind.

And the guests at this wedding saw that to live for one another, for love, and to be treated as if they were all one family, was an incentive of greater power than orthodoxy could furnish. It seemed on this occasion as though every one was inspired with the Holy Ghost. They had the example set them by their Father, and, was to be, Mother— Dr. Juno and Miss Armington. They all loved and respected the happy couple for their great achievements, and when they saw that these heroic reformers lived to make all mankind sound and happy, they praised God from the abundance of their hearts, to think that the spirit of righteousness, the spirit of Christ and spirit of God, dwelled in the leaders of this new era.

Truly, the Millennium dawn and the second appearing of Christ were being made manifest; all were happy in the spirit; all felt joy in the gratification of the thinking faculties, which gave them power to control the lower propensities, and they were in "one place with one accord;" verily, the doctrines of Christ seemed to have become natural, and nothing was craved but the desire to make each other happy.

This was a delightful state of affairs, and it only went to prove that it is as easy to do right, under physiological or natural circumstances, as it is to do wrong, under artificial and diseased circumstances.

Under the unphysiological orthodox circumstances, swearing came naturally to young and old, without requiring public, private or Sunday schools; whilst, under the genuine Christ-like or natural circumstances, praises and intuitive prayers come naturally, and eloquent inspiration from the fountain-head of Jehovah teaches all to speak as with cloven tongues that which is necessary to be spoken.

The hour had arrived for the nuptial ceremony to be performed; the minister announced it, and all arose to their feet, and with reverence listened to the eloquent words of the Progressive apostle, as he spoke as follows:

"Dearly Beloved in the Lord:—It hath again pleased the Lord of hosts to permit us to meet together in peace and spiritual communion. And although our beloved hosts have gone through many fires, yet have they ever been guided by the infallible hand of God, whose fixed laws are always a safe guide to the people of His heritage.

"We have gathered together on this delightful occasion to join this man and woman in holy matrimony, which is commanded by the highest ordinance of the Creator; but it is not a function that should be lightly or unadvisedly entered; but reverently, discreetly, soberly and physiologically, in the fear of committing new sins, provided the applicants for these holy orders were not fitted physically and mentally to propagate their kind in the image of God.

"If any man can show any defect in either this man or woman, or just cause why they may not lawfully be joined together, let him now speak, or else hereafter hold his peace.

"Victor Juno, wilt thou have this woman to be thy wedded wife, to live together so long as ye both shall live?"

"I will," responded Victor.

"Lucinda Armington, wilt thou have this man to be thy wedded husband, to live together so long as ye both shall live?"

"I will," responded Lucinda.

"Inasmuch as it has pleased Almighty God to grant unto this man and woman the talent, the health and the understanding of his fixed laws; and inasmuch as this man and woman have come here to be joined together *for pure love for each other* as man and wife, I now pronounce the holy ordinance: 'What, therefore, God hath joined together let no man put asunder.'

"Let us all pray. Father of mercies, and Giver of all necessary things, we praise Thy hallowed name for having made us in Thine own blessed image. We worship Thee by obedience to Thy fixed mandates, and we glorify Thy name for the munificent gifts that heaven and earth bestow upon Thy faithful children. And, O Lord, we thank Thee for having given us this man and woman as exemplars for Thy people. May they live long on Thy footstool, and bless the nations with that knowledge of Thy kingdom which surpasses all sinful understanding. And to Thee be all the power and the glory forever. Amen."

At this point, Pat O'Conner and Judy McCrea came modestly forward, hand in hand, and Pat said:

"May it plaze yer Riverence tow do they same tow us?"

This caused a laugh throughout the assemblage, but the minister obeyed the solicitation, and Pat and Judy were equally happy.

Thus ended the nuptials of two faithful couple, and Victor and Lucinda seemed to have a brilliant crown of glory surrounding their heads. The happy couple were now taken by the hand by all present, and were congratulated with all sorts of expressions, from the most eloquent eulogies to silent tears; the latter spoke with double emphasis. Indeed, all things seemed to work together for good, because all loved the Lord in a practical manner, and a crown of glory awaited every man and woman in the large assemblage.

The guests had commenced to congregate at nine o'clock in the morning, the ceremony was performed at twelve at noon, and they left at five in the afternoon, which was all in keeping with the new order of things, and which made it a day of thanksgiving. Thanks that came from the heart; and not vain lip service, whilst the mind was unconcerned as it is in pharisaical circles.

Happiness, the aim and end of man, seemed to smile upon Dr. Juno, but all was not permanently serene yet.

CHAPTER XCVIII.

FAMINE AND PESTILENCE COME TO THE AID OF THE NATURALISTS.

IT may be easily imagined that thousands of hardened, lost men and women lived at that day, when the supremacy of Nature's laws were in the ascendant; and although these people feared Dr. Juno worse than Satan, still they could not yield in their determination to pursue their own downward course.

Famine first came, and pestilence next, to aid the cause of reform, by destroying those who led dissipated lives, who were stimulated and enervated by the orthodox habits. These people died like flies; and as they would not accept the reformed hygienic treatment, but persist in employing stealthily the poison practices of medical science (?), they passed away so speedily that not a remnant scarcely was left of them after the pestilence raged a month; hence the path for the Naturalists was cleared of all its deteriorating rubbish, and the work of God and man went exultingly along.

It may seem very curious to orthodox minds why it was that famine and pestilence should make their appearance just in the nick of time to aid the Reformation! Some may ask, did God suspend any of His fixed laws for the benefit of the Naturalists, and thereby send famine and pestilence?

We answer, No; but the earth has been stimulated for centuries, has been forced by artificial means, the same as the orthodox people, and at last could no more produce food, nor give pure air to its inhabitants, who, instead of holding dominion over everything, ran riot; thus were poisonous gases continually generated, until both earth, atmosphere and man became so depraved as to cause rebellion in the spirit of each; hence war, famine and pestilence are brothers, and they are caused by violations of God's fixed laws, whilst the penalty is a natural result instead of a suspension of His immutable mandates!

Immediately after Dr. Juno was married, and as soon as he had published his new constitution to the world, the earth ceased to produce food for man or beast, and nearly two years of famine and starvation existed.

The Naturalists, who live not by "bread alone, but by every word that proceedeth out of the mouth of God," had, of course, the advantage over the remaining portion of the orthodox people, who would not be converted in due season. The former, who were grown up, suffered very little for the want of food, because they were comforted by the clear understanding that this scarcity of food was to be their salvation; but the poor little children, whose systems were growing, and whose hunger therefore was very great, suffered awfully; many cases were heart-rending in the extreme.

We give a few examples as illustrations how these little angels suffered all over the globe. The Naturalists' children suffered less than the orthodox.

In the New England States you could hear little children cry for bread! "Oh, dear mamma, give me some bread!

Oh, I am so hungry; I cannot live. Please, oh, please give me some bread!" Mothers and fathers would eat the poorest quality and smallest quantity of what little they could procure, and give the best to their children.

A wealthy farmer, who had joined the Naturalists, had a large family of little children, the oldest was a son of twelve summers. One morning they all sat around their table, which contained nothing except mouldy bread. These children, until now, always had plenty, and when the son of twelve saw the mouldy piece of bread lie on his plate, he looked at his father disdainfully, and said:

"Father, I hope you do not expect me to eat this stale and mouldy bread?"

When his father seemed to turn pale, and flushed alternately, which surprised the boy, when the parent lifted *his* piece of bread and said:

"My son, I have cut you and my dear babies the best of all we have, look how mouldy and spoiled *my* piece is!"

This brought great tears into the boy's eyes, and he said, sobbing:

"Father, forgive me, I did not know that we had no better; I am satisfied."

All seemed to enjoy their mouldy bread after this conversation except the father, who seemed to have lost his appetite entirely, and when the smallest children, mere babies, had eaten their portion, and saw that some was left by their father, one asked:

"Papa, don you want dat bed?"

"No, my beloved babies," was his reply.

"Den give to Benny an I," said a little girl. The father could not resist, but gave the sour, mouldy bread to them, when they devoured it with a gusto that caused the older boy to weep as if his little heart would break, and the parents were compelled to leave the scene. Flour and bread were saved so long as to cause them to grow mouldy.

The Naturalists could live on very little compared with the orthodox people, and the latter cared little what quality of stuff they swallowed, so long as it filled their stomachs and appeased their hunger; but whilst they feasted rather better than the Naturalists during the famine, they were being made terrible victims for the jaws of the pestilence, a thing they did not expect, nor did they understand these matters any more than they ever did; hence it only proved again that orthodoxy and self-defiling were synonymous, and when the hour of accountability for the deeds done *in* the body and *to* the body came, these people fell dead by the thousands; whilst the Naturalists understood that as the quality of food is that you swallow so also is the quality of the bodily textures; therefore they lived on a very little of pure food, and had nothing therefore inside of them that would easily decay, whilst the orthodox people were filled with gross agencies, hash and drugs from crown to toe, which ignited instantly when the miasmatic effluvia touched their vitals, and the combustion under these circumstances was so great that instant extinction of life was certain.

Dr. Juno issued a proclamation of warning to those who had lived reckless orthodox lives, as follows, the moment that the looked-for pestilence made its appearance:

"PROCLAMATION.—To those of the people who did not heed the many warnings that I gave them for many years, I proclaim and order that they will at once flee to the mountains and subsist upon the plainest food that they can procure, and those who will not or cannot do so, if they are taken with the pestilence must expect to be burned up in their houses, for we shall remove the valuables from the cities where the plague exists and set the cities on fire, which will burn out the miasma and aid in creating rain, which will bring the elixir of life with it in the shape of oxygen!

"In time of war, famine and pestilence it cannot be expected that the guilty ones alone shall be made to suffer; therefore, if there are any innocent ones who are unfavorably situated, we advise them to observe this proclamation and flee from the wrath to come; and if such are penitent, we shall exert ourselves to save them, otherwise we cannot aid them, having enough to do to take care of ourselves, and to stop the plague from spreading more and more.

"Given this twentieth day of ———, 19—, by
"Victor Juno."

This plague exceeded everything in its extent of destruction of human life that was ever known or heard of. Hundreds of thousands fell dead daily, which so horrified the balance of the orthodox and rebellious worldlings that they were anxious to become Naturalists, as they saw that very few of the latter died, and the few who did die with it were those who had only recently turned reformers, and whose bodies had not yet had time to be remodelled sufficiently to bear the brunt of so great a pestilence.

The dead bodies were ordered to be burned, and thousands who were lying on their death-beds were consumed by the burning of the various cities, which seemed a visitation too horrible to be anticipated; but what could be done beside this course?

Drug doctors fell dead in hundreds, and they seemed to know nothing about the disease; in fact, they do not, and never did, understand the true nature and causes of diseases, or they would not poison a person just because he had been ill through one or more violations of God's laws of health, thereby adding insult to injury. However, these hypothetical vipers dared, in past ages, to assume the attitude of the "Regular Standard" lights of healing of the sick, when every step in life's great battle proved them charlatans and stuck up and opinionated impostors!

If what is here asserted be not true, then are Jesus Christ and nature false doctors; but the fiat has gone forth, and these quacks have died and vanished by their own achievements; therefore peace to their ashes, but a warning to all generations to come!

CHAPTER XCIX.

THE NEW CONSTITUTION.

WE, who understand the fixed laws of the Creator, hereby form the following constitution, which shall be the supreme and *only* law of the land:

SECTION I. We recognize the unalterable, fixed laws of nature and wonderful natural works of God as the sovereign power of heaven and earth, and love to God and man are the fruition of obedience to the same.

SECTION II. We regard the acts of Jesus Christ as worthy of imitation, and no citizen of these United States of America shall profess or claim to be a Christian or Naturalist unless he leads, as near as possible, the natural life that Christ led. And the fifth, sixth, seventh, tenth and twenty-third chapters of St. Matthew of the New Testament shall be learned, and their teachings become the principles by which all things shall be compared, and upon which everything is to be based.

SECTION III. All anti-natural and anti-Christ customs, statutes and precepts shall be treated as felonious. Fashions and all useless or unnecessary things and customs shall also be treated as criminal, and the victim shall be imprisoned in the institutions of instruction.

SECTION IV. Individuals shall not own property of any kind, but each shall receive the necessaries of life as he or she has need of, in common with the rest, and in keeping with the laws of nature and capacity of the means of the country.

SECTION V. The apt, zealous and faithful disciples shall become the apostles, who will make proper scientific interpretations of the fixed laws of God. The people who will not voluntarily learn the right and obey it shall be *made* to do so, as school boys of yore were compelled to do.

SECTION VI. The oldest, ablest and most faithful apostle shall be esteemed an infallible interpreter of the fixed laws of the Church of God! But if found wanting shall be deposed.

SECTION VII. Dr. Victor Juno's sermons, teachings, proclamations and army orders shall be the standard for all generations; because they are sound beyond cavil.

SECTION VIII. That there shall be no public opinion, but knowledge of all the essentials pertaining to human affairs shall banish opinion! Opinions shall not be tolerated in matters where science or fixed law exists. Beliefs, conjectures and hypotheses on matters of human affairs shall not be allowed to be advanced and promulgated in public or private.

SECTION IX. The printing press shall only be open to those who understand God's fixed laws, who are authorized to use it for His kingdom, and to print or publish anything that is erroneous, false, useless or in conflict with the infallible laws of nature or nature's God shall be esteemed treason toward high heaven; and the penalty for the first offence shall be imprisonment in the institutions of instruction, and for any future violation of this section shall be *death*. The so-called "Free Printing Press" has proved the most dangerous vehicle to debauch the people; therefore the heaviest penalty shall be attached to the misuse of it.

SECTION X. Little children shall be cared for as if they constituted the angels in heaven, no matter who are their parents, or whether they inherited good or bad constitutions; but parents who generate human souls under unphysiological circumstances, and bring sickness, deformity and so forth upon their offspring, shall at once be imprisoned in the separate department for the sexes of the institutions of instruction; and marriages shall not be allowed except from love and when in a natural state. The head of "The Church" will further direct these matters in keeping with the "Body and Blood of Christ."

SECTION XI. All who fail to comprehend and do not

live out the teachings of our king—Fixed Law—shall be imprisoned in what shall be known as the "*institutions of instruction*," which institutions shall be conducted upon natural principles, as set forth in Dr. Victor Juno's great *proclamation of peace*, section third; but we hope the time will speedily come when no such institutions will be needed.

SECTION XII. The orthodox method of educating the young and old shall be totally abandoned, and obedience to the fixed laws of growth and development of body and soul shall be the only schooling, when intuition or the Holy Spirit will teach all they ever need know; but to so raise and train both young and old as to become the purified temples of God, the apostles and Naturalists who are grown up shall have books wherein the fixed laws are explained.

SECTION XIII. The Bible shall only be in the hands of the apostles, who can scientifically interpret the meaning of the authors, and obsolete Biblical history, like every other history, shall be abandoned.

SECTION XIV. Conversation for recreation, mirth and mere pastime shall not be restricted so long as blasphemy and profanity are omitted; but when it is given as instruction or advice a heavy penalty shall be attached to false doctrines; in fact, the latter *shall not* be tolerated under any pretext by pen, tongue, printer's ink, or in any other manner.

SECTION XV. To speak evil of any one, or to herald evil, or to show forth evil of any kind, shall be esteemed the highest crime amongst men, and shall be punished as in section nine of this constitution.

SECTION XVI. Hypocrisy and deception shall be esteemed the highest crime against God and man, and if any person indulges in them, or if any individual knows persons who practise them, and does not inform on the hypocrites, they shall *all* be counted guilty of felony,—the hypocrite and shielder of the deceiver,—and shall be punished as in section nine of this constitution.

SECTION XVII. All municipal laws and ordinances made by mankind shall be in harmony with the fixed natural laws of God; and love to God and man shall be the highest law of earth.

CHAPTER C.

DAWN OF THE MILLENNIUM.

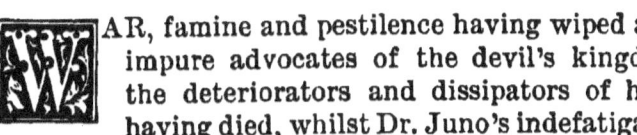AR, famine and pestilence having wiped away the impure advocates of the devil's kingdom, and the deteriorators and dissipators of humanity having died, whilst Dr. Juno's indefatigable acts, war proclamations, orders and so forth, have compelled the balance to obey God's holy laws, which are for the joy and everlasting glory of all rational creatures alike; so now an entire new era has been established, and those who live, live to let live, live for health, for one another, for happiness, for glory to God and mankind; thus the *Second Advent of Christ* is everywhere manifest.

A new Eden is established; the image of God is enthroned; one continual Sabbath day is celebrated; the dressing of the garden of perpetual peace and innocence is the legitimate work of each man and woman; God is praised without ceasing; love is as free as the mountain air, and is ushered forth toward God and man from the abundance of the heart or depth of the soul.

The year of jubilee has come! Peace and good will to God and man reign supreme and on high! His will is done here, in earth, as it is in heaven! Dr. Juno and his beloved wife, Lucinda, sit regally clad in the habilaments of heavenly glory upon the throne of grace! They are the acknowledged victors and chief apostles of the Naturalists, who, in company with the happy sons and daughters of Victor and Lucinda, surround their father and mother, whilst the grandfather—General Washington Armington —in the sere and yellow leaf, daily asks blessings on the heads of all the children of earth, and the old man fairly worships his noble son and daughter, whilst the grandchildren dote on their blessed grandpapa.

Words cease to express the joy, the happiness and good will that reigns continually amongst *all* the people. There is more than plenty of everything to supply all their natural, real wants, and also plenty of time daily for all to gather together for mutual sociability and intuitive thanksgiving to Him who has made everything for the whole people's good!

Every living mortal now sees the folly and sinfulness of the old barbarous orthodox customs, and they praise Dr. Juno, and the Almighty Creator for having been brought into the light of the hallowed Millennium!

The second coming of Christ—which means the second appearing of God's righteousness in the shape of obedience to His fixed laws—is consummated in full power and heavenly grandeur; and the immaculate and infallible spirit of Christ, or spirit of God's science of human life, holds sovereign sway and masterdom, which makes the earth a heaven, and inspires the temple of God with holy fire and heavenly zeal, baptizing all nations and peoples with power and grace divine!

Foreign countries are being hastily baptized with the same exuberant blessings, and a new heaven and a new earth have been established, for the old having passed away to make way for the second coming of Christ, and the hosts of the New Jerusalem are sounding their talismanic lyres with enchanting effect upon the minds of all the children of His footstool!

Peace and good will are not one tithe the blessings that surround the human family; but love to God and one another, magnified by thrills from the Holy Spirit, which enhances the pleasures and joys of earth so extensively that God's will has become the universal will of the people. Thus death is swallowed up in victory, and all rejoice in the transmission from earth to mansions in the skies.

Language fails to express the acknowledged munificence of God, and the rapturous bliss that His unalloyed influence exercises over the purified temples of God is overwhelming, which causes the human mind to quaff living water, whose properties are exuberantly, magically and divinely spiritualistic, that thrill and enliven every avenue of the soul, until the body becomes a normally toned instrument, whereupon the Spirit of God, or Holy Spirit, plays enchanting music that electrifies every atom of all animated creation!

Now Victor Juno is blessed with everything that his great heart yearned for, with everything that his muscles labored for, with everything that his giant will struggled for, with a congenial and heroic Christian wife and mother by his side, with children, in God's blessed image, surrounding him, with all the people falling before the throne of grace and doing homage to God and man, and all this for the love they bear for him, for God and for one another.

This pays him ten million times for the pains, deprivations, persecutions and struggles through which he was compelled to go for the purpose of establishing this Millennium dawn. The Spirit of Jesus Christ now holds sacred his manly body and soul, and those who have exhausted their strength of body, mind and purse to disgrace and persecute him, have sunken into the depth of disgrace, and have become fuel for the evil one to satiate his venom upon, whilst a beloved Victor and his people enjoy the gifts of an unchangeable Creator, and a mansion, not made by human hands, but eternal in the sky, awaits the blessed Naturalist, whose greatness, goodness and indomitable energy are indelibly inscribed upon the hearts of the entire race of mankind!

Thus, *truly, worthy* have proved the operations of the noble and heroic "Son of Toil," who has lived and labored for the salvation of his race; his reward is made manifest to the inhabitants of heaven and earth, whilst he is the HAPPY MAN!

MORAL.

I HAVE written this novel with the intention of showing the danger of entrusting the government of Church and State in the hands of theoretical speculators, who carry on their trades or callings without opposition, or without permitting open criticisms on their conduct and logic.

Ministers of the sectarian denominations have thus grown impudent and hardened in their sanctimonious work, who dare not be opposed with impunity; and they claim a holy right to usurp every means, good and ill, to sustain their false positions, which has been shown in their acts toward myself, as partly portrayed in this story.

My trial and imprisonment for publishing a scientific physiological book, and the several attempts to assassinate me, also the newspaper libels and sectarian connivings, as laid down in this novel, are all truer than most of the preaching that we hear from the fashionable rostrums.

I have drawn a heavy picture on both sides; however, I am convinced that the Protestant sectarian leaders, if they were a unit, as the Roman Catholics are, would do worse deeds than are given in this story; but instead of being a unit, they have several hundred sects, each hating the other, which may be the only benefit of the many sects.

The hero of the plot, as well as the heroine, Victor and Lucinda, are two people after mine own heart, and I would do things precisely as they are portrayed by them if I had it in my power! Moreover, I hope all thinking people will appreciate the charity of dealing summarily with those who misrepresent God, Nature and Jesus Christ, and who by so doing have bankrupted everything until the immutable laws of the Creator are spurned, whilst the traditions of men receive respect at the sacrifice of millions of the human kind!

The deacon is only a fair sample of what many of our self-righteous modern deacons are, only with this difference, that Deacon Rob Stew is far more brave, heroic and fearless than our modern bigots, who in their hearts feel like doing as Deacon Stew did, but have neither the tact nor courage to do so.

I hope that I am not misunderstood in presenting the extreme views of good and evil, or the acme of heavenly zeal or demoniacal ambition! I love the genuine Christian and honest official, but despise the ways of the hypocrite and politician.

All should be governed by the fixed law of God, and the good of the many should be sought at the sacrifice of the good of the few, which reverses the customs of the day. And until the aim and end of able men point in the direction that this novel sets forth, the broad road will be lined, whilst the narrow path will be deserted!

My secret prayers are for the welfare of all, and my physical and mental energies shall be expended in the direction just spoken of, hoping that the Millennium *will* dawn ere many years pass away!

THE AUTHOR.

THE END.

www.ingramcontent.com/pod-product-compliance
Lightning Source LLC
Chambersburg PA
CBHW051245300426
44114CB00011B/899